# Ethical Sentimentalism

In recent years there has been a tremendous resurgence of interest in ethical sentimentalism, a moral theory first articulated during the Scottish Enlightenment. Ethical sentimentalism promises a conception of morality that is grounded in a realistic account of human psychology, which, correspondingly, acknowledges the central place of emotions in our moral lives. However, this promise has encountered its share of philosophical difficulties. Chief among them is the question of how to square the limited scope of human motivation and psychological mechanism – so easily influenced by personal, social, and cultural circumstances – with the seemingly universal scope and objective nature of moral judgment. The essays in this volume provide a comprehensive evaluation of the sentimentalist project with a particular eye to this difficulty. Each essay offers critical clarification, innovative answers to central challenges, and new directions for ethical sentimentalism in general.

REMY DEBES is Associate Professor of Philosophy at the University of Memphis, and has published numerous articles and book chapters on moral theory with an emphasis on human dignity, respect, metaethics, moral psychology, empathy, and understanding. He is the editor of *Dignity: A History* (2017).

KARSTEN R. STUEBER is Professor of Philosophy at the College of the Holy Cross. He is the author of, among others, *Rediscovering Empathy: Agency, Folk Psychology, and the Human Sciences* (2006), and co-editor of *Empathy and Agency* (2000) and *Debating Dispositions* (2009).

# Ethical Sentimentalism

*New Perspectives*

*Edited by*

**Remy Debes**

*University of Memphis*

**Karsten R. Stueber**

*College of the Holy Cross, Massachusetts*

**CAMBRIDGE**
**UNIVERSITY PRESS**

# CAMBRIDGE
## UNIVERSITY PRESS

University Printing House, Cambridge CB2 8BS, United Kingdom

One Liberty Plaza, 20th Floor, New York, NY 10006, USA

477 Williamstown Road, Port Melbourne, VIC 3207, Australia

314-321, 3rd Floor, Plot 3, Splendor Forum, Jasola District Centre, New Delhi - 110025, India

79 Anson Road, #06-04/06, Singapore 079906

Cambridge University Press is part of the University of Cambridge.

It furthers the University's mission by disseminating knowledge in the pursuit of
education, learning and research at the highest international levels of excellence.

www.cambridge.org
Information on this title: www.cambridge.org/9781107461307
DOI: 10.1017/9781316105672

© Cambridge University Press 2017

First published 2017
First paperback edition 2019

*A catalogue record for this publication is available from the British Library*

ISBN 978-1-107-08961-7 Hardback
ISBN 978-1-107-46130-7 Paperback

Cambridge University Press has no responsibility for the persistence or
accuracy of URLs for external or third-party internet websites referred to in
this publication, and does not guarantee that any content on such websites is,
or will remain, accurate or appropriate.

# Contents

# Contributors

SIMON BLACKBURN, a former Professor of Philosophy at the University of Cambridge, is a Distinguished Research Professor of Philosophy at the University of North Carolina at Chapel Hill.

JUSTIN D'ARMS is Professor of Philosophy at Ohio State University.

REMY DEBES is Associate Professor of Philosophy at the University of Memphis.

MICHAEL L. FRAZER is a lecturer in Political and Social Theory at the University of East Anglia.

TERRY HORGAN is Professor of Philosophy at the University of Arizona.

DANIEL JACOBSON is Professor of Philosophy at the University of Michigan.

ANTTI KAUPPINEN is an Academy of Finland Research Fellow at the Department of Philosophy at the University of Tampere.

MICHELLE MASON is Associate Professor of Philosophy at the University of Minnesota.

DIANA TIETJENS MEYERS is Professor Emerita of Philosophy at the University of Connecticut.

JESSE PRINZ is Distinguished Professor of Philosophy at the City University of New York, Graduate Center.

PETER RAILTON is the Gregory S. Kavka Distinguished University Professor and Arthur F. Thurnau Professor at the University of Michigan.

KARL SCHAFER is Professor of Philosophy at the University of California at Irvine.

KARSTEN R. STUEBER is Professor of Philosophy at the College of the Holy Cross.

MARK TIMMONS is Professor of Philosophy at the University of Arizona.

DAVID B. WONG is the Susan Fox Beischer and George D. Beischer Professor of Philosophy at Duke University.

# Acknowledgments

Anthologies like this come into existence because of the good will among the contributors, and we are very grateful for the admirable spirit of cooperation among our authors. We would like to thank the *McFarland Center for Religion, Ethics, and Culture* at the College of the Holy Cross for sponsoring a conference allowing the authors to discuss their first drafts. We would also like to thank Hilary Gaskin at Cambridge University Press for believing in this project. Finally, we are grateful to our families for their support and encouragement.

# Introduction

*Remy Debes and Karsten R. Stueber*

In recent years, there has been a tremendous resurgence of philosophical interest in sentimentalism, an ethical and meta-ethical tradition first articulated during the Scottish Enlightenment and particularly associated with David Hume and Adam Smith. This renewed interest is due to a convergence of factors ranging from the development of sophisticated meta-ethical positions inclined toward sentimentalism, a renewed scholarly emphasis on its historical source, ongoing feminist engagements with concepts of empathy and care, and the growing influence of empirical research in moral psychology. The essays in this anthology provide a comprehensive and critical evaluation of the contemporary sentimentalist project, clarifying its central claims, evaluating the merits of its promises, and suggesting ways of thinking through its problems.

## 1  The Basic Position

It is difficult to give a perfectly straightforward definition of sentimentalism. As the various contributions to this anthology reveal, "sentimentalism" accommodates a rather diverse group of meta-ethical positions. Still, a few important commitments continue to connect the various contemporary accounts together, as well as contemporary accounts to classical ones. First and foremost, ethical sentimentalists are unified by a conviction in the "response-invoking" nature of (at least some) ethical concepts and judgments; that is, the thesis that (at least some) ethical concepts or judgments must be analyzed in terms of human emotional responses (broadly construed). Accordingly, in both the eighteenth century and contemporary contexts, sentimentalists have adamantly opposed rationalist and intuitionist accounts of ethical knowledge, and, in particular, those accounts that argue for a priori or non-inferential access to the truth of a moral proposition (or at least some moral propositions). For example, intuitionists claim that certain moral propositions can be known merely by employing our capacity to "attentively consider" and "adequately understand" them, or to

1

"think about them in the right way."[1] In this respect, knowledge of the normative domain is often claimed to be akin to our grasp of logical and mathematical propositions.[2] For example, in something like the way we "grasp" that "2 + 2 = 4," intuitionists think we can grasp that "the deliberate humiliation, rape, and torture of a child, for no purpose other than the pleasure of the one inflicting such treatment, is immoral."[3] By contrast, sentimentalists insist that to analogize moral thinking to mathematical reflection fails to acknowledge the full range of mental reactions wound up with moral judgment. To think that the deliberate torture of a child is wrong, for example, necessarily involves *feeling* something about such an action – perhaps, grief over the child's suffering and anger toward the person who caused it. The point is, sentiments are not accidental features of correct moral thinking, or its mere by-products.

Beyond this, it seems best to evaluate sentimentalism in terms of the dimensions of ethical discourse and practice that philosophers have typically been most concerned with explaining. These dimensions are formal and common to sentimentalist and non-sentimentalist theory alike. It is *how* the sentimentalist explains these dimensions, and *why* exactly the sentimentalist is concerned to explain them in the first place, that distinguishes sentimentalism from other moral theories, such as rationalism or intuitionism. To be clear, we are not implying that philosophers associated with sentimentalism have put equal weight on all of the dimensions of moral discourse we shall identify, or even that all the dimensions have been accepted as genuinely essential features of ethical discourse and thus as criteria for judging their position. Nevertheless, in the traditional and contemporary debate, the plausibility of candidate theories has always been judged according to how well these dimensions were either met or explained away as mistaken criteria in the first place.

First, sentimentalism has always been concerned with the *practical relevance* of moral judgment. Sincerely judging child abuse or torture as "wrong," for example, should have implications for how we conduct our life. But if moral judgments depend on the existence of an emotion, and emotions are motivating mental states, then sentimentalists have an attractive explanation for this first dimension of morality. At any rate, sentimentalists have tended to be (at least implicit) proponents of what philosophers nowadays refer to as "judgment internalism," the view that sincerely making a moral judgment necessarily implies that one has a motive to act accordingly.[4] Correspondingly, sentimentalists usually maintain that moral philosophy is possible only in light of a plausible moral psychology.

---

[1] Audi (2013: 94); Shafer-Landau (2003: 247); Scanlon (2014: 70).
[2] Clarke (1964); Ross (1930); Scanlon (2014).
[3] Shafer-Landau (2008: 83).    [4] Darwall (1983).

Second, and again like most moral theories, sentimentalism seeks to address the apparent *objectivity* of moral discourse, at least in the minimal sense of explaining how moral judgments can be intersubjectively valid. Some sentimentalists who famously rejected realist objectivity (the claim that moral judgments have literal truth value), like Alan Gibbard, have still seen it fit to explain how moral discourse operates with a *kind* of objectivity, namely, of a sort that could answer to relativist worries. And even those, like A.J. Ayer, who seem to bite the bullet on the *lack* of objectivity afforded by their views, still address the appearance of objectivity in moral discourse and try to show how their theories can explain away this dimension (as a requirement of a suitable theory). Granted, the success of these attempts has been contentious. But this doesn't change the point at hand, namely, that sentimentalists have always taken seriously the intuition that moral judgments and rules purport to have universal scope and for this reason are distinguishable from mere social conventions. Closely related to this point of objectivity, most sentimentalists accept the further expectation to explain how the wrongness of a given practice provides every human being with a reason not to engage in such practices, and vice versa for right ones. In other words, most sentimentalists understand the objectivity of morality to require an attending account of how such moral judgments express normative obligations for all human agents, regardless of whatever local practices and customs a given agent might subscribe to. Call this third dimension the *normative character* of ethical discourse and practice.

Finally, to provide an account of morality that explains its *practical relevance* in a psychologically plausible way, and that acknowledges its *objectivity* and *normative character*, sentimentalists have been committed to a naturalistic perspective. They have assumed that they must offer a theory that is *epistemically* and *metaphysically* plausible in view of our best scientific theories about the world.

## 2    Classical Sentimentalism

In the eighteenth century, "sentimentalism" was not a classification of moral theory. In fact, the term had virtually no currency in the eighteenth century. Even when it did gain currency (in the nineteenth century) it first referred to an eighteenth-century literary genre known for exaggerated and glorified emotional sensitivity and tenderness.[5] Instead, the Enlightenment

---

[5] Canonical examples include Samuel Richardson's *Pamela, or Virtue Rewarded* and Jean-Jacques Rousseau's *New Heloise*. This literary movement was not unrelated to its philosophical cousin, as Rousseau's own authorship partly testifies. For a stimulating inquiry into sentimentalist literature in the eighteenth century and some of its connections to philosophical sentimentalism, see Festa (2006).

innovators of the position – Shaftesbury (Anthony Ashley Cooper), Francis Hutcheson, David Hume, and Adam Smith – were first collectively identified as "moral sense" theorists. This label stuck until about 1960, at which point "sentimentalism" slowly took over as the new term of art.[6] This change was overdue. For, while Shaftesbury and Hutcheson defended the idea of a moral sense (albeit, they had very different conceptions of it), Hume and Smith successively moved away from it.[7] We will return to this point later.

What precipitated the rise of sentimentalism? It hardly needs saying that the scientific revolution and conjoined rise of empiricism during the Enlightenment profoundly affected all philosophical thought of the period. This influence was buttressed by the reinvigoration of skeptical debates that started in the late sixteenth and early seventeenth centuries, and that seemed to many to undermine the appeal of traditional alternatives, especially theological dogmatism and ancient rationalism. Among these are thinkers like Hobbes, Locke, and the early French materialists, who thought the deep lesson of skepticism was whole-hearted naturalistic empiricism. This commitment set the stage for sentimentalism, in two closely connected ways.

On the one hand, endorsing skeptical and materialist foundations meant rejecting or at least suspending conviction in a metaphysically free will. On the other hand – and most obviously in the case of Hobbes and the other early materialist thinkers – empiricism seemed to call for a fresh scrutiny of human psychology and behavior. The puzzle wasn't that something like justice and morality seem to exist, but how to explain the seeming objectivity and normativity of justice and morality without reference to mind independent truths or a metaphysically free will. Materialists addressed this puzzle by appealing to the passions as fundamental facts of human nature. Thus Hobbes explicitly classified ethics as merely the study of "consequences from the passions of men."[8] And the French materialist Vauvenargues – a

---

[6] It is not clear precisely when "sentimentalism" came into usage as a description of the moral and meta-ethical theory we associate with that term today. Baumrin's introduction to the 1964 edition of Selby-Bigge's "British Moralists" uses "sentimentalism" more or less as we do now. A more likely bridge for its introduction to metaethics, however, may be Mackie's usage in his 1980 *Hume's Moral Theory* (though of course Mackie may have referenced Baumrin). In any event, the term clearly does not have much currency before 1980. We are grateful to Stephen Darwall and Donald Ainsle for discussion on this point.

[7] Hume critiques (what one assumes must be Hutcheson's) moral sense theory in Treatise 3.1.2, for being at risk of positing an infinite number of sensory capacities to humans. But even if Hume retained elements of a moral sense, Smith rejects moral sense theory altogether; see the concluding part of, *The Theory of Moral Sentiments* [hereafter TMS] (1759/1982), esp. VII.iii.3.16. In this volume, all references to Smith's work are to part, section, chapter, and paragraph numbers.

[8] Hobbes (1994: IX).

forerunner to more famous French determinists like d'Holbach and Helvetius – implied the same when he wrote, "Nos passions ne sont pas distinctes de nous-memes" (the passions aren't distinct from who we are).[9]

Of course, turning to the passions was the methodological starting point, not the explanatory conclusion. For, while Hobbes and his fellow materialists famously reduced justice and morality – or at least, the practice of justice and morality – to self-love and the products of prudent fulfillment of private interest, the sentimentalists arrived at more optimistic conclusions. Thus, like Hobbes, the sentimentalists seized the opportunity early modern empiricism and materialism helped create, namely, to explain justice and morality in terms of natural facts about human nature, especially human passion and sentiment. But, unlike Hobbes, their analysis of human nature ultimately vindicated the "sociable" side of humanity. Indeed, resisting self-love theories emerged as an explicit, distinguishing feature of sentimentalist thought – though not, as one might think, on account of Hobbes's influence. Instead, it was the influence of a new egoistic challenge, Bernard Mandeville's then notorious, *Fable of the Bees*.[10]

Mandeville registered two primary complaints against more optimistic views of human sociability. First, he challenged the "Reality" of morality, and specifically credence in immutable moral truths, which an innate human "Sense" (as Shaftesbury had explicitly called it), allows us to discern. Thus Mandeville emphasized the fact that moral judgment seems malleable. Our moral beliefs are highly susceptible to the influence of custom, to change over time, and cultural differences – points that must have pricked the doubt of Enlightenment readers who were witnessing rapid cultural changes and astounding discoveries about foreign civilizations.[11] In short, Mandeville called into question the *objectivity* of moral judgment.

---

[9] Vauvenargues (1857: 31). Notably, some empiricists took the materialist focus on passion further; that is, beyond a passion-centered study of moral motivation – to a theory about epistemological relations generally. Most famously, Hume claimed that belief was itself a peculiar feeling: "An idea assented to," Hume argued, "*feels* different from a fictitious idea." (Hume 1739–1740/2000, 1.3.10.3; SBN 119 & 1.3.7.7; SBN 628–629). In this volume, all citations to Hume's *Treatise of Human Nature* are followed by book, part, and section number, and, in the case of explicit quotations, also to paragraph numbers. All citations to Hume's *Abstract* to the *Treatise* are abbreviated by "Abs" followed by paragraph number. All citations to Hume's *An Enquiry Concerning Human Understanding* and *An Enquiry Concerning the Principles of Morals* are to part and section numbers, and, in the case of explicit quotations, also to paragraph numbers. Explicit quotations are in all cases also followed by the Selby-Bigge/Nidditch edition page numbers, abbreviated as "SBN."

[10] Chronologically speaking, Mandeville attacked Shaftesbury's optimism in human "sociability" (though that isn't a term Shaftesbury relied on), and Hutcheson, Hume, and Smith in various ways defended the more optimistic view.

[11] Mandeville presents many examples, moral and non-moral. He especially points to differences in religious belief: "Which is the best Religion? is a Question that has caused more Mischief than all other Questions together. Ask it at *Peking*, at *Constantinople*, and at

Second, Mandeville challenged optimism in human *moral motivation*. For Mandeville, no one actually possesses virtue because our ultimate motive to be virtuous is itself vicious – namely the pleasurable pride we take in thinking (falsely) that we are virtuous. "The humblest Man alive," Mandeville concludes, "must confess, that the Reward of Virtuous Action, which is the Satisfaction that ensures upon it, consists in a certain Pleasure he procures to himself by Contemplating on his own Worth."[12]

Hutcheson was the first to rebuff Mandeville's pessimism, which he did by a sustained defense of moral sense theory and the claim that humans are imbued with universal benevolence, that is, some innate love of mankind.[13] However, it was ultimately the moves that Hume and Smith made to counter Mandeville that proved most influential for the development of sentimentalism. Regarding Hume, his empirical and skeptical commitments obviously told against moral realism and even the semblance of rationalism to explain moral motivation and human sociability in particular. "Reason," Hume famously wrote, "is, and ought only to be the slave of the passions."[14] Instead, his explanation of sociability turned on what he called, the principle of "sympathy," a natural mechanism of psychological association by which emotions are communicated from one person to another (what today we would call "empathy"). Very roughly, Hume thought that when we witness the outward signs of emotion in another person, we internally associate these signs with an *idea* of that emotion, which idea is then "enlivened" into an *impression* – that is, into an actual emotion itself. Hume then concluded, regarding sociability:

'Tis true, there is no human, and indeed no sensible, creature, whose happiness or misery does not, in some measure, affect us, when brought near to us, and represented in lively colors: But this proceeds merely from sympathy, and is no proof of such an universal affection to mankind, since this concern extends itself beyond our own species.[15]

This appeal to sympathy, however, even if effective for explaining human sociability without egoism, doesn't explain moral approbation. Thus, suppose we approve of someone's motive, for example, her gratitude. Even if we grant that our approval *feels* like something, it doesn't obviously seem to feel like *gratitude*, or any other prototypical emotion for that matter. And yet, it is precisely prototypical emotions like gratitude that Hume claimed

*Rome*, and you'll receive three distinct Answers extremely different from one another, yet all of them equally positive and preemptory" (1988b: 331).
[12] Mandeville (1988a: 57).
[13] In the preface to his *Inquiry*, for example, Hutcheson announces his goal "to prove what we call the Reality of Virtue" (2004: 8). Whether Hutcheson was genuinely espousing moral realism, however, has been the subject of intense controversy in contemporary scholarship.
[14] Hume (1739–1740/2000, 2.3.3.4; SBN 414).     [15] Ibid. 3.1.2.4; SBN 471.

sympathy communicates to us. Nor can we explain approbation by appealing to the mere *agreeableness* of whatever sympathy communicates to us;
that is, approbation cannot be merely the pleasant valance of gratitude or
any other prototypical emotion we feel by sympathy. For, in that case, we'd
have no way to distinguish our approval of good wine from good action.
Worse, we'd have no way to distinguish our approval of "truly" moral
actions from our approval of actions that please us because they serve our
private interest.

But Hume anticipated these worries. Approval is not only a sentiment,
he claimed, but a "peculiar" one. Hume elaborated: "'Tis true, those sentiments, from interest and morals, are apt to be confounded, and naturally
run into one another ... But this hinders not, but that the sentiment are, in
themselves, distinct; and a man of temper and judgment may preserve himself from these illusions."[16] This statement is worth underlining. By explicitly claiming that moral approbation is a distinctive species of sentiment,
Hume highlights a feature of classical sentimentalism not obviously shared
with its contemporary counterparts, namely, the idea that approbation is
itself a kind of emotion.[17] Of course, one might worry that Hume's emphasis on the peculiarity of this sentiment forces him to accept some version
of moral sense theory after all. For, how else can we explain the origin of
this peculiar feeling? Indeed, it may well have been exactly this worry that
led Smith to take a different approach to answer the challenges of self-love
theory.

First, Smith reconceived sympathy.[18] According to Smith, sympathy is a
process of imaginative simulation. We imagine ourselves in the situations of
other people and take up, as it were, a first person perspective on the object
of their emotions. As a consequence, sometimes we come to feel something
toward those objects ourselves. Second, Smith argued, we observe whether
or not the feeling that this simulation produces in us matches, or at least
closely resembles, what the actual "actors" in those situations feel. And
if the emotions do match, he further argued, then we cannot help but to
approve what those people feel.[19] Finally, Smith argued that to observe
this agreement or "mutual sympathy" between the two emotions – what
we as spectators feel and what the other person as actor feels – is always
pleasurable. Similarly, to observe that we are not in mutual sympathy is
always painful. This, for Smith, is the sense in which moral approbation is
itself a *felt* response: moral approbation just is the pleasurable feeling of

[16] Ibid. 3.1.2.4; SBN 471.
[17] The most obvious exception is Michael Slote. But see also Prinz in this volume.
[18] Smith concedes that sympathy is sometimes, but only rarely, the pure product of a Humean
associationistic contagion; see TMS I.i.1.6–9.
[19] Ibid. I.i.3.1.

mutual sympathy. To Smith's mind, these observations already rebuffed at least part of self-love theory. For, he argues, "the pleasure and the pain" of mutual sympathy or its absence, "are always felt so instantaneously, and often upon such frivolous occasions, that it seems evident that neither of them can be derived form any such self-interested consideration."[20]

Hume's and Smith's innovations in moral psychology, especially on sympathy, were strong counter arguments to Mandeville's attempt to reduce the phenomenology of approbation to self-love. But what of Mandeville's challenge to account for the *objectivity* of moral judgment? Hume and Smith did not fail to offer a reply to this point as well, and in fact made very similar replies.

In the first place, without the constraints of moral realism, Hume and Smith could easily admit that moral judgments vary and change – indeed, that they change partly for the very reason Mandeville suggested, the influence of custom. However, Hume and Smith were quick to add, this is what we should expect given the pivotal role of sympathy in moral judgment. For, on both their accounts of sympathy, sympathy naturally tends to favor the sentiments of persons close to us by dint of affection, time, or distance, as well persons like us in manner, belief, or appearance. And yet, Hume and Smith argued, these same facts about the variance of moral judgment pressure us to search for *common* points of agreement. Very roughly, Hume emphasized that moral language and belief would be too unstable to be intelligible without such points of agreement. And Smith reemphasized the fact that mutual sympathy (which marks agreement) is in itself pleasurable, and its absence painful, and thus we are naturally always motivated to seek agreement. In either case, the only way to establish such agreement is to reflect on our own sentiments from a viewpoint that is not "peculiar to ourselves" (as Hume put it[21]). That is, we must seek a standpoint abstracted from our personal biases, which standpoint might allow us to form general standards of correctness for our sentiments and in turn general concepts of morality. Hume called this, "the general point of view" or the viewpoint of the "judicious spectator";[22] though it is perhaps better known by the name Smith gave it, the viewpoint of the "impartial spectator." In this way, Hume and Smith combined a normative account of moral judgment with their meta-ethical one, thereby answering Mandeville's challenge to explain the objectivity of morality without appealing to moral realism.

But what of the final dimension of morality we noted in our description of the basic position of sentimentalism, namely, the need to explain the *obligation* to be moral? Even if we accept Hume's and Smith's general

---

[20] Ibid. I.i.2.1.     [21] Hume (1751/1998, 5.2.42; SBN 229).
[22] Hume (1749–1750/2000, 3.3.1.14–15; SBN 581).

strategy to explain the objectivity of moral standards, still, what requires us to abide by those standards? How do Hume and Smith, or Shaftesbury and Hutcheson for that matter, explain the *normativity* of morality? The classical sentimentalists seem to have appreciated the conceptual point. Shaftesbury, Hutcheson, Hume, and Smith each in their own way distinguish the need to explain what they called our "interested" obligation to morality (which in some way reduces to self-interest) from our "moral" obligation (which is not so reducible). However, scholars disagree about how these various explanations are supposed to go. One is thus left wondering whether there is a definite answer to the "normativity" question in the classical view? Then again, perhaps it will turn out to be a distinctive contribution of contemporary sentimentalism to fill in this part of a tradition that started over two and half centuries ago. Indeed, some of the contributions to this volume take up exactly this challenge.

### Contemporary Sentimentalism

Historically, the appeal of sentimentalism has been complicated and diminished by both utilitarian and Kantian alternatives to morality. In the Kantian perspective, reason itself is conceived of as containing an inherently practical aspect. That is, reason no longer merely recognizes the truth of moral propositions in virtue of adequately conceptualizing them, as intuitionist rationalism suggests. Rather, the validity of moral propositions and beliefs is tied to our commitment to rules and procedures already implicit in our deliberation about what to do. Or, at least, this is the central claim of so-called constructivist interpretations of the Kantian position, which are presently so influential.[23] Within this framework, the sentimental aspect of human nature plays at most a supportive role, namely, to reinforce the rule of moral reason through proper education and habituation. In other words, for a Kantian, our emotional reactions cannot *ground* the intersubjective and supposedly universal validity of moral judgments.[24] Moreover, as **Michael Frazer** argues in his essay, philosophers did not merely follow Kant's rationalist "lead" when it came to ethics. Many took his approach as paradigmatic for philosophy as a whole. And in doing so they generally ignored, to the detriment of philosophy, a more interdisciplinary and empirically grounded conception of philosophy so cherished by classical sentimentalism and its German sympathizer Johann Gottfried Herder.

Within the more narrow confines of Anglophone ethics, utilitarianism displaced ethical sentimentalism in the nineteenth century as the dominant "empiricist" ethical view. Hume had already made much of the importance

---

[23] Korsgaard (1996a).    [24] See particularly Wood (1999).

of "utility" to moral judgment, and in various ways the early utilitarians seem to have tried to co-opt Hume's position. In particular, and seemingly following Hume, John Stuart Mill attempted to ground the normative authority of the greatest happiness principle by linking it to our sympathetic and "social feeling of mankind."[25] However, utilitarians did not think of ethical concepts and judgments as being grounded in our emotional responses invoked in specific situations when we encounter other agents in their concrete individuality. Accordingly the impartial and sympathetic spectator seems to have been reconceived by Mill and his heirs as "the perfectly rational individual who identifies with and experiences the desires of others as if these desires were his own," allowing us – as Rawls later described it – to apply "the principle of one man" to the society as a whole.[26] But this conception of the impartial spectator came in for quick criticism. Writing in the latter half of the nineteenth century, Sidgwick argued that this manner of defending the utilitarian principle was empirically implausible. And this pejorative view continued well into the twentieth century. Thus Rawls complained that such a conception of impartial sympathy mistakes "impersonality for impartiality."[27] One can assume only that the long critique of "impartial spectator" models of ethics contributed to the neglect of classical sentimentalism.

Despite this inherited burden of resistance from critics of utilitarianism, however, the fortune of sentimentalism began to change around the beginning of the twentieth century. This change started in the context of logical positivism and its empiricist conception of the meaning of ethical statements. Ethical statements, the positivists stressed, do not seem to be directly verifiable by sensory experience. Yet it seems to be too radical to suggest that they are completely without meaning. A. J. Ayer first attempted to dissolve this conundrum by suggesting an emotive analysis of the content of ethical statements as merely expressing – rather than reporting – an approving or disapproving attitude toward certain kinds of actions.[28] In merely expressing certain attitudes, ethical statements do not report any moral or psychological facts and so cannot be shown to be true or false. Charles Stevenson further articulated the emotivist position outside of the confines of logical positivism by attempting to account for the seemingly rational character of ethical discourse and for the possibility of interpersonal disagreement.[29] Ultimately, however, to view ethical judgments merely as expressions of a feeling of approval seems not to square very well with our ordinary intuitions about the realist, objective, and universal character of ethical discourse.

---

[25] Mill (1963, chap. 3).     [26] Rawls (1971: 27).
[27] Sidgwick (1981: 499–503 and 387–388); and Rawls (1971: 190).
[28] Ayer (1936, chap. 6).     [29] Stevenson (1944 and 1963).

More recently, Simon Blackburn and Alan Gibbard have proposed quasi-realist and expressivist accounts of the meaning of our ethical statements that combine a non-cognitivist and anti-realist understanding of the ethical domain while acknowledging our prima facie realist intuitions within ordinary ethical discourse. They try to save the appearance of objectivity by providing a more detailed specification of the attitudes expressed in ethical statements, which allows us explicate the function of these attitudes in logically complex inferences. In turn we "earn the right" to regard these statements as having the appearance of being truth-apt. For expressivists, ethical discourse cannot be merely understood as the expression of a first-order mental attitude, such as anger, resentment, or guilt. Rather ethical discourse is best seen as being constituted by a complex of first- and second-order attitudes about one's own and others' first-order attitudes. For example, to judge the torture of innocent children to be wrong is not merely the expression of my personal anger or outrage. It also involves being angry at other people who are not angry about such events, and, correspondingly, approving of such anger in other people and oneself.[30] In this anthology, **Simon Blackburn** provides a forceful defense of such contemporary expressivism, drawing in part on the classical sentimentalist understanding of moral objectivity to counter contemporary forms of moral realism.

Contemporary expressivists also seem to acknowledge the normative dimension more directly in their analysis of ethical concepts than classical sentimentalists. Moral judgments and concepts are response-invoking not only because they express certain causal dispositions (first- or second-order). Rather, they are expressing second-order judgments or attitudes about the *appropriateness* or *fittingness* of such first-order sentiments. For example, Gibbard analyzes our judgments of moral wrongness as expressing an attitude of "acceptance" for norms prescribing feeling guilty when we commit certain acts and resentment when others commit them.[31] Justin D'Arms and Daniel Jacobson have usefully suggested the term "neo-sentimentalism" as a label for such fittingness accounts of moral concepts, which are now wide-spread in the contemporary context. In contrast to classical sentimentalism, neo-sentimentalists seem to acknowledge the inherently normative dimension of our moral judgments, which cannot be accounted for easily by identifying a moral concept in terms of specific causal dispositions. Obviously, it has to be asked whether and how the notion of fittingness can be analyzed so that it is compatible with the general sentimentalist framework. **Antti Kauppinen** suggests here that this

---

[30] Blackburn (1998: 8).
[31] Gibbard (1990: 47). Gibbard has since developed and modified his position; see Gibbard (2003).

problem can be solved by referring to the reactive attitudes of an adequately specified impartial spectator, while **Justin D'Arms** and **Daniel Jacobson** emphasize in the final essay of this anthology that an explication of fittingness has to proceed piecemeal in light of an investigation of the specific emotions involved in our evaluative judgments.

Sentimentalist or neo-sentimentalist analyses of moral concepts and judgments do not logically entail a particular stance regarding the metaphysics of moral properties.[32] They can be associated with an anti-realist and projectivist account of moral properties according to which our sentiments paint the world in moral colors. Ethical sentimentalism is also compatible with a modestly realist and response-dependent account, according to which such properties are constituted in light of our responses to the world.[33] Similar to secondary properties like color, moral properties can then also be perceived given the right education and skillful attunement toward the world. In principle, a sentimentalist account of moral concepts can even be combined with a robustly realist – that is, response-independent – explication of moral properties, regardless of whether such an account views moral properties as being reducible or irreducible to natural properties. For a robust realist, our sentiments or emotions would then play primarily an epistemic role for recognizing or affectively perceiving moral properties that are constituted independent of our sentiments. Sentimentalists would normally regard a non-reductive account of moral properties to be incompatible with the naturalist framework that they favor. Indeed from an evolutionary perspective it would seem to be rather mysterious that our cognitive and sentimental faculties are selected to track such "non-natural" properties. Thus, adopting a *robustly realist* yet reductive account of moral properties seems to be a more plausible option for a sentimentalist, even if contemporary sentimentalists so far have been more attracted toward anti-realism or versions of modest realism. A number of the following essays address these metaphysical topics and mirror the variety of meta-ethical positions associated with sentimentalism. **Karl Schafer** shows that from an epistemological perspective arguments based on evolutionary considerations – so-called debunking arguments – cannot be easily used to argue for sentimentalist antirealism. **Terry Horgan** and **Mark Timmons** argue that realism is not implied by the phenomenology of moral perceptual experiences as is often assumed by contemporary philosophers but is also compatible with a position of cognitive expressivism. Moreover, **Peter Railton** shows in his essay that there is reason to think Hume himself adopted a robustly realist yet reductive conception of moral properties while also accepting a sentimentalist account of moral concepts.

---

[32] See also Kauppinen (2014a).    [33] See Blackburn (1988) and McDowell (1998).

Alongside these theoretical spurs to sentimentalism, interest in contemporary sentimentalism has been greatly bolstered by a trending tendency of philosophers to connect ethical hypotheses to empirical research. In particular, sentimentalism has benefited from empirical studies of the psychological mechanisms underlying our capacities for moral judgment and moral agency (see for Haidt 2001; Greene and Haidt 2002; and various articles in Sinnott-Armstrong 2008). Some philosophers, most notably Shaun Nichols and Jesse Prinz, have even suggested that traditional meta-ethical considerations are best decided solely in light of such evidence.[34] Interestingly, both Nichols and Prinz take the empirical evidence as counting against a neo-sentimentalist or fittingness conception of moral judgment and as supporting more traditional sentimentalist positions, which analyze moral concepts in terms of first order emotional responses. In his essay, **Jesse Prinz** provides further arguments for this claim while at the same time emphasizing that Hume's sentimentalist stance provides current empirical research in moral psychology with hitherto overlooked directions.

Surprisingly, but maybe also due to a lingering influence of Rawls' critique of the utilitarian conception of sympathy mentioned above, most contemporary sentimentalists focus narrowly on the importance of emotions in their analysis of ethical concepts. Comparatively few have emphasized Hume's and Smith's claim that sympathy – or what we now call empathy, that is, our ability to share another person's state of mind and imaginatively take up his perspective – is the central underlying psychological mechanism enabling us to take an evaluative and moral stance toward each other. But this is starting to change. For instance, Michael Slote (2007, 2010), being also influenced by a feminist ethics of care, has argued that moral approval and disapproval is constituted in light of our ability to empathically recognize an agent's benevolent or sympathetic motivations for his actions. In contrast to Hume and Smith, however, Slote embraces the natural limitations and biases of our empathetic capacities in his defense of the moral significance of empathy. That is, he does not appeal to an impartial spectator perspective as a corrective for such biases. At yet, it is precisely this susceptibility to bias that has led some sentimentalists like Prinz to limit their endorsement of the classical tradition; indeed, Prinz has vigorously argued against empathy as an essential ingredient in human morality.[35] In her essay, **Diana Tietjens Meyers** evaluates this important point about bias and some of these arguments against empathy, but she ultimately argues that empathy is necessary for overcoming problems of difference.

Regardless of one's stance toward empathy, the question of bias raises a more fundamental question for the sentimentalist project: How do we

---

[34] Nichols (2004) and Jesse Prinz (2007).     [35] Prinz (2011a and 2011b).

square a realistic account of human psychology with the apparent universal scope and intersubjective validity of moral judgments? If human motivation and psychological mechanisms (even prima facie other-oriented ones) are of rather limited scope and easily malleable by personal, social, and cultural influences – how can sentimentalism make sense of morality's objectivity and normativity? More robustly realist and Kantian constructivist positions in metaethics seem to have an easier time answering the question about the universal scope of our moral judgments even if sentimentalists provide a much richer description of our emotional life. Taking their cues from Strawson's seminal essay "Freedom and Resentment," some authors[36] have therefore suggested to think about the nature of reactive attitudes as already being infused with Kantian notions of deontic moral responsibility and moral autonomy, a conception that **Michelle Mason** in this volume argues needs to be broadened to what she calls an appellative understanding of the reactive attitudes. But maybe, as various authors in this anthology suggest rethinking the stance articulated by classical sentimentalists, particularly Adam Smith with his emphasis on empathy and the impartial spectator perspective, allows us to find underutilized resources within the sentimentalist tradition that would enable us to squarely address this fundamental challenge. More specifically, **Karsten Stueber** argues that impartiality and the impartial spectator perspective should be seen as an implicit commitment of our folk-psychological practice of making sense of each other through empathic perspective taking. And **Remy Debes** suggests that empathic judgments about the propriety of emotion are sometimes grounded in a conception of ourselves as persons with dignity. Moreover, in recognizing the value of ethical sentimentalism one might be also one step closer to properly appreciate the ethical perspective of early Confucianism, which rejects a strict distinction between reason and sentiments as **David Wong** argues in his contribution to this anthology.

---

[36] Darwall (2006a) and Wallace (1996).

# 1     Interdisciplinary before the Disciplines: Sentimentalism and the Science of Man

*Michael L. Frazer*

## 1     Introduction

One of the obstacles that we face when interpreting the philosophy of another era is the fact that key terms change their meaning over time. The very word "philosophy" is itself rather protean. In eighteenth-century English, the terms "science" and "philosophy" could still be used interchangeably to refer to intellectual investigation as such. To isolate the "philosophy" of the Enlightenment as a distinct subject of scholarly inquiry – one to be interpreted by a community of philosophical specialists, separate from those devoted to the history of science – is therefore to risk serious misunderstanding.[1]

Once we use two protean words together, the possible confusion only magnifies. This is precisely the problem with the phrase "moral philosophy," since the word "moral" also meant something rather different in the Enlightenment than it does today. In a narrow sense, "moral" could mean something like it does now, but it could also be used in a broader sense to refer to anything having to do with the mental or social lives of human beings. A professor of moral philosophy was expected to teach what we still call by that name, but also what we now call psychology, philosophy of mind, sociology, anthropology, history, political science, and economics. In eighteenth-century English, "moral philosophy" in this broad sense was also often called "the science of man."

As is so often the case, these changes in language reflect deeper changes in social practices. The narrowing of the word "philosophy" represents a narrowing of the philosophical profession itself, as philosophers take their place alongside a host of other specialists in the modern university. Moral philosophy, in turn, is reduced to a mere subfield of this one small discipline. Outside of that subfield, most of the subjects once considered part of

---

[1] In a new introduction to the new edition of *Leviathan and the Air Pump*, Shapin and Schaffer (1985/2011: xxxv) complain that their work has not been able to overcome the division between those who study Hobbes the "philosopher" and those who study Boyle the "scientist."

moral philosophy are now investigated using allegedly value-neutral methods modeled on those of the natural sciences.

Although all Enlightenment philosophers felt free to cross what would later become disciplinary boundaries, not all of them did so in the same way. Kant famously begins his critical moral philosophy with the a priori metaphysics of morals, only then turning to empirical investigation to determine how imperfect, real-world creatures such as ourselves may be better brought in line with morality's authoritative demands. By contrast, other philosophers seamlessly integrate empirical and normative analysis throughout their work – asking how creatures such as we are, possessing the kind of psychological constitutions that we do, can agree on standards of happiness and virtue tailored to our particular nature. This approach can be seen as culminating with Kant's estranged student J. G. Herder, whose comprehensive "history of humanity" was intended as a grand synthesis of all of our knowledge about human virtues and vices.

We can follow contemporary custom and call the former camp "rationalist" and the latter "empiricist," but only with the caveat that categories developed to organize the history of other branches of philosophy and science must be used with care when applied to moral philosophy and the science of man. In Germany at the time, the same two approaches to moral subjects could be called "metaphysical" and "anthropological," respectively – with "anthropology" used to mean all forms of empirical study of human beings, and not the narrower discipline with which we are familiar today. In Britain, the first approaches could be called "abstract" and the latter "experimental" – with "experiments" used at the time to mean simply "observations," not necessarily the controlled experiments of the laboratory. Unfortunately, all of the available names for these approaches are liable to cause one form of confusion or another (see Debes 2014).

Regardless of the labels we use, the important point for purposes of this volume is that Hume, Smith, and the other authors whom we now call sentimentalists all follow empiricist procedures. There is no necessary connection between empiricism in other fields and sentimentalism in ethics; Locke was more or less a moral rationalist. Nor is there even a necessary connection between moral sentimentalism and specifically moral empiricism; empirical study of the human condition might reveal that the road to hell is paved with good sentiments, as Mandeville argued. There is, however, an elective affinity between the empiricist methods and sentimentalist conclusions. Careful investigation of the origins of our actual moral commitments, and of the empirical requirements of human happiness, typically reveals that human ethics is based in large part on emotion, and that we can only hope to be happy by pursuing the virtues toward which our emotions point us. Many eighteenth-century moral empiricists who are not typically thought of as sentimentalists, Herder most prominent among them, can readily be reclassified as such.[2] Scientists and philosophers examining empirical moral psychology today have also endorsed roughly sentimentalist positions, while those opposed to empiricist methods in ethics are more often moral rationalists.[3]

Those who reject both moral empiricism and moral sentimentalism have often taken their inspiration from the critical-period Kant. Neo-Kantians are generally comfortable with the narrow confines of the modern discipline of philosophy. As has been widely observed since Hegel, Kant's critical philosophy is built around a series of divisions: divisions between phenomena and noumena, between theoretical and practical reason, between virtue and justice, and, between the a priori metaphysics of morals and the empirical study of practical anthropology. The modern Anglo-Germanic university – with its many autonomous disciplines and its commitment to scholarly specialization – is the institutional embodiment of intellectual distinctions that make sense from a Kantian perspective.

Still, it is important not to exaggerate Kant's responsibility for today's division of intellectual labor, which can also be defended in a wide variety of other ways. It is particularly ironic that many defend the division of labor between moral philosophers and scholars in the other arts and sciences by reference to a misinterpretation of Hume, the view that "Hume's law" draws a sharp boundary between "is" and "ought." Closer attention to Hume's work and that of his fellow sentimentalists cures us of this confusion. As Macintyre (1966: 242) memorably points out, Hume himself regularly breached his own alleged law. Similar violations were committed by all of Hume's immediate sentimentalist predecessors (such as Shaftesbury, Butler, and Hutcheson) as well as his immediate followers (such as Smith, Herder, and the pre-critical Kant).

There is a growing sense that the current structure of disciplinary divisions is both arbitrary and unduly constraining. Interdisciplinarity is the watchword of the day, but most scholars are so utterly socialized into their segregated disciplines that it is often unclear how interdisciplinary research can proceed. Enlightenment sentimentalism's greatest potential contribution to scholarship today is thus not a matter of humanistic scholarship, empirical social science, or normative ethics, but rather an agenda for fruitful collaboration between these fields. Eighteenth-century sentimentalists were united in a common project synthesizing all of what are now

---

[2] For a full defense of my reclassification of Herder as a moral sentimentalist, see Frazer (2010, chap. 6: 139–167).

[3] For some examples of recent empiricist sentimentalism, see Haidt (2001), Nichols (2004), and Prinz (2007).

the humanities and social sciences so as to both understand and improve human nature, a project that could serve as an inspiration to analogous work in the twenty-first century.

Section 2 of this chapter will further elucidate the empirical approach of eighteenth-century moral sentimentalism by contrasting it to the alternative approaches that came both earlier and later. Section 3 will then use Hume and Herder as methodological models for interdisciplinary research on the moral sentiments. This interdisciplinary approach will then be defended against two important objections. Section 4 will respond to the objection that an empirically informed approach to human ethics is unacceptable because it cannot produce a moral code binding on any rational being as such. Section 5 will respond to the objection that this approach cannot establish the categorical authority that moral principles have over us. Section 6 will conclude with some sociological and psychological hypotheses that might help explain why the sentimentalist approach to ethics, for all its philosophical virtues, has not been adequately appreciated.

## 2    The New Science

There was widespread agreement in the eighteenth century that something new and exciting was going on in moral philosophy. The standard analogy is to the radical changes that "natural philosophy" (that is, science) had undergone in previous centuries. Like his teacher Kant, Herder calls for a second Copernican revolution, but he has a rather different revolution in mind. Just as "the Ptolemaic system became the Copernican system," Herder heralds the coming of a day when "our entire philosophy has become anthropology" (Suphan 1967–1968 v. 32: 61).[4] "You are already a philosopher," he enjoins his fellow intellectuals. "Oh, be a human being, and think for human beings, that they may act and be happy" (Gaier 1985 v. 1: 118; Forster 2002: 15).

The echo of Hume's injunction "Be a philosopher, but amidst all your philosophy be still a man" (Hume 1748/1999, 1.6; SBN 9)[5] is surely intentional. Herder – an excellent reader of English – was aware that the revolution he advocated in German philosophy was already underway in Britain. Hume himself cites his sentimentalist precursors Shaftesbury, Hutcheson, and Butler alongside their interlocutors Locke and Mandeville as among the "late philosophers in England who have begun to put the science of man

---

[4] There are two widely used editions of Herder's works in German: Gaier (1985) and Suphan (1967–1968). Whenever a translation has also been consulted, it is listed after the citation to the German edition. In other cases, translations are my own.

[5] When the editors of the editions cited themselves failed to do so, I have modernized and Americanized the spelling and punctuation of eighteenth-century English texts.

on a new footing" (Hume 1739–1740/2009 Intro.7; SBN xvi). Although "they differ in many points among themselves," Hume praises these authors for all "founding their accurate disquisitions of human nature entirely upon experience" (Hume Abs. 2; SBN 646).

The analogy to the earlier revolution in natural science was taken seriously by all of the British authors that Hume mentions. In his preface to the posthumously published *System of Moral Philosophy*, Hutcheson's colleague William Leechman recalls that Hutcheson

> ...had observed that it was the happiness and glory of the present age that they had thrown off the method of forming hypotheses and suppositions in natural philosophy and had set themselves to make observations and experiments on the constitution of the world itself ... He was convinced that in like manner a true scheme of morals could not be the product of genius and invention, or of the greatest precision of thought in metaphysical reasonings, but must be drawn from proper observations upon the several powers and principles which we are conscious of in our bosoms, and which must be acknowledged to operate in some degree in the whole human species. (In Hutcheson 1755/2005, v. 1: xiii–xiv)

It is important to realize that eighteenth-century moral empiricists consciously decided to reject what they saw as the previously dominant approach to the subject. Seventeenth-century moral rationalists – such as Spinoza and the Cambridge Platonists – had employed methods surprisingly similar to those used by twentieth-century Anglo-American analytic ethicists. It was not that the seventeenth-century approach to moral philosophy was purely metaphysical or aprioristic, at least not with the kind of purism that would emerge later. In Butler's formulation, the distinction between the "two ways in which the subject of morals may be treated" is a matter of different starting points. The old method, he says, "begins from inquiring into abstract relations of things"; the new "from a matter of fact, namely, what the particular nature of man is, its several parts, their economy or constitution; from whence it proceeds to determine what the course of life it is, which is correspondent to this whole nature" (Butler 1983, Preface 12: 13).

In the twentieth century, the a priori approach to ethics was thought to be the only possible means of escaping what Moore (1903/1993) called the naturalistic fallacy. Even as they consciously chose to reject the seventeenth-century ancestors of this approach, eighteenth-century empiricists were well aware of the danger of blurring the distinction between empirical and normative claims. Hume is of course famous for making a distinction along roughly those lines, and Smith too describes how the bulk of his moral philosophy "is not concerning a matter of right, if I may say so, but concerning a matter of fact" (Smith 1759/1982, II.i.5.10).

Yet while we must indeed distinguish between matters of fact and matters of right – and may not be able to derive one from the other – it is nonetheless the case that coming to understand the facts concerning human moral sentiments will, as a matter of psychological fact, have an effect on those very sentiments. While identifying the psychological effects of this factual knowledge is itself a matter of empirical investigation, Enlightenment sentimentalists did not merely identify the psychological effects of self-knowledge in a value-neutral way, but also evaluated them normatively, and concluded that they were overwhelmingly changes for the better. "By examining the various turns, inflections, declensions and inward revolutions of the passions," Shaftesbury explains, "I must undoubtedly come the better to understand a human breast, and judge the better of others and myself" (Shaftesbury 1711/2001, v. 1: 182).

Moral philosophers must begin with our moral sentiments as they are; they must devote most of their time and energy to ensuring that their descriptions of all the relevant facts are empirically accurate. Smith nonetheless notes that "by the justness as well as delicacy of their observations they may often help both to correct and to ascertain our natural sentiments with regard to the propriety of conduct, and suggesting many nice and delicate attentions, form us to a more exact justness of behavior, than what, without such instruction, we should have been apt to think of" (Smith 1759/1982, VII.iv.6).

Here, the appropriate analogy is not to the natural science of the sixteenth and seventeenth centuries, but to the ethics of a much earlier era. The Enlightenment science of man represents a return to the Hellenistic conception of moral philosophy as a kind of practical therapy, the art of learning to think, act, and feel properly, and hence to live well and become happy. Modern empirical science is valued, not for its own sake, but insofar as it is the best means available to help us achieve the ancient ideal of happiness through self-awareness. Shaftesbury – the most self-consciously neo-Stoic of all the Enlightenment sentimentalists – is convinced that the proper "harmony and proportion" of the soul is only "discoverable in the characters and affections of mankind, in which are laid the just foundations of an art and science superior to every other of human practice and comprehension" (Shaftesbury 1711/2001, v.1: 218).[6]

## 3     The Experimental Method

Once we have decided to attempt an empirical investigation of human virtue, the next question is how such an investigation should be

---

[6] On the neo-Hellenistic character of Enlightenment sentimentalism, see, among others, Immerwahr (1989), Martin (1994), and Potkay (2000).

conducted. Admittedly, Enlightenment sentimentalists were not always the most methodologically sophisticated researchers. In an era before the discovery of the full depths of the subconscious mind, most were convinced that the human soul was fully transparent to introspection. As a result, Hutcheson could reasonably claim that to discover truth on the subject of human psychology "nothing more is necessary than a little attention to what passes in our own hearts, and consequently every man may come to certainty in these points, without much art or knowledge of other matters" (Hutcheson 1728–1742/2002: 4).

Yet moral philosophy could not ignore the methodological changes that had occurred in natural philosophy. The remarkable effectiveness of new scientific approaches convinced Hume that with any "question of fact we can only expect success by following the experimental method" (Hume 1751/1998, 1.10; SBN 174). Today's methodological innovators would certainly seem to agree. Current proponents of "experimental philosophy" (e.g., Appiah 2008: 5–28) explicitly defend this movement in an attempt, in the spirit of Hume, to reintroduce "the experimental method of reasoning into moral subjects" (Hume 1739–1740/2009, Title Page).

Unfortunately for X-Phi-ers seeking to claim Hume as one of their own, "experimental" (as was already noted) is yet another protean term that has changed its meaning since the eighteenth century. Rather than recommending the controlled tests of today's laboratory science, Hume instead equates "careful and exact experiments" with the "observation of those particular effects which result from ... different circumstances and situations" (Hume 1739–1740/2000, Intro). If experimentation in general is to be equated with careful observation, in the case of "moral subjects" experimentation will merely involve close observation of the operations of the social world around us and the psychological forces within us. For Hume, who was most famous in his own time as a historian and an essayist, these observations were not to be conducted in the laboratory under controlled conditions, but in the uncontrolled reality of human life, a reality whose complexity is captured in history and literature. Although controlled experimentation will always be invaluable in psychology – as it is in so many other fields – humanistic inquiry also has an invaluable contribution to make when we are investigating the nature of human virtue.

Experimental psychologists are well aware that careful work in the laboratory is better at establishing what they call "internal validity" of their findings than what they call their "external validity." While there is often little doubt that, in a particular controlled environment, it was indeed the experimental treatment that caused the observed effects, it is often unclear to what extent an experiment's results can be generalized to other settings. For Hume, by contrast, "following the experimental method," is primarily about "deducing general maxims from a comparison of particular instances" (Hume 1751/1998, 1.10; SBN 174). The model here was Newton, who famously used his theory of gravity to explain everything from the orbits of the planets to the falling of an apple. As a result, Hume sought a general theory to explain all the diverse empirical phenomena which he observed in the moral realm. If the phenomena being explained are not sufficiently diverse, then the theory derived from them will lack the global applicability necessary to qualify as a general theory of human virtue. In this regard, evidence rigorously collected from a handful of (typically undergraduate) volunteers in the local laboratory is little better than evidence drawn from the intuitions of a group of professional philosophers gathered around a seminar table, or even from solitary introspection.

Herder was particularly concerned that the theories of virtue put forward by his contemporaries were unduly parochial. "Woe ... to the philosopher," he writes, "who, in making theories on humanity and manners and morals, knows only his own scene ... " (Suphan 1967–1968, v. 5: 653). Herder, like Hume before him, thinks history is the only cure for philosophical myopia – but in this case, history, not only of England, or even of Europe, but of the world as a whole. "Whoever does not make it his main focus ... to put together in imagination the taste and character of each age," Herder writes, "and to travel through the various periods of the world events with the penetrating look of a traveler hungry to learn, he, like that blind man [of Mark 8:23–25] sees human beings as trees, and consumes in history a dish of husks without a kernel, in order to ruin his stomach" (Gaier 1985, v. 1: 158).

Herder's goal is still to identify human happiness and human virtue, but when he studies diverse cultures across all times and places – including their arts, literature, and religion as well as their philosophy, politics, and economics – he sees that "in humanity there lies one invisible seed of receptivity for happiness and virtue on the whole earth and in all ages which, differently developed ... appears in different forms" (Suphan 1967–1968, v. 5: 558; Forster 2002: 335). While grounding universal claims about virtue in human nature is often thought to rely on an unduly "uniformitarian" understanding of our species,[7] Herder's oeuvre shows us that "human nature is no container of an absolute, independent, unchangeable happiness as the philosopher defines it." The human psyche is not a rigid structure but "a flexible clay, in the most different situations, needs and pressure, forming itself differently." In this way, "the very image of happiness changes with each condition and region" (Suphan 1967–1968, v. 5: 509).

---

[7] For two classic statements of this position, see Collingwood (1946/1994) and Meinecke (1936/1972).

That said, Herder insists that there are many important similarities underlying these different conceptions of happiness, so much so that he predicts they are gradually converging on a single ethical consensus. "There lies in the human species an infinite variety of sentiments, thoughts and efforts towards the unity of a true, effective purely moral character which belongs to the whole species," Herder insists. "An infinite variety striving for a unity that lies in all, that advances all" (Gaier 1985, v. 7: 750; Forster 2002: 423–424).

Just as Hume and Smith insisted that their moral philosophy was based more on matters of fact than on matters of right, so too does Herder often insist that he is merely an empirical historian. "I merely want to gather historical examples of how far the diversity of human beings can extend, to bring it into categories, and then to try to explain it," he writes. "I shall lead my readers out onto a knoll and show them how in the valley and on the plain creatures stray about that are so diverse that they hardly have a common name left; however, they are our fellow brothers, and their history is the history of our nature" (Gaier 1985, v. 1: 151; Forster 2002: 249). This historical project produced Herder's masterworks: the methodological essay *Auch Eine Philosophie der Geshichte zur Bildung der Menschheit* (*Yet Another Philosophy of History for the Education of Humanity*) of 1774; and the magisterial, if incomplete, application of this methodology in the four volumes of *the Ideen zur Philosophie der Geshichte der Menschheit* (*Ideas towards the Philosophy of the History of Humanity*) published between 1784 and 1791.

Just like the British sentimentalists, however, Herder is well aware that true understanding of the nature of moral sentiments does not, and should not, leave those sentiments unchanged. Herder calls on us to build empathetic understanding across otherwise insurmountable barriers of difference, not for its own sake, but to provide the insight necessary to take the morally appropriate stance on practical issues. Most importantly, Herder urges Europe to give up on her monstrous imperial goal of "compelling all the nations of the Earth to be happy in her way" (Gaier 1985, v. 6: 335; Churchill 1966: 224).

## 4 Humans and Other Rational Beings

It is the fact that virtue is what Shaftesbury calls a "constitution or economy of a particular creature or species" (Shaftesbury 1711/2001, v. 2: 53) that allows us to identify it through empirical investigation of the species in question: *homo sapiens*. Insofar as this method can prove effective, it can only do so for real-world human beings such as ourselves, creatures inescapably bound by the contingent features of our biology, our psychology, and the unchangeable features of our social life. Other sorts of beings might require other sorts of virtues; Smith suggests that the kinds of moral judgments which might be appropriate for God to make are not appropriate for us (Smith, 1759/1982, III.5.7). The virtues might look very different indeed if our species were, as Hume puts it, "so framed by nature as that each individual possessed within himself every faculty, requisite both for his own preservation and for the propagation of his kind" or if "all society and intercourse" were "cut off between man and man by the primary intention of the Supreme Creator" (Hume 1751/1998, 3.1.20; SBN 191).

What of the critical-period Kantian intuition that morality, to be worthy of the name, must be binding on any rational being as such? This intuition was simply one that sentimentalists did not share; for most of them, it barely even needed to be addressed. Later philosophers would try to fill in this apparent lacuna for them; Schopenhauer, for example, argues that the concept of a "rational being as such" is incoherent. We know the faculty of reason, he says:

...as the exclusive attribute of the human race, and are by no means entitled to think of it as existing outside that race, and to set up a genus called "rational beings" differing from its sole species, "man." Still less are we justified in laying down laws for such imaginary rational beings in the abstract ... We cannot help suspecting that Kant here gave a thought to the dear little angels ... (Schopenhauer 1840/1995: 63.)

There is no need, however, for sentimentalists to accept Schopenhauer's argument on this point. The concept of a rational being as such might be perfectly coherent, and it might be entirely possible to develop a moral philosophy out of principles binding on all members of that class – be they humans, gods, extraterrestrials, or even "dear little angels."[8] It is an interesting question whether there are any moral principles that apply both to us, as we are, and these imagined beings, as they are, but the sentimentalists never attempt to answer this question. Their goal was simply a different one – virtue "for earthlings," as Miller (2013) calls it today. Such virtue is appropriate only for us. "Were the question to be whether the human being could become, and should become, more than human," Herder admits, "a super-, an other-man [*ein Über-, ein Aussermensch*] beyond the realm of the species, every line written in response would be in vain" (Gaier 1985, v. 7: 125; Adler 1997: 99).

Insofar as eighteenth-century sentimentalists hint at an argument for choosing this goal over Kant's, the argument is primarily a moral one. Just

---

[8] The possibility of rational creatures on other planets was of particular interest to Kant. See Dick (1984), Crowe (2008), and Szendy (2013).

because a puzzle is coherent and interesting does not mean that it is worth spending our time trying to solve it. Life is short, and human needs are pressing. Sentimentalists therefore argued that it was their responsibility to their fellow humans to address moral questions of particular relevance to us as we happen to be. "If philosophy is to become useful for human beings," Herder writes, "then let it make the human being its center." (Gaier 1985, v. 1: 125; Forster 2001: 21).

For those with a deep concern for imaginary, non-human rational creatures, the results of the empiricist approach can be rather troubling. This is particularly true when we imagine fantastic beings interacting with realistic humans, and try to puzzle out not only whether they should be governed by the moral principles with which we are familiar, but whether we should be governed by these principles when we are interacting with them. In a discussion of what Rawls (1971/1999: 110) would later call the "conditions of justice," Hume writes:

Were there a species of creatures, intermingled with men, which, though rational, were possessed of such inferior strength, both of body and mind, that they were incapable of all resistance, and could never, upon the highest provocation, make us feel the effects of their resentment, the necessary consequence, I think, is that we should be bound by the laws of humanity to give gentle usage to these creatures, but should not, properly speaking, lie under any restraint of justice with regard to them. (Hume 1751/1998, 3.1.18; SBN 190)

Hume goes on to point out, however, that such a situation has never arisen in reality. "Civilized Europeans" may be tempted to imagine that they have a position of superiority of this sort over "barbarous Indians," and men may be tempted to imagine that they have such a position over women, but in both cases they would be mistaken (Hume 1751/1998, 3.1.19; SBN 191). The fact that Hume is willing to bite the bullet regarding such a disturbing hypothetical, and defend his position merely on the grounds that this possible world has never been actualized, leaves more recent philosophers rather unsatisfied (e.g., Baier 1980).

Hypothetical scenarios, often of an outlandish nature, are the stock in trade of ethicists today; a moral theory stands or falls on the basis of its ability to resolve them in ways that we find intuitively appealing. The implicit assumption seems to be a sort of moral modal realism – that our moral judgments about all possible worlds are genuine moral judgments, and that they are as important as our judgments about the actual world. This assumption is unquestioned even among those undertaking empirical research on moral psychology, whose modus operandi typically involves observing experimental subjects asked to solve the same scenarios used by philosophers. A distinctively human moral system, however, can only be expected to properly address situations in which human beings, with all their contingent features, actually find themselves. Eighteenth-century sentimentalists are entirely comfortable with the principles of morality being contingent in their reliance on these features of humanity, while the critical-period Kant and those who take their inspiration from him generally are not. As a result, where ethicists today produce their own short-form science fiction, sentimentalists like Hume, Smith, and Herder typically draw real-world examples from history, current events, and everyday experience.

## 5     Sources of Normativity

Yet it is not only those with a deep moral concern for extraterrestrials or angels who have reason to be concerned about sentimentalism's humanistic and empirical approach to moral philosophy. Those who are convinced that the naturalistic fallacy really is a fallacy will worry that defining virtue as an empirically-discoverable harmony of the human psyche will rob it of any unconditional claim it might have, even over us earthlings. Shaftesbury acknowledges that this is a concern worth addressing, since "what virtue is, and to whom the character belongs" is a separate matter from the question of "what obligation there is to virtue, or what reason to embrace it" (Shaftesbury 1711/2001, v. 2: 45).

As this quotation indicates, "obligation" is another English term that had a broader meaning in the eighteenth century than it does today. An obligation to perform an action simply meant an overriding reason to do it, one which ruled out the possibility of omitting it. This determinative reason could easily be self-interested. "If by obligation," Shaftesbury says, "we understand a motive from self-interest sufficient to determine all those who duly consider it, and pursue their own advantage wisely to a certain course of actions, we may have a sense of such an obligation ... by considering how much superior we esteem the happiness of virtue to any other enjoyment" (Shaftesbury 1711/2001, v. 2: 177).

Of course, there may be other sources of the "obligation to virtue" as well. The work of many eighteenth-century moral sentimentalists – with the adamant exception of Hume – is filled with frequent appeal to natural teleology and the intentions of nature's designer (see Gill 2000). Yet while these religious and metaphysical foundations may play a significant role in establishing morality's authority, they play a surprisingly marginal role in sentimentalist moral philosophy. "In this art, as in all others," Hutcheson explains, "we must proceed from the subjects more easily known, to those that are more obscure." As a result, he insists, we must not "deduce our first notions of duty from the divine will, but from the constitution of our nature, which is more immediately known, that from the full knowledge of it we may discover the design, intention and will of our Creator as to our conduct" (Hutcheson 1742–1747/2007: 24).

As in modern natural science, final causes are to be avoided when more mundane explanations based on empirically observable efficient causes are available. Since virtue can be discovered as the form of psychic harmony necessary for our happiness, those who are already committed to the purposiveness of the cosmos and the benevolence of God can deduce that it is both the intention of our creator and the *telos* of our nature for us to be happy in this way. Yet neither divine intentions nor natural teleology are necessary for us to unearth either the substance of virtue or the necessary role it must play in our happiness.

Metaethicists today tend to be dissatisfied both with a mere "interested obligation" to virtue and also with the religious and metaphysical foundations that were once thought to lend virtue an authority independent of its necessary contribution to human happiness. As a result, they have often looked elsewhere for the sources of morality's authority. Many have written approvingly of Enlightenment sentimentalists' discussions of reflective self-approbation as something of which only a virtuous mind is capable (e.g., Baier 1991 and Korsgaard 1996b). For most eighteenth-century authors, however, reflective self-approbation is a necessary element of happiness rather than an independent source of normative authority. As Shaftesbury argues, peace of mind can come only when "together with the most delightful affection of the soul there is joined a pleasing assent and approbation of the mind to what is acted in this good disposition and honest bent" (Shaftesbury 1711/2001, v. 2: 61). Only "a mind ... well composed, quiet, easy within itself and such as can freely bear its own inspection and review" (Shaftesbury 1711/2001, v. 2: 66) can be harmonious and tranquil, and therefore happy.

Here is hardly the place to determine whether self-approbation can function as a source of normativity independent of its role in promoting happiness, let alone whether a view of normativity along these lines can be attributed to any Enlightenment sentimentalists.[9] Such issues may be safely bracketed because the project of identifying virtue through the empirical investigation of humanity is compatible with a wide variety of positions on normativity. If we accept some version of eudemonism, then the fact that virtue is necessary for creatures such as ourselves to be happy may be sufficient to establish its authority over us. If we do not, then some further authority may be sought from a teleological Nature or Nature's

---

[9] In Frazer (2010), I argue that a view along roughly these lines can be attributed to Butler and the later Hutcheson, but that Hume, in his correspondence with the latter, offers a devastating refutation of it. See also Gill (1996) and Loeb (2002).

God, from a quasi-Platonic realm of reified "reasons," or perhaps from the reflective stability of the virtuous soul itself. Regardless, these concerns were marginal to the project of the Enlightenment sentimentalists – typically confined to introductions, conclusions, or passing asides. If anything, this should make their theories more rather than less attractive in today's diverse societies, as we search for a moral and political consensus that can unite those divided by their religious and meta-ethical worldviews. There is no denying that the sources of normativity are of profound philosophical interest, but they must not be allowed to monopolize our intellectual energy when there are so many more pressing issues for human minds to address.

## 6    Concluding Socio-Psychological Speculations

There is no denying that the empiricist, sentimentalist agenda for moral philosophy represents a path not taken in modern scholarship. Insofar as the path we did take can be attributed to a single philosopher, Kant is as good a candidate as any. It is therefore a great historical irony that, at the time that he was Herder's teacher, Kant was an adamant proponent of the sentimentalist approach. "The sole moral rule ... is this," Herder records Kant as proclaiming in his lectures of the early 1760's: "Act according to your moral feeling!" (Kant 1997: 10; KGS 27:16).

Kant also makes clear his commitment to British-style sentimentalism in the *Inquiry Concerning the Distinctness of the Principles of Natural Theology and Morality*, written in 1762 but published two years later. Here, Kant notes that "Hutcheson and others have, under the name of moral sentiment [*des moralischen Gefühls*] provided us with a starting point from which to develop some excellent observations" (Kant 1992: 274; KGS 2:300). In the announcement of his program of lectures for the 1765–1766 winter semester, Kant again asserts that "the judgment of moral rightness can be known, easily and accurately, by the human heart through what is called sentiment [*Sentiment*]." The word that Kant uses here isn't even proper German; he has simply left the English term untranslated. "The attempts of Shaftesbury, Hutcheson and Hume," he explains, "although incomplete and defective, have nonetheless penetrated furthest in the search for the fundamental principles of all morality." Kant promises that, in his lectures, the moral theories of these British sentimentalists "will be given the precision and the completeness that they lack." He continues:

In the doctrine of virtue I shall always begin by considering historically and philosophically what happens before specifying what ought to happen. In so doing, I shall make clear what method ought to be adopted in the study of man ... My purpose will be to establish what perfection is appropriate to him ... This method of moral enquiry is an admirable discovery of our times. . . . (Kant 1992: 298; KGS 2:311)

In later years, of course, Kant was to reverse this procedure: establishing what ought to happen metaphysically before considering what really happens anthropologically. This is not to say that Kant ever lost interest in the empirical features of human virtue. Recent commentaries on Kant's mature ethics have moved away from the rationalist foundational theories of *Groundwork* and the second *Critique* to see even the critical-period Kant as engaging with the contingent features of specifically human morality, in works of what might be called "impure ethics," or, more closely following Kant's own terminology, "practical anthropology" (e.g., Louden 2000, Shell 1996, and Sherman 1997). In the lectures of 1784–1785 preserved by G. L. Collins, Kant explains that this sort of inquiry must "build upon the characteristic feature[s] peculiar to the human race" (Kant 1997: 55; KGS 27:261–262).

In correcting interpretations unduly focused on his metaphysics of morals, however, we must be careful not to overstate the later Kant's estimate of the moral or philosophical importance of practical anthropology. To be sure, Kant recognized that human beings are not purely rational beings, and that the empirically observable, non-rational features of the human soul neither can nor should be entirely extirpated. Instead, they must be cultivated so as to help our behavior conform with reason's authoritative demands. Yet if they are not put in service of the moral law legislated a priori by reason, distinctly human virtues are nothing but vices. Though they may "seem to constitute part of the inner worth of a person," Kant writes, such traits "lack much that would be required to declare them good without limitation (however unconditionally they were praised by the ancients), for, without the basic principles of a good will they can become extremely evil (Kant 1996: 50; KGS 4:394).

Kant's own reasons for his radical about-face on the methodology of moral philosophy are far too complicated to address adequately here. The question of whether we have any good reason to join him in this turn is more complicated still.[10] There is some cause to worry, however, that Kant's later position on the matter might not have gained ascendancy – either in his own mind or in the wider academic community – on purely intellectual grounds.

---

[10] On the former, biographical question, see Beiser (1992) and Schlipp (1938/1960). On the latter, philosophical question see Cartwright (1987), Henson (1979), Korsgaard (1996b), Mendus (1985), and Sherman (1990).

In Kant's individual case, we cannot rule out psycho-biographical explanations rather than philosophical justifications. Zammito (2002: 83–135; see especially 131–135) hypothesizes that – suffering from severe melancholy at having turned forty the previous year and having been spurned in his quest for marriage – Kant underwent a "conversion experience" sometime in the mid-1760's, renouncing the emotional component of his psyche and identifying his true self with philosophical reason alone. Kant's biographer Kuehn (2001: 148) concurs that Kant underwent a sort of "rebirth" after a mid-life crisis, though he suspects that this may have had more to do with the death of Kant's friend Johann Funk than with any romantic failure.

Socio-economic causes may play an analogous role in explaining why Kant's melancholic rationalism came to dominate academic moral philosophy. The nineteenth and twentieth centuries saw an incredible increase in academic specialization spurred by a conviction that the division of labor is as good a means of achieving efficiency in the intellectual sphere as it is in commerce and industry. Universities were reorganized, with disciplinary departments given significant autonomy – first in Germany, then in the United States, and gradually in the rest of the world. Ethics was denied a department of its own and eventually became part of a new discipline given the old name of "philosophy." Kant's distinction between the metaphysics of morals and practical anthropology could be used to justify this convenient bureaucratic arrangement. Ethics, when conducted in an aprioristic fashion, can use analytic tools akin to those used in other philosophical subfields. Confident of the autonomy of their enterprise, moral philosophers can now sit proudly among the specialists who surround them, both in their own particular discipline and in the university as a whole.

As a semi-independent guild of trained professionals, moral philosophers today have an interest in the rejection of empiricist sentimentalism wholly independent of its intellectual merits. Were it to prove impossible to segregate ethical questions from psychological, sociological, political, biological, historical, or literary ones, then moral philosophers would find themselves either having to collaborate with experts on these matters or attempt to develop these myriad forms of expertise themselves. While there is admittedly much excitement about interdisciplinary work in the academy today, it is still very difficult to resist the professional awards, which accrue primarily to specialists.

Admittedly, this hypothetical explanation of empiricist sentimentalism's decline is not only highly speculative but also unacceptably uncharitable to those involved. There are both moral and intellectual reasons for assuming that our interlocutors hold the positions they do for good reasons, and that there are no ulterior motives at work – whether consciously or unconsciously. Yet what makes for good practice in scholarly debate can lead to bad practice in intellectual history, as we come to make the Pollyannaish assumption that the best arguments always win, and that the evolution of scholarship is always a matter of Whig-historical progress. Rejecting this assumption allows intellectual history to be of much more than mere antiquarian interest. By returning to the philosophical past, we can correct for wrong turns and missed opportunities, reclaiming lost ideas and approaches that should have never been abandoned in the first place.

There is no doubt that the most important Copernican revolution in the philosophy of the eighteenth century belonged to the critical-period Kant, not his estranged student Herder. It may only now be time for Herder's anthropological revolution – a revolution that is at the same time a restoration. In the twenty-first century, moral philosophers may once again remember that they are human, and forget about the dear little angels once and for all.

# 2    Neo-Classical Sentimentalism

*Jesse Prinz*

## 1    Introduction

Sentimentalism is a theory of moral judgment which emphasizes the emotions. It emerged in the late seventeenth century in Great Britain, reaching its most influential formulation in the eighteenth century, in the work of David Hume. Sentimentalism waned in popularity under the influence of various subsequent traditions, including utilitarianism and Kantian ethics, but has been revived within analytic ethics. New formulations, sometimes referred to as "Neo-Sentimentalism," owe much to Hume and his predecessors, but there have also been important departures. Meanwhile, there has been a rapid growth of interest in sentimentalism coming out of social psychology, social neuroscience, and empirically informed philosophy. The twentieth century was dominated by a linguistic turn in philosophy, and the twenty-first launched with an empirical turn. Here I will argue that the picture suggested by new empirical approaches comes closer to the classical position than do the Neo-Sentimentalist theories of recent analytic philosophy.

I will begin by identifying four core tenets of Hume's moral psychology. I will then indicate some of the ways in which twentieth-century sentimentalists departed from Hume. Finally, I will review recent empirical findings that support Hume's classical approach. The emerging picture can be called "Neo-Classical Sentimentalism."

## 2    Hume's Classical Sentimentalism

### 2.1    Background

The idea that emotions contribute to moral judgment has a rich history. Related ideas can be found in ancient Greek philosophy (Cooper 1999) and in Confucian ethics (Luo 2007). There are also relevant ideas in French thought, particularly in the philosophy of art. Dominique Bouhours claimed that successful art incites positive feelings by virtue of having an ineffable, *je ne sais quoi*; Charles de Saint-Évremond and Chevalier de Méré began writing about good taste, as a metaphor for aesthetic sensibility (following the Spaniard, Gracián); and Jean-Baptiste Du Bos examined aesthetic pleasure and the emotions aroused by poetry, painting, and theater. These authors emphasize the role of the sentimental in aesthetic evaluation, also making observations about the moral domain. For example, Du Bos comments that, "Nature has implanted in us all an instinct, to discern the character of men" (1719: 79). Such ideas took hold in Britain as well, and they found their most influential champion in the Scottish philosopher, David Hume. His ideas will be the focus of this discussion.

Hume was not the only British moralist to take up sentimentalism, nor was he the first. His two most notable precursors were Anthony Ashley Cooper, Third Earl of Shaftesbury and Francis Hutcheson, whose accounts I will not review here. I will present Hume's position as the classical view, since its impact has been greater. I will also suggest that it enjoys enduring support.

Hume dedicates the third part of his *Treatise of Human Nature* (1739–1740/2000) to morals, and it opens with a critique of rationalism – the view that moral judgments can be arrived at through pure reason. Two arguments are particularly important. The first is based on what we now call motivational internalism. Moral judgments, Hume claims, are intrinsically motivating (1739–1740/2000, 3.1.1). We talk of such things as duties and obligations, and these compel us to act. Hume also claims that reason is motivationally inert: when it comes to action, reason is a slave of the passions (2.3.3). Thus, moral judgments cannot derive from reason alone. Hume's second argument (or series of arguments) concerns limits of reason. Reason, he tells us, can be used to discern relations or to derive facts from facts, but is not apt to derive moral truths (3.1.1). Reason tells us how things happen to be, not how they should be. Thus, we can examine an action, and not find anything in it that adds up to moral wrongness. In the *Treatise*, he offers "willful murder" as an example, which he carries over to *An Enquiry Concerning the Principles of Morals* (the "second *Enquiry*"), now using Nero's remorseless murder of Agrippina as a specific illustration (1751/1998: Appendix 1). Nero was not ignorant of any facts in this case, yet he viewed it with moral indifference; this suggests that our outrage at the crime cannot be deduced by reason, but rather reflects a difference in our sensibility.

Hume uses his anti-rationalism to argue for sentimentalism: if morality does not derive from external facts, then it must be internal. He supplements this argument by elimination with an appeal to phenomenology: the apparent wrongness of willful murder can be found only when we introspect our emotions (Hume 1740/2000, 3.1.1). These basic aspects of Hume's theory provide the usual textbook gloss. But details of his positive account – in particular, four central claims – deserve closer examination.

## 2.2     Constitution

First and foremost, it is important to be clear on what makes Hume a senti-mentalist. One can define sentimentalism as the view that moral judgments are based on emotions. We can define a moral judgment as a mental state that attributes a moral quality (e.g., being morally bad, immoral, evil, pro-hibited, wrong, and their contraries) to something (e.g., a character type or an action). For the sentimentalist, these psychological states essentially involve emotions. This formulation can be fulfilled in a variety of different ways. For Hume, sentimentalism is fulfilled by what I will call "the Consti-tution Thesis."

The Constitution Thesis is a conjecture about moral psychology. It says that our moral judgments comprise emotional states. Here's Hume:

> [W]hen you pronounce any action or character to be vicious, you mean nothing, but that from the constitution of your nature you have a feeling or sentiment of blame from the contemplation of it. (Hume, 1739–1740/2000, 3.1.1.26; SBN 469)

This Constitution Thesis would also be endorsed by Hutcheson and Shaftesbury. Authors of the period believed that moral judgments literally are emotional responses. The particular formulation here, however, hints at a crucial difference between these authors. Whereas for Hume a moral judgment is "nothing but" a sentiment, his predecessors might add that these sentiments track a mind-independent moral reality. Hume couples his Constitution Thesis, which concerns the psychological nature of moral judgments, with a metaethical thesis, which concerns the nature of morality as such. I will return to this with my fourth Humean Thesis below.

## 2.3     Character

The second of Hume's theses I will address concerns the emotions that con-tribute to moral judgment. Hume offers an analysis of what makes moral emotions distinctive. His analysis, I will suggest, is functional, and the cen-tral upshot is that moral emotions concern character. I will refer to this as "The Character Thesis."

Hume is committed to the view that there are distinctive emotions impli-cated in moral judgments, and he raises an interesting question about how these can be distinguished from other emotions. He says, "[Not] every sen-timent of pleasure or pain, which arises from characters and actions, [is] of that peculiar kind, which makes us praise or condemn" (1739–1740/2000 3.1.2.4; SBN 472). Some scholars read this as saying that the moral emotions are *sui generis* (Debes 2012b), but the term "peculiar" can also be read more modestly as meaning that the moral emotions can be differentiated from other forms of pleasure and pain. Here I do not want to take up the issue of whether Hume believed in *sui generis* moral emotions. He clearly didn't think it would suffice to just stipulate that moral emotions have a characteristic phenomenology. Instead, he develops another strategy for distinguishing moral emotions: he argues that they have a distinctive functional role. Hume's functional analysis of moral sentiments has three aspects, which I will refer to as outputs, objects, and inputs. Let's look at these in turn.

Hume's appeal to the distinctive outputs of moral judgments appears immediately after he asks how moral sentiments can be distinguished from nonmoral sentiments. This suggests it is his main answer to the question. In the crucial passage, he says that moral sentiments cause us to experience what he elsewhere calls "indirect passions." An indirect passion is one that brings to mind the idea of a subject, either self or other. Hume proposes that moral sentiments, " ... give rise to [*pride, humility, love*, or *hatred*]; which clearly distinguishes them from the pleasure and pain arising from inanimate objects" (Hume 1739–1740/2000, 3.1.2.5; SBN 473). He also suggests that different indirect passions will arise on different occasions; for example, we love the amiable Caesar and esteem the ambitious Cato (3.3.4; see also, Hume 1751/1998: Appendix IV). Confusingly, Hume makes another remark, later in the *Treatise*, that *identifies* moral sentiments with indirect passions (1739–1740/2000, 3.3.5), but his official view seems to be that these typically *follow* the sentiments that can constitute our moral judgments.

The indirect passions thesis can distinguish moral pleasures and pains from the pleasures and pains that arise in response to inanimate things, such as wine or weather. But one might worry that it cannot distinguish moral pleasures from the pleasure we take in other personal attributes. For instance, we might esteem someone for her wit. Hume bites this bullet, saying that there may be no psychological difference between moral approbation and the approbation we have for appealing personality traits. He does, however, have other resources that could help address this concern. In the *Treatise*, Hume suggests that moral judgments are always judgments about people's motives:

Tis evident, that when we praise any actions, we regard only the motives that produced them, and consider the actions as signs or indications of certain principles in the mind and temper. The external performance has no merit. We must look within to find the moral quality. This we cannot do directly; and therefore fix our attention on actions, as on external signs. But these actions are still considered as signs; and the ultimate object of our praise and approbation is the motive, that produc'd them. (1739–1740/2000, 3.2.1.2; SBN 477)

Motives add to Hume's account of how moral emotions have a distinctive functional role. Unlike other pleasures and pains, moral sentiments have motives as their "ultimate objects." Wit, on this interpretation, would not be a moral trait, since it is not directed toward motives.

The final part of Hume's functional analysis concerns the inputs that cause our moral emotions. Here Hume appeals to sympathy, which he defines as our capacity to experience the feelings that we witness or imagine to be appropriate in other people (what we now usually call empathy). For Hume, sympathy is a precursor to moral judgment in most cases. When evaluating an action, we reflect on its impact – the degree of pleasure or pain that it did or would cause. When we bring this impact to mind, it causes a like response in us. One might interpret Hume as suggesting that moral sentiments are to be identified with these vicarious feelings, but I think he is more accurately interpreted as holding that these vicarious feelings cause us to feel moral sentiments. Hume cautions that sympathy is biased; we are more sympathetic to those who are close to us than distant strangers. So we must work to adopt a more general point of view and imagine how an action would impact those in its vicinity, rather than focusing on how it affects us or our close affiliates (cf. 1739–1740/2000, 3.3.3). So, a moral judgment is caused by a sympathetic emotional response constrained by this perspective shift.

Summarizing, when we consider an action and sympathetically review its effects, we have vicarious feelings (the inputs); these cause pleasure or pain, which is directed at the motives of the person who performed the action (the object); this then leads us to form an indirect passion toward that person (the outputs). The pleasure and pain directed at some object constitutes the moral judgment. Phenomenology aside, pleasures and pains are clearly distinguished by their causes, objects, and effects.

Moral judgments usually begin by contemplating actions and their impact. But actions can be evaluated only by their underlying motives, which Hume regards as indicative of character: "If any action be either virtuous or vicious, tis only as a sign of some quality or character" (1739–1740/2000, 3.3.1). Our esteem or blame is elicited because we see actions not as mere movements or effects, but as originating in the constitution of those who perform them. This is Hume's Character Thesis; it suggests that moral assessments of actions lead directly to assessments of persons.

## 2.4     Artificiality

Next I introduce what I call "The Artificiality Thesis." Following Hutcheson, Hume believes that human beings are naturally benevolent and thus motivated to do good things. However, as with sympathy, we are disposed to be kind to our near and dear but have little natural regard for strangers. To acquire a moral orientation, we must extend our fellow-feeling outward to others. This happens through social conventions that recondition our moral emotions. Hume's chief example is "justice," by which he means, broadly, respect for others' property. Hume tells us that, "the sense of justice and injustice is not derived from nature, but arises artificially, through necessarily from education, and human conventions" (1739–1740/2000, 3.2.1.17; SBN 483). For Hume, justice is an artificial virtue because it has to be invented to promote social stability.

Hume gives other examples of artificial virtues, including laws, modesty, and manners (1739–1740/2000, 3.3.1). He also says that some virtues are natural. A key example is generosity, which derives directly from our natural dispositions toward sympathy and benevolence. Hume notes, however, that our natural state of generosity is limited to our near and dear (ibid.). So, in calling generosity a natural virtue, Hume is not implying that we are naturally disposed to extend generosity to strangers. Thus, Hume's term "natural virtue" must be read cautiously (see 3.1.2), for, to become a moral virtue, our prosocial instincts must be artificially extended through moral education. All moral virtues are, in this sense, artificial – hence the Artificiality Thesis. The main difference between so-called natural virtues and those dubbed artificial is that the latter are cultural extensions of natural dispositions, and the latter are introduced ex nihilo for the betterment of society.

Despite the Artificiality Thesis, Hume does not conclude that morality is completely relative to culture. For example, he says, "The convenience, or rather necessity, which leads to justice is so universal, and everywhere points so much to the same rules, that the habit takes place in all societies" (1751/1998, 3.2.47; SBN 203). Our shared concern for stable society together with our shared capacity for sympathy leads to similar values cross-culturally.

Nevertheless, Hume's insistence on the artificiality of morals opens up the possibility of substantial moral divergence. His most sustained discussion of this appears at the end of the second Enquiry (Hume 1751/1998: Dialogue). There he describes cases in which "civilized" societies diverge dramatically on moral matters. His main examples are drawn from ancient Greece: "an Athenian man of merit might be such a one as with us would pass for incestuous, a parricide, an assassin, ungrateful, perjured traitor, and something else too abominable to be named" (Ibid. 17; SBN 329). The unnamable item at the end is homosexual love. His second key example is contemporary France. Here, the list of shocking customs includes open affairs with the spouses of friends, dueling, and giving the family fortune to only one child. He also lavishes special attention to the way French men subordinate themselves to women: "But this nation gravely exalts those, whom nature has subjected to them, and whose inferiority and infirmities are absolutely incurable. The women, though without virtue, are their masters and sovereigns" (Ibid. 24; SBN 332). Hume clearly thinks that some cases of moral variation are correctable mistakes. "Greek love" was mistakenly believed to promote friendship, he surmises, and dueling is a misguided way to promote good manners. In both examples, he emphasizes that morals are grounded in more universal aspirations (though, recall, that Hume regards manners as artificial). Hume does not seem to suppose that our shared sentiments can settle every moral dispute. Some sources of variation lead to irreconcilable differences: nations that are at war or in peace, rich or poor, monarchies or republics, or places that happen to settle on different tradeoffs between utility and pleasure. Hume compares the moralities of the world to rivers that spring from the same source – our shared sentiments – but "different inclinations of the ground, on which they run, cause all the difference of their courses" (Ibid. 26; SBN 333). Thus, while Hume seems optimistic about moral convergence, he does recognize the impact of chance and context.

## 2.5    Taste

This brings us to the final aspect of the Humean theory. Hume's sentimentalism comes packaged with a metaethical position, which I will call "The Taste Thesis." Hume relates morals to secondary qualities, "Vice and virtue, therefore, may be compared to sounds, colors, heat and cold, which, according to modern philosophy, are not qualities in objects, but perceptions in the mind" (Hume 1739–1740/2000, 3.1.1.26; SBN 469). This analogy is important for Hume, but also imperfect. For Locke, secondary qualities are creations of the human mind, but they nevertheless have fixed correlates in the objective world. He analyzes them as external powers, and suggests that certain physical magnitudes have the power to cause specific sensations in us. The color blue is not a feature of the mind-independent world (it would not exist without us), but there is some mind-independent configuration of matter that reliably causes blue experiences. One might say that secondary qualities are neither mental nor non-mental but rather relational, and one of their relata is objective – supervening on the world together with human nature. Hume's position on secondary qualities is harder to pin down. He sometimes insists that there are no things in the world to which they correspond (Ibid. 1.4.4), but he worries that this position will lead to skepticism, and recognizes that secondary qualities do have correlates in the external world (see Winkler 2011). In contrast, he clearly denies morals having objective external existence. Though he frequently mentions utility as a correlate of moral goodness, he also mentions agreeableness, implying that agreeableness is prior to utility insofar as good outcomes, such as health, are good insofar as we find them agreeable (1751/1998: Appendix 1). Hume also emphasizes the open-ended nature of moral rules and the ways in which they can be created by custom (as emphasized in the Artificiality Thesis). Thus, vice and virtue should not be characterized as relations to fixed mind-independent properties, or powers.

Hume sometimes expresses his metaethical position by saying that:

[O]ur passions ... are not susceptible of any such agreement or disagreement ... It is impossible, therefore, they can be pronounced either true or false, and be either contrary or conformable to reason. (1739–1740/2000, 3.1.1.9; SBN 458)

A similar claim is advanced in the second *Enquiry*:

Thus the distinct boundaries and offices of REASON and of TASTE are easily ascertained. The former conveys the knowledge of truth and falsehood: the latter gives the sentiment of beauty and deformity, vice and virtue. The one discovers objects as they really stand in nature, without addition and diminution: the other has a productive faculty, and gilding or staining all natural objects with the colors, borrowed from internal sentiment, raises in a manner a new creation. (1751/1998: Appendix 1.21; SBN 294)

Hume makes clear that judgments of taste (i.e., those that are grounded in sentiment) fail to convey mind-independent truths.

This ideal of gilding and staining has sometimes been read as a kind of projection thesis, according to which we falsely project our passions onto the world (see D'Arms and Jacobson 2006). But, Hume says that we can come to recognize that morality is in us, and not in the world (as when he discusses willful murder) – something that is much more difficult in the case of color. Earlier in the *Treatise*, he also contrasts secondary qualities with pains and pleasures, saying that the former are treated as external, the latter not (Hume 1739–1740/2000, 1.4.2). His equation of moral sentiments with pleasures and pains seems to imply that these are not projected onto the world, but rather experienced as reactions to the world. I read Hume as implying that the phenomenology is actually ambiguous between these options, prior to careful examination.

Though Hume eschews talk of truth and locates moral feelings in the mind, he still makes room for moral error. For one thing, Hume insists that moral judgments are not expressions of personal preference, but are instead made from a "common" or "general" point of view (Ibid. 3.3.1); they are intended to be abstract rules that generalize beyond our own case. One could err in making a moral judgment by failing to accurately adopt a general point of view. One might also make a moral judgment based on an erroneous belief, such as the belief that something harmful is helpful, or conversely. Hume chooses to say that such judgments lack truth or falsity, since their error can be located in the precipitating beliefs (Ibid. 3.1.1). But he certainly thinks that such judgments are mistaken. This, again, might be compared to other emotional responses. One might take a bite of food and find it disgusting only to realize that one's taste was tainted by something else. Or one might attempt to generalize one's verdict about the food, only to discover that others find it delicious. Judgments of taste can go wrong, even if they do not represent external reality.

Putting this together, we can describe Hume's metaethics as follows. When we say that something is morally right or wrong, we are not attributing some objectively describable power to it, as a strict reading of the secondary quality analogy would suggest. Nor are we saying something that is immune to correction. Rather we are saying something about how it feels when viewed from the right perspective. The correctness conditions hinge on whether what we feel does in fact align with what one would be disposed to feel under good conditions of evaluation (e.g., if one had a personal concern for parties involved). I call this the Taste Thesis, since I think the analogy to taste best captures Hume's effort to deny that moral judgment corresponds to external facts, while also leaving room for error. It also reflects the importance of taste as an analogy in the sentimentalist tradition, as well as the deep parallels that the early sentimentalists saw between morality and aesthetics.

Critics shudder at the idea that morality might be a mere matter of taste, because taste is assumed to be subjective. But one needn't worry, since Hume rejects such variability. In the aesthetic domain, he posits ideal critics, and in the moral domain, he says our personal preferences must be checked by a common point of view. Both maneuvers leave room for some relativism: ideal critics can differ in temperament, and shared vantage points may, as we have seen, be relative to culture. Still, moral taste will be less variable than personal preferences – for example, culinary taste. Hume's Taste Thesis could also be called a Shared Taste Thesis, since it has this social dimension. Though shared does not necessarily mean universal.

Here I have summarized central tenets of Hume's moral philosophy. I take the four theses here to capture distinctive features of Hume's sentimentalism, which I will label "classical sentimentalism." I will now suggest that tenets of the classical view lost traction in the twentieth century, but may be gaining momentum in the twenty-first.

## 3      Neo-Sentimentalism

The twentieth century saw a proliferation of moral theories, and many of these have historical roots in authors other than Hume, such as Aristotle, Bentham, or Kant. Here I want to focus on theories that are often characterized as Humean. In particular, I will consider views that have been classified as sentimentalist. Most of these are said to owe their greatest debt to Hume, among the sentimentalists, since other authors from the period have been comparatively neglected. My thesis is that that recent Humean views have drifted away from the letter of Hume's theory, and to their detriment.

In the first half of the twentieth century, the major sentimentalist theory was emotivism (Ayer 1936; Stevenson 1944). This approach took Hume's remarks on truth very seriously, saying that moral judgments are mere expressions of feeling without any truth-values. To many critics, this was unsatisfying, since moral judgments appear to aim at truth. As a result, ethicists in the second half of the twentieth century tried to find ways to preserve the spirit of the Humean approach without giving up on truth. Two traditions emerged out of the fallout from emotivism.

The first of these traditions is expressivism. Blackburn (1998) adopted Stevenson's line that moral judgments express emotions, but he also developed a semantic and ontological theory, called quasi-realism, designed to preserve the surface form of moral discourse. Moral judgments, he claimed, can be quasi-true. Gibbard (1990) developed a different kind of expressivist theory. He claimed that moral judgments express our endorsement of norms, and the norms in question are norms of feeling: they instruct us to feel emotions such as anger or guilt under certain circumstances. Gibbard (2003) also proposes a semantic theory to accommodate the assertoric form of moral discourse.

The other tradition that has emerged in the wake of emotivism is called the sensibility theory. Its defenders take up the analogy between moral and secondary qualities, where moral judgments refer to response-dependent properties (Wiggins 1987; McDowell 1998). This move secures truth talk without need for a special semantics. Sensibility theorists have tended to assume that moral truths are universal, though they often offer little defense of this supposition.

As these examples illustrate, descendants of Hume have divided into two metaethical camps. This bifurcation reflects a twentieth-century preoccupation with language, particularly to fine-grained semantic distinctions. Some authors try to explain projection by proposing that moral concepts don't refer, while others say they refer to response-dependent properties. Hume did not distinguish these two options, and one might interpret them as attempts to clarify his half-baked views. On the other hand, one might argue that neither gets Hume right. As remarked above,

Hume's use of the secondary quality analogy is best interpreted loosely. According to the Lockean tradition, secondary qualities have correlates in the external world and are best construed relationally. This is not how Hume understands morality. Likewise, though Hume officially eschews truth-values for moral sentiments, he never implies that this requires an alternative semantics for moral discourse. Nor does he suggest that moral judgments are like exclamations. Rather he compares moral judgments to judgments of taste. I don't think it is accurate to describe Hume as vacillating between the secondary quality view and expressivism. His Taste Thesis steers a course between contemporary alternatives.

I will not attempt to say what a semantics of taste discourse should look like. That is a topic for another occasion. I will simply remark that the taste analogy opens up space for a position that is neither referential, in the way that a secondary quality theory might require, nor expressive. Contemporary semantic theory has been so preoccupied with reference that we come to think we must choose between referential assertions and pseudo-assertions. Discourse about taste is not necessarily best described in either of these ways and so contemporary sentimentalism is misled by restrictive semantic categories.

Contemporary theories also fail to do justice to the other tenets of Hume's classical sentimentalism. Consider the Constitution Thesis, which is central to Hume's position. Here is one of the sharpest divides between contemporary ethicists and the pioneering British moralists. Shaftesbury, Hutcheson, and Hume all embraced a moral psychology according to which moral judgments are constituted by emotional states. Contemporary heirs to this tradition have largely dropped this commitment, saying instead that moral judgments involve moral warrant (see Darwall et al. 1992). Thus, for Gibbard, an expressivist, moral judgments express norms according to which moral emotions are warranted, and, for McDowell, moral assertions convey the judgment that something merits disapproval. D'Arms and Jacobson (2000) consider this the major unifying theme in contemporary sentimentalist theories. They use the term "neo-sentimentalism" to designate accounts of this kind. Such views are distinct because moral judgments are defined as being *about* emotions, rather than containing emotions.

What about the Character Thesis? This, recall, is a commitment to a character-focused account of the difference between moral and non-moral emotions. Neo-sentimentalists largely ignore this issue. They do not comment on Hume's suggestion that moral emotions are directed toward motives and cause indirect passions. Most contemporary sentimentalists say little about character, leaving this topic to Aristotelians (though see Driver 2001 and Slote 2003, for work on Humean virtue ethics). More generally, there is little effort in the neo-sentimentalist tradition to explain which emotions contribute to moral judgment. This unfinished aspect of Hume's program idled in the twentieth century. The question has rarely been raised, and Hume's machinery, especially the indirect passions, have received so little attention that one can infer that they have gone unnoticed.

The Artificiality Thesis has also been neglected (and relativists tend to neglect sentimentalism). Most contemporary authors say little about where morals come from (e.g., McDowell), and when they do, they tend toward evolutionary explanation (e.g., Gibbard). Gibbard indicates a potential role for learning in the creation of moral rules but places emphasis on language and reason-giving, rather than on the construction of rules for social cohesion. There is scant discussion of Hume's examples of artificial virtues (such as justice and modesty), and treatments of natural virtues tend either to assume that we are innately benevolent to strangers, or else argue that our biases are normatively acceptable (Slote 2010). Little energy is expended on how our innate dispositions develop into the elaborate moral rules that govern our lives.

In summary, twentieth-century heirs to sentimentalism have departed in certain ways from the classical tradition. Core Humean theses are either flatly rejected (Constitution), misunderstood (Taste), forgotten (Character), or ignored (Artificiality). It is fair to say that, by the end of the twentieth century, the Humean picture had fallen into disfavor. Sentimentalism remained in vogue, but key aspects of his theory have been abandoned or ignored. In the twenty-first century, there has been a move back toward Hume's classical sentimentalism. This change has been spurred by the introduction of empirical methods into philosophical theorizing. Moral philosophers who are informed by empirical research find themselves confronted with new reasons to rekindle Hume's old torch. Some of these reasons have been extensively discussed in the literature, but others have received less attention. In the next section, I will make an empirical case for embracing and updating classical sentimentalism.

## 4    Neo-Classical Sentimentalism

There has been scant attention paid to identifying specific moral emotions, and the few authors who do allocate intellectual energy to that exercise tend to emphasize semantic features of emotions (see, e.g., Greenspan 1995). The neglect of emotions may stem from the fact that twentieth-century philosophy was shaped by the linguistic turn. Within that intellectual framework, emotions have difficulty finding a place. Because emotions are not linguistic items, they tend to either get neglected or interpreted semantically. This has been changing with the recent empirical turn.

The twenty-first century has witnessed a dramatic rise in efforts to bring empirical results to bear on philosophical questions, and some of the most seminal findings directly concern the emotions. Examples include Damasio's (1994) popularized neurology book on the role of emotions in reasoning, Greene et al.'s (2001) fMRI study of the way emotions and reason operate in moral dilemmas, and Haidt's (2001) psychological defense of an intuitionist – which is to say, emotional – model of moral decision-making. The researchers in question have divergent views, and many would resist sentimentalism. I will not review these differences here (see Prinz 2016 for a sentimentalist critique of Greene and others who suggest that some moral judgments derive from reason alone). Rather, I will offer a philosophical interpretation of recent empirical work that comports with classical sentimentalism. What follows updates an earlier work, in which some aspects of Hume's position, especially the Character Thesis and the analogy to taste, were rejected or neglected (Prinz 2007).

## 4.1    Constitution

If one were to caricature neo-sentimentalism, one might call it sentimentalism without the emotions. For neo-sentimentalists, emotions are no longer regarded as components of moral judgments. That is, they abandon the Constitution Thesis. This has changed with the advent of empirical approaches to moral psychology. Much of the recent empirical work supports the Constitution Thesis. Numerous studies have investigated the role of emotions in moral judgment, suggesting that emotions are actively involved. I will illustrate with some examples and offer a Humean interpretation.

A number of recent studies have shown that moral judgments co-occur with emotional responses. This work can be divided by three kinds of evidence. First, there are neuroimaging studies that show activation in brain structures associated with emotion in a wide range of moral tasks: moral judgment, moral dilemmas, moral picture viewing, moral decision making, and so on (for a review, see Prinz 2016). It has been occasionally suggested that some of these studies do not show emotion response in every condition. That claim, however, is unfounded. The few studies that do not report increased emotionality in some conditions suffer from design flaws and when these are corrected, emotions seem to be active in every task that engages moral assessment (ibid.).

Second, there are studies that induce emotions and measure the effect on moral judgment. These studies have used multiple induction techniques, and several emotions have been investigated, including disgust, anger, and happiness. In each study, increasing emotion has resulted in stronger moral evaluations. For example, anger and disgust tend to increase the intensity of moral condemnation (Seidel and Prinz 2013a), and happiness increases the intensity of moral praise (Seidel and Prinz 2013b).

Finally, there are studies that examine the effects of reductions in emotional responsiveness. These are hard to conduct, since there is no lab manipulation that can eliminate emotions, and patient populations with global emotional impairments tend to be entirely non-responsive (Damasio and Van Hoesen 1983). There are, however, special populations that have selective reductions in emotional responsiveness. Individuals with Huntington's disease have diminished disgust response and a corresponding reduction in sensitivity to moral norms having to do with sexual conduct (Schmidt and Bonelli 2008). Individuals with psychopathy, on the other hand, have reductions in sadness, guilt, and empathy, and they seem to regard norm violations involving violence less seriously than comparison populations (Blair 1995).

Together these findings support the Constitution Thesis. Neuroimaging studies suggest that emotions are active when people make moral judgments; induction studies show that people consult emotions when asked to report moral opinions; and deficit studies suggest that, when emotions are less available, capacity for moral judgment is compromised. This is most naturally explained by the assumption that emotions are components of moral judgment. If emotions were merely contingent accompaniments, one would not expect such reliable correlation or diminished capacity with diminished emotionality. The findings also support the Humean thesis that positive and negative emotions are implicated in positive and negative moral judgments, respectively.

Empirical findings cannot decisively settle modal questions, about whether it is conceptually possible to have moral attitudes without emotions. I do not think, however, that Hume was much concerned with this. He wanted to give account of how we actually make moral judgments, not how we conceive of them. Indeed, he would likely be unimpressed with a finding showing that people can seem to make moral judgments in the absence of emotions, since we can, for example, report our food preferences without experiencing gustatory pleasure. The Constitution Thesis concerns the normal case, and, thus far, the evidence aligns with Humean predictions.

Crucially, the evidence fits the classical sentimentalist model better than it fits neo-sentimentalism. Neo-sentimentalists assume that moral judgments concern appropriateness, in contrast with the classical view that moral judgments contain emotions. Therefore, neo-sentimentalism makes no direct prediction about whether emotions are active when we make moral judgments, or whether judgments will gain and lose intensity with corresponding changes in emotional states. Neither feeling bad nor failing to feel bad settles whether it is warranted to feel bad. Furthermore, Nichols (2004, chap. 4) presents empirical evidence that children make moral judgments long before they develop a mature capacity to attribute moral emotions. For example, children think that victimizers will be happy, not sad (Nunner-Winkler and Sodian 1988). There is also evidence that four-year-olds do not differentiate between transgressors who show or fail to show guilt, even though they understand that the transgressions are wrong (Vaish et al. 2011).

### 4.2     Character

Neo-sentimentalists have been relatively reticent on the topic of character, and they have ignored Hume's account of indirect passions, which implies a characterological focus in moral judgment. Much of the recent empirical work also ignores character. Indeed some empirically minded philosophers are skeptical about the existence of character, though everyone grants that people make character attributions (Doris 2005). I think that character exists (Prinz 2007: 155), and some recent studies support the Character Thesis – establishing a spontaneous inference from bad behavior to bad character.

This pattern is already evidenced in early development. Infants who have watched animations of characters performing helpful or hindering actions will subsequently prefer contact with the characters who helped over the characters who hinder. In adults, too, there is ample evidence that we make inferences about character on the basis of moral conduct (Pizarro and Tannenbaum 2012). It is well known from the literature on person perception, that people spontaneously infer personality traits from behavior. Ross and Nisbett (1991) call this "lay dispositionism." This is especially clear for morally relevant behaviors. For example, Winter and Uleman (1984) show that we infer that someone is helpful, generous, kindhearted, inconsiderate, bigoted, or rude based on a single action. Such findings indicate that morally construed acts lead to moral character assessments.

The link between character and moral judgment has also been explored in the other direction: showing that negative character attributions lead to more negative moral judgments. In a pioneering study, Alicke (2000) showed that people are more likely to blame a driver for causing a car accident if he was driving for reasons that reflect badly on his character (heading off to hide some drugs). In a series of replications and extensions of this work, Nadler and McDonnell (2012) show that people with bad character are regarded as more responsible and blameworthy in situations where harm is accidently caused by something that they own (such as flammable materials or dogs). Such findings are not directly predicted by Hume, since he says that character attribution follows judgments about harm, rather than the other way around. Still, the findings fit with Hume's theory, since they establish a close relationship between moral judgment and character. We might explain these results by assuming that prior beliefs about bad character increase the emotional sensitivity to harms and inform assessments of motives, leading to a series of moral responses that is more negative in every dimension.

The connection between moral judgment and character attributions is robust, but not always proportionate. Some bad actions lead to more negative character attributions than others (Uhlmann and Zhu 2014). For example, a racist slur can lead to stronger and longer lasting inferences about bad character than a physical assault (Uhlmann et al. 2014). Similarly, harming a person is worse than harming an animal, but the latter is more indicative of character (Tannenbaum et al. 2011). There is also an asymmetry of valence: bad acts are seen as more indicative of character than good acts, because good acts can stem from ulterior motives (Reeder and Brewer 1979). There are even cases where good behavior can lead to negative character appraisals, as when one pushes someone off a lifeboat to save others (Uhlmann et al. 2013). Thus, the relationship between moral judgments and character is multifaceted and context-sensitive. This is, nevertheless, consistent with Hume's view. Hume does not say that moral judgments are constituted by character judgments, but rather that they characteristically bring about such judgments. He also indicates, in contrasting love and esteem, that our character assessments can depend on specific aspects of moral actions.

Overall, I see the aforementioned research as a confirmation of Hume's Character Thesis, and a welcome correction to neo-sentimentalism and other views that treat actions as the primary locus of moral judgment. The link between moral judgment and character suggests that morals are bound up with identity in ways that Hume anticipated (see Prinz forthcoming).

## 4.3    Artificiality

Hume's Artificiality Thesis concerns the history of morals. Many of the major figures in the history of Western moral philosophy speculated about morality's origin (Hobbes, Rousseau, Hume, Nietzsche, Marx, Hegel), but that question lost currency after the linguistic turn. Most neo-sentimentalists have little to say about the history of morals. Gibbard (1990) is a notable exception among analytic philosophers, but his efforts got little traction initially. Still, they signal a segue into the twenty-first century, since his interest in the history of morals is informed by his methodological naturalism. As ethics makes its empirical turn, some dimensions of classical sentimentalism have been resurfacing.

Anthropologists, sociologists, and historians have long endorsed the artificiality of morals, and recent work on cultural evolution supports this. For example, the anthropologists Richerson et al. (2003) argue natural selection has furnished us with "tribal social instincts," leading us to favor our near and dear. Cultural forces are then required to extend our capacity for cooperation to unrelated others. They describe cultural "work-arounds," such as military uniforms or religion, that people in large-scale societies use to view each other as members of the same tribe. Though the details differ, this is very much in line with Hume's idea that morality is a kind of trick for extended natural benevolence (a "natural virtue") to distant others. On both models, such extensions are motivated by the benefits they confer but cannot be psychologically implemented by explicit self-interest.

Experimental research has also been brought to bear on artificiality. For example, studies using economic games have found that different groups have different conceptions of fairness. In our society, when a game player is asked to fairly divide a resource with another player, the split tends to approximate a 50/50 division. Among the Machiguenga, an Amazonian group in Peru, people are willing to settle for much less equitable divisions (Henrich 2000). The explanation seems to be linked to the economic system in which they traditionally live – a system in which cooperation with family members is more important than cooperation with strangers.

Within psychology, artificiality is studied by looking at proximal mechanisms of moral change. For example, Rozin and collaborators investigate the role of disgust in changing attitudes toward meat eating (Rozin, Markwith and Stoess 1997) and smoking (Rozin and Singh 1999). He finds that people who avoid meat for moral reasons are more disgusted by it than people who avoid meat for health reasons. This fits with the Humean idea that emotions can be shared by social forces, making moral concern more inclusive.

One can also investigate artificiality by studying moral change. To take up Hume's example of Greek love, we are seeing a dramatic international change in marriage laws, reflecting new tolerance for same-sex relationships. Why? One answer is that economic conditions no longer favor large families, and as a result procreation is no longer seen as a fundamental life goal (Werner 1979). People are getting married less frequently, later, and many are choosing not to have children (Pew Research Center 2010). These behaviors would have seemed strange or stigmatizing a generation back. Same-sex unions tend to have less reproductive orientation, and can thus be interpreted as part of this cultural trend. Historians, economists, anthropologists, and sociologists have studied other examples of moral variation and change that are relevant to Hume's Artificiality Thesis: property laws, dueling, infanticide, and transformations in women's rights, for example.

Such studies challenge Hume's confidence that the sexist and homophobic mores of eighteenth century Scotland are more natural and reasonable than those of other societies but would support his broader contention that moral values are human constructions (the possibility of consensus remains open for debate).

## 4.4    Taste

Let us turn, finally, to the Taste Thesis, which concerns Hume's metaethics. The analogy between morality and taste was crucial for the emergence of sentimentalism. One study has taken this analogy very literally: pleasant and bitter tastes were shown to influence moral judgments (Eskine et al. 2011). But the real interest of the thesis lies in its metaethical implications: the idea that morality derives from us. Here, the most historically important analogy is not culinary taste, but aesthetic taste. Comparisons between morality and beauty waned in the later half of the twentieth century. Most neo-sentimentalists ignore aesthetic evaluation and would resist an aesthetic treatment of morality.

Rather than comparing morality to beauty, neo-sentimentalists have more often pursued the secondary quality analogy, or Hume's suggesting that moral sentiments lack truth-values, developing formal semantic theories for moral discourse. With the empirical turn, both avenues may lose popularity. Empirically oriented philosophers are more apt to ask, what psychological processes lead people to arrive at moral verdicts? At this point, one might look to the secondary quality analogy, which has a psychological cast but runs into difficulties. We do not seem to locate moral qualities in external objects, as we do with color or heat. Phenomenologically, it is unclear where the badness of stealing is felt to be, and in this respect it is more like judgments of taste: Where is deliciousness? Where is beauty? Neither is obviously external nor obviously internal.

This point raises a challenge for the empirical investigation of metaethics, since it won't be obvious to most moralizers that morality originates from within. There is research underway that attempts to investigate metaethical questions more directly. A study by Goodwin and Darley (2008) asked people to say whether various moral disputes can be settled (one position is true, the opposing position is false), or whether they are merely matters of opinion. The basic finding (at least with their American sample) is that people divide on these questions, suggesting uncertainty about the matter, just as the taste analogy predicts. Moreover, the tendency to say that an issue is a matter of opinion increases significantly when the issue in question is the subject of considerable disagreement. Thus, the abortion debate is overwhelmingly said to be a matter of opinion rather than fact. This seems surprising because people have strong views about abortion. On the projection analogy, one might expect those strong views to translate into greater confidence of absolute truth. Instead people recognize the lack of universality (perhaps the lack of a common viewpoint) and come to see the divide as between feelings rather than a disagreement about facts.

In a similar spirit, Sarkissian et al. (2012) examined intuitions about moral relativism, and found that people tend to adopt non-relativist views about debates between members of the same culture but become increasingly relativist as cultural distance increases. Through a Humean lens, this might be interpreted as an implicit recognition that the local case allows a common perspective, but more distant comparisons do not. People can see that their moral principles have an internal origin when they reflect on how widely they apply.

In one of the most direct explorations of the relationship between morality and taste, Nichols and Folds-Bennett (2003) compare intuitions about moral objectivity and culinary preferences. They do find far greater relativism about food, but this is consistent with Hume's view that moral taste aims for generality. Moreover, in this study, and a follow-up (Nichols 2004), many respondents give non-objectivist responses about the moral domain, or morals are regarded as less objective than facts. This comports with the Taste Thesis insofar as Hume sees morals as subjective but shared.

Empirical work has been consistent with Hume's Taste Thesis, but efforts to identify people's metaethical beliefs often end up revealing a lack of consistency (e.g., Wright et al. 2012). This suggests that ordinary intuitions may be a poor guide to metaethics. In a way, that is precisely the point. Many philosophers make metaethical claims by appeal to intuition (think of Mackie on queerness). I read Hume as saying that we have no immediate awareness of where judgments of taste originate. Metaethical positions cannot be easily read off our moral concepts.

We are still without a truly illuminating empirical metaethics. Some of Hume's claims cannot be tested with opinion polls (e.g., whether divine command theory is true). Still, preliminary evidence is consistent with the analogy between morality and (shared) taste. If we discover that Hume's Taste Thesis aligns with ordinary understanding, that could undercut some of the allure that realist theories have had.

## 5     Conclusions

I began by presenting four tenets of Hume's classical sentimentalist theory. These have either been neglected or rejected by many of the neo-sentimentalists. I think this shift has been regrettable. Recent empirical work provides some support for Hume's views. This invites a turn back from neo-sentimentalism to neo-classical sentimentalism.

At this point, one might ask about the "neo" in "neo-classical." The "neo" simply indicates that Hume's views are likely to undergo some revision and embellishment after empirical inquiry. For example, recent work has sought to identify specific emotions, such as anger and disgust, that underlie moral judgments. This is a step forward in articulating the Constitution Thesis. Other work has investigated the scope and limit of sympathy in prompting our moral judgments. If sympathy is not always operative, then Hume's Character Thesis stands in need of amendment. There is also much work on the origins of morality that add needed details to the Artificiality Thesis, and may undercut some of Hume's optimism that human nature will secure moral convergence. The Taste Thesis, too, may be refined as we investigate how people adopt a general point of view.

I suspect that the moral theory emerging from sentimentalist research will differ from Hume's in many ways. There will also be striking points of agreement. Empirical evidence for emotional constitution, new work linking moral judgments to character, prevailing models of cultural evolution, and recent studies of metaethical intuitions all lend support to Hume's speculations. Sentimentalism took some detours in the twentieth century, motived in part by the linguistic turn, but the empirical turn has revived aspects of the eighteenth century tradition. Emerging evidence suggests Hume's views were remarkably prescient, and, in attending to what he and his contemporaries actually said, we may gain further insights and directions for research.[1]

---

[1] I am extremely grateful to audiences at the College of the Holy Cross and the École Normale Supérieure. I received invaluable feedback on the manuscript from Remy Debes, Karsten R. Stueber, and, especially, Fiona Schick. I am indebted to the editors for their patience, wisdom, and support.

# 3    Moral Epistemology for Sentimentalists

*Simon Blackburn*

> We must not begin by talking of pure ideas – vagabond thoughts that tramp the public highways without any human habitation – but must begin with men and their conversation.
>
> C. S. Peirce (*CP* 8, 112)

## Introduction

There is an influential view, perhaps an orthodoxy that has surfaced in moral philosophy in recent years. It is what Sarah McGrath has nicely christened "relaxed realism," and is common to Tim Scanlon, Ronald Dworkin, Derek Parfit, and perhaps many others bobbing in their wake.[1] McGrath discerns four central theses of this position. Rewording them slightly these are:

(1) There are objective, irreducibly normative moral truths.
(2) Moral properties are not causally efficacious and do not figure in the best explanations of why we believe anything.
(3) Harman's test, in which explanatory indispensability is a litmus test for the reality of a property, is not one that morality needs to pass.
(4) Morality lacks controversial metaphysical or empirical presuppositions. It is therefore invulnerable to being "debunked" by metaphysical or empirical discoveries.

If it is complained that this makes the subject matter of morality entirely mysterious, relaxed realism often seizes on a comparison with mathematics; if it is complained that it leaves the epistemology of morality entirely mysterious, soothing noises are made either by mentioning reflective equilibrium, or a combination of reflective equilibrium and intuition.[2] Intuition is not, of course, a causal receptivity but is supposedly akin to our

---

[1] McGrath (2014).    [2] Kelly and McGrath (2010).

mathematical intuition.[3] Dworkin preferred the word "interpretation" to the idea of reflective equilibrium, but what he called interpretation was in effect the same procedure.[4]

Relaxed realism in its modern incarnation tends to be attached to a "reasons-first" doctrine, according to which the entry point to understanding morality is not by way of traditional concepts, such as those of obligation, duty, or value, but by way of practical reasons and rationality. This may, or may not, be an important distinction in first-order ethics, but it makes no substantial difference to my concerns in this paper, since it is in effect simply pushing the bump around the normative carpet. Whatever is puzzling about moral knowledge in general, or relaxed realism in particular, will remain whether we start with "musts" applied to behaviour and motive or "musts" applied to letting our minds be guided in particular ways, by taking one thing to be in favour of another.

The time-tested sentimentalist objection to relaxed realism is that it leaves the subject matter of morality so high up in the air that we might as well ignore it. What explanation can relaxed realists offer for why we worry about moral truths? What goes wrong if we confine our attention to the natural world, and take our motivations from the properties we find there: notably things being pleasant (in many different ways), or painful (also in many different ways)? Have we not got enough on our plate coping with these things, especially when we consider our sympathetic concern for the pleasures and pains of other people, and future people, and animals, and our aesthetic concerns for the environment? What was the benefit that a costly cognitive add-on, the ability to achieve moral knowledge, is supposed to have provided for us? Or, to put it another way, what dire consequences are supposed to follow if we mistake the true distribution of moral properties? Since they cause nothing and explain nothing, this would seem to be as innocent an error as could be imagined, a mistake of no more intrinsic interest than, say, a false entry into a crossword puzzle that is put aside once finished. Derek Parfit's agonized quest to give his life meaning by hunting down the true distribution of these properties would be as quixotic and pointless as the alleged medieval concern with how many angels can dance on the head of a pin. Counting the blades of grass in the lawn could, conceivably, one day have some practical import; charting the airy denizens of the non-natural world and their relationships can have none.

---

[3] Disliking the comparison with mathematics, McGrath, a self-confessed realist, still finds a need for intuition to help out but does not think we should be relaxed about it.

[4] Dworkin (2011) claims that it goes beyond reflective equilibrium by interpreting values in the light of each other until the "best theory" of how they fit together emerges, but it is difficult to see this as sustaining any real difference.

This problem does not arise for mathematics: whatever your account of applied mathematics, if you wrongly think that $12 \times 12 = 132$ you are poised to fail at tiling your 12 ft. square room, and the best explanation of why you fail is that you ordered 12 tiles too few. But with moral properties, on the relaxed realist picture there is not even a good reason for supposing that the distribution of properties in the non-natural world bears any fixed relationship, such as supervenience, to earthbound facts. They may be like Peirce's vagabonds, wandering stars in the ethereal firmament; fickle in their presence, here today, elsewhere tomorrow.

In other words, there is no explanation of why a fifth wheel, the "moral property," should lie anywhere between sentiment and its more natural and intelligible objects, the pleasures and pains and their distributions, that we know matter to us. Relaxed realists often fail to get this question into focus, instead assuring us that, tautologically, we have reason to care about reasons, or ought to pay attention to obligations.[5] But that isn't the issue: the problem for them is to explain why, on their picture, we do so care.

I think this question is salient, completely unanswerable in the terms the realist has provided, and therefore devastating to the philosophical credentials of the package. It is just as much so in application to its relaxed form as it was to the old-fashioned (but more or less identical) realism of Moore or Ross. So to do better I am going to set it aside, and ask instead what the sentimentalist tradition offers by way of a moral epistemology.

# I

It will seem strange to some philosophers to talk about a moral epistemology at all, in conjunction with sentimentalism. After all, sentimentalism is often casually called "non-cognitivism," and thus in many peoples' minds it holds that there is nothing to know: no subject matter and no truth or falsity, or at least no "objective" truth or falsity. Isn't that what is distinctive about the position? Indeed, isn't that what makes it so rebarbative to right-thinking, well brought-up people: for isn't it on the contrary obvious that we just *know* that it is wrong to stamp on blind babies for fun, and so on and so on?

This reaction seems hardly to have bothered the founding fathers of the sentimentalist tradition, from whom worries about moral knowledge seem at first blush to be largely absent. The phrase itself does not occur in either Hume's *Treatise*, or the second *Enquiry*, or in Adam Smith's *The Theory of Moral Sentiments*. Indeed, even the term "scepticism" does not feature in

---

[5] Parfit (2011, vol. 2: 621ff).

the last of these texts and is clearly of no concern to Smith. But when we look more closely we find that Hume himself devotes a good deal of attention to pouring cold water on the pretensions of moral skepticism. His rebuttal of the skeptic, or the "disingenuous opponent" who denies the "reality of moral distinctions" is consistently robust. He is majestically dismissive of any "threat" such a character may be imagined to pose.

> The only way, therefore, of converting an antagonist of this kind, is to leave him to himself. For, finding that nobody keeps up the controversy with him, it is probable he will, at last, of himself, from mere weariness, come over to the side of common sense and reason.[6]

For Hume, three elements in human nature are enough to get a reasonable morality started. There is first our own self-interest, a desire for those things that are pleasant and an aversion to those that are painful, coupled with an ability to take a long view of such things. There is a tincture of humanity, a sympathy with others that renders the pleasures of others pleasant to us, and their pains painful to us. And there is the ability to take up the "common point of view," which will include imaginative reflection on ourselves as we appear to others, one amongst many, and the sentiments generated by such reflection. These make up the foundation of the moral judgments we make about ourselves and others, as well as historical and fictional characters. If the philosophical skeptic arrives with thought-experiments in which we imagine a person lacking these qualities or abilities, then Hume says, as any sentimentalist should, that "it is in vain to expect, that any logic, which speaks not to the affections, will ever engage him to embrace sounder principles." He is a monster, not a man, so you just leave him alone, or if necessary, quarantine him. Hume's contemporary Diderot suggested, more robustly, that we smother him.[7]

I shall come back to Hume's reply to the moral skeptic, but meanwhile we can approach the issue from a different direction. Moral realists, whether relaxed or strenuous, take it for granted that moral knowledge is a Good Thing, to be pursued and fought for. But Bernard Williams, rightly, argued that there is something naïve about this.[8] Drawing on a work by Edward Craig, Williams asked whether the purposes served by our having a concept of knowledge in the first place, transfer straightforwardly to the ethical or moral domain. Craig's "practical explication" of the concept of

---

[6] Hume (1751/1998, 1.2; SBN 170).

[7] Diderot discusses the social defector in his 1755 *Encyclopédie* article on natural rights: "what then shall we reply to this violent interlocutor before smothering him?" I am grateful to Remy Debes for the reference.

[8] Williams (1995a).

knowledge highlights the question of why we have such a concept.[9] Why don't we content ourselves with talking of true belief? Craig finds the answer in the need to assess sources of information, policing each other and ourselves as being in the *kind* of position from which information can properly be received. One might also add, being in the kind of position that renders further inquiry otiose: having the status to call the case closed. In normal circumstances a witness to a scene may be in a position to close the question of what happened, whereas anybody absent is not; a proof closes a mathematical question whereas a speculation does not, and so on. Of course, quite delicate judgment may be involved in supposing that an answer is known, even in cases of witnesses and apparent proofs, and the verdict that the answer to some question is known is often defeasible, and sometimes plain wrong.

Given this explanation of the point of knowledge claims, applying them to the domain of ethics and morality is not straightforward, as Williams notes. Consider, for instance, the vexed but fundamental issue of balancing our largely private concerns against more public concerns. This is at least a matter of estimating how stringent the duties of charity are, or of how much we are permitted to withdraw into a private space, and how much we need to make ourselves into "servants of the world." Does theory give us one answer to this real, practical conundrum? It does not appear to do so. Ronald Dworkin, for example, was convinced that a unique correct moral system, that of his hedgehog, can be found hidden underneath the foxy complexities of everyday thought. He thought it delivered the dictum that everybody's life is of equal objective importance. But he also held that it is nevertheless permissible for him to prioritize his own children as he dispensed largesse or charity ("they are after all my children"[10]). It is hard to suppress the unkind thought that, apparently, when it comes to putting one's hand in one's pocket, objective importance is not all that important. It is hard as well to imagine how the one true moral theory can sidestep that issue, and harder still to imagine how, once it is confronted, it will give one a definitive answer, that is, an answer that all reasonable people will take to close the question. It is rather a question on which it is virtuous to feel pulled both ways, and to be in two minds. Of course if we became convinced of this, we might claim to know that the moral truth is that there is no one right answer, meaning that it is permissible to give to charity as

---

[9] Craig (1990). I had raised the question of the practical value of the concept myself in an earlier paper, "Knowledge, Truth, and Reliability," collected in my *Essays in Quasi-Realism*, but Craig was the first to see the full potential of the approach.

[10] Dworkin (2011: 274). Of course Dworkin does not duck the problem, but neither does he present a convincing solution to it.

much as you can or as little as you wish. But the claim to know that would naturally meet opposition from both ends.

Even putting aside the idea common to an earlier generation of intuitionists, that we have a plurality of potentially conflicting principles which will admit of no systematization, it is still obvious that new experience, new institutions, new conceptions of how much is owed to society and how much to the individual, are always possible. It would be mere dogmatism to think that such an issue could ever be done and dusted, settled by some surprising piece of moral mathematics, or logical inference from unquestionable "intuitions" or axioms. All this leads Williams, rightly, to hold that "the picture of rationality for ethics expressed in terms of theory and system is inadequate," and with the failure of that picture it becomes inappropriate, at best, to talk much in terms of moral knowledge.[11]

Although this much is right about sufficiently abstract, theoretical questions, it does not ban us from deploying the locution of someone knowing that $p$ in suitable contexts and with suitable ethical or moral substitutions for $p$. The most obvious cases will be where a simple empirical judgment, such as a witness can make, ties in with a shared background assumption. Zoe knew that her brother-in-law was a scoundrel when she saw him hitting her sister. The shopkeeper knows that Abel does wrong when he sees him shoplifting. Here the background moral conditional that bridges the observation and the evaluation is shared, or goes without saying, and the observation clinches the verdict, putting it beyond further question (similar certainty can attend judgments made with thick concepts, where the link between description and evaluation is often not in question).

But we can hold the same in more abstract contexts as well. Who is going to deny that it is wrong to stamp on blind babies for fun? An imagined monster, someone in whom the humane sentiments are completely non-existent? But he gets no purchase on us: we can't imagine arguing with him, since if he holds *that* then who knows what other perversities he holds? What we are perfectly sure about is that the issue is not even discussable; it is done and dusted; the case is closed. And this is what we signal by saying that we know it to be true. Our question about the bizarre dissident is not "what strange theory does this person hold, that gives this result?" but more directly "What is wrong with him?" And like Diderot, we may quietly wish to take up a pillow.

Another way of putting this is that in moral matters an opponent gets a purchase on us only insofar as he can put some alternative in a favourable light. Nozick could shake a Rawlsian claim to know that a just society would embed the difference principle by putting the principle that it

---

[11] Williams (1995b: 183).

is fundamentally individuals who own things and not the collective in a favourable light, and of course Rawlsians can do the reverse to Nozick's unfettered individualism. The specific attachments we all feel to friends and family put a monolithic act-utilitarianism in a dimmer light, while the needs of the poor cast a shadow over our more local partialities. Here, just where we might have looked to theory to help us, moral philosophy can do little more than point out the conflicting pulls. But when it comes to the idea of stamping on blind babies for fun, killing at random, having a thing about Tuesdays, and the other monstrous doctrines sometimes put into the mouths of "skeptics," there is simply no conflicting pull in play. Were anybody who sincerely holds such things to come along – but we can be pretty sure they will not – conversation would be useless. Cure, quarantine, or suffocation is the only answer.

I now want to suggest that the message of the last few pages vindicates one aspect of both Hume and Smith. Each of them moves seamlessly from what we are actually like to recommendations about the shape our practical lives should take. In other words, they make no difficulty about the transition between an "is" and an "ought." Hume tells us at the end of Section 1 of the second *Enquiry* that he is trying to "find those universal principles from which all censure or approbation is ultimately derived," and this, he affirms, "is a question of fact, not of abstract science" which is to be settled by "the experimental method."[12] But in the course of the work he not only describes what he thinks are our natural, universal, human tendencies, but announces how much he likes them, affirming in no uncertain terms the values to which these give rise, and in particular the virtues, the qualities of mind "useful or agreeable to ourselves or others" and which "give to a spectator the pleasing sentiment of approbation."

It requires but very little knowledge of human affairs to perceive, that a sense of morals is a principle inherent in the soul, and of the most powerful that enters into the composition. But this sense must certainly acquire new force, when reflecting on itself, it approves of those principles, from whence it is derived, and finds nothing but what is great and good in its rise and origin. Those who resolve the sense of morals into original instincts of the human mind, may defend the cause of virtue with sufficient authority; but want the advantage, which those possess, who account for that sense by an extensive sympathy with mankind.[13]

Extensive sympathy is one of humanity's moving principles, and, being human, Hume voices his approval of it and its progeny, our sense of morals, moving without shame from being an anatomist to being a painter, to use his own metaphor (sometimes, half-jocularly, he confesses that in order to

---

[12] Hume (1751/998, 1.10; SBN 174).    [13] Hume (1739–1740/2000, 3.3.6.3; SBN 619).

maintain his persona as an anatomist he has to check this natural tendency of his thought[14]). Philosophers who suppose themselves to have learned from Hume a ban on inferring an "ought" from an "is," or a value from a fact, may be shocked at what they think of as a trespass against his own famous principle. But there is no trespass, because he never issued any such ban, and indeed would have been idiotic to do so. Whenever we deploy standards of conduct we infer an "ought" from an "is"; the entire business of ethics and morality consists in shaping that bridge correctly. The "is/ought" principle Hume actually affirms is that it is not purely by means of a logical deduction or relation of ideas that the transition is effected. It takes a different kind of movement of the mind, and one that proceeds by "speaking to the affections" as he put it in the passage quoted above.[15] It is by mobilizing desire or aversion, hope or fear, that the "is" of a character or action brings about approbation or the reverse.

Similarly Adam Smith's great treatise starts simply by describing one aspect of human nature, namely our capacity for fellow-feeling, for sympathizing with the pain and distress or joy and happiness of other people. For Smith the "manner by which we judge of the propriety or impropriety of the affections of other men" is by their "concord or dissonance with our own":

> When we judge in this manner of any affection, as proportioned or disproportioned to the cause which excites it, it is scarcely possible that we should make use of any other rule or canon but the correspondent affection in ourselves.... Every faculty in one man is the measure by which he judges of the like faculty in another. I judge of your sight by my sight, of your ear by my ear, of your reason by my reason, of your resentment by my resentment, of your love by my love. I neither have, nor can have, any other way of judging about them.[16]

An affirmation of someone else's moral claim will issue in "oughts," sure enough, but it will be issued because of an "is": the fact of correspondence between the person with whom we agree and the person doing the judging. This correspondence in turn will be the result of attention to the "is" of whichever situation has prompted the reaction, for Smith is clear that what we try to do, as we move toward a correspondence or dissonance, is to appreciate the situation which brought about the feeling. It is natural properties whose instantiation make up the circumstances of the case, and these are the ones to which we respond.

---

[14] Hume (1751/1998, 2.1.5).

[15] A misreading of Hume on just this point pervades Dworkin's attempt to show the irrelevance of facts about the aetiology of our moral opinions to views about their cogency, or the confidence with which we may feel entitled to hold them. Dworkin erroneously supposed that taking such facts to be relevant is ruled out by Hume. See also McGrath (2014).

[16] Smith (1759/1982, I i.3.1).

Smith's view by no means implies that a correspondence and a resulting sincere judgment are bound to be correct. Looking at *you* entering a favourable judgment of *him*, I may find you both wanting, if in my judgment the situation did not call for the "affection" it appears to have excited. But if so I will be voicing my own discord with the way you both feel about the situation. Your concord makes your judgment of him sincere, but it does not ensure that I am to share it. When I do not, I will call you both wrong.

Smith is right that whatever I judge, it is I who is doing the judging. He is right too that I can deploy only my own standards, although of course both he and Hume think it is inevitable that those will be widely shared, since human nature is sufficiently uniform to ensure this. But Smith leaves unexplained what is surely a possible thought, which is that my own judgment may perhaps be faulty.[17] I may be insecure about my verdicts, just as I can issue judgments of merit in aesthetic matters, but be insecure about them, fearing that they could be improved. But this is not a significant problem: I have, of course, standards for improvement and can fear that a more rigorous, or more imaginative, or better informed application of those standards would reverse even ones among my current considered judgments. As in aesthetics, I might come across a sound critic – someone of more delicate taste, highly practiced across wide domains of experience, with good sound sense and free of all prejudice, whose opinion therefore matters to me, and whose example encourages me to readjust my sentiments, or in other words re-evaluate myself, and perhaps change.[18] It would be a case of my imagined self, improved in ways I can also only imagine, out of concord with my present self. Of course, the possibility that this other self would be better by standards that I endorse has to remain theoretical, for if I knew what the improvement would be, and knew that it would be improvement all the way, and knew that that judgment would displace my present one, then I would not stand behind my current judgment in the first place.

It may be natural for some moral philosophers to complain that we are not finding objectivity by these means. We remain mired in subjectivity, or at best the intersubjectivity of contingent consensus. But it is telling that neither Hume nor Smith shows any interest in those evil twins of modern moral philosophy, subjectivity, and objectivity. Neither of these nouns, nor their correspondent adjectives, occur in either the *Treatise* or

---

[17] He does, however, acknowledge this possibility, especially in the sections on the influence of fortune or moral luck, where he confesses that our sentiments are "somewhat irregular," and that the Deity judges rather differently. But the Deity is better informed than us.

[18] The virtues of the sound critic are of course those of Hume's essay "Of the Standard of Taste."

the *Enquiry*; none of them occurs in *The Theory of Moral Sentiments* either. They are simply no part of the agenda. No doubt this is partly because of the deeply social cast of their writings. The days of the solitary, isolated subject conducting his practical life in a private mental space lay ahead, beyond Rousseau, Kant, and the Romantics. It didn't occur to the sociable gentlemen of the eighteenth century that ethics and morality could be anything other than the shared upshot of a joint practical enterprise. So for Hume the very language of evaluation is molded by respect for the "common point of view," and for Smith the standpoint of the impartial spectator provides the perspective at an angle to a person's own private concerns, but morally authoritative and on occasion, peremptory. Our social sentiments and sympathies, the ways in which our minds mirror each other, ensure that the moral point of view matters to each of us. Just as "a man will be mortified if you tell him he has a stinking breath, though 'tis evidently of no inconvenience to himself" so the moral mirror ensures that we cannot avoid the gaze and the judgment of the other members of the "party of humanity." We neither need, nor can have, an "objectivity" that lies above and beyond this standpoint, a vagabond objectivity that tramps the public highways without any human habitation, as Peirce so nicely put it.

With this in mind it is melancholy to contemplate the historical as well as the philosophical ignorance and insensitivity with which contemporaries calling themselves moral realists sneer at expressivists and sentimentalists as *merely* "sounding off" or *merely* voicing their own reactions to things. These charges ignore the multiple ways in which socialization, education, reflection, and experience can modify the ways we feel about things. There is nothing "mere" about attitudes and motivations, and there is nothing mere about the social processes that by a continual process of adjustment and coordination keep the social vaults, which we construct in sufficiently good repair to support the arduous task of enabling us to live and flourish together. By comparison, earnestly delineating the non-natural world, making entries in crossword puzzles that can then be immediately shelved, is as mere an activity as can well be imagined.

Finally, it is evident that the sentimentalist is uniquely well placed to fend off any threat of the moral equivalent of Cartesian skepticism. Our sentiments pick out and applaud the social and personal virtues and there is simply no intelligible question of whether they "should" do so or whether we might be "wrong," for instance, to applaud clemency, prudence, and justice as opposed to cruelty, thoughtlessness, and injustice. This is how we are, and thank heavens for that, and there is the end of it. Earnest discussions of these things, just like anyone genuinely doubting them, should be smothered rather than given the oxygen of academic respectability.[19] Moral truth is not a vagabond bereft of human habitation.

It may not be quite so easy to put to rest fears of dragons like bias and relativism. It is easier to get rid of the second, since a properly deflationary theory of truth suffices to do so. It is not easy to get rid of the first, since many studies in social psychology show that humans are biased toward bias. But we can be alert to the problem, and we can cultivate the acquaintance of Others against whom we might have implicit or explicit prejudice. We can listen to the humane critics with delicate taste and wide experience, who have overcome bias. We can aspire to objectivity: it is set us as a task. Relativism is not a problem, but dealing with difference, and knowing what to tolerate, what to admire, and what to oppose is similarly set us as a task. Education, experience, a decent modesty, and a desire to cultivate our better sentiments are the cure for both ailments.

## II

What, then, is the relation between sentimentalism and the "relaxed realism" with which I started? I was careful to say above that the problem of explaining the practicality of morality was devastating not to relaxed realism itself, but to its philosophical credentials. By this I mean that sentimentalism need have no quarrel with many of the things relaxed realists say, but it mocks the belief that these provide any kind of explanation, or any kind of Wittgensteinian *"übersichtliche Darstellung"* or perspicuous view of things. In other words, if we revisit McGrath's four defining theses of relaxed realism, there is actually quite little with which the sentimentalist need quarrel. It is not the theses themselves, but rather the thought that they provide an "-ism," a good stopping point, a satisfying explanation or story, that is so depressing.

First: "There are objective, irreducibly normative moral truths" – certainly: here is one: it is wrong to stamp on blind babies for fun. Second: "Moral properties are not causally efficacious and do not figure in the best explanation of why we believe anything" – just so, although a sentimentalist should be disinclined to talk of moral properties at all. But she can sign up to instances of this: the fact that someone is good, for instance, is seldom the best explanation of why we like her. At best it sums up, or points toward the best explanation. That would look to the underlying natural

---

[19] A similarly human moral epistemology neutralizes Sharon Street's peculiar charge that quasi-realism leads to the moral equivalent of Cartesian skepticism. See her 2011, and my rebuttal "Sharon Street on the independent moral truth as such," at www2.phil.cam.ac.uk/~swb24/PAPERS/Meanstreet.htm.

properties of, for instance, benevolence, prudence, tact, or cheerfulness, that both make her good and explain why we like her. Third: "Harman's test is not one that morality need pass" – certainly: evaluating things, expressing our sentiments about them, is not usefully identified with describing some new set of properties, and is therefore not impugned or worried in the least by the apparent explanatory impotence of those properties. If we want to talk of moral properties and relations, then we must remember that they are merely the semantic shadows cast by moral predicates; they have no metaphysical life of their own. That the boys ought not to be doing what they are doing is not a different, new fact floating in a mathematical, or rational, or metaphysical empyrean, the normative sphere beaming (non-causally) the lights in which we see and feel things. It is the verdict with which you had better agree, not part of the inventory of a New World. It does not hover in an abstract firmament above and beyond the fact that they are setting a cat on fire for fun.

Fourth and finally "morality lacks controversial physical and metaphysical presuppositions" – absolutely, since the only presuppositions of our giving our verdict are first, the description of what the boys are doing, which grounds and justifies the verdict, and second, the uncontroversial empirical ones about the human sentiments, by way of explanation of our revulsion. We then justify from within, participants in these sentiments, not exiles from them.

To put it another way, sentimentalists should agree that G. E. Moore had a perfectly good ear for the distinctive semantics of moral sentences. He was right that they are not natural descriptions of the natural world but have their own distinctive meanings. He was right to contrast them with natural descriptions. But his instinct for explanation failed him, as it fails his contemporary followers, when he kept the word "description" without asking himself what other functional story could remove the perplexity that this leaves.[20] Sentimentalists remove those perplexities, such as the difficulty of seeing why morality should matter to us, or why moral verdicts are to be issued in the light of natural facts. We give instead a metasemantic story, which places our use of moral sentences in the perfectly ordinary human activity of comparing, adjusting, endorsing, and criticizing the practical reasonings that govern our lives.[21] So the sentimentalist ends up happily trading in the currency that realists prize so much: truth, fact, normativity, the autonomy of ethical thought, and reasons for action.

---

[20] Moore confesses that this idea had never struck him. See Schilpp (1942: 544).

[21] Huw Price holds that the kind of role an idea of moral truth clearly plays in these social activities is the same as the role truth plays across the board; this is the core of his global expressivism. See his 2003.

It is just that as we do so, we know what backs the currency, whereas realists, whether relaxed or not, offer nothing at all at that crucial point. We are concerned about morality not because "moral properties" possess some mysterious non-natural magnetic pull on us, strangely rivaling the pull of natural objects of desire or aversion (although of course in their very own unintelligible, ethereal, non-causal and non-explanatory way) but because we are concerned about the myriad ways in which things can go well or ill, and our moral language is that in which we voice, adjust, coordinate, or insist upon those concerns.

Moral epistemology for realists relaxed or otherwise, is a fraught business. For there is no discernible reason why "intuition" should have a default title to reliability. As we have seen some, like Scanlon, take refuge in a comparison with mathematics, in spite of the glaring contrasts between, on the one hand, working out the properties of abstract structures described axiomatically, and on the other hand, knowing to put your hand over your mouth when you cough, or taking pleasure in finding that your feelings about some matter coincide with those of your friend. By contrast the sentimentalist tradition deals in plain, down-to-earth facts. We like it when things go well for ourselves and others. Our sympathies interest us in the conditions that further the safety, prosperity, tranquility, ease, happiness of ourselves, our families, and those who surround us. As we have seen the question whether we are "right" to have this interest does not arise. To make it trouble us, a doubter would have to do something to put these values and wishes in an unfavourable light, but what could that be?

Perhaps in the civilized Edinburgh of the eighteenth century, this question would simply not worry anyone. But in the twenty-first century we are all too aware of people who do put humanity, peace, benevolence, or justice in an unfavourable light. The three goads of grievance, greed, or God fill people with the righteous certainty that it is a duty to unleash rapine and terror on those on the other side. People are always able to behave inhumanely to one another, out of fear or anger or jealousy or resentment, sectarianism or greed. Even in Europe the appalling belief that war has a glorious and cleansing power was promoted by influential warmongers like Gabriel d'Annunzio at the beginning of the twentieth century. Such beliefs grow in specific historical soil, as does the allure of Holy Wars and genocide. D'Annunzio was not refuted by intuitions and reflective equilibria, but by the First World War. But even resentment, religious frenzy, and plain greed do not give rise to a general party of inhumanity or a desire to see a global increase in suffering and distress or a desire to see a general aversion to safety and tranquility, prosperity or happiness. There is only the belief that others have more of these things than they deserve, and at our expense, and therefore we have a holy cause to seize the goods and rectify the balance. Otherwise, there is no party of sociopaths. They inevitably come singly, for even a pirate ship requires internal loyalty, solidarity, and rules governing property and promises. The sociopath of moral philosophers' nightmares either belongs to the disingenuous disputants whom we ignore, or at worst would be the kind of monster whom we would hope to quarantine or smother. Either way, we sail on, unruffled. We know that a good will, happiness, and safety, prosperity, ease, and tranquility are better than misery and fear, destitution and discomfort. The heart speaks with only one voice, and the question is closed, even if the routes to these desirable states are often dim and difficult to discern.

# 4 Evolutionary Debunking Arguments, Explanatory Structure, and Anti-Realism

*Karl Schafer*

Any non-skeptical moral theory claims that our moral judgments are not systematically false. Thus, such theories take these judgments to be reliable in at least a minimal sense. But how is our reliability about moral questions best explained? One option is to explain the reliability of these judgments by making the moral facts dependent upon our moral reactions or judgments. For example, suppose that the moral facts depend upon our moral sentiments – and that our moral judgments are also sensitive to these sentiments. In this case, it seems relatively easy to explain why our moral judgments and the moral facts generally agree. After all, on this view, both the moral facts and our moral judgments are a function of a single common factor – namely, our moral sentiments.

Explaining the reliability of our moral judgments becomes more difficult, if we think of the fundamental moral facts as wholly mind-independent. For example, consider a more realist version of sentimentalism, which takes our moral sentiments to be our primary means of access to the moral facts but takes many of these facts to be independent of our sentiments. Unlike the previous view, this second position cannot explain the reliability of our moral sentiments via an explanatory connection that runs from our moral sentiments to the moral facts. And the most obvious alternative to this strategy raises worries of another sort. For suppose our realist sentimentalist tries to appeal here to an explanatory connection in the opposite direction by, say, taking our moral sentiments to be partially caused or constituted by certain moral facts. While this might help explain the reliability of these sentiments, it would also call into question whether they can be understood in purely naturalistic terms. Thus, this sort of "robust realism" about moral facts has seemed to many to conflict with a purely naturalistic understanding of moral psychology.[1]

---

[1] A simpler style of debunking argument can be found in Harman (1977). The debate over this style of argument is complex, but it seems to many to beg the question against the moral realist, by assuming that we ought to form our beliefs *solely* through scientific forms of inference to the best explanation.

The most fashionable way to bring out this sort of conflict appeals to an evolutionary account of the origins of our moral faculties. In particular, such "evolutionary debunking arguments" claim that evolutionary considerations show us that our moral faculties cannot give us knowledge of mind-independent moral facts. Thus, if such debunkers are right, we must choose between a robust and non-skeptical form of moral realism and a naturalistic picture of human psychology and its origins.[2]

Not surprisingly, debunkers do not agree on the proper response to these arguments. For some, they apply very broadly – so that an error-theory about morality is the only rational response to them.[3] For others, these problems are best dealt with by turning to a non-cognitivist metaethical theory on which questions of reliability are arguably misplaced.[4] But many debunkers believe that the proper reaction to them is something more modest – namely, a turn away from robust forms of moral realism toward a view on which the moral facts are dependent upon our psychology.[5] Thus, many debunkers take these arguments to support a cognitivist form of sentimentalism or constructivism on which there are moral facts, but these facts are a function of our moral sentiments or attitudes.

For the most part, I will focus on the last of these alternatives in what follows. I believe that a moral error theory is best avoided if at all possible. And while I have a good deal of sympathy with quasi-realist forms of expressivism, the issues such views raise lie outside the scope of this paper. So while some of what I say will be relevant to these views, I will focus here on debunking arguments that aim to establish that moral facts are mind-dependent, while remaining within the context of cognitivism about moral judgment. Such arguments aim to undermine – not the very existence of moral facts – but rather the "robust realist" claim that these facts are independent of our moral psychology.

But should we find such arguments convincing? To consider this question, I first distinguish two basic forms such arguments can take – focusing on the epistemological assumptions that drive their skeptical conclusions. Then I argue that we have good reason to be skeptical of these assumptions on general epistemological grounds. In doing so, I note that many moral anti-realists also have reason to reject these assumptions – for they are powerful enough to jeopardize moral knowledge even given many forms

---

[2] Of course, one may be skeptical of the project of giving a wholly naturalistic or non-normative characterization of the mind. I am not unsympathetic to such views, but for the sake of argument, I will mostly concede to the debunker that a wholly naturalistic account of the nature and development of the human mind is preferable. For an argument against this, see Wedgwood (2007).

[3] Joyce (2007).      [4] Blackburn (1998); Gibbard (2003). Compare Schafer (2013).

[5] Street (2006); Bedke (2009); Setiya (2012).

of anti-realism. Thus, as will become clear, what drives these "evolutionary debunking" arguments often has less to do with the distinction between realism and anti-realism *per se*, and more to do with the details of the explanatory structure of one's metaethical views.

In this way, the majority of this essay will be dedicated to defending moral realism against the debunker. But in the end, my attitude toward these arguments is more ambivalent. For while I do think that even "very robust" moral realists can resist the hard choice between anti-realism and skepticism the debunker wishes to force upon them, I also agree with the debunker that her arguments point to a legitimate source of dissatisfaction with many forms of moral realism. Thus, even if these arguments fail as arguments from robust moral realism to skepticism, they succeed in raising real questions about the explanatory structure of many forms of moral realism – questions that might very reasonably be taken to motivate a broadly mind-dependent view of morality of a sentimentalist or constructivist sort.

## 1    Two Varieties of Debunking

Let's begin by defining the kind of moral realism that will be our focus. Although some debunkers have attempted to debunk *all* forms of moral realism – and, indeed, all forms of quasi-realism – the clearest target of such arguments are "robust" forms of *non-naturalist moral realism*: views on which the fundamental moral facts cannot be reduced to or wholly explained by any combination of facts about our mind or other natural facts:

**Robust Realism**: There are moral facts; and the *fundamental* moral facts are explanatorily independent of facts about our normative attitudes, as well as other evolutionarily significant natural facts.[6]

Thus, the Robust Realist claims that there is a domain of fundamental moral facts – facts that hold independently of facts about moral psychology – or any other relevant naturalistic facts.[7]

---

[6]  See Cuneo (2007), Enoch (2011), Fine (2002), Fitzpatrick (2015), Nagel (1986), Parfit (2011), Scanlon (2014), Shafer-Landau (2003/2005), and Wedgwood (2007).

[7]  The latter qualification is important, because in order to block the debunking arguments considered below, it will be sufficient that the fundamental moral facts are explained by features of the human species that also explain our moral judgments and reactions. Thus, in order to resist these arguments, we need not draw a *direct* explanatory connection between the moral facts and our moral judgments or reactions. It will be enough if we can draw an explanatory connection (of the right sort) between each of these elements and some third factor, which is itself amenable to naturalistic explanation. (Kauppinen in this volume).

**Robust Realism** may seem an implausibly strong metaethical view. But in considering it, it is important to stress that it does not insist that the moral facts are mind-independent or human-independent in the sense of having *nothing to do with* the nature of human beings or their minds. For example, one popular candidate for the status of fundamental moral truth is the fact that pain is bad, which concerns the badness of certain psychological states. Indeed, on such views, the fundamental moral facts may themselves establish *explanatory* connections between, say, the fact that something is painful and the fact that it is bad. What is crucial for the Robust Realist is simply that *these most fundamental* moral facts are not themselves explained in terms of further natural facts.

Thus, on any such view, more determinate moral facts about human beings will be explained in part by natural facts about us, in conjunction with more fundamental moral facts. The important point for the Robust Realist is simply that the fundamental fact that, say, *pain is bad* is a product neither of our evaluative reactions to being in pain (at least naturalistically described) nor any other natural fact. Thus, the Robust Realist need not deny that morality is especially concerned with (say) pleasure and pain. And they need not deny that many moral facts are partially explained by natural facts. All they must insist is that the *fundamental* moral facts are not explained in this way.

One way of understanding the core claim of **Robust Realism** is in terms of the idea that the most fundamental moral facts do not depend on anything contingent or parochial to a specific culture, community, or species. Again, in saying this, the Robust Realist need not deny that the vast majority of moral facts about human beings *do* depend on such facts. Rather, what is important to the Robust Realist is simply the idea that these more determinate moral facts about human beings in particular are explained by more fundamental moral facts that hold independently of contingent natural facts.

How, then, do debunking arguments attack **Robust Realism**? Unsurprisingly, they begin with some sort of empirical claim about the origins of our normative faculties and judgments. Quoting Sharon Street, we might put this claim as follows:

**Assumption**: We have come to make the normative judgments we do because "the mindless process of evolution by natural selection shaped us that way."[8]

---

[8] Street (2006 and 2009). An interesting question is whether a focus on biological as opposed to cultural evolution matters here. This, of course, will depend greatly on one's views about the nature of cultural explanation. But I will follow Street in assuming that the influence of biological evolution on the development of our faculties and judgments is sufficient on its own to raise these concerns.

For our purposes, what matters most about **Assumption** is not the details of how this process of evolution is understood. Rather, what is important is that **Assumption** implies that the full explanation of why we make the normative judgments we do does not appeal to moral or normative facts, at least when these facts are characterized in moral or normative terms.[9] Of course, establishing this does not require any appeal to evolution by natural selection *in particular*. All that is required is a high degree of confidence that the best explanation of why we make the moral judgments we do is purely naturalistic. But nonetheless evolutionary theory remains relevant here insofar as the success of evolutionary theory increases our confidence in the possibility of this form of explanation.

Given **Assumption**, the basic form of these arguments is quite simple. From **Assumption**, the debunker argues that, if **Robust Realism** were true, any fit between our moral judgments and the moral facts would, at least at the most fundamental level, be an *accident* or *coincidence* in an epistemically problematic sense. And from this they conclude that these judgments cannot be regarded as genuine instances of moral knowledge because of the presence of the relevant form of accidentality or luck.

Crucially this last step can be made in two quite different ways. First, the debunker may argue that we should regard accidents of this sort as *highly unlikely*. If she proceeds in this way, she will then conclude that, conditional on the conjunction of **Assumption** and **Robust Realism**, we should regard it as highly unlikely that our moral judgments are reliable.[10] In short, on this version of the argument, we would have to believe something quite *incredible* in order to regard our normative faculties as reliable (given **Assumption** and **Robust Realism**). Thus, even if we do possess an initial entitlement to treat our moral judgments and faculties as reliable, this entitlement will be defeated by the recognition that they are highly unlikely to be reliable, given what we know about their origins.[11] I'll refer to this style of argument as the **Argument from Incredibility.**

---

[9] This qualification is important to allow for the possibility that the moral or normative facts are identical with certain naturalistic facts. For the most part, I will focus on the moral case, but similar considerations apply to normative judgments more general, and it will sometimes be useful to include these in the scope of my discussion.

[10] Compare Street's discussion. See also Joyce (2007) and Bedke (2009) among others.

[11] The initial entitlement at issue here can be understood in at least two ways. First, we might understand it in terms of an *a priori* entitlement to *believe* that our moral faculties are reliable. Or, second, we might understand it in terms of the idea that we are entitled to form moral judgments through the *use* of our faculties, without thereby having any sort of entitlement (prior to the use of our faculties) to *believe* that these faculties are reliable. The first option corresponds to so called "rationalist" responses to skepticism. (See, e.g., White 2005). The second represents a form of "dogmatism" in Jim Pryor's influential sense of this term (Pryor 2000). The difference between these views won't matter for our discussion – but I am inclined to view both of them as capturing part of the truth about these matters. In particular, the first may accurately characterize our *propositional* justification to believe

This is perhaps the most familiar way for such arguments to proceed. But there is another way the debunker could appeal to claims about "accidental reliability" to attack moral knowledge. Rather than entering into a debate about our entitlement to believe that our moral faculties are reliable, she might simply appeal to the attractive idea that knowledge requires non-accidentally true belief to argue for this conclusion *directly*. For example, she might claim that a belief can only count as knowledge if it is formed by a method that is non-accidentally reliable:

**No Accident**: When S knows that P, she knows it by a reliable method, and it is no accident that her method is reliable.[12]

If this is right, and if the sense of "accident" that this condition appeals to is the same as the one that is involved in the debunker's earlier claims, then the debunker would be in a position to conclude that knowledge of the fundamental mind-independent moral facts is impossible for us (given **Assumption**) simply in virtue of our moral beliefs lacking the relevant sort of non-accidental connection with the moral facts. Thus, while the first of these styles of argument attacks moral knowledge via attacking our entitlement to believe that we are reliable about moral questions – and then infers from this that the relevant sort of moral knowledge is impossible – the second style of argument attacks the possibility of such moral knowledge directly, by arguing that the realist cannot satisfy a basic condition on *what it is* for a belief to count as knowledge. I'll refer to this second argument as the **Argument from Non-Accidental Truth**.[13]

As we will see, there are costs and benefits to each of these strategies. But the upshot of them is quite similar. Given **Assumption**, both aim to leave us with a choice between moral skepticism and the rejection of **Robust Realism**. Thus, those unsympathetic to moral skepticism, and sympathetic to a naturalistic account of the nature and origins of the mind, are left with a powerful argument in favor of some form of moral anti-realism – or least, some "less robust" form of realism or quasi-realism.

## 2        The Argument from Incredibility

But does either of these arguments really require us to choose between moral skepticism and anti-realism in this way? There is reason to be skeptical in both cases. To see why, let's begin with the first style of argument. In considering it, it is important to recognize that it is not meant to devolve

---

that our faculties are reliable, and the second may characterize our *doxastic* justification for such beliefs. See Willenken (2011).

[12] See Yamada (2011) and Setiya (2012).

[13] This is Setiya's preferred version of the argument.

into a general skeptical argument against our entitlement to trust *all* of our faculties. Rather, the debunker means to offer a targeted skeptical argument – one that (given **Robust Realism**) effectively undermines our entitlement to trust our moral or normative faculties, while leaving our entitlement to trust our faculties for perception or non-moral reasoning intact.[14]

Given this, the debunker should allow that we are equally entitled *a priori* to rely on all of our faculties – both moral and non-moral. And she should concede that this *a priori* entitlement is equally robust and resilient in the moral and non-moral cases. Otherwise, her argument will beg the question against the realist who claims that prior to any empirical discoveries about our faculties, our moral and non-moral faculties deserve the same epistemic respect.[15]

Accordingly, the debunker should be understood as claiming that what we have discovered about the empirical origins of our moral judgments is sufficient to *undermine* our initial entitlement to treat these faculties as reliable. To put things in Hume's terms, what is at issue here is a form of consequent, not antecedent, skepticism.[16]

Of course, there is nothing very odd about this idea. For there are many cases in which discoveries about the origins of some belief or faculty or method has this effect. For example, consider the following, due to Dustin Locke:[17]

**Martian**: Jack has not received the training of an ordinary physics student. Rather, Martians brainwashed Jack to believe that certain kinds of streaks are caused by protons. Moreover, they brainwashed Jack to have this disposition, rather than a disposition to believe that something else causes such streaks, not because they themselves had done any physics, but simply because they liked the sound of the word "proton." You can even suppose, if you like, that there is some deep law of Martian psychology that makes them like the sound of the word "proton," and so it was in a certain sense inevitable (given the initial conditions) that Jack would come to have this disposition. Now Jack sees a streak and believes there goes a proton. However, just after coming to believe this, Jack learns that he was brainwashed in just the manner described above, and that he has not received the training of an ordinary physics student.

As Locke notes, it is very plausible that Jack's discovery about the origins of his disposition to believe that certain kinds of streaks are caused by protons

[14] Plainly this is essential to her aims – otherwise the debunking argument would be self-undermining.
[15] Again, this is the basic problem with Harman's argument. This section draws on the discussion in Schafer (2010). For related discussion see Enoch (2010b), Wielenberg (2010), Clarke-Doane (2012), Shafer-Landau (2012), Vavova (2014), Berker (2014), and Fitzpatrick (2015).
[16] Hume (1748/1999).    [17] Locke (2014: 231).

is sufficient to undermine whatever entitlement he might otherwise have to treat this disposition as reliable. But Jack's case is very different from the debunking arguments we are discussing. In particular, Jack presumably has a great deal of background evidence in favor of the proposition that dispositions for forming beliefs about matters of empirical fact are generally only reliable when they are caused in certain ways. Thus, in Jack's case, we can explain the debunking effect of his discovery via a straightforward appeal to his background knowledge about when dispositions for the formation of empirical beliefs are reliable – plus his discoveries about the nature of his disposition in this case.

This is a plausible model for many *local* debunking arguments, which target only some of our moral judgments. For many of these do appeal to conflicts between what empirical psychology tells us about some of our moral judgments and our background moral beliefs. But this style of argument does not seem promising for the debunker who aims to undermine *all* our moral judgments and faculties simultaneously. After all, any knowledge we might have of the conditions under which our moral faculties are reliable is itself (at least in part) a species of moral knowledge. And if we are allowed to appeal to background moral beliefs about *this* in the present context, we should also be allowed to appeal to other background moral beliefs as well. But if we are allowed to appeal to our background moral beliefs in evaluating the reliability of our moral faculties, the result of this evaluation will often be vindicating as opposed to debunking. After all, the debunker has given us no reason to think that our moral faculties generally produce results that conflict with our background moral beliefs. Indeed, given that these background beliefs are the product of these very faculties, it would be very surprising if this were the case across the board.

On the other hand, suppose we do bracket all of our background moral beliefs, and consider the significance of the discoveries we have made about the development of our moral faculties. In this case, the problem for the debunker is that, given this, it is unclear that these discoveries give us *any* evidence about whether these faculties are likely to be reliable. Such discoveries do tell us that the development of our moral faculties was sensitive to certain natural facts, but without drawing on *some* background moral beliefs, we seem at this stage to have no reason to regard this influence as *either* distorting *or* truth tracking with respect to the moral facts.

In short, if we rely on our background moral beliefs, many of these influences will (unsurprisingly) appear to have put us in a position to track the moral facts. But if we bracket our background moral beliefs, we seem to have insufficient evidence to judge whether these influences are likely to be distorting. So from neither of these perspectives do we gain the *positive evidence of unreliability* that the debunker needs to provide us with in order to undermine our initial entitlement to rely on our moral faculties.

Against this one might insist, as Locke does, that we can *generalize* from conclusions about the conditions under which empirical faculties are reliable to conclusions about conditions under which moral faculties are reliable. Thus, the debunker might argue that we do not need to rely on our moral faculties or any background moral knowledge in order to arrive at conclusions about the conditions under which moral faculties are likely to be reliable. But any such analogy is likely to be contested in the present dialectical context. For example, the realist is likely to insist that the proper epistemology for the moral domain differs from the proper epistemology of sense perception in ways that make such analogies misleading.[18]

At this point, the "incredibility" debunker may turn from cases like Locke's to cases in which it is intuitive that the origins of our *moral* beliefs has a dramatic debunking effect. For example, suppose I know that my basic moral beliefs were implanted in me via a random process that has a fixed 10 percent chance of giving me true moral beliefs. Plainly in this case, I should lose whatever confidence I might have had in these beliefs. But this case is importantly different from the actual developmental history of our moral beliefs in at least two crucial respects. First, in this case we *know* that our moral beliefs are the product of a random process, and second, we *know* that this process has a low chance of producing true beliefs.

Crucially, neither of these is true of the evolutionary origins of our moral beliefs. For while the evolutionary processes that produced our moral beliefs may not have been sensitive to the moral facts *as such*, these processes were hardly random. Indeed, the results of contemporary evolutionary theorizing suggest that these processes are likely to lead creatures like us to develop importantly similar moral faculties and judgments, even beginning from a fairly wide range of initial conditions.[19] Thus, rather than being a random process, evolution tends to produce creatures who treat certain sorts of naturalistic properties as morally significant. For this reason, the comparison of evolutionary processes to truly random processes like coin flips or dice rolls is quite misleading.[20] In particular, given this, the

[18] Compare Parfit (2011) and Scanlon (2014).
[19] Enoch (2010), Schafer (2010), and Wielenberg (2010).
[20] Against this, one might argue that the *diversity* of possible moral systems gives us sufficient reason for skepticism. But given that evolutionary processes are not random, this style of argument has very little to do with the evolutionary origins of our moral faculties. Rather it relies on claims about the epistemic significance of *possible moral disagreement*. I leave the skeptical significance of *that* to the side, but see Schafer (2015a) for some relevant discussion.

question facing us is whether the *non-random* outputs of these evolutionary processes are likely to be reliable at tracking the moral facts. And we have yet to see a way of tackling this question without drawing upon some sort of background moral (at least normative) knowledge.

## 3       The Argument from Incredibility Reconsidered

In response to this, the debunker may concede that we do in fact have to draw on *some* background moral (or at least normative) claims to make the **Argument from Incredibility** work. But they may go on to insist that these claims are so minimal and uncontroversial that this need not call the argument into question.[21]

To see how some debunkers have tried to take this step, it is helpful to ask how the realist can explain the proposition *that our normative judgments are generally reliable*, given **Assumption** and **Robust Realism**.[22] Now, the realist may have a good deal to say about why this proposition is true.[23] But, at least according to the debunker, if **Assumption** is true, whatever explanatory story they tell will end up having something like the following structure:

(1) A naturalistic explanation of why our moral faculties treat certain naturalistic properties as having normative significance.
(2) Certain further moral claims about the moral significance of the properties these faculties track – claims that at some stage bottom out in certain fundamental moral facts for which no further explanation can be given.

Thus, if the debunker is right, the realist's explanation of our moral reliability will ultimately rest on a *basic and unexplained connection* between the domain of moral facts and domain of evolutionarily significant natural facts – one that delivers the happy result that our faculties are reliable at tracking the moral facts. This *is* a sense in which the realist's explanation of our reliability about moral questions must rest on an "accident" or "coincidence." Thus, if this were right, there *would* be a sense in which our reliability about moral questions is ultimately the product of a happy coincidence.

One way to challenge these claims would be to question whether it is possible to give a purely naturalistic characterization of the nature and development of our moral attitudes and judgments.[24] I have some sympathy with this sort of partially normative conception of the mental. But taking this

---

[21] Street.      [22] This is exactly what debunkers like Street have done.
[23] See Enoch (2010), Schafer (2010), Wielenberg (2010), and Berker (2014).
[24] Fitzpatrick (2015).

line in the present context calls into question the truth of **Assumption**, which we are taking for granted. Thus, I'll leave this response to the side.

Instead, what I want to argue is that, even if this is the shape the realist's account must take, we should be skeptical of the epistemological conclusions the debunker wants us to draw from this fact. For even if the debunker is right about the structure of the realist's view, what we have discovered about this view is simply that it rests on a basic and unexplained connection between certain basic moral facts and certain evolutionarily significant natural facts. Thus, whatever debunking force this argument has must derive from the idea that we should assign a low prior probability to possibilities that involve such "coincidences."

Now, there is some plausibility to the thought that we ought to assign a relatively low prior probability to "coincidences" of this sort, all things considered. Indeed, a commitment to this idea appears to follow from the rationality of inference to the best explanation as a method of belief formation.[25] But the debunking arguments under consideration greatly overstate the force of such considerations. To see why, it is helpful to consider the following points:

(1) Any non-theistic theory of reality (other than perhaps Spinoza's) will in the end appeal to a number of basic, unexplained connections of this sort.
(2) While these unexplained facts may not be relevant to the explanation of the reliability of our moral attitudes on every such theory, they will be relevant to the explanation of *some* facts. Thus, in comparing such theories, it is important not to focus *exclusively* on their ability to explain *one* fact in particular.
(3) Furthermore, while the non-skeptical moral realist may have to posit certain basic connections of this sort between the evolutionarily significant naturalistic facts and the moral facts, it is far from obvious that he will have to posit *very many* – or that these connections will be at all *implausible*.

Thus, while the non-skeptical moral realist may have to posit certain basic connections between the evolutionarily significant naturalistic facts and the moral facts, it is far from obvious that he will have to posit *very many* or *very costly* connections of this sort. So the costs of **Robust Realism** along this dimension may not be very great. Indeed, it is not clear that the realist will have to posit *more* connections of this sort than debunker's preferred form

---

[25] It is important to distinguish this concern for explanation from related concerns about ontological parsimony. Such concerns also raise questions about **Robust Realism**, but their relationship to these explanatory questions is complicated.

of anti-realism does. After all, many anti-realist views require us to make a number of basic, unexplained claims about the manner in which our moral attitudes *determine or ground* the moral facts. And it is possible for the realist to conceive of the fundamental moral facts as facts about how certain natural facts ground or determine certain non-fundamental moral facts. In which case, the basic structure of these two views on this score will be quite similar. Thus, it is not clear that the combination of anti-realism and an evolutionary account of our views scores better in this regard than the combination of non-skeptical moral realism and an evolutionary account does.

Of course, the force of this point might be mitigated by treating these fundamental connections between the moral and the natural as identities or reductions – e.g. by seeing them as essential to the relevant moral properties.[26] But such a move is equally open to *both* realists and anti-realists – *provided* they are willing to give up on the fully non-reductive ambitions associated with **Robust Realism**. Thus, this possibility doesn't undermine the basic symmetry between realist and anti-realist views here – although it may put pressure on *both* to move toward a more reductive understanding of the relationship between the moral and the natural facts.

Moreover, and more importantly, while I agree that the existence of such connections *is* a potential cost of the non-skeptical realist's view, it is not nearly as great a cost as the debunker's argument suggests. Most theories of reality will in the end appeal to some number of basic, unexplained connections of this sort. So while we should aspire to a complete theory of everything that involves as few such connections as possible, this concern for explanatory simplicity must be treated as *defeasible* in the face of our total evidence. Even if such "coincidences" are *a priori* somewhat unlikely, they are not *so* unlikely that it is always unreasonable to believe that they have occurred. For we can, and often do, acquire evidence that just this is the case.[27]

Thus, even if these considerations mean that a naturalistic explanation of our moral faculties and views should *somewhat* lower the probability that we assign to these faculties reliably tracking mind-independent moral facts, no reason has been given why it should lower this probability to such a degree that our moral faculties lose *all* evidential significance. To think otherwise is precisely to make the presence of a "coincidence" or unexplained connection of this sort a decisive theoretical failing. And this would give considerations of explanatory simplicity an importance they do not have.

---

[26] For the significance of essentialism in this context, see Rosen (2010) and DasGupta (2015).
[27] Setiya (2012).

Thus, the realist should agree with the debunker that "coincidences" of the sort at issue are *relatively* unlikely *a priori*. But he can nonetheless maintain that our total moral and non-moral evidence supports the proposition that we have developed faculties that are generally reliable at tracking the mind-independent moral truth. After all, debunking arguments aside, it appears that evolutionary factors often *have* produced moral faculties that track properties that we *take* to have the relevant sort of moral significance. And while the debunker's argument should perhaps diminish our confidence in the reliability of such judgments to some degree, we have yet to see any reason to believe that it should do so to a degree that would completely undermine our reliance on them.

Against this, the debunker might complain that we have no *independent* source of evidence that such a coincidence has occurred. After all, our only source of evidence for this proposition rests on a reliance on the very moral faculties that are under attack. But while this challenge does raise deep epistemological issues – these issues are perfectly general, and have very little to do with the causal origins of our moral beliefs *in particular*. After all, it is just as difficult to give evidence for the reliability of our perceptual faculties that is wholly independent of *any* reliance on those faculties. So while there are genuine questions here, I don't think they support a *targeted* debunking argument of the sort the **Argument from Incredibility** aims to be.

### 4     The Argument from Non-Accidental Truth

With this in mind, let's turn to the second, more direct, manner the debunker might appeal to claims about "accidental reliability" to attack the possibility of moral knowledge?

Once again, this style of argument relies – not on claims about the probability we should assign to hypotheses with a certain sort of explanatory structure – but rather on the idea that a *condition* on knowledge is that a belief can only count as knowledge if it is formed by a method that is *non-accidentally reliable* in some sense:

**No Accident**: When S knows that P, she knows it by a reliable method, and it is no accident that her method is reliable.

This condition will only be relevant in the present context, if we understand the notion of "accidental reliability" it appeals to so that it makes contact with the explanatory structure of **Robust Realism**, given **Assumption**'s claims about the origins of our moral faculties. In order for this to be the case, we must read **No Accident** so that the developmental history of our moral faculties is relevant to whether their reliability is an accident in the intended sense. As a result, in order for **No Accident** to have the "desired" debunking effect, it is normally understood to require an explanatory connection between two facts: first, the fact that some method M is reliable and, second, the fact that the believer is disposed to use M:

**Strong No Accident**: When S knows that P, she knows it by a reliable method, and there is an explanatory connection between (i) the fact that this method is reliable and (ii) the fact that she uses it.[28]

Such an explanatory connection can take many forms. For instance, it might involve a variety of different forms of explanation – including not just causal explanations but also constitutive or teleological explanations. And more importantly, the explanatory connection of interest to us may be the product of a variety of different *directions* of explanation. So, for example, the reliability of some method might (in part) explain why we use this method – as would be true if the reliability of our moral methods helped to explain why use them. Or this method's reliability might be explained by our use of it – as would be the case if the moral facts themselves were mind-dependent. Finally, there might be some more complicated story about how the two facts in **Strong No Accident** are explained by a common factor.

Having said all that, the debunker is ready to object to *any* story the **Robust Realist** offers to explain the connection between our moral methods and the reliability of that method. For given **Assumption**, the **Robust Realist** faces a dilemma in trying to connect together the two facts at issue in **Strong No Accident**: (i) the fact that we use method M to form moral beliefs and (ii) the fact that M is reliable at tracking the fundamental moral facts:

On one hand, the Robust Realist cannot claim that (i) is explained by (ii). For (ii) is itself a moral fact. Thus, by **Assumption**, neither it, nor the fundamental moral facts that explain it, plays any role in the explanation of (i).

On the other hand, the Robust Realist cannot claim that (ii) is explained by (i). After all, (ii) is explained by the fundamental moral facts. And, given **Robust Realism**, these facts are not explained by (i) or by any other naturalistic fact relevant to the explanation of (i).

Thus, given these assumptions, there seems to be no way of satisfying **Strong No Accident** – at least with respect to the fundamental moral facts.[29]

This is the heart of the argument. But it is worth noting that **Strong No Accident** also raises similar worries for forms of moral *anti*-realism that make positive metaethical claims about how the moral facts are determined

---

[28] For a full development of this argument, see Setiya (2012).

[29] Importantly, the same is not true of the *non-fundamental* moral facts. So one option is to concede to the debunker that knowledge of the fundamental moral facts is impossible, but to insist that this result is not overly skeptical so long as knowledge of the non-fundamental moral facts *is* possible.

by the psychological facts.[30] For example, consider an anti-realist view that takes as basic some version of the claim that *the facts about value hold in virtue of our attitudes of approval or disapproval.* Call this metaethical fact **Approval**.

Then we can ask whether knowledge of **Approval** is possible, given **Strong No Accident**. Once again, to explain how this is possible, we have to show that there is an explanatory connection between the fact that (i) we use method M to form metaethical beliefs and (ii) the fact that M is reliable at tracking the basic metaethical facts like **Approval**. And this raises the same issues that **Strong No Accident** generated for the realist. In particular:

On the one hand, we cannot claim that (i) is explained by (ii). After all, provided that irreducible metaethical facts like **Approval** are not part of a naturalistic account of the human mind, then given **Assumption**, (ii) will play no role in the explanation of (i).

On the other hand, we also cannot claim that (ii) is explained by (i). After all, (ii) is explained by **Approval** – a fact that is explained neither by (i) nor by any other naturalistic fact relevant to the explanation of (i).

Thus, once again, on this form of anti-realism, **Strong No Accident** seems to make the fundamental facts about how our attitudes determine the moral facts unknowable. More generally, while a view that accepted **Approval** *could* use **Approval** to explain how we can satisfy **Strong No Accident** with respect to the first-order moral facts, this only pushes the basic challenge that **Strong No Accident** raises with respect to our knowledge of *fundamental* facts back a step.

In order to avoid this, the anti-realist might dig even deeper – by offering a further explanation of facts like **Approval** – one that allows her to establish the explanatory connection **Strong No Accident** requires of us in *that* case. But this will only invite an infinite regress of such explanatory claims.[31]

In this way, principles like **Strong No Accident** naturally invite an explanatory regress, on pain of making whatever facts they take to be fundamental unknowable simply in virtue of the non-accidentality of knowledge.[32] I think this should make us suspicious of **No Accident**'s

---

[30] Of course, neither quasi-realists nor error-theorists will be tempted to make such claims. So these comments only apply to one form of metaethical anti-realism.

[31] A better possibility might be to understand the relationship between the basic facts about value and our attitudes of approval or disapproval as one of *identity* as opposed to grounding or determination. But it is unclear that **Strong No Accident** will not generate the same problems for our ability to know the relevant identities. In any case, this move would be equally available to a realist, provided that they were willing to give up on the non-reductive ambitions of **Robust Realism**.

[32] As Berker (2014) notes, such a regress may not be totally unnatural with respect to some forms of anti-realism. For example, someone who accepts **Approval** might also find it natural to see the truth of **Approval** as *itself* grounded in facts about our attitudes – and so on *ad infinitum*.

interpretation of the connection between knowledge and non-accidental truth. In saying this, I do not mean to suggest that there is *no* sense in which knowledge is incompatible with accidental truth or accidental reliability. Indeed, I think there are at least two ways in which this is true – having to do with the non-accidental connection that the truth of a piece of knowledge must have with both the *subject* who possesses the knowledge and the *objects* that are known. These two connections can be roughly glossed as follows:[33]

**Reliability**: If a belief is to count as knowledge, that belief must satisfy some sort of intuitive "reliability" condition – be that a matter of safety or reliability or something less reductive. In this sense, the belief's truth must have a non-accidental connection with the manner in which it was formed.

**Attributability**: If a belief is to count as knowledge, it must be reasonable to attribute the truth of that belief, as well as the positive epistemic features that are relevant to the **Reliability** condition, to the believer so that these features are regarded as relevant to one's *epistemic evaluation of the believer*.

In the end, I believe that these two forms of non-accidentality can be traced to the role played by our practice of knowledge attribution. But what is crucial for our purposes is that neither of them suggests that anything as strong as **Strong No Accident** is a condition on knowledge. Thus, we can accept that knowledge requires non-accidental truth in both senses without accepting the principle that drives the second debunking argument.

To see why, suppose that I have a basic, innate faculty that provides me with intuitions about some subject matter – say, morality – in a highly reliable, safe, and sensitive manner. And suppose I form a belief through normal reliance on this faculty. Plainly such a belief will satisfy **Reliability** – since we can simply stipulate that the faculty in question is reliable in whatever sense is relevant. And whatever else might be true of such a case, it seems reasonable to attribute the truth of this belief to me as a believer, if in fact it is true. After all, it seems plausible that whenever I form a belief through normal reliance on one of my basic epistemic faculties, the positive epistemic features of this belief are relevant to the epistemic evaluation of me.

Crucially, this seems to be the case however the reliability of this faculty is *ultimately* explained. For instance, it seems reasonable to give me this weak sort of "credit" for the truth of this belief whether or not the reliability of

---

Another option for the proponent of **Strong No Accident** might be to think of **Approval** as constitutive in some sense of the meaning of the relevant concepts. In this case, these facts would have an explanatory connection with beliefs involving these concepts. But then we could ask, as above, how **Strong No Accident** allows for knowledge of *these* facts about meaning.

[33] Schafer (2014). Compare Pritchard (2012).

this faculty is *ultimately* the product of some grand cosmic accident deep in the developmental history of creatures like me. Indeed, it is hard to see how such a fact *could* be relevant to the attributability of these features of my beliefs to me in the sense at issue.

This fact about **Attributability** in the case of *basic* faculties or methods for belief formation is easily obscured by a focus on *derivative* methods for belief formation – that is, methods whose use is explained by the use of some other method. In the case of derivative methods, it is plausible that the positive epistemic features of some belief can be attributed to me only if the method that led me to use the derivative method in question was itself reliable.[34] It is this idea that drives the intuitions behind **Strong No Accident**. But while this thought is plausible in the case in which our use of some method depends on the use of a further method, it seems to me unmotivated and, indeed, counterintuitive in the case of basic methods.[35]

In this sense, at least in the case of basic methods or faculties, **Reliability** and **Attributability** are relatively "local" conditions on belief formation – neither is sensitive to the deep explanatory history of my beliefs or faculties. Thus, contrary to what **Strong No Accident** implies, the *ultimate* explanation of why such basic methods or faculties are reliable need not play a role in either of these two conditions on knowledge.

That having been said, I know that my intuitions about such cases are not universal. But I can see no reason to think that the two non-accidentality conditions noted above will imply anything as strong as **Strong No Accident**. Thus, it seems to me that **Strong No Accident** should *at best* be regarded as a highly controversial epistemological principle – one that goes well beyond the established sense(s) in which knowledge requires non-accidental truth. Given this, it is hard to see why the realist should feel compelled to accept it – or any debunking argument that relies on it.

---

[34] For example, suppose that John accepts some highly complex but ultimately truth-conducive *non-basic* method M, but does so on obviously irrational grounds – such as a recommendation of M by the *National Inquirer*. Intuitively the beliefs that John forms via M do not count as knowledge. And this seems to be because it would be unreasonable to attribute the truth-conduciveness of this method to John in the sense discussed above. This shows that the causal history of our methods is sometimes relevant to the conditions above – my point is simply that this is not always the case in the manner **Strong No Accident** requires. For a view on this topic that does not support the **Argument from Non-Accidental Truth**, see Bernecker (2011).

[35] For example, consideration of basic methods makes clear that it must sometimes be possible for the positive epistemic features of a method to be attributable to someone even though they have no independent evidence of its reliability. See Enoch and Schechter (2008).

## 5        Dissatisfaction with the Explanatory Structure of Robust Realism as a Motivation for Anti-Realism

Thus, each of the two debunking arguments ultimately rests on epistemological claims that are highly controversial. As a result, a non-skeptical moral realist can resist these arguments by taking issue with the epistemological presuppositions at their heart. Of course, in doing so, she will take on epistemological commitments of her own. But these commitments are not implausible. Indeed, they are far more modest than the epistemological commitments on which the debunking arguments rely. And it is hardly surprising that the moral realist will have to take a stand on certain epistemological issues in resisting moral skepticism.

Unfortunately for the realist, this is hardly the end of the story. For whatever we think of these epistemological questions, these arguments point to something about the explanatory structure of **Robust Realism** that we *should* find unsatisfying – even if this dissatisfaction is not nearly as dramatic as the debunker suggests. In particular, I believe that the debunker is correct in her insistence that the very structure of many robust forms of moral realism limits the degree to which such views can offer us a *satisfying* explanation of our reliability about moral questions. After all, so long as we think that the most fundamental explanation of why we think what we do about moral questions is naturalistic, any attempt by Robust Realists to explain our reliability in the moral domain will, at least at the fundamental level, rest on a conjunction of this naturalistic story with a moral explanation of why the relevant natural properties are morally significant. Of course, there are various moves the Robust Realist can make to minimize the explanatory costs of this aspect of his view. But in the end, any form of moral realism with this structure will be limited in its ability to offer us a truly satisfying explanation of our reliability about moral questions.[36]

This is a real cost of forms of realism with this structure, one that it would be best to avoid or at least to minimize – something which helps to explain the perennial appeal of debunking arguments. For while these arguments may fail at establishing that moral realism leads inevitably to

---

[36] An important question is whether moving to a reductive form of moral naturalism is helpful in this regard. In thinking about this, it is important to stress that a reduction of the moral to the natural will only be helpful insofar as it establishes a genuine *explanatory* connection between the moral facts and the relevant natural facts. Thus, it is not sufficient to simply claim that the moral facts are identical with or reducible to certain natural facts on the metaphysical level, these claims must also provide us with an explanation of why the moral facts are as they are claimed to be.

skepticism, they nonetheless point to a real cost of many forms of robust moral realism – and a real potential advantage of their competitors.

In particular, even if a mind-dependent account of normative facts does come to rest on certain basic, unexplained claims about how our attitudes ground the normative facts, the structure of such accounts seems to offer us *more* of an explanation than their realist competitors of *why these attitudes are reliable*. After all, this sort of anti-realism makes the reliability of our normative faculties *essential* to the nature of the normative facts and attitudes themselves, which seems to answer that question in as satisfying a manner as may be possible.

Moreover, while this is only one explanatory task among many, it is one with *considerable* significance for the success or failure of a metaethical theory. Thus, it is no surprise that even realists feel drawn to the sorts of intuitions that drive mind-dependent or constructivist views of the normative:

The connection between objectivity and truth is therefore closer in ethics than it is in science. I do not believe that the truth about how we should live could extend radically beyond any capacity we might have to discover it (apart from its dependence on nonevaluative facts we might be unable to discover).[37]

In short, these explanatory considerations do provide considerable support for the idea that there should be some sort of *constitutive connection* between the nature of our normative attitudes and the normative facts themselves.[38] Thus, even if these arguments fail to reduce **Robust Realism** to skepticism, they do help to demonstrate what is so attractive about less robustly realist accounts of the normative domain.

Indeed, this way of understanding the dialectic may actually make anti-realism more attractive than the understanding of the dialectic many debunkers prefer. Given an understanding of these arguments like Street's, we must either reject these arguments or be pushed, like Street, to a very extreme form of anti-realism. But if we understand these arguments in terms of *how good* an explanation of our reliability a theory makes possible, we are free to reject this choice between extremes in evaluating the metaethical significance of these considerations. Doing so is important because it allows us to see the nuanced costs and benefits of different forms of realism and anti-realism with respect to these explanatory questions. Thus, it opens the door to a variety of views that are intermediate between the most "robust" forms of realism and the most "extreme" forms of anti-realism.

[37] Nagel (1986: 139).
[38] There are views that might reasonably be regarded as forms of "realism" that provide us with a connection of this sort. Compare Schafer (2015b).

Of course, to properly evaluate these different views, we would need to carefully consider the costs and benefits associated with their explanatory structure. But it is there, as opposed to simple attempts to show that some form of realism implies skepticism, that we should focus our attention on these debates.

# 5     Sentimentalist Moral-Perceptual Experience and Realist Pretensions: A Phenomenological Inquiry

*Terry Horgan and Mark Timmons*

Recently there has been much interest in perceptual experience as a basis for moral knowledge. Some contemporary moral realists have sought to defend an empiricist moral epistemology, arguing that it is possible for one to know moral propositions that are grounded in moral-perceptual experience.[1] Some defenders of perceptually grounded moral epistemology conceive of moral-perceptual experience as ordinary *sensory* perceptual experience of a select sort.[2] Others defend the idea that there is such a thing as *affective* moral-perceptual experience.[3] According to views of the former sort, it is possible, for example, to literally see (visually perceive) the injustice of an action one is witnessing by becoming immediately, visually, aware of the instantiation, by the action, of the property of injustice. By contrast, those who defend the idea of affective moral-perceptual experience argue that it is possible for one to detect instantiations of moral properties by means of one's affective capacities. For instance, according to one version of the latter view, one's emotional responses of, say, disgust and indignation are (under the right conditions) means by which one can experience instantiated moral properties – experiences that are arguably perceptual in nature. Given the central role that affect plays in these views, they may be referred to appropriately as sentimentalist accounts of moral perception, which thereby fit into a broadly sentimentalist approach to morality.

As our title indicates, we plan to focus exclusively on sentimentalist accounts of moral-perceptual experience. In particular, we are interested in exploring the question whether one can determine on the basis of

---

[1] Use of the term "moral perception," on one natural understanding, implies that one does not have it unless one is in perceptual contact with instantiated moral properties. So to avoid misunderstanding, in what follows we will use "moral-perceptual experience" as an expression intended to be officially neutral about whether the sorts of psychological state that figure centrally in the moral perception literature involve contact with moral properties.

[2] See, for instance, Cuneo (2003), McGrath (2004), McBrayer (2010a, 2010b), and Audi (2013).

[3] See Johnston (2001), Prinz (2007), and Döring (2007).

introspectionist methodology *whether* such experiences have or "carry" what we call *strong ontological objectivist (realist) purport* – henceforth, "realist purport."[4] For purposes of this chapter, we understand moral realism as an ontological view, according to which there exist (instantiated) moral properties whose nature and existence is independent of conventions and idiosyncratic attitudes, whether such properties are response-dependent (as are color properties, on some views) or response-independent. In order for some concrete moral experience to carry moral realist purport, then, the experience must purport to present a (putatively) instantiated moral property, understood as one or another form of moral realism conceives of such properties.

Some philosophers think that one can determine *on the basis of introspectionist methodology* that moral experience does carry such purport (more presently on the nature of such methodology). The rough idea is that by focusing attention on certain aspects of one's moral experiences one can reliably confirm that these experiences have intentional propositional content that represents putatively instantiated moral properties, construed as moral realists conceive of such properties. This claim about the content of moral experience figures as the main premise in what we call *the argument from introspection* whose upshot is that phenomenological inquiry – inquiry that relies on introspectionist methodology – grounds pro tanto justification for believing that some form of moral realism is true. An argument from introspection that features sentimentalist moral-perceptual experience would thus have as its central premise that one can reliably determine, based on introspectionist methodology, that such affective experiences carry moral realist purport. It is this particular version of the argument from introspection we are concerned to evaluate.

In what follows we argue for what we call "the neutrality thesis," according to which one cannot reliably determine by introspectionist methods whether affective experiences of the sort featured in the sentimentalist perception literature carry such purport. We do not here argue that such experiences *do not* have realist purport. For all we have to say in this chapter, they might. But whether they do is not something one can reliably determine by introspectionist methodology, so we argue. We begin with some further clarificatory remarks about the dialectic our chapter addresses.

## 1      Phenomenological Inquiry and the Neutrality Thesis

What we are referring to as phenomenological inquiry involves the use of first-person introspection for the purpose of ascertaining aspects of one's

---

[4] We set aside, for reasons of space, rationalist conceptions of moral objectivity, which we consider to be a species of strong moral objectivism.

conscious experience. What we will call *direct* introspection is the activity of turning one's attention inward, as it were, and attending carefully to one's ongoing experience in order to describe some aspect of that experience. In addition, there is what we will call the *indirect* method of introspection. This method is a way of abductively establishing phenomenological claims about the presence or absence of experiential features that are not open to direct introspection. Suppose it is controversial whether experiences of some type include phenomenal feature P. The indirect method proceeds by pointing to some aspect of one's overall experience that is directly intro-spectible, and then argues that the best explanation of this aspect is that the experience in question also includes P. What we are calling introspectionist methodology includes both the direct and the indirect methods.

Focusing for the moment on conscious mental states that are being referred to as states of affective moral-perceptual experience, we will make the following three assumptions. First, such states have intentionality of some sort.[5] Second, these states enjoy a phenomenal character – there is something it is like to undergo or have them. For instance, there is something it is like to undergo an experience of, say, indignation. Finally, we will assume that such states, as experiences, each have a phenomenal character that is (a) proprietary (i.e., is uniquely specific to the kind of attitude involved – e.g., indignation), (b) distinctive (i.e., is uniquely specific to the particular intentional content of the given state), and (c) is individuative (i.e., it can be individuated in virtue of its proprietary and distinctive character taken together).[6]

The question we are raising about the intentional content of relevant affective states is really two-fold. First, what is one able to determine about the elements of one's moral-perceptual experiences through the use of introspectionist methodology? Second, how do these elements bear on the question whether such affective experiences purport to be about something objective. In particular, do such experiences carry realist purport? Here are three competing answers to this two-part question:

*Affirmative*: Use of introspectionist methodology can establish that at least some types of affective moral-perceptual experience do carry realist purport.
*Negative*: Use of introspectionist methodology can establish that no type of affective moral-perceptual experience carries realist purport.

[5] The intentionality of a psychological state need not be (or only be) *propositional* intentionality. For instance, a state of fear with respect to a snake one perceives has *singular* intentionality: its intentionality is directed toward the snake. (It might also have propositional intentionality, e.g., that the snake is dangerous.)
[6] For elaboration and defense of these claims, see Horgan and Tienson (2002), and Horgan and Timmons (2008).

*Neutrality*: Use of introspectionist methodology cannot establish whether any type of affective moral-perceptual experience carries realist purport.

A few comments about Neutrality are in order.

Neutrality presupposes that certain questions about the intentional content of the sorts of experience in question do not have answers that can be established by introspectionist methodology, despite the fact that the experiences themselves are introspectively accessible. One might be suspicious of this claim, thinking that this couldn't be so, since the subject matter is supposed to be that which is available to introspection. However, one needs to distinguish between what is *present in experience* on one hand, and, on the other, which aspects of what is given are reliably *ascertainable* on the basis of introspectionist methodology. They need not coincide. For example, with respect to the question of whether the content of agentive experience is compatible with state-causal determinism, one might hold that the answer to this question is *fixed* just by the nature of the experience itself, as the experience is self-presented to the agent. Arguably, however, introspectionist methodology alone will not allow one to reliably ascertain that answer.[7] Again, consider the question of whether in visually perceiving something one's experience typically represents high-level properties and relations such as kind properties and causal relations, in addition to such low-level properties as colors and shapes. Assuming that the answer is affirmative, can one determine by such methodology that one's visual experience represents such high order properties? In response to this question, Susanna Siegel writes: "No matter how much you introspect, it isn't obvious one way or another" (2011: 14). By introspection Siegel has in mind the direct method. We agree with her that one should not assume that everything presented in experience is open to direct introspection. (Siegel goes on to argue abductively for the view that visual experience has rich content, by explicitly considering various candidate explanations of certain directly introspectible phenomenal contrasts and explicitly rejecting the candidates that are alternatives to an explanation that appeals to rich visual-perceptual content. This argument deploys the *indirect* method of introspection.[8])

There are certain potential limitations in the extent to which claims about experiential character can be established by means of the methodologies of introspection. Perhaps, for instance, (1) there is a definite fact of the matter about whether moral-affective experiences carry realist purport, and yet

---

[7] See Horgan (2012 and 2015), and Horgan and Timmons (2011).

[8] What we call the indirect method, Siegel refers to as the method of phenomenal contrast. We prefer our label, since the method of direct introspection can proceed by directly introspecting two or more experiences for purposes of calling attention to some subtle yet directly introspectible feature one of them has which the other lacks.

(2) this fact of the matter (whatever it is) cannot be reliably confirmed by either the direct or indirect methods of introspection. Then the argument from introspection featuring affective experiences will be in serious trouble, even if those who propound the argument are correct in their contention that such experiences do carry realist purport – and even if fans of the argument are also correct in claiming that such experiences constitute affective *perceptions* of (instantiations of) the kinds of ontologically robust moral properties whose existence is affirmed by moral realists and is denied by moral irrealists.

In defending our neutrality thesis, we proceed in several steps. In the next two sections, (*i*) we describe what we take to be one of the most plausible accounts of affective moral-perceptual experience (defended by Sabine Döring), (*ii*) we provide a rich phenomenological description of an instance of indignation as a representative moral-emotional experience, and then (*iii*) we explain how Döring's perceptual theory of emotion can accommodate the phenomenology in question. In Section 4, we sketch the expressivist metaethic we favor, a construal of moral judgments that we call *cognitivist expressivism* (step *iv*), and (*v*) we explain how this view can accommodate the introspectively accessible phenomenal features of moral judgments. Finally, in Section 5 we present a cognitivist expressivist account of moral emotion (step *vi*), and (*vii*) we explain how this view can accommodate the phenomenal character of our representative moral emotion, smoothly and without distortion. Having done this, we will have defended Neutrality. Section 6 is our conclusion.

## 2     Moral Emotion as Affective Moral Perception

As lately noted, one of the most plausible accounts of affective moral-perceptual experience is developed by Sabine Döring. Central to her account is a perceptual theory of emotion, according to which emotions have *propositional intentionality* that is (as we will put it) "affectively charged." Furthermore, because emotions play the same kind of role in justifying (as well as explaining) evaluative beliefs as do sensory perceptual experiences in justifying (as well as explaining) sensory perceptual beliefs, she claims that emotions *are* perceptions, although, due to the nature of their affective phenomenology, they are to be distinguished from sensory perceptions (Döring 2007: 376). So, in her view emotions (or at least prototypical ones) are affective perceptions.

With respect to affective *moral* perception, Döring illustrates her view with the example of witnessing a parent harshly punish her child, a toddler, who accidentally drops his ice cream. *First*, upon witnessing this event, you experience indignation and in "experiencing the indignation at the harsh punishment of the toddler, it seems to you that the punishment is unjust: your occurrent emotional state puts forward your indignation's content as correct" (Ibid.: 377). Given that "emotional evaluations imply an 'ought-to-be' judgment, experiencing the punishment as unjust means that it is an event in the world which ought not to have happened" (Ibid.: 386). *Second*, in taking your emotion at face value, you come to judge that the punishment ought not to have occurred (an evaluative judgment). *Third*, if you then judge that it is possible (and justifiable) to take action, practical reasoning leads you to judge that you ought to intervene (a normative judgment) by, for example, protesting this child's treatment, which, if determinatively effective in your deciding what to do, leads you to protest. The guiding idea, then, is that what you witness causes in you an emotional response with moral-evaluative propositional intentionality – an affective perceptual state in which it seems to you that the punishment is unjust and ought not to have happened. This seeming-state can serve as spontaneous input that can rationally ground (without inference) content-relevant evaluative judgments which themselves can serve as premises in practical reasoning leading to appropriate action.

It is not our purpose here to evaluate Döring's particular version of the perception theory. Given our neutrality thesis, what is important about this view is that it constitutes a clear example of a sentimentalist account of moral-perceptual experience that could figure in the argument from introspection. We now proceed to elaborate a phenomenological description of a concrete experience, based on the example from Döring, followed by an explanation of how her account of affective moral perception can accommodate the various components of such an experience so described. This explanation constitutes a prima facie case for Affirmative.

## 3     Indignation: A Phenomenological Description and a Pro-Tanto Case for Affirmative

Consider Döring's own example of the moral indignation experienced by the bystander who witnesses the harsh treatment of a toddler. The following list is an attempt to provide a rich, but by no means complete, phenomenological description of this particular emotional episode as we imagine it.

Projecting into the position of the bystander having just witnessed the harsh treatment in question:

I. – At the most generic level of description, one experiences one's indignation as causally *grounded* in what one has just witnessed –

the "external" state of affairs or event that one saw as unjust. Particular aspects of one's indignation (again, as we imagine it) include the following:

II.  – Experiencing one's *attention* captured by the event one has just witnessed: one's *focus* is outward; not on one's self or how one is feeling at the moment.

III.  – Experiencing one's indignation as flowing from oneself and *directed* or "aimed" outward toward the external event.

IV.  – Experiencing one's indignation as involving a *feeling with negative valence*: one experiences oneself as being against the event in focus. Moreover, one's negative feeling in this particular case is experienced as particularly *intense.*

V.  – One's intense negative feeling, while directed outward, also involves *bodily experiences* (even if they are not the focus of one's attention) including, perhaps, experiencing an accelerated heart rate, tenseness in one's muscles, teeth beginning to grit, one's face grimacing, etc.

VI.  – One's againstness feeling (directed outward) is itself experienced as co-occurring with (though not necessarily distinct from) an ought-not-to-be *seeming experience*, or more accurately in this case, an ought-not-to-have-happened seeming experience that itself is experienced as grounded in what one has just witnessed. Call this the "evaluative core" of one's indignation.

VII.  – Assuming one has no reason to take one's seeming experience as non-veridical, one experiences one's response as *fitting* the external state of affairs, which includes one's seeming experience having a *categorical feel* to it – as being independent of one's pre-existing desires.

VIII.  – This categorical feel is accompanied by a *feeling of authoritativeness*, a feeling of one's indignation grounded in reasons – in this case one's taking the parent's punishment as unjust, and as unjust because small children are so prone to incur such minor accidents unintentionally.

IX.  – One feels poised to react in various ways on the basis of one's indignation – one's emotional experience includes a *motivational-evaluative "pull,"* perhaps as strong as a felt demand, to do something, such as protest the child's treatment.

There is much to say about this phenomenological description, but we limit ourselves to two clarificatory comments. First, we claim that these elements are introspectively accessible. However, this is not to say that all of these aspects are immediately obvious in a "look see" way. For instance, in order to bring into view aspects VII and VIII – the categorical, authoritative feel of one's evaluative experience – one may need to patiently interrogate one's experience by, for example, contrasting one's experience of indignation with an experience of intense frustration in reaction, for example, to one's horse having lost the Kentucky Derby. In this latter case, one does not experience one's frustration as independent of one's pre-existing desires or as having the kind of authority intrinsic to one's indignation experience. Contrasting such cases helps foreground the categorical, authoritative feel of one's indignation, allowing one to become aware of these aspects through introspection. Second, in light of items VI–VIII, it is certainly correct to describe this experience of indignation as having an *overall objective feel* to it. One experiences oneself as responding to the external state of affairs with a sense that one's indignant response is authoritatively correct.

How, then, does Döring's account of affective moral-perceptual experience accommodate the introspectively accessible phenomenal features I – IX listed in the previous section, and, in particular, features VI–VIII? The obvious answer is that in her view the phenomenology of indignation includes the following characteristic, one with moral-realist purport:

X – One's affective moral-perceptual experience of indignation carries propositional intentionality that is given by correctness conditions that include the instantiation of the (putative) evaluative property, *ought-not-to-have-happened.*[9]

An advocate of a view like Döring's might appeal to direct introspection and claim that just by attending to one's experience of indignation, one can reliably determine that, in addition to features I–IX, one's experience

---

[9] One might complain that this misrepresents Döring's view, because, in her example, the so-called affective intentional (propositional) content of one's experience of indignation represents the action as being *unjust* and does not also represent the property of ought-not-to-have-happened. After all, we quote her as saying that emotional evaluations *imply* ought (not)-to-be judgments. We reply as follows. First, on Döring's view, insofar as one's affective-perceptual experience of indignation has accurate *evaluative* propositional intentionality, it must purport to represent a property whose nature is evaluative. Second, insofar as an instantiation of the (putative) property of injustice (being represented in one's emotion) is the instantiation of a thick evaluative property involving both non-evaluative descriptive aspects and an evaluative aspect, its evaluative aspect would seem to be its ought-not-to-be-ness, or perhaps its particular *way* of being a state of affairs that ought not to be. So, given these two points, it would seem to follow that on Döring's view the propositional intentionality of one's indignation must include the action's ought-not-to-be-ness. Finally, regardless of how Döring is best interpreted, were one to defend a view somewhat like hers according to which (in the indignation example) one's overall experience includes an ought-not-to-be *judgment* that normally is inherited (perhaps automatically, rather than as a conscious inferential transition) from the propositional intentional content of the emotion, it would not matter for our pro-Neutrality argument. All that matters is that the sort of expressivist attitudinal account of emotion we describe below in Section 5 can accommodate the relevant phenomenological data that is accessible to introspection.

includes feature X. If so then Affirmative is true, and one has made a pro tanto case for moral realism. Alternatively, one might defend abductively the claim that X is present in one's experience of indignation, by arguing that the presence of this feature explains why one's feeling of againstness co-occurs with its seeming to one that the state of affairs in question ought not to have happened. It would also explain the categorical and authoritative feel of one's indignant response to the child's treatment. And if this is the clearly best explanation of the phenomenology in question then by the method of indirect introspection, the pro tanto case for Affirmative is secure.

A defender of the argument from introspection might not explicitly distinguish the direct method from the indirect method and might not explicitly articulate the intended form of the argument. We suspect that many of the argument's fans would regard as overwhelmingly obvious the contention that the directly introspectible features VI–IX can be plausibly explained only by the presence of feature X – so obvious that this contention might not even come to mind explicitly. For such a person, the indirect and direct methods of introspection effectively converge with one another: given that feature X is the obvious-seeming explanatory basis for features VI–IX, feature X is apt to seem so intimately bound up with features VI–IX that the direct introspective accessibility of those features will seem virtually tantamount to the direct introspective accessibility of X itself. (This is especially likely to happen if the contention that X is the explanatory basis for VI–IX gets implicitly assumed, rather than becoming consciously thematized.)

This completes what we described in the introduction as the first three steps in our evaluation of the argument from introspection. We now proceed to the fourth and fifth steps: sketching cognitive expressivism (our own favored metaethical position regarding the nature of moral judgment), and explaining how this view smoothly accommodates the introspectively directly accessible phenomenal features of moral judgments. This will set the stage for Section 5, where we will extend cognitivist expressivism to moral emotion and then offer an expressivist account of features VI–IX. The viability of this account, as an alternative to the account that appeals to claim X, will be the key element in our case against Affirmative and in favor of Neutrality.

## 4     Cognitivist Expressivism and the Phenomenology of Moral Belief

Two dialectically important features of our upcoming line of argument should be kept well in mind. First, the argument will assume only that cognitivist expressivism is a credible candidate for being a correct metaethical position – not that it *is* the correct position. And the same holds with regard to the cognitivist expressivist theory of emotion that we will set forth in Section 5. But if (*i*) our metaethical view (and the theory of emotion situated within it) can accommodate the introspectively accessible aspects of the relevant phenomenology, and moreover (*ii*) this form of accommodation is no less viable than is a theory of moral emotion that attributes realist purport to these emotions, then that is enough to show that introspective methodology (either the method of direct introspection or the indirect method) does not yield a positive answer to the question about whether moral-emotional phenomenology carries realist purport. An indirect argument from introspection will be undermined by the availability of the alternative explanation of the pertinent phenomenological data. A putative direct argument from introspection will be undermined this way too, because the availability of the alternative explanation both (a) will prevent the indirect and direct methods from converging, and also (b) will make it very likely that those who claim to directly introspect feature X in their affective moral-perceptual experience are actually *interpreting* such experience in an ontologically realist way.

Second, the argument as we develop it will take for granted the very plausible claim (which we ourselves are happy to concede) that metaethical positions that attribute realist purport to moral experience *also* can smoothly accommodate the phenomenal features of moral experience to be discussed in this section and the next one. That is why our cognitivist-expressivist construal of the pertinent moral phenomenology, if viable, will constitute evidence for Neutrality rather than constituting evidence for Negative.

### *Cognitivist Expressivism: A Very Brief Introduction*

Cognitivist expressivism involves a general conception of belief according to which a belief is a certain kind of commitment state with respect to a non-evaluative propositional content that we call the belief's *core* descriptive content. The view recognizes three logically distinct fundamental belief types, with respect to a core descriptive content: *is*-commitment, *ought*-commitment, and *not-ought* commitment.[10] For example, the belief that

---

[10] It is convenient too to speak of negative ought-commitments, sometimes calling them "ought-not" commitments (and we will do so below); but an ought-not commitment vis-à-vis a core descriptive content *that-p* is really just an ought-commitment toward the corresponding negative core descriptive content *that-**not**-p*. *Not-ought* commitments, on the other hand, are logically fundamental, because being *not-ought* committed with respect to a core descriptive content is distinct from being ought-committed with respect to the negation of that descriptive content, and is also distinct from *not* being ought-committed with respect to that core descriptive content. For elaboration, see Horgan and Timmons (2009). Cognitivist expressivism also posits a recursive hierarchy of logically complex belief-types, whose constitutive inferential roles in cognitive economy constitute our way of addressing

the parent harshly punished her child, and the belief that the parent ought not to have done so, are respectively an is-commitment vis-à-vis the core descriptive content *that the parent harshly punished her child*, and an ought-commitment vis-à-vis the (negative) core descriptive content *that the parent **not** have harshly punished her child*.

This general conception of belief treats moral judgments as genuine beliefs, but, strictly speaking, it is noncommittal with respect to whether such beliefs also have overall *moral* propositional content. Thus, the framework could be embraced by a moral realist: the claim would be that, for example, the belief that the parent ought not to have harshly punished her child is both an ought-commitment with respect to the non-moral propositional content *that the parent not have harshly punished her child* and an is-commitment with respect to the putative moral propositional content *that it ought to have been that the parent did not harshly punish her child*. However, the framework is also compatible with denying that moral beliefs have moral propositional content. In some of our past writings, we have defended a non-error version of metaethical irrealism, in which we combine a cognitivist view of moral judgments (a view that construes them as genuine beliefs) with a nondescriptivist/irrealist view about such judgments. This is the position we are calling "cognitivist expressivism." On this view, then, there is no such way the world might be as, for example, *the parent harshly punishing her child being an action that ought not to be*. But there is a distinctive type of ought-commitment with respect to a non-moral way the world might be, as in *the parent not having harshly punished her child*. One might capture the idea here by saying that, on this conception of moral belief, the *ought* is in the attitude, rather than in a putative moral proposition. A moral belief is an ought-ish commitment with respect to a *non*-moral proposition, and is not an is-ish commitment with respect to a putative *moral* proposition.[11] How to understand this "ought-ish way" of becoming committed brings us to our next point.

The three kinds of belief, call them *is-beliefs*, *ought-beliefs* (both positive and negative), and *not-ought beliefs*, each involving a distinct kind of commitment state with respect to a core descriptive content, are each *sui generis*: none is reducible to any of the others, and none is reducible to some other kind of nonbelief state such as an attitude of approval or a mental state appropriately expressible via an imperative sentence. The way to understand the nature of the beliefs we are calling ought-commitments

the infamous Frege-Geach and negation problems for expressivism. For elaboration, see Horgan and Timmons (2006b, 2009).

[11] We do not deny the meaningfulness, or the aptness in many contexts, of sentences like "The proposition that the woman was wrong to harshly punish the toddler is true." For elaboration, see for instance Horgan and Timmons (2006a, 2006b).

and not-ought commitments is not by trying to reduce them to something else, but rather by delineating their key features – both the generic features they share in common with ordinary descriptive beliefs (is-commitments), and the distinctive features that set them apart from descriptive beliefs.[12] This task requires dwelling on both the phenomenological and functional-role features of the two types of belief, a task we have undertaken at some length elsewhere. Since our primary concern here is with phenomenology, we will make only passing mention of matters of functional role.

The issue of strong ontological purport arises not only for moral emotions, but also for moral beliefs. Here too there are three theses to consider:

*Moral-Belief Affirmative*: Use of introspectionist methodology can establish that at least some types of moral belief carry realist purport.

*Moral-Belief Negative*: Use of introspectionist methodology can establish that no type of moral belief carries realist purport.

*Moral-Belief Neutrality*: Use of introspectionist methodology cannot establish whether any type of moral belief carries realist purport.

In the remainder of the present section we will argue that Moral-Belief Neutrality is the correct view. We will do so by explaining how cognitivist expressivism can smoothly accommodate the pertinent features of moral belief that are directly introspectively accessible – both the phenomenological features that are common to all beliefs, and those that are specific to moral beliefs. Smooth accommodation involves not just being *compatible* with such phenomenological features but also constituting a plausible and natural way of *explaining* them. (We take it to be uncontroversial that these phenomenological features can also be smoothly accommodated by views asserting that moral beliefs do possess realist purport.) Smooth accommodatability via cognitivist expressivism would undermine the attempt to argue abductively, via the method of indirect introspection, that (at least some) moral beliefs have realist purport, because the correct – and therefore the best – explanation of the pertinent phenomenology might well be the cognitivist expressivist explanation. The attempt to argue for realist purport by the method of direct introspection would be undermined too, because the availability of a viable-looking cognitivist expressivist explanation would make it hard to deny that those who claim that they can directly discern realist purport in their moral-belief phenomenology are really imposing an interpretation on this phenomenology that outstrips what is reliably introspectively accessible.

---

[12] Hereafter, for simplicity of exposition, we will usually deploy the locutions "ought-commitment" and "ought belief" more broadly, to cover ought-commitments both positive and negative and also not-ought commitments.

We will focus first on the generic phenomenal characteristics of occurrent belief – characteristics shared by the two species of belief. This will put us in a position to explain how cognitivist expressivism accommodates the phenomenology of ought-beliefs.

### The Phenomenology of Two Types of Belief

Generally speaking, occurrent beliefs involve: (*i*) psychologically "coming down" on some issue, in a way that (*ii*) classifies (often spontaneously) some "object" of focus as falling under some category, where one's classificatory coming down is experienced as (*iii*) involuntary, and (*iv*) as a cognitive response to some sort of consideration that is experienced (perhaps peripherally in consciousness) as being a sufficient reason for categorizing as one does.[13] So, in the case of occurrently believing that, for instance, the bird on one's back fence one is now looking at is a goldfinch (a descriptive is-belief) one experiences oneself (*i*) coming down on the identity of the object one is looking at by (*ii*) classifying it as falling under some category applicable to physical objects (being a goldfinch), where one's coming down (either spontaneously or after some process of reflection) is experienced as (*iii*) involuntary, and as (*iv*) a cognitive response to its seeming to be one, based largely on one's immediate visual perceptual experience, which one takes to be a sufficient reason for believing that the bird one is looking at is a goldfinch.[14]

### Moral-Belief Neutrality

We are now poised to defend the neutrality thesis concerning moral belief, construed as pertaining to what is reliably introspectible via direct introspection. We begin with the following question. Is one able to reliably determine by introspectionist methodology whether moral beliefs carry moral-realist purport? We say no. Despite the phenomenological similarities we have just pointed out between experiences of occurrent non-normative

---

[13] We might add to this description that (*v*) one experiences one's occurrent belief (as just described) as apt for assertion and hence as naturally expressible in a public language by a sentence in the declarative mood. This aspect of belief is plausibly understood as involving both phenomenological and functional role features.

[14] Feature (*iv*) need not involve an *explicit conscious belief* that one's visual experience is a reason for so classifying the perceived object; indeed, this construal of feature (*iv*) would be far too intellectualistic. Normally, rather, feature (*iv*) would be an aspect of one's phenomenology that is constituted by an *implicit appreciation* of that reason-conferring relation – an aspect that could be present even if one is conceptually fairly unsophisticated (say, because one is a small child). Implicit-appreciation aspects of experience – aspects that we call *chromatic illumination* – are an important and ubiquitous dimension of human phenomenology, something we argue at length elsewhere (Horgan and Potrč 2010; Horgan and Timmons, in preparation).

beliefs and occurrent moral beliefs, we maintain that moral beliefs can exhibit these features without having moral propositional content. In other words, we maintain that our cognitivist expressivist metaethic, which construes moral belief as consisting of an ought-commitment vis-à-vis a core descriptive content, accommodates the introspectively accessible phenomenology of moral belief.

To proceed with our defense of Moral-Belief Neutrality, let us first consider the phenomenological features of a moral belief, (*i*)–(*iii*). We maintain that one can experience an occurrent ought-commitment as an involuntary, classificatory, coming-down state vis-à-vis some core descriptive content, even though this state does not have moral propositional content. The experiential classificatory aspect of this coming-down state need not be a matter of experiencing oneself to be mentally attributing some putative in-the-world moral property to some act, agent, or state of affairs. Rather, it can perfectly well be the experiential manifestation of the specific *mode of affirmatory commitment* (or negatory commitment) that the agent now instantiates with respect to the given descriptive content – namely, ought-commitment (or ought-not commitment or not-ought commitment). And if one's phenomenological classificatory coming-down experience need not be a matter of experiencing oneself as attributing a putative in-the-world moral property, then, for example, one's becoming ought-not committed to the state of affairs constituted by the parent harshly punishing her child need not involve regarding this state of affairs as instantiating an in-the-world ought-not-to-be property.

In response, one might think that the very nature of classification involves attributing in-the-world properties to things. When one classifies a bird as a goldfinch, one experiences oneself as attributing to the bird the property of being a goldfinch. So, phenomenologically speaking, doesn't classifying an action as one that ought not to occur involve experiencing oneself as attributing the property *ought-not-to-be* to the action? Again, if one relies solely on methods of introspection (no matter how carefully employed) and considers what one can ascertain by these methods, we think the answer is no. It can perfectly well be the case that in classifying an action as a state of affairs or event that ought-to-be or ought-not-to-be, one's experience in doing so *just is* a matter of becoming committed *in a certain way* toward the state of affairs or event in question. In spelling out this "certain way" – an "oughtish" way of being committed – one appeals to the phenomenal character of this sort of state, which constitutes the categorical basis of a host of agentive dispositions vis-à-vis the state of affairs under consideration.

Turning for a moment to the fourth generic phenomenological feature of belief – that one experiences one's involuntary, classificatory coming down as grounded in reasons – it is this phenomenological aspect that gives one's ought-belief the categorical and authoritative feel. How does cognitivist expressivism accommodate this feature of one's experience? In this case (and others) an occurrent ought-commitment is based psychologically upon descriptive considerations that are experienced as *rationally grounding* this commitment state independently of the morally judging agent's pre-existing desires, even though the commitment state is not descriptive. Experiencing one's ought-commitment as being independent of one's pre-existing desires is what gives the experience its *categorical* feel. Relatedly, experiencing one's ought-commitment as grounded in descriptive considerations in this way gives the experience its *authoritative* feel. One experiences one's ought-commitment as grounded in considerations that reflect a *non-self-privileging, impartial* ought-commitment (or ought-not commitment) vis-à-vis the pertinent non-evaluative state of affairs.[15]

In response, one might think that experiencing one's ought-commitment as "rationally grounded," in the manner just described, involves an introspectively accessible experience as of a normative relation being instantiated – that is, as of one's commitment *fitting* the external state of affairs as one takes them to be. And thus (one might think) this particular aspect of one's experience has realist purport: one's experience purports to represent an in-the-world un-fittingness relation obtaining between the circumstances and one's ought-commitment. Again, however, so far as what direct introspection can reveal, the introspectible phenomenology is properly captured in a way that need not involve realist purport. In experiencing oneself as being ought-committed vis-à-vis some state of affairs, perhaps one experiences oneself as (*i*) *becoming ought-committed in a non-self-privileging way*, and (*ii*) as becoming so committed *because* of certain non-normative factual considerations. The idea is that such ought-commitments possess a kind of phenomenological unity: not only is one aware of certain objective, non-evaluative features of some object of evaluation, and not only does one experience oneself as becoming ought-committed with respect to a certain non-evaluative descriptive way-the-world-might-be (or might-have-been), but one experiences oneself as becoming ought-committed *because* of those features, and (as we have said) *in a non-self-privileging way*.

Here, it is important to notice that the "because" is not simply a causal "because." Phenomenologically, one's awareness of certain pertinent non-evaluative features of the object of evaluation is experienced not primarily

---

[15] Our remarks in the preceding footnote apply again here. In many instances of moral judgment-formation, especially instances where the judgment arises quite spontaneously in response to a perceived or envisioned state of affairs, the rational-grounding aspects are present in consciousness not explicitly but only implicitly, as chromatic illumination.

as a *causal source* of one's ought-commitment (although in the typical case, presumably it is in fact a causal source), but rather as exerting a certain *experiential grip* upon oneself, relative to that ought-commitment – a "being a reason for" experiential grip. In elucidating this structurally complex aspect of moral experience, cognitive expressivism will approach it similarly to how the view approaches ought-beliefs themselves. That is, it will stress (*i*) the aspect of phenomenal character that is distinctive of being thus "reason-for-ishly-gripped" by one's non-evaluative awareness-state vis-à-vis one's ought-commitment, and (*ii*) various associated agentive dispositions whose experiential categorical basis is that phenomenal-character aspect itself. It also will stress that this phenomenal element, like the moral belief, arises involuntarily and is independent of self-interest. To be thus gripped by one's non-evaluative awareness-state vis-à-vis one's ought-commitment, involuntarily and independently of self-interest, is to experience the pertinent non-evaluative state of affairs as an *authoritative* reason for being so ought-committed.[16] The structurally complex experiential aspect of "reason-for-ish grippedness," as thus elucidated, need not be construed as carrying strong ontological purport either to in-the-world moral property-instantiations and moral facts, or to in-the-world reasons-relations one of whose relata are in-the-world moral facts.

To summarize: cognitivist expressivism can smoothly accommodate each of the four key phenomenological features of moral ought-beliefs, and can do so despite denying that such beliefs are attitudes directed toward a putative moral evaluative proposition. Because this is so, neither the direct nor the indirect method of introspection can establish that moral beliefs carry realist purport. So, the upshot is that Moral-Belief Neutrality is correct. Let us now consider how cognitivist expressivism can and should construe moral emotion, and how such an account can be harnessed in support of the neutrality thesis about affective moral-perceptual experience.

---

[16] On an expressivist view, this experienced authority lies in oneself; it does not lie in the experienced detection of an in-the-world supervenience relation between certain instantiated non-evaluative properties and an instantiated in-the-world moral property. But again, being thus "reasonishly gripped" is involuntary and is independent of self-interest. Kantian terminology seems apt here (albeit under an expressivist, and hence sentimentalist, interpretation): in experiencing a given non-evaluative state of affairs as a reason for a certain moral ought-commitment, one may be viewed as in effect *giving oneself the moral law* (though, this is not to say that this construal can be read off from the phenomenology). One can give *oneself* the moral law, in the pertinent sense, whether or not this self-given moral law *pertains* to oneself, or pertains *merely* to oneself. The moral law that I give myself could pertain to you but not to me; or it could pertain to everyone; or it could pertain to everyone in such-and-such potential circumstances; etc.

**5    Moral Emotion as Evaluative: A Cognitivist Expressivist Account**

In this section we will first extend cognitivist expressivism to incorporate moral emotions, by construing such states by analogy to how cognitivist expressivism construes moral beliefs. We will then return to our representative example of moral indignation. We will argue, again by analogy with what we just said about moral belief, that the proposed cognitivist expressivist account can smoothly accommodate the phenomenological features I–IX described in Section 3, including in particular features V–VIII – the ones that might initially seem to underwrite the contention that experiences of moral indignation carry realist purport. (Feature IX also needs addressing, because the pertinent motivational-evaluative "pull" of a moral emotion is experienced as emanating from features VI–VIII, rather than as being a matter of pre-existing desire.) Because of the availability of this metaphysically irrealist way of accommodating the phenomenology, the upshot will be parallel to one at the end of Section 4: the thesis we called Neutrality is correct. Hereafter will call this thesis *Moral-Emotion Neutrality*. If, as we have supposed, the most plausible understanding of moral-perceptual experience is moral-emotional experience of the sort defended by Döring, then our defense of the latter will be sufficient for defending our original neutrality thesis set forth in Section 1.

*Extending Cognitivist Expressivism to Moral Emotions*

There is a natural way to extend cognitivist expressivism to moral emotions, as follows. Construe a moral emotion as having two constitutive components: attitude and content. The content is a non-evaluative proposition – what we call a core descriptive content. The attitude is a specific kind of *agentive stance* vis-à-vis that proposition. Any such moral-emotional stance-type – e.g., indignation – will have a specific, affect-laden, phenomenal character and will underwrite specific agentive dispositions regarding the putative state of affairs represented by the core descriptive content. (The pertinent dispositions will depend on the distinctive phenomenal character of the given moral-emotional stance-type, while of course also depending on the core descriptive content.) Also, the core descriptive content of a given moral emotion will have the aspect of *seeming to be true* – although the person experiencing the emotion might not, or anyway might not *yet*, actually mentally affirm that content. (To mentally affirm it would be to believe it, i.e., to form an is-commitment regarding it.) Furthermore, the phenomenal character of the emotion will underwrite, at a minimum, a *tendency* to form a moral belief (i.e., an ought-commitment or a not-ought commitment) vis-à-vis the core descriptive content – although in some cases such a moral belief will arise concurrently with the moral emotion, and in other cases the moral belief will arise prior to the moral emotion (and perhaps trigger it).

Consider once again the experience of indignation upon witnessing a woman harshly punishing her toddler for dropping his ice cream. On the proposed account, the propositional content of this emotional state – its core descriptive content – is *that the woman is harshly punishing her toddler for dropping his ice cream.* (This propositional content is inherited from a belief with the same content, which itself is inherited in turn from a perceptual seeming with that same content.) The attitude component of this emotional state is a particular agentive stance vis-à-vis the state of affairs characterized by that (non-evaluative) proposition – the stance called indignation. This stance is a distinctive kind of affect-laden orientation toward that state of affairs, with a distinctive phenomenal character; and the phenomenal character constitutes the experiential categorical basis of various associated dispositions with respect to the situation prompting one's emotional response – e.g., a disposition to form an ought commitment with respect to the core descriptive content *that she **not** harshly punish him for dropping his ice cream* (i.e., a belief that her performing the action was morally wrong), and a disposition to intervene by protesting to the woman that the child's innocent accident was no legitimate basis for reprimanding him in such an angry and blame-conveying manner.

Similarly, mutatis mutandis, for other moral emotions – and indeed, for many other kinds of emotions too. The emotion will be directed toward a putative, non-evaluative, state of affairs, characterizable by a non-evaluative proposition; and the attitude component will be a distinctive kind of agentive orientation toward that putative state of affairs, with a distinctive phenomenal character that is the experiential categorical basis of an associated range of behavioral dispositions. And (as we will argue next) emotions, so construed, can be smoothly accommodated within the rubric of cognitivist expressivism: they can perfectly well have all these features without carrying realist purport.

### *Moral-Emotion Neutrality*

Here we can be brief, because the earlier-mentioned considerations in support of Moral-Belief Neutrality extend quite straightforwardly, mutatis mutandis, to moral emotions. For concreteness, let us return yet again to Döring's example of indignation at the mother's harsh treatment of her toddler and features VI–IX in our phenomenological description of it in Section 5. (These four features of the case, you will recall, are the ones most likely to be regarded as supporting (moral-emotion) Affirmative, viz., "Use of introspectionist methodology can establish that at least some types of affective moral-perceptual experience do carry realist purport.") We will address each of features VI–IX in turn.

Feature VI is the emotion's co-occurring with an ought-not-to-have-happened seeming experience. Our expressivism accommodates this feature as follows. First, the emotion itself is construed expressivistically, as a state comprising a specific agentive stance-type (viz., the type *indignance*) and a core descriptive content (viz., *that the woman is harshly punishing the toddler for dropping his ice cream*). As with our cognitivist expressivist treatment of moral belief, the moral-evaluative aspect is "in the attitude" (i.e. the agentive stance of indignance), rather than in the emotion's propositional intentional content. Second, the emotion's phenomenal character strongly inclines one toward a full-fledged negative ought-commitment with respect to the mother's harsh treatment of the toddler, i.e., a full-fledged moral belief that this episode ought not to have occurred (although in some cases, the felt agentive stance might experientially pull toward a corresponding belief without such a belief actually arising – e.g., perhaps because one finds oneself wondering, "Is she perhaps scolding the toddler for something *else*?"). Third, the *seeming* aspect of the emotion – i.e., the woman's behavior toward her toddler *seeming* to be something that ought not to have happened – consists not in a moral-evaluative propositional content which purports to represent a putative in-the-world moral fact (and which seems to be true), but rather in the fact that one's agentive stance of indignation toward her behaving as she did has a phenomenal character that, constitutively, strongly inclines one toward an outright negative ought-commitment toward her behavior (i.e., an outright moral belief that she should not have so acted).

Feature VII is the emotion's being experienced as fitting the external state of affairs to which one is responding – with this fittingness being experienced as categorical, and hence as independent of one's pre-existing desires. Our expressivism accommodates this feature by construing it in terms of our expressivistic construal of reasons-for phenomenology, as described in Section 4: in undergoing the emotion, one finds oneself "reason-for-ishly gripped" by one's awareness of the state of affairs represented by the emotion's core descriptive propositional constituent (viz., the woman's harsh treatment of her toddler) – gripped with respect to the ought-not-to-have-happened seeming-experience, feature VI. This experiential grip occurs involuntarily and also occurs categorically, i.e., independently of self-interest and of one's pre-existing desires.

Feature VIII is the feeling of authoritativeness that accompanies the emotion's categorical feel. Our expressivism accommodates this aspect of the emotion by stressing, in combination, (*i*) the categoricalness itself, (*ii*) the aspect of involuntariness, and (*iii*) the fact that the experiential "becausal" connection between one's awareness of the woman's behavior and one's emotional response is not primarily as-of a mere causal relation but rather is the distinctive, experientially sui generis, phenomenal character of "reason-for-ish grippedness." We contend that this combination of phenomenal aspects plausibly *constitutes* the phenomenology of authoritativeness, and furthermore that all three aspects – and feature (*iii*) in particular – can be construed expressivistically.

Finally, feature IX is the motivational dimension of one's indignation experience – a form of motivation that is not a matter of pre-existing desires. This we accommodate by emphasizing that the overall, constitutive, functional role of the emotion of indignation, as subserved by its distinctive phenomenal character, includes motivating roles of certain kinds. Remember: on our account, one's indignation at the woman's treatment of her toddler is an experienced *agentive* stance with respect to the situation, and specifically with respect to the woman herself. The indignation motivates one, for example, to intervene and protest that this treatment is unjust.

So, cognitivist expressivism can smoothly accommodate features VI–IX. Moreover, our expressivist construal of this representative example of a moral emotion looks to be straightforwardly extendable to indignation in general, and indeed to moral emotions in general.[17] Because expressivism is ontologically irrealist with respect to putative in-the-world moral properties and moral facts, the upshot is that introspectionist methodology cannot reliably ascertain whether moral emotions carry realist purport, i.e., Moral Emotion Neutrality is correct. Although our case in this chapter for Neutrality regarding the realist purport of moral-emotional experience has not been fully developed and defended, we believe that we have at least done much to weaken if not topple the argument from introspection that features affective moral-perceptual experience. Finally, as we have said a number of times, it may be that moral-emotional experiences do carry realist purport (although we doubt it), but we have argued that one cannot determine whether or not this is so on the basis of introspectionist methodology alone.

---

[17] In cases where a moral judgment precedes an accompanying moral emotion and cases where the two arise concurrently, the phenomenal character of the emotion typically will subserve, inter alia, a judgment-reinforcing disposition, i.e., a disposition to render the strength of the moral judgment even greater than it would be otherwise.

## 6    Conclusion

We conclude with a brief remark about moral objectivity. In commenting on our phenomenological description of an episode of indignation, we noted that this experience has an overall "objective feel" to it. Moral realists attempt to explain this quality of the experience by claiming (*i*) that one's experience purports to represent an instantiated in-the-world moral property, and (*ii*) that in propitious circumstances, one's experience is a response to the putative moral property (or properties) being instantiated. But this is not the only way to understand the objective feel of such episodes. On the expressivist picture we favor, the objective feel of an experience of indignation (and of other moral emotions), and likewise the objective feel of an occurrent moral belief, emerges from the two aspects of the phenomenology we have been describing. First, one experiences oneself as judging (or in the case of a moral-seeming state, being disposed to judge) in a non-self-privileging way – taking, as it were, an impartial perspective – and thus as less self-centered and more other-centered. Second, one experiences oneself as becoming (or being disposed to become) positively or negatively ought-committed toward some state of affairs in what we have referred to as a "reasonish-because way." Thus, one experiences oneself as involuntarily "coming down" on the matter (coming down into an agentive stance, and perhaps also into an outright positive or negative ought-commitment) in an impartial, non-arbitrary reason-based manner. Call this conception of moral objectivity *small 'o' objectivity*. We contend that this modest conception generalizes to all moral experience that has an objective feel, and also nicely captures the kind of objectivity that is available to introspection (both direct and indirect) when reflecting on moral experience. As we have insisted all along, it remains possible that moral-emotional experiences (and moral experiences generally) also carry commitment to some strong, high-octane form of objectivity. But this is not something that can be determined by introspectionist methods.[18]

---

[18] Thanks to Remy Debes and Karsten R. Stueber for their very helpful comments on a previous version of this chapter.

# 6    Sentimentalism and Realism in Epistemology and Ethics

*Peter Railton*

## 1    Introduction

Over the past two decades, a surprisingly wide range of philosophers have claimed to be realists of some sort about morality. But the claim is made less surprising by the fact that many of these are "quasi-realists," who offer an expressivist or fictionalist account of moral language, which formally reproduces the surface continuity between ordinary moral discourse and more prosaically factual language and logic but avoids the "metaphysical" commitments of naturalistic or non-naturalistic realisms. Realists and quasi-realists seem to be deadlocked, the former treating the descriptive character of moral discourse as primary, the latter treating the prescriptive character as primary, and it has become increasingly unclear what reasons can be given for adopting one position over the other.

Perhaps for that reason, the appearance of a newcomer on the meta-ethical scene seems welcome. The newcomer, moreover, has a distinguished ancestry – it is seen as descending from the moral philosophy of figures like Hume and Adam Smith. *Neo-sentimentalists*, as we will call them, promise to unite descriptive and prescriptive elements of moral thought and language by arguing that sentiment is a kind of mental state that both presents the world as being a certain way (in the manner that fear presents its object as dangerous) and motivates a response appropriate to that representation (in the manner that fear motivates us to find ways of coping with, or avoiding, danger).

Is the upshot of such neo-sentimentalism a realist or quasi-realist account of the metaphysics of morals – or some quite different "third way?" Some quasi-realists wish to claim Hume for their own, insisting that Hume recognized a sharp distinction between beliefs, which are straightforwardly cognitive, and sentiments, which are quasi-cognitive at best (Blackburn 1998). By contrast, "fitting attitude" versions of neo-sentimentalism suggest that Hume's view is best interpreted in terms of a novel metaphysics of "response-dependent properties," corresponding to the "response-dependent concepts" that figure in sentimental attitudes

(D'Arms and Jacobson 2000a). Realism seems to be out of the picture once it is conceded that moral judgments express sentiments, rather than beliefs. But in this paper, I will be arguing that the most plausible interpretation of Humean sentimentalism is in fact realist – an interpretation that can accord full recognition to distinctive, "response-dependent concepts" in sentimental attitudes, while denying that the *properties* to which such discourse answers are either response-dependent or quasi-real. Instead, I'll argue, "fitting attitudes" are fitting because they represent, and track, *bona fide* properties of the physical and social world – and that this is Hume's view as well.

To make my case, I will follow an indirect route. Against the quasi-realist (and the contemporary neo-Humean orthodoxy, see Smith 1994), I will argue that Hume was a sentimentalist about *belief* – that is, he took the state of mind that constitutes belief, and that assertions express, to be a distinctive kind of "passion." Against the neo-sentimentalist, I then argue that Hume's account of belief offers a model of how irreducibly "response-dependent" concepts, like <credible>, can function to pick out worldly phenomena that are independently characterizable. Taking belief itself to be a "peculiar sentiment" might be thought *a fortiori* to lead to a non-realist or even anti-realist (error-theoretic) epistemology. That is something like the position taken by Christine Korsgaard in writing of Hume that "his view is that beliefs are sentiments which are caused in us by perceptions and habits," leaving no place for normative questions about what we have reason to believe (Korsgaard 1997, n. 23). As against neo-Humeans and neo-Kantians alike, I will be arguing that Hume's claim that belief is a sentiment is a crucial element in his *vindication* of human processes of belief-formation as (to use Hume's terms) capable of being "solid and legitimate" and "reasonable," and thus of possessing "authority" (1739–1740/2000, 1.3.13; SBN 143, 154).

Hume himself was adamant that belief is a "peculiar sentiment" – viewing this as one of his key innovations in philosophy, and central to his critique of rationalism. He does not, however, expect to win ready converts. In his anonymous "Abstract of a Book Lately Published," summarizing the main claims and arguments of the *Treatise*, he admits that this view of belief "seems a little surprizing," yet "we are led to it by a chain of propositions, which admit of no doubt" (Hume 1740: 24, 22). Understanding Hume's "surprizing" sentimentalist account of belief, I claim, will enable us to see more clearly the normative purport of Humean sentimentalism in the epistemic and moral domains alike.

Of course, my interest in connecting Hume's name with realism is not impartial – I have long defended a naturalistic realism in meta-ethics, and would be delighted to be able to inherit some of Hume's authority. But perhaps what I argue below will have interest even for those who place no stock in such realism. The neo-Humean program in philosophy has had enormous influence, as has the fundamental contrast it draws between two broad families of mental states: *belief-like states*, which are seen as representational in nature and as characterized by a "mind-to-world" direction of fit, and *desire-like states*, which are seen as motivational or "conative" in nature and thus as possessing "world-to-mind" direction of fit.[1] Since moral judgments are widely held to be "practical" in nature, that is, as having an "internal" connection to dispositions to *act*, neo-Humeans have argued that they must belong to the desire-like family.[2] Such a conception of the contrast between belief-like and desire-like states thus lies at the foundation of a number of key disputes in meta-ethics, and in philosophy more generally. If there is a problem with the way the belief/desire or theoretical/practical distinctions are being drawn by neo-Humeans, then a number of debates will need to be revisited.

Looking beyond such meta-ethical or meta-normative issues, it seems to me that Hume's sentimentalism about belief is a profound philosophical insight in its own right, one which is now receiving important support in empirical psychology and neuroscience. I am inclined, then, to agree with Hume that this "surprizing" conclusion is one of his most important philosophical contributions – however little this has subsequently been appreciated.

## 2      Hume on Belief

The *locus classicus* for contemporary neo-Humean accounts of belief is the distinction Hume draws in the first section of Book III of the *Treatise* between mental states that have "active principles," such as "passions and volitions," and those that lack such an active principle, such as the representation of "mere ideas" by "reason." Hume is launching a sustained attack on rationalism in morality by arguing that rationalists place moral judgment in the latter class of mental states, because they hold that "morality, like truth, is discern'd merely by ideas, and by their juxta-position and comparison . . . from reason alone" (Hume 1739–1740/2000, 3.1.1.4; SBN 456–457).

---

[1] For example, Simon Blackburn (1998: 100) calls the first family "Apollonian" and the second "Dionysian," and holds that "the eighteenth century got it right" in drawing this distinction between "cognitions" and "passions".

[2] This is a very simplified way of expressing a very complex set of issues. For some of the diversity of formulations of "internalism" about moral judgment, see Darwall (1997).

Hume's attack then proceeds from what he views as a truism accepted by philosophers and commonsense alike, namely, that "morality . . . 'tis supposed to influence our passions and actions" (Ibid. 3.1.1.5; SBN 457). So his question becomes, can "reason" and the "juxta-position and comparison" of "mere ideas" have such an influence? To answer, Hume must tell us something about what he takes "reason" to be. For the purpose of this argument, he offers what he again takes to be a widely accepted truism: reason aims at "the discovery of truth or falshood." This, then, tells us over what domain reason must operate:

Truth or falshood consists in an agreement or disagreement either to the *real* relations of ideas, or to *real* existence and matter of fact. Whatever, therefore, is not susceptible of this agreement or disagreement, is incapable of being true or false, and can never be an object of our reason. (Ibid. 3.1.1.9; SBN 458)

Hume then goes on to claim that "passions, volitions, and actions" are states of mind "compleat in themselves" which are non-representational in the sense that they imply "no reference to other passions, volitions, and actions" (Ibid.). As a result, they are "not susceptible of any such agreement or disagreement" with relations of ideas or matters of fact (Ibid.). He concludes:

'Tis impossible, therefore, they can be pronounced either true or false, and be either contrary or conformable to reason. (Ibid.)

Since action requires the motivating force of "passions" or "volitions," and these states by their nature lie outside the scope of reason,

Reason is wholly inactive, and can never be the source of so active a principle as conscience, or a sense of morals. (Ibid. 3.1.1.10; SBN 458)

What are the mental "representations" admitting of "truth and falshood" with which Hume is contrasting passions and volitions? Most have assumed that they must be *beliefs* – since we know that beliefs admit of truth and falsehood, and can be the objects of reasoning. The moral standard drawn from Hume's argument, then, is that since moral judgments are supposed to "influence the will," they cannot express mere beliefs – they must express some qualitatively different kind of state, a state with an "active principle" which has an inherent, "internal" relation to volition and motivation, a "world-to-mind" direction of fit.

Hume's compact argument here thus would undermine not only the rationalist project of founding moral distinctions on reason, but also any purely cognitivist, belief-based account of moral judgment. It would also afford a natural entry point for a Humean sentimentalism about the nature of moral judgment, since sentiment by its nature *does* have an influence on volition and action. Moreover, as he famously remarks, if you examine "any action allow'd to be vicious" seeking a "matter of fact, or real existence" that is its viciousness, you will find nothing until "you turn your reflexion into your own breast, and find a sentiment of disapprobation, which arises in you, towards this action" (Ibid. 3.1.1.26; SBN 468–469). Hume concludes:

> Vice and virtue, therefore, may be compar'd to sounds, colours, heat and cold, which, according to modern philosophy, are not qualities in objects, but perceptions in the mind. (Ibid.)

This passage should puzzle us somewhat, however. That the extensions of "red" and "cold" depend upon the peculiar properties of the actual human perceptual system – that redness and coldness are in some sense "response-dependent" – is readily admitted. But as perceptual features they *do* purport to represent some putative states of the world – the color or temperature of a plum on an autumn morning, say. Whatever the role of "perceptions in the mind" in fixing the reference of "red" or "cold," this does not preclude redness and coldness judgments from expressing beliefs that will be true or false in the most prosaic way. So perhaps the contrast Hume has in mind is *not* between belief-like and desire-like states?

Let's look at the other passage that has been most influential in buttressing the idea that Hume is arguing against the possibility that moral judgments could express beliefs, which is found in Book II:

> A passion is an original existence, or, if you will, modification of existence, and contains not any representative quality, which renders it a copy of any other existence or modification. When I am angry, I am actually possest with the passion, and in that emotion have no more a reference to any other object, than when I am thirsty, or sick, or more than five foot high. (Ibid. 2.3.3.5; SBN 415)

Here we encounter again the notion of passions as "original existences" rather than copies, and we again are told that they "have no . . . reference to any other object." But Hume's example here is *anger*, and again that should be puzzling. It hardly seems possible that as acute an observer of the sentiments as Hume could have thought we cannot be angry *at* someone, or angry *that* we have been passed over for promotion. To be sure, the passion of anger *itself* is not a mere representation – it is an "original existence" or psychic state with which I am "possest," and no more a "copy" of something else than is thirst, illness, or height. But anger is paradigmatically an *intentional* passion – one that is *about* something beyond itself, and can take a propositional object.

So what *is* the contrast Hume is after in this passage? Here's a proposal: he is not distinguishing between mental states that have representational content and those that do not, but between mental states that are *mere copies* and those that are not. What sorts of mental states *are* mere copies? Ideas and those "relations... which depend solely upon ideas," namely, *contrariety*, *similarity*, *degrees in quality*, and *proportions in quantity* (Ibid. 3.1.1.2; SBN 70). And why are these especially relevant to Hume's argumentative purpose? Because these are relations that can be discerned by reason alone – and the rationalist is claiming that *moral* distinctions can be discerned by reason alone. Given the idea **x is red**, say, reason can produce the ideas **x is not-red** (via contrariety), **x is a similar red to y** (via similarity), **x is redder than y** (via varying quality), and **x has more red than y** (via varying quantity).[3] These "mere ideas" and "relations among ideas" are certainly "susceptible of [the] agreement or disagreement" in which truth and falsity consist (Ibid. 3.1.1.9; SBN 458). Thus the idea **x is red** agrees with the color of a stop sign, and **x has more red than y** is agrees with the ordered pair, {Canadian flag; US flag}, but, as mere ideas, these are certainly not *beliefs* – reason can freely form compound ideas, negations, etc., with these ideas at will, whereas belief is not voluntary (Hume 1739–1740/2000, Appendix 2; SBN 623–624).

So Hume's point in contrasting a "passion" vs. a mere "copy" in this passage is not to contrast passions with beliefs (which are *not* mere "copies"), but to contrast passions with "mere ideas" and "relations among ideas" (which *are* mere "copies" – and thus within the power of reason (Hume 1739–1740/2000, 3.1.1). And when Hume is arguing that moral judgment has a "connexion" with the will, he is not contrasting moral judgments with beliefs, but with mere "relations among ideas" of a kind reason can judge. Such judgments could constitute moral judgments only if one could establish a "connexion betwixt the relation and the will" such that we can:

... prove that this connexion is so necessary, that in every well-disposed mind, it must take place and have its influence; tho' the different betwixt these minds be in other respects immense and infinite. (Ibid. 3.1.1.22; SBN 465)

And Hume takes himself to have "already prov'd, that even in human nature, no relation [of these four kinds] can ever alone produce any action ... " (Ibid. 3.1.1.22; SBN 466).

Hume's use of the term "reason" in the *Treatise* has been subject to much debate and must always be handled with care. Here we will adopt a reading of "reason," in which it is essentially co-extensive with "demonstrative and probable reasonings" (Ibid. 1.3.9.19n; SBN 117n) that take the form

---

[3] In contexts where there might be confusion between the idea *that p*, considered as an abstract object, and the idea **that p**, considered as a mental state with the idea *that p* as its content, I will use the convention of putting abstract ideas in *italics* and mental states and their contents in **boldface**.

of "relations among ideas." Such ideas might include principles of probabilistic inference (of which more, below), and so "reason" in this sense does
not exclude causal reasoning. What is important for our purposes, however,
is that such reasonings can be assessed for their formal validity, independently of whether the premises or conclusions are true or believed. Thus, we
can *reason* perfectly well from mere "copies" or "ideas" without requiring
that these premises be *believed* – for example, when we reason from suppositions or hypotheses. Such purely hypothetical reasoning, however, will
not by itself lead to action. Let's say that we are exploring an abandoned
building. I can reason, "Suppose the floor would support us, then we could
reach the stairs by crossing this room." A quick look at the floorboards,
however, reveals that they are thoroughly rotten, so we drop any plan of
attempting to cross them. Does this new evidence in any way disqualify the
hypothetical reasoning? Counterfactual supposition is in no way defective,
and neither is reasoning based upon such supposition invalid. By contrast,
the new evidence counts against, and would tend to undermine, any *belief*
we might have had that the floor would support us, or any *intention* we
might have had to cross it.

How is it that *belief* stands in such different relations to action and evidence from supposition? If, as the rationalists tell us, thought is just a succession of ideas, then what distinguishes successions that are suppositions
from successions that are beliefs? Hume points out in the *Appendix* to the
*Treatise* that rationalists have not so much as noticed the need to ask this
question: "what the nature is of . . . belief, . . . few have had the curiosity to
ask themselves" (Hume 1739–1740/2000, Appendix 2; SBN 623).

To understand Hume's own account of belief, we can begin by noting
the familiar distinction between the belief *attitude*, **belief [ ]**, and the *idea*
that is its object, **that *p***:

**belief [that *p*]**

The very same idea **that *p*** occurs in **imagine [that *p*]** or **suppose [that *p*]**.
So the difference must lie in the belief attitude itself, **belief [ ]**. Moreover,
this difference must be "distinguishable to the mind" in some immediate
manner – otherwise we would be at a loss, when **that *p*** is present in our
mind, whether to act on this or not. Hume thinks the rationalist must find
a difference that *reason alone* could distinguish – that is, some other "idea"
or "relation of ideas." But Hume argues that this is impossible:

That [belief] is not a new idea, annex'd to the simple conception [that *p*], may be
evinc'd from these two arguments. *First*, We have no abstract idea of existence, distinguishable and separable from the idea of particular objects. . . . *Secondly*, The
mind has the command over all its ideas, and can separate, unite, mix, and vary

them, as it pleases; so that if belief consisted merely in a new idea, annex'd to the conception, it wou'd be in a man's power to believe what he pleas'd. (Ibid. Appendix 2; N 623–624)

Let's focus on the second point. Hume takes belief to be a "secondary impression," "feeling," or "sentiment" arising involuntarily from sensation in much the same way that sensations give rise to fear, surprise, anger, or sadness. But what might this "peculiar" feeling or sentiment be in the case of belief? Hume admits that it is difficult to characterize it exactly, but he gives a clear account of its functional role – the "job description" the sentiment must satisfy:

> . . . belief consists not in the nature and order of our ideas, but in the manner of their conception, and in their feeling to the mind. . . .
> I confess, that 'tis impossible to explain perfectly this feeling or manner of conception . . . it is something felt by the mind, which distinguishes the ideas of judgment from the fictions of the imagination. It gives them more force and influence; makes them appear of greater importance; infixes them in the mind; and renders them the governing principles of all our actions. (Ibid.1.3.7.7; SBN Appendix 629)

He identifies this feeling as a "firm manner of conceiving" the object of belief, rather than a vividness or clarity of that mental object itself. I can vividly imagine a fire-breathing dragon in fine detail, without being in the least inclined to believe there is such a beast. For example, such "conceptions of the imagination" are "loose" in the mind – I can freely make the imagined dragon rearing up or attacking, or as injured or not. That isn't the case with the "firm conception" of belief, which imparts to its object a "fixity" or "firmness" that makes this object *resist* such self-conscious, voluntary tampering. The terms Hume especially associates with the belief attitude therefore are not visual metaphors such as the vividness or clarity of an idea, but terms that describe the "force," "life," or "fixity" of the object of belief in our mental economy:

> I conclude, by an induction which seems to me very evident, that an opinion or belief is nothing but an idea, that is different from a fiction, not in the nature, or the order of its parts, but in the *manner* of its being conceiv'd. . . . An idea assented to *feels* different from a fictitious idea, that the fancy alone presents to us: And this different feeling I endeavor to explain by calling it a superior *force*, or *vivacity*, or *solidity*, or *firmness*, or *steadiness*. (Ibid.)

This "force" and "vivacity" is akin to, and indeed arises originally from, the "force" and "vivacity" of directly sensing the presence of an object or state of affairs in perception – a "force" and "vivacity" that is translated immediately to the idea of that object or state. Of a perceptual belief, Hume writes:

... it may be ask'd, from what are the qualities of force and vivacity deriv'd, which constitute this belief? And to this I answer very readily, *from the present idea.* For as this idea is not here consider'd as the representation of any absent object, but a real perception of the mind, of which we are immediately conscious. (Ibid. 1.3.8.15; SBN 106)

The contrast is with "loose conceptions of the imagination," like the leopard-spotted lion, which lack the distinctive "force" and "vivacity" of perceptual acquaintance with an object. Or we might contrast the character of experience when one is having a "dissociative" episode and the external world seems to be a movie one is watching rather than a reality one is inhabiting. A similar contrast in "vigor and firmness" marks the difference between ideas furnished by *memory* as opposed to "loose" imagination (Ibid. 1.3.8.16; SBN 106) – when I recall an episode from a lecture this morning I lack the freedom to readjust the features of the idea I am holding in mind that I would have if I were painting mental images of giving a morning lecture.

It is this "firm manner of conception" that Hume calls the "peculiar sentiment" of belief. He believes that this sentiment is familiar to us all in immediate experience, though he recognizes that it is of the nature of this sentiment to direct our attention to its content, and induce us to rely upon this content in thought and action, without drawing attention to itself. Therefore, to convince us that there really *is* a sentiment here, he must describe cases where belief is *gained* or *lost*, such that difference in "feeling to the mind" is discernable. For example, the mental states **doubt [that *p*]** and **belief [that *p*]** share the same object – when the mind makes the transition from one to the other, the difference must lie in the "manner of conception," not in the conception **that *p*** itself:

This is the subject of plain experience. If ever this experience can be disputed on any occasion, 'tis when the mind has been agitated with doubts and difficulties; and afterwards, upon taking the object in a new point of view, or being presented with a new argument, fixes and reposes itself in one settled conclusion and belief. In this case there is a feeling distinct and separate from the conception. (Ibid. Appendix 4; SBN 625)

If it be objected that belief cannot be a sentiment since all sentiments or affect are connected with some positive or negative valence, Hume will point to the active *discomfort* of "doubts and difficulties," which makes them inherently difficult to bear – and to the fact that, when the mind *does* acquire evidence that enables it to "fix and repose itself in one settled conclusion and belief,"

[t]he passage from doubt and agitation to tranquility and repose, conveys a satisfaction and a pleasure to the mind. (Ibid. Appendix 4; SBN 626)

And now we are in a position to tackle the otherwise rather obscure remark in Book II, quoted above, that "a passion is an original existence, or, if you will, modification of existence, and contains not any representative quality" (Ibid. 2.3.3.5; SBN 415). Recall that the example of such an original existence he gives is puzzling, *anger*, which not only can take an individual or event as its object, but which can be more or less *fit* to its object, more or less *justified* by the evidence, or simply more or less *mistaken*. For example, my anger at you for missing a rendezvous can be *unjustified* if I haven't verified whether today actually *is* the date and time we arranged. And that anger will be *mistaken* or *unfitting* if it turns out that the rendezvous was in fact scheduled for yesterday, and that I was the one who failed to show up, not you. Why would Hume deny such obvious facts about anger – facts that are congenial to his general enterprise of attributing content and aptness conditions to sentiment?

To see what is actually at work in this passage, let *p* be "You missed our rendezvous." Consider now the attitude:

**anger [that *p*]**

Recall Hume's argument from the *Appendix*. **That *p*,** we know, is an idea – the same idea that figures in the content when I freely imagine, hypothesize, or suppose *that you missed our rendezvous*. Focus, then, on what sort of thing **anger [  ]** adds to the idea **that *p*.** Could it be "a new idea, annex'd to" the idea **that *p*** – say, the idea *that you slighted me*? Then my mind would contain *two* conjoined ideas: **that you missed our rendezvous** and **that you slighted me**. Could having this conjunction of ideas in mind be what it is for me to be angry that you missed our rendezvous? Hardly, since one could have these two ideas before one's mind as a bare supposition, without any attendant affect at all. And one could freely dismiss one or both ideas from one's mind, with no concomitant change in mood. But none of this is true of anger, which I cannot contrive or dismiss at will, and which does not come and go, leaving my mood unchanged. Indeed, even in my chagrinned and apologetic state after myself missing our rendezvous, I am still free to entertain the counterfactual thought *that you missed our rendezvous & you thereby slighted me* – I just can't believe it and won't feel the associated anger.

So **anger [  ]** must be something other than a "new idea" annexed to **that *p*.** Indeed, it must be a very different *sort* of thing from an idea. And we know perfectly well what: it is a non-voluntary *state* of mind and body, an "original existence" or "modification" of my existence, with which I am "possest," refocusing my attention, churning up my feelings in its distinctive way, accelerating my metabolism, reorienting my thought, and changing how I am disposed to act – whether I like it or not. This sort of coordinated, spontaneous "modification of my existence" is the essence of anger.

Thus, Hume's claim that a passion is a state with which we are "poss-est," and not a mere representation, tells us nothing about whether passions can take a person or proposition as their objects, or be more or less *justified* given one's evidence, or be more or less *fitting* or *mistaken*. When I look in my calendar and see that our rendezvous was scheduled for yesterday, I realize at once that my anger toward you is unjustified, unfitting, and mistaken, and while I will continue to feel churned up, both the object and the nature of my passion will have changed – what anger I feel is now directed toward myself, and toward you I feel embarrassed and apologetic. A new "original existence" or "modification" of my existence – which is not *itself* a copy or mere idea – will involuntarily have come into being.

Thinking of the belief attitude, **belief [ ]**, as a passion or sentiment involves thinking of it, too, as a "modification" of the agent's existence with respect the idea **that** *p* – a state with which she is "possest" that changes how she feels, thinks, and acts in systematic ways. Of course, belief is typically not itself an *aroused* state like anger or chagrin. Instead, it is a rather subtle, "calm and indolent...firmness" that can be hard to distinguish from the idea **that** *p* itself – which gives rise, Hume thinks, to the illusion that reason can produce belief, since we *can* produce ideas by reasoning.[4] However, as we saw, Hume believes this subtle passion becomes palpable whenever we shift from doubt to belief.

Hume despairs of giving an exact name for the sentiment of belief, but we can get a fix on it by appealing to two well-known sentiments that often crop up in his discussions of *belief*, *trust*, and *confidence*. These sentiments have the advantage for our purposes of having an important role in empirical social science – for example, early development of relationships of trust seems to be of vital importance for normal cognitive and social development in infants, and dysregulation of confidence is a key indicator in diagnosing and treating a number of mental disorders (Trevarthen 2001). Moreover, trust and confidence pass Hume's test of adequacy for any theory of mind: the theory must account for the mental states we attribute to infants (and animals, Hume 1749–1750/2000 1.3.16). Since infants are said to have beliefs, the "feeling to the mind" of belief that *p* must be of a kind readily discernable even by the very young from, say, fear that *p* or doubt that *p* – and trust and confidence that *p* are such states.

---

[4] As Remy Debes reminded me, Hume attributes people's willingness to believe that *moral* judgments are the product of reason to this tendency to confuse a "quiet," unaroused attitude with the idea that is its object (Hume 1749–1750/2000, 2.3.3.8; SBN 417).

Like belief, trust, and confidence can take an "idea" as their object – one can *trust that p* or *be confident that p*. Following the strategy of Book II of the *Treatise*, we can additionally observe that the attitudes of trust and confidence also have characteristic causes and effects akin to belief. For example, trust and confidence, like belief, are non-voluntary states that are spontaneously strengthened or weakened in response to positive or negative evidence. Moreover, trust and confidence that *p*, like belief that *p*, have a *direct* influence upon thought- and action-tendencies – one will *expect* that *p* and *rely* upon *p* in inference and behavior, thereby removing the threat of a regress of judgment that concerned Hume.[5]

Trust and confidence also manifest the *phenomenology* of belief. They are "calm passions," distinguished in their "feeling to the mind" from "agitated doubts and difficulties." Their action-guiding force, like that of belief, is "indolent" and assured, rather than anxious and insecure. Such assurance gives to their objects a degree of "firmness" or "fixity" in the mind, providing a stabilizing role in the "governance" of thought, feeling, and action. For example, in proportion as you trust or are confident that I will come to this afternoon's meeting, you will expect to see me there, presuppose my presence in your thinking about the meeting, and be surprised if I do not show up. By contrast, imagining or pretending that I will be there involve no such expectation, or surprise if I'm absent. Finally, like belief, we can speak of trust or confidence that *p* as more or less *warranted* insofar as one has evidence that *p*, and as more or less "reasonable" (to use Hume's term) insofar as their strength corresponds to the strength of one's evidence.

### 3    Sentimentalist Epistemology and Meta-Epistemology

Suppose that we follow Hume in understanding belief as a "peculiar sentiment." How might this affect our thinking in epistemology or meta-epistemology? Perhaps if we can answer these questions, we will be in a better position to determine whether sentimentalism in ethics might call for a "third way" in meta-ethics.

To help find an answer, let us look a bit closer at neo-sentimentalist approaches to ethics. In their seminal essay, "Sentiment and Value" (2000a), Justin D'Arms and Daniel Jacobson raise the question whether sentimentalism *as such* has a distinctive place in the meta-ethical landscape, and they begin by locating a common core doctrine:

---

[5] For arguments that expectation and reliance are more basic states that can be characterized without invoking belief, as well as more extensive discussion of the ways in which belief operates within the psyche akin to affective states like trust and confidence, see Railton (2013).

The great underlying agreement between the neosentimentalists ... is that they are all committed to what we will call the "response dependency thesis" (RDT). The crucial idea, which we take to be the defining characteristic of neosentimentalism, is that an important set of evaluative concepts (or terms or properties) is best understood as invoking a normative assessment of the appropriateness (or merit or rationality) of some associated emotional response. (729)

They then go on to distinguish response-dependency about evaluative concepts vs. evaluative properties. Let us use φ as a second-order variable for *properties*, and designate the *concept* of a property φ as <φ>:

(RDT-<φ>) to think that $X$ has some evaluative property φ is *to think it appropriate* to feel $F$ in response to $X$. [729, emphasis added]

(RDT-φ) for $X$ to instantiate some evaluative property φ is *for it to be appropriate* to feel $F$ toward $X$. [cf. 732, emphasis added]

We will consider the conceptual thesis first. D'Arms and Jacobson offer a further explanation of the thought on the right-hand side of (RDT-<φ>):

For the neosentimentalists, to think a sentiment appropriate in the relevant sense is a normative judgment. . . . Or, rather, it is a consideration in favor of feeling it in certain contexts. (729)

As their gloss reveals, (RDT-<φ>) is not a *reductive* thesis, explaining normative language and thought in non-normative terms. Rather, it seeks to *situate* normative thoughts in a distinctive way in our mental economy. They involve two elements: (a) a recognizable psychological attitude or sentiment toward $X$, and (b) a normative judgment that one *ought* to feel this sentiment toward $X$.

Now it is well-known that there are two significantly different readings available for "appropriate" in formulations like (RDT- <φ>). It could mean something like "supported by the balance of reasons." In this sense, pragmatic advantages or disadvantages of feeling $F$ in response to $X$ can come into play. Consider:

(RDT-<good>): to think that $X$ is good is to think it appropriate to *approve* $X$.

I might think it appropriate on balance to approve of my teenager's initial efforts in the direction of autonomy, so long as they are not actively dangerous, as a way of encouraging him to develop self-confidence. But this is not the same as thinking that these efforts are, in any given instance, *good*. To capture *that* thought would require a different sense of "appropriate" – one akin to thinking that my teenager's decisions *themselves* merit approval, so that it would be *correct* or *fitting* in some sense for me to approve of them.

To make clear this "fittingness" reading of "appropriate" in (RDT-<good>), the neo-sentimentalist might rewrite it as:

(RDTF-<good>): to think that $X$ is good is to think $X$ merits approval.

Similarly, the neo-sentimentalist in aesthetics might say:

(RDTF-<beauty>): to think that $X$ is beautiful is to think $X$ merits appreciative enjoyment in virtue of $X$'s sensory qualities.

Well, then, what about the third member of the triumvirate, "the good, the true, and the beautiful?" Should the Humean sentimentalist in epistemology embrace as our fundamental understanding of the concept <truth>:

(RDTF-<truth>): to think that $p$ is true is to think $p$ merits belief?

This seems a good bit stranger than its brethren. (RDTF-<truth>) would make <truth> into a normative concept, and, while that might ultimately be the right view to hold, it would be difficult to maintain that this belongs to competent speakers' mastery of the concept <truth> in the way recognizing <good> and <beauty> as normative concepts belongs to mastery of these concepts. There is, after all, a long history of thinking <truth> to be on the *is* side of the *is/ought* gap.

   Perhaps, then, a Humean sentimentalist epistemology should start out from what unquestionably *is* a core normative epistemic concept. The response-dependent theorist might hold that:

(RDTF-<credible>): to think that $p$ is credible is to think that $p$ merits belief.[6]

This certainly has a stronger claim to be something we grasp when we master the relevant concept, so let us start from there. More precisely, let us grant that (RDTF-<credible>) provides us with the *irreducible, core* meaning of <credible>, such that we cannot push an informative analysis further.

   Given the irreducibility of the concept <credible>, what follows about the irreducibility of the property, *being credible*? That is, are we also obliged to accept

(RDTF-credible) For $p$ to instantiate the normative property *being credible* is for $p$ to merit belief

as the point where an informative philosophical account of the property *being credible* bottoms out?

I can't see why. Generations of epistemologists have sought to specify in some non-circular way conditions or processes such that a belief formed in those conditions or by these processes is warranted or justified – or, given (RDTF-<credible>), merits belief. For example, a Bayesian will say that a

---

[6] For simplicity, I suppress in these initial formulations any reference to the epistemic context, $C_E$, relative to which the belief is credible.

degree of belief $r$ that $p$ is merited just in case $r$ is the result of conditionalizing our initial degree of belief that $p$ on the totality of our current evidence. It would certainly be odd to say that Bayesian conditionalization belongs to the *concept* <credible>; rather, Bayesianism is a proposal about the property that best satisfies this concept. Bayesianism is, to be sure, a controversial proposal about this property, but it has in recent decades made very substantial inroads into formal epistemology, statistical testing in the natural and sciences, formal learning theory, and machine learning. How far Bayesians will be able to carry their program seems to me an open question at this point, not something we can settle by insisting that (RDTF-credible) is as far as we can go in saying what credibility is.

Moreover, there is very good reason for hoping that *some* non-circular account of credibility will be possible. Evaluative properties *supervene* on non-evaluative ("natural") properties – a principle that holds in epistemology as much as ethics. Acts or beliefs are always justified in virtue of reasons, and reasons themselves are, or supervene upon, facts. So, if there were *no* set of natural facts sufficient to make it the case that a given belief is credible in a given epistemic context, then this would seem to be a victory for skepticism, not sentimentalism.

And as I understand Hume's project in Book I of the *Treatise*, he wants skepticism to go only so far. His first goal is to show that the rationalists' story of belief cannot work – reason alone simply cannot produce belief, so "pure reason" cannot be the foundation of justified or (to use Hume's terms) "reasonable" or "probable" belief (Hume 1739-20/2000, 1.3.13) – a skeptical conclusion about the long-vaunted power of reason. His second goal is anti-skeptical and constructive: to show that a sentimentalist account of belief *can* work and give us a foundation for "reasonable" or "probable" belief.

We have already discussed some of Hume's arguments to the effect that a sentimentalist account can give an adequate *descriptive* theory of belief – capturing in a non-circular way how the belief attitude is constituted, how it distinctively functions, and what its characteristic phenomenology is like. What remains is to say something about Hume's account of how sentimentalism could underwrite an adequate *normative* theory of belief – capturing in a non-circular way the processes that can yield belief that is "reasonable," "probable," or "merited," *even in the face of* all the arguments leading toward skepticism. Put another way, is there a non-circular account of when a given degree of credence is *fitting*, given the evidence?

Hume's clearest and most systematic discussion of this question, at least, to my knowledge, is found in his account of "philosophical" vs. "unphilosophical" probability in Book I of the *Treatise*. Philosophical probability – roughly, "justified degree of belief" in contemporary terms – begins with sensory perception. Experience provides us with *ideas*, but it also supplies us with something more, namely "force and vivacity" (Ibid. 1.3.8.2; SBN 98). Perception thus furnishes us immediately ("non-inferentially") with both the elements necessary for belief: an idea **that** *p*, and an attitude or sentiment toward that idea, **belief [  ]**, which gives the content that *p* a regulative role in our psychic economy. The *immediacy* of this process is essential for Hume, since the rationalist idea that perceptual belief involves a distinguished mental act of *judgment* or *inference* risks launching a regress (Ibid. 1.3.7.5n; SBN 96n), requires an abstract idea of existence (Ibid. Appendix 2; SBN 623), and would rely upon a principle of cause and effect that could never be established without presupposing perceptual evidence already in hand (Ibid. 1.3.8.11–17; SBN 103–106). For belief formation to get off the ground, it must avoid these pitfalls.

Perhaps the "force" of immediate experience can get perceptual belief off the ground, but this is still far short of what we need if belief is to afford a "regulative principle" for action. All perceptual experience is singular, and limited to the present or past. Yet all action takes place going *forward* in time – into territory of which we have no direct experience. So perceptual experience must be *generalized* and *projected* if it is to support action-guiding expectations about actual or possible futures. Here is where belief's *sentimental* character becomes important – for sentiment such as anger, fear, hope, doubt, and trust readily project forward in time, as a *direct* response to experience, without requiring a conscious act or judgment or inference. These are states of mind and body with which we are "possest," and which have as their characteristic function reorienting in a coordinated way what we expect, attend to, notice, prepare for, and are disposed to do.

This forward-looking shift in my psychic state is not, however, all or nothing – it varies with the quantity and severity of experience. How confident I am that the neighbor's dog is friendly will be responsive to the frequency with which encounters with this dog have gone well or badly. On Hume's view, the tendency of sentiment to strengthen or weaken in experience explains how belief can acquire its action-guiding force. Thus, if I have had a succession of good encounters with this dog, I will have a succession of "agreeing images" of those encounters, and:

> . . . agreeing images unite together, and render the idea more strong and lively, not only than a mere fiction of the imagination, but also than idea, which is supported by a lesser number of experiments. Each new experiment is as a new stroke of the pencil, which bestows and additional vivacity on the colours, without either multiplying or enlarging the figure. (Ibid. 1.3.12.11; SBN 135)

The "figure" or mental content (**that the neighbor's dog is friendly**) remains the same across the "experiments," but the "force" or "vivacity" with which

I conceive this idea grows – and this greater or lesser sentiment of trust or confidence will directly affect how much I expect harm from my next encounter with this dog, how much I therefore focus upon it when passing by, whether I am primed to avoid it, etc.

But what about those cases where the pattern of experience is irregular? Here the sensory images do not all agree. Hume claims that the "impulse" to believe in such cases is "broke into pieces," and "diffuses itself" over the various patterns observed, in proportion to the frequency of those patterns in experience (Ibid. 1.3.12.10; SBN 134). This calibration of the degree of strength of belief to the evidence is grounded in a parallel feature of "the affections":

... when an object produces any passion in us, [this] varies according to the different *quantity* of the object.... (Ibid. 1.3.12.24; SBN 141; emphasis added)

These experience-shaped variations in degrees of belief constitute for Hume a "philosophical" probability, that is, a probability of a kind "receiv'd by philosophers, and allow'd to be reasonable foundations of belief and opinion" (Ibid. 1.3.13.1; SBN 143).

But variation in the force and influence of beliefs arising from the regularity or irregularity of patterns in immediate experience is not the only way in which "philosophical probability" can be increased or decreased, Hume argues. There also is probability "by resemblance" and "by analogy." Sentiment operates by *association* as well as *projection and feedback*. If, in a new environment, I am surprised by what I see, then I will expect more surprises in similar circumstances, and the strength of this expectation will vary with the degree of similarity. Thus, associative "spreading activation" stimulated by perception can produce increase in belief in related ideas that are furnished by the imagination.

If you weaken either the union or the resemblance, you weaken the principle of transition, and of consequence that belief, which arises from it. (Ibid. 1.3.12.25; SBN 142)

Hume notes that this kind of strengthening or weakening of belief via links of resemblance in content is also received by philosophers as a reasonable foundation of belief and opinion (Ibid. 1.3.13.1; SBN 143).

In these ways, then, the Humean sentiment that underlies belief participates in an experience- and imagination-based *probabilistic learning system* that attunes the strength of belief that $p$ in proportion to what are generally recognized as "solid and legitimate" forms of evidence that $p$ (T 1.3.13.1; SBN 143). Thus far, his introduction of sentiment into belief formation and revision is *epistemically vindicatory* – though described entirely in naturalistic terms, it fits with widely-held norms of credibility ("reasonable foundations of belief and opinion"), and thus is a plausible candidate for satisfying the normative concept <credible>.

However, Hume also notes that, owing to the fact that "'tis on the degrees of force and vivacity, that the belief depends, according to [my] system," belief formation and revision will be subject to failures to track "solid and legitimate" evidence (Ibid. 1.3.13.1; SBN 143). He thus turns to giving an account of "unphilosophical probability" that anticipates in a number of ways recent decades' work on cognitive "biases and heuristics" in cognitive social psychology (Kahneman and Tversky 2000). Hume observes that differences in the strength of belief not reflecting "degrees of evidence" can arise from the *recency* of experience, the *ease* with which a memory is recalled or an inference followed, and the tendency to *generalize* hastily from biased samples (e.g., the general rules which we "rashly" form about national or ethnic character upon meeting a few members of a group, "which are the source of what we properly call Prejudice") (Ibid. 1.3.13.7; SBN 146).

These forms of "unphilosophical probability" threaten to derail the vindicatory project, except that Hume argues that our characteristic dispositions in belief formation tend to be *self-correcting*. For example, he argues that the remedy for "rashly" formed general rules on the basis of experience is to gain *more* and *more varied* experience and to be "enlarging the sphere of my experiments as much as possible (Ibid. 1.3.15.11; SBN 175).

Our spontaneous tendency to project patterns in experience as *expectations* for novel cases – which in itself is "so little founded upon reason" – sets us up for *learning*, by turning subsequent experience into "experiments" that test hypotheses and enable us to "fine tune" the belief sentiment. The projective role of this sentiment is essential to such learning: it is only relative to expectations that new experiences will be either confirming instances or disconfirming discrepancies, and it is only with expectations that we can take actions guided by the pursuit of evidence. It is via this process, Hume argues, that we learn to distinguish accidental generalizations from genuine causal regularities:

> ... when we find that an effect can be produc'd without concurrence of any particular circumstance, we conclude that that circumstance makes not a part of the efficacious cause, however frequently conjoin'd with it. (T 1.3.13.11–12.; SBN 149)

In this way, Hume claims:

> The following of general rules is a very unphilosophical species of probability; and yet 'tis only by following them that we can correct this, and all other unphilosophical probabilities. (Ibid. 1.3.13.13; SBN 150)

Indeed, in the decisive closing pages of his discussion of skepticism in Book I, Hume writes it is only by a feature of "unphilosophical probability" that "we save ourselves from [a] total scepticism" that undermines not only rationalist epistemology but all "philosophical probability" and "leaves not the lowest degree of evidence in any proposition" – namely, that "we enter with difficulty into remote views of things, and are not able to accompany them by so sensible an impression, as we do those, which are more easy and natural" (Ibid. 1.4.7.6–8; SBN 267–268). This self-protective feature of sentiment is, however, not mere resistance to remoter views and elaborate arguments. Rather, it is another example of a "reflexive act of the mind," in which the greater acquired force of rules "more extensive and consonant" with our experience counteracts the force of principles "of an irregular nature, and destructive" of established belief, such as the skeptical hypotheses (Ibid. 1.3.13.13; SBN 150).

Hume attributes such reflexive self-equilibration in belief to "the understanding," resulting in a further species of "philosophical probability."

In every judgment, which we can form concerning probability, as well as concerning knowledge, we ought always to correct the first judgment, deriv'd from the nature of the object, by another judgment, deriv'd from the nature of the understanding. ... Here then arises a new species of probability to correct and regulate the first, and fix its just standard and proportion. (Ibid. 1.4.1.5; SBN 181–182)

In speaking of "correction" and of a "just standard and proportion," Hume clearly means to be making *normative* claims about credibility in the face of skepticism. The sentiments involved in human belief formation and revision will tend, by their nature, to confer greater confidence or trust in the authority of more broadly based generalizations:

'Tis certain a man of solid sense and long experience *ought to have*, and usually has, greater assurance in his opinions, than one that is foolish and ignorant, and that *our sentiments have different degrees of authority*, even with ourselves, in proportion to the degrees of our reason and experience. (Ibid. 1.4.1.6; SBN 182; emphasis added)

Thus, even though Hume holds that *"belief is more properly an act of the sensitive, than of the cogitative part of our natures"* (Ibid. 1.4.1.8; SBN 183), this underwrites rather than undermining normative epistemology. His theory of human belief formation and revision, taken as a whole, is vindicatory, not debunking, in both letter and spirit.

And there is something more – from the standpoint of meta-epistemology, Hume's naturalistic account of the property *being credible* affords the materials needed for an "inference to the best explanation" in support of an *a posteriori* naturalistic realism in epistemology. Hume's account of the dynamics of "probability" learning resembles in its main features "hierarchical Bayesian causal modeling" – an approach that is increasingly becoming dominant in the design of "optimal" artificial learning systems. Cognitive scientists who set out, not to do normative epistemology, but to design programs capable of the most efficient and effective extraction of information from data, have developed models of learning that parallel Hume's. Further, as studies of the brain have become more detailed at the neural level, it seems to be emerging that the neural processes underlying learning are themselves largely similar to these optimal learning strategies based upon hierarchical causal modeling.[7] The "coincidence" that, over hundreds of millions of generations, natural selection appears to have settled upon neural learning mechanisms in intelligent animals that approximate ideal finite formal learning models is perhaps no coincidence at all – it is "best explained" by the epistemic *merits* ("optimality") of this design. Importantly for the Humean, it is the *affective system* of intelligent animals that lies at the core of these learning mechanisms – it is there that expectation and uncertainty are encoded, that discrepancy-reduction learning occurs, and that environmental mapping is carried out and combined with expectations to generate decision weights that "govern" actions.[8]

The pieces are thus in place for a Humean to embrace a naturalistic realism about the property of epistemic credibility on the strength of its explanatory role. This embrace is not forced – other meta-normative accounts are compatible with Hume's naturalistic account of belief formation and revision. But the crucial point for our purposes is to note that a thorough-going Humean sentimentalism about belief, and a response-dependent or "fittingness" account of the concept <credible> does not drive one *away* from such naturalistic realism in meta-epistemology. On the contrary, it can sustain a strong case for such realism.

## 4    Sentimentalism in Ethics and Meta-Ethics

Now that we have considered Humean sentimentalism in epistemology and meta-epistemology, have we learned anything relevant to Humean sentimentalism in ethics and meta-ethics? I will argue that, structurally and substantively, the two cases are parallel.

To understand how sentimentalism might apply in ethics and meta ethics, let us again follow the suggestion of D'Arms and Jacobson and

---

[7] See Beierholm *et al.* (2009), Soto *et al.* (2014), and Tenenbaum *et al.* (2011).

[8] For some recent work, see: Courville *et al.* (2008), Dayan and Daw (2008), Pessoa (2008), Schultz (2002), Schwarz and Clore (2003), Storbeck and Clore (2007), and Tobler *et al.* (2006).

begin with a response-dependency thesis about the relevant core normative concepts. In particular, since it is the central concept in Humean
moral thought, we will consider *virtue*. A fittingness version of a response-
dependency theory (RDTF), as applied to the concept <virtue> might take
the form:

(RDTF-<virtue>) To think that a character trait *C* is a moral virtue is to think that
*C* merits disinterested approval.

We cannot, I think, say with any confidence what Hume himself thought
about the concept <virtue>, or other moral concepts, since even when he
"defines" a term, or states what an expression "means" – e.g., for "cause"
(Ibid. 1.3.14.32; SBN 170), "reason" (2.3.8.13; SBN 437), "will" (2.3.1.2;
SBN 399), "knowledge" (1.3.11.2; SBN 124), "necessity" (1.3.14.22; SBN
165–6), etc. – he characteristically does not give a conceptual analysis.
Rather, he supplies something more like a "real definition" or "reforming
definition" of the associated property or capacity – for example, *what it is
to be a cause*, or *what sort of mental processes constitute reasoning*, etc. His
"definitions" are meant to be clear, substantive, non-circular, and empirical, not to be analytic truths.

Since Hume seems to leave the field of conceptual analysis largely open,
let us explore the possibility of accepting (RDTF-<virtue>) on his behalf.
That would allow Hume to say that the concept <virtue> is irreducibly
normative and response-dependent. At the same time, however, as we saw
in the case of <credible>, accepting that a concept is irreducibly normative
and response-dependent is compatible with giving a straightforwardly naturalistic account of the *property* associated with the concept. Here is one
of Hume's formulations of *what it is to be* a "natural virtue."

When any quality, or character, has a tendency to the good of mankind, we are
pleased with it, and approve of it; because it presents the lively idea of pleasure;
which idea affects us by sympathy, and is itself a kind of pleasure. (Ibid. 3.3.1.14;
SBN 580)

And here is *what it is to be* an "artificial virtue":

there are some virtues, that produce pleasure and approbation by means of an arti-
fice or contrivance, which arises from the circumstances and necessities of mankind.
Of this kind I assert justice to be.... (Ibid. 3.2.1.1; SBN 477)

The "approval" in both natural and artificial virtue is, for Hume, not itself
a *moral* judgment or a distinctively *moral* sentiment. Moreover, something
substantive is said about what the approval tracks: "a tendency to the good
of mankind" or "the necessities of mankind."

Hume, it seems to me, is concerned to offer a clear, substantive, non-circular, and empirical explanation of the origin of "moral distinctions" and their relation to the guidance of action. For example, concerning the "connexion" between moral qualities and motivation, he explicitly rejects the idea that this is grounded (as many contemporary philosophers have claimed) in a grasp and application of the concept <virtue> or <moral goodness>:

no action can be virtuous, or morally good, unless there be in human nature some motive to produce it, distinct from the sense of its morality. (Ibid. 3.2.1.7; SBN 479)

Motivation in the case of virtue, he argues, arises as an effect of "sympathy" – which is itself an affective response to the effects on human well-being of actions or traits of character. The interpretation of Humean sympathy is controversial, but a plausible and empirically realistic way of understanding it is as a form of *simulation* of the mental states of others by an imaginative placing of one's in their situation, which engages one's own affective responses. Via these affective responses, we gain "non-inferential" information about other's beliefs, desires, intentions, emotions, and so on. Sympathy is motivating, on this picture, *because* the simulation uses our own sentiments as its "test bed."

Empathically simulating the pleasure of another, we saw, "is itself a kind of pleasure," and this pleasure is reinforced by one's own pleasure in seeing a benefit conferred. Just as infants lacking normative epistemic concepts can hold beliefs, infants lacking normative moral concepts can experience this species of approval, and be pleased with a story in which individuals who act helpfully toward others are happy in the end, while those who act harmfully are not (Hamlin and Wynn 2011). The fact that virtuous fictional characters, who are in no position to benefit us, readily attract our approval is evidence that this approval is *disinterested*, and indeed Hume likens it to disinterested approval of what is beautiful (Hume 1739–1740/2000, 3.3.6.1; SBN 618).

In perceiving both that which is beautiful and that which is generally beneficial, we experience an affective response, disinterested approval, capable of motivating without assuming any other desire or advantage to ourselves – and also without assuming that we endorse any distinctively moral principle or make a distinctively moral judgment. Indeed, as noted above, even judging an action or trait to be "in the public good" would leave us "indifferent," "except so far as sympathy interests us in [the public good]." Hume would appear *not* to be the "motivational judgment internalist" (Darwall 1997) he often is portrayed as.

Disinterested sympathy, especially when developed and refined through extensive social experience, *attunes* us to just those acts or traits of character that promote outcomes of a kind impartial benevolence would approve. So now the "sense of virtue" itself, and "the principles, from whence it is deriv'd" can be "approv'd of" on reflection – by its nature, this sense tends to track what actually is "laudable and good." In short, Hume's account enables us to make a case that our "sense of virtue" is reliable and well-grounded.

This might be clearest, in fact in the case of the "artificial virtues," where there is the greatest worry that our sentiments might simply be the product of arbitrary social conventions and acculturation, so that they do not have any tendency to "track" what genuinely is "laudable and good." Instead of the artificial virtue of justice, Hume writes:

Most of the inventions of men are subject to change. They depend upon humour and caprice. They have a vogue for a time, and then sink into oblivion. It may, perhaps, be apprehended, that if justice were allowed to be a human invention, it must be placed on the same footing. (Hume 1739–1740/2000, 3.3.6.5; SBN 620)

Yet here too, he makes a case for justification and well-foundedness. He continues:

But the cases are widely different. The interest, on which justice is founded, is the greatest imaginable, and extends to all times and places. It cannot possibly be served by any other invention. It is obvious, and discovers itself on the very first formation of society. All these causes render the rules of justice stedfast and immutable; at least, as immutable as human nature. And if they were founded on original instincts, could they have any greater stability? (Ibid.)

As before, if a sense of justice were implanted in us as an "original instinct," this would in itself say nothing about whether it is tracking anything that might actually *merit* normative evaluation as just. And, as before, Hume believes there is a *bona fide* learning mechanism underlying our intuitive normative "sense" – a mechanism that makes us sensitive to the sorts of features that make a social arrangement have a "tendency to the public good," and disposed to approve of these features owing to disinterested sympathy.

And thus we find a close parallel – indeed, a mutual dependency – between Hume's account of the epistemic and the moral.[9] In both domains, reason alone cannot explain how we make the discriminations necessary

---

[9] One might add, that this approach also foreshadows Hume's later account of the role of "the test of time" in aesthetic evaluation – over time, particular fashions and partialities tend to wash out as growing experience produces convergence in judgment upon "beauties" that are "naturally fitted to excite agreeable sentiments" when appropriately attended to (Hume 1987: 233, 237). For discussion, see Railton (1997).

to distinguish the credible from the non-credible, or the virtuous from the vicious, or the just from the unjust. Neither can reason explain why these distinctions have an effect on what we are disposed to believe or do. In both domains, vindicating our normative distinctions requires showing that our discriminations *do* track normatively relevant features – "philosophical probability" or "general benefit," respectively – through processes that deserve to be called *learning*, not mere "prejudice" or "instinct."

Of course, as in belief, there are certain inherent tendencies toward partiality and bias in our attitudes of approval and disapproval, for example, the tendency to "prefer whatever is present to the distant and remote, and makes us desire objects more according to their situation than their intrinsic value" (Ibid. 3.2.7.8; SBN 538).

The chief remedy for perspectival limitations and partiality in empathy, like the chief remedy for perspectival limitations in belief formation, is more extensive and varied experience, and the development of a more "steady," general view of things that can counteract perspectival biases and over-hasty generalizations. The sentiments involved in approving and promoting virtue and justice, like those in the formation and revision of belief, have an inherent tendency to *project* to novel cases. This in turn leads to expectations – if we approve an action on one occasion, we expect to approve this action, or one very similar to it, on the next occasion. And discrepancy with expectation generates feedback to refine our moral assessments to conform more closely with "intrinsic value." As in the case of "philosophical" vs. "unphilosophical" probability, a disposition to generalize hastily – which *itself* cannot be justified – ramifies through wider experience and feedback into a process in which our moral assessments become less biased, more discriminating, and more stable over time. Hume writes of such processes:

> ...every particular man has a peculiar position with regard to others; and 'tis impossible we cou'd ever converse together on any reasonable terms, were each of us to consider characters and persons, only as they appear from his peculiar point of view. In order, therefore, to prevent those continual *contradictions*, and arrive at a more *stable* judgment of things, we fix on some *steady* and *general* points of view; and always in our thoughts, place ourselves in them, whatever may be our present situation. (Ibid. 3.3.1.15; SBN 581–82)

As our "expectations" of our fellows become more interdependent, we tend to converge upon certain principles of justice, and to approve via disinterested sympathy the keeping of these general rules, even to the point of disapproving of injustice when this does not accord with our own interest:

> When therefore men have had experience enough to observe, that whatever may be the consequence of any single act of justice, performed by a single person, yet

the whole system of actions . . . is infinitely advantageous to the whole, and to every part; . . . Every member of society is sensible of this interest [and] . . . expresses this sense to his fellows. . . . (Ibid. 3.2.2.22; SBN 497–498)

Hume concludes Book III:

Thus upon the whole I am hopeful, that nothing is wanting to an accurate proof of this system of ethics. (Ibid. 3.3.6.1; SBN 618)

To the contemporary ear, Hume's view might seem hopelessly naïve. While many in contemporary psychology have come around to Hume's view that moral judgment is primarily based in sentiment, most see this in a very different light from Hume. The relevant sentiments reflect a history of evolution for social cooperation but also for intergroup competition and intragroup relations of domination and subordination – the evolutionary past of *Homo sapiens* is but a recent overlay of a much longer evolutionary history of less pacific social animals, and our adaptation for modern notions of equality, fairness, and tolerance is very incomplete. The affective responses underlying "moral intuition" are seen as evolutionarily ancient, fast, blunt, "push-button," "point-and-shoot," relatively "inflexible" or "hard-wired," and "heuristic based" rather than quantitative – very far from the well-calibrated disinterested sympathy that is so prominent in Hume's picture of the moral sentiments.[10]

However, just as contemporary work in cognitive neuroscience has revealed increasing evidence that the affective system in humans and intelligent mammals is involved in a spontaneous learning process that approximates optimal learning theory, so has contemporary work in affective neuroscience found increasing evidence that intuitive *evaluative* responses in intelligent animals and humans approximate decision-theoretic ideals.[11] Moreover, these intuitive evaluations concern not only immediate, egocentric reward but multiple dimensions of value, including social values – including the evaluation of a cooperation partner and "third-party" evaluations of actions.[12] And Hume appears to have been right in placing "sympathy" in a central role. Empathy, understood as a form of simulation, appears to be a core capacity for prudential as well as social effectiveness, continuously active, and capable of generating evaluations that do not reflect the interests of the individual herself.[13] Of course, empirical research is subject to more or less dramatic change over time, and Hume

[10] For some recent work in this vein, see Haidt (2001), Greene and Haidt (2002), and Kahneman (2013).
[11] For some examples, see Courville *et al.* (2008) and Dayan and Daw (2008).
[12] For some examples, see Behrens *et al.* (2008), Melis *et al.* (2006), and Behrens *et al.* (2009).
[13] See Decety and Chaminade (2003) and Lamm *et al.* (2007).

may be overly optimistic about the power of sympathy to overcome various darker forces in the human psyche and social dynamics, but, in providing a theory of how evaluative and moral learning can take place via sentiment and sympathy, he appears not naïve, but prescient.

### Conclusion

We have seen here how a Humean sentimentalism in epistemology and ethics is compatible with a naturalistic account of the properties that answer to core normative concepts in these domains – <credible> and <virtue> – even if these concepts themselves are interpreted in an irreducibly normative, response-dependent way. In both sentimentalist epistemology and sentimentalist ethics, Hume's view attributes a central role to learning processes inherent in the sentiments themselves, which enable us to track such properties as *credibility* and *virtue* to arrive at beliefs and evaluations that can withstand critical reflection. Hume's ambitious account thus supplies the materials for a realist vindication in epistemology and ethics – not in spite of their sentimental character, but because of it.[14]

[14] For further discussion of affective learning mechanisms in evaluation and ethics, see Railton (2014). I am grateful to my fellow participants in the Workshop on Moral Sentimentalism (College of Holy Cross), at the 2015 Scots Philosophical Association Meeting (University of Glasgow), and especially to the editors, for providing penetrating comments on earlier drafts.

# 7 Sentimentalism, Blameworthiness, and Wrongdoing

*Antti Kauppinen*

It is relatively easy for a sentimentalist to make the case that someone is, say, admirable or enviable if and only if it is fitting to admire or envy her. And it is plausible that whether such attitudes are fitting depends on something about those attitudes themselves, or even facts about human tendencies to respond to certain things in certain ways, as sentimentalists say, although this is much more controversial. But for sentimentalism to be a serious rival to competing theories in metaethics, it must also account for central moral properties such as blameworthiness and praiseworthiness of agents and rightness and wrongness of actions in terms of some kind of emotional response. In this paper, I will focus on two tough questions for such *ambitious neo-sentimentalism*. The first concerns the basis on which blaming attitudes are fitting. There is broad agreement that blame is merited on the basis of the quality of the agent's will, but it is not trivial to delineate genuinely sentimentalist criteria for a blameworthy quality of will. The second issue concerns the relationship between blame and wrongdoing. While it is *agents* who are to blame, it is *actions* that are right or wrong. The question, then, is how fitting attitudes toward agents can ground the moral status of actions as obligatory, permissible, or impermissible.

On the issue of fitting blame, I begin by sketching a general sentimentalist picture of what makes any attitude fitting. Roughly, on my ideal subjectivist view, fittingness of an attitude is determined by the nature of the attitude together with the related desires of a suitably idealized subject. Blame, I claim, consists of negative reactive attitudes that target an undesirable quality of the will of the agent. I argue that the best motivated characterization of a morally authoritative subject is of a self-respecting rational agent who serially occupies the position of each affected party and gives equal weight to the strength of emotional responses in everyone's shoes without aggregating the numbers – for short, a Nagelian Imp. The consequence of these views for the question of fitting blame is that someone is blameworthy when and because she has a quality of will that a Nagelian Imp would not want her to have – roughly speaking, when she fails to sufficiently constrain or shape her planning by the will of others.

Second, I address a key challenge to ambitious sentimentalism. When it comes to rightness and wrongness, it is fairly clear that an action can be wrong or impermissible even if the agent is not blameworthy. It is, after all, possible for a person to have an *excuse* or be exempt from blame, even if what they do is wrong. But it is tempting to think, as Allan Gibbard (1990) and Stephen Darwall (2006a) do, that if someone either is blameworthy or *would be* blameworthy as a result of an action if they lacked an excuse or exemption, then the action is wrong. Call this the Blame-Wrongness Link. Many philosophers have recently challenged it. In particular, they have argued that people can be blameworthy for permissible actions. If so, it seems the link between assessing an agent's quality of the will and the permissibility of her action is decisively broken. How, then, could sentimentalists hope to ground the moral status of actions on attitudes toward agents?

In response to this challenge, I grant that there are cases of blameworthiness without wrongdoing. Nevertheless, I maintain that even in these cases, the permissibility or impermissibility of actions indirectly hangs on fitting attitudes based on a possible quality of will of the agent. Roughly, when it is *possible* to perform an action while meeting all the conditions of accountability without meriting blame, it is permissible. When it is *not possible* to perform an action without meriting blame, unless one has an excuse, it is impermissible. In such cases, there is what I call an *external support* for blame.[1] If this move, call it the *Indirect* Blame-Wrongness Link, is successful, questions about the agent's possible quality of will (and external support for blame) turn out to be central to normative inquiry.

The Indirect Blame-Wrongness Link has interesting normative consequences. In particular, since one's quality of will is centrally a matter of the kind of plans one acts on in the circumstances, and there are often several possible plans for bringing about the same outcome, blameworthiness turns out to depend not only on *what* one intends to bring about but also on *how* one intends to bring it about. Since permissibility or impermissibility, in turn, is determined by *possible* quality of will, it will depend on how it is *possible* to bring about an outcome; that is, on the causal paths available to the agent and how other agents are involved in the causal paths, not just on the impersonal desirability of the possible outcomes. For example, if the only way to bring about an impersonally desirable outcome requires subordinating the good of one to the good of many, as in the Footbridge trolley case (pushing a heavy person on the tracks to save five others), a Nagelian Imp will predictably resent the agent who chooses the option (insofar as she is accountable), and the act will be impermissible. Roughly, this is because a

---

[1] This proposal builds on the work of Frances Kamm and others.

Nagelian Imp's attitude depends on the *strength* of emotional response in each affected person's shoes, not on the *number* of people who have the response, and that the resentment caused by imagining being used as a means to advance another's good at the expense of a like good of one's own is stronger than the resentment caused by failure to be saved. In short, an independently motivated sentimentalist account of moral metaphysics turns out to provide indirect support for nonconsequentialist normative theory – although some might reasonably argue that this shows only that metaethical and normative projects must be pursued hand in hand.

## 1      Fitting Attitudes and Actual Sentiments

While one can be a sentimentalist about moral judgment or epistemology, in this paper I focus on *metaphysical sentimentalism*. Metaphysical sentimentalists hold that moral properties are grounded in a subject's sentimental response. As Hume summarizes,

The hypothesis which we embrace is plain. It maintains, that morality is determined by sentiment. It defines virtue to be *whatever mental action or quality gives to a spectator the pleasing sentiment of approbation*; and vice the contrary. (Hume 1751/1998: Appendix 1.10; SBN 289)

When Hume talks about a spectator, he does not mean just anyone. As other passages make clear, he is thinking of someone who adopts a general point of view when considering the consequences the agent's motives or traits tend to produce. It is the approbation of such subjects that determines what is a virtue.

While Hume is happy to talk about the relationship between sentimental responses and the properties that give rise to them in causal terms, such reductive approaches are rejected by most contemporary sentimentalists. According to the neo-sentimentalist view, insofar as moral properties are determined by our attitudes, it is *fitting* attitudes that count. We can't simply observe what *causes* approbation to discover what is right or good, but must reflect on what *merits* it. The fact that we're disposed to approve of something doesn't mean it's good or right, since it is always an open question (as Moore said) whether something we're disposed to approve of is good. This is at least in part because moral properties are *normative* for us in a way that powers to cause responses in some subjects are not.

There is a lot to be said for this new orthodoxy. Nevertheless, I want to push back a little bit. There is nothing sentimentalist about Fitting Attitude (FA) accounts as such. After all, non-naturalist intuitionists such as A.C. Ewing (1947) have endorsed FA analyses. For all that FA says, the fact that resentment, say, is fitting toward an agent might be a primitive mind-independent fact that obtains regardless of what sentimental responses people have or could have. The distinction between a generic FA analysis and a *neo-sentimentalist* FA analysis must lie in there being some significant role for sentimental responses or dispositions in making a response fitting. When we ask whether a joke merits amusement, for example, the correct answer will have *something* to do with what actually amuses people. At the extreme, it makes no sense to say that something merits amusement if you cannot get anyone to laugh at it.

What, then, makes an attitude fitting for a sentimentalist? I will set aside nominally sentimentalist views that appeal to the correctness or accuracy of a belief or presentation contained in an emotional response. Such accounts presuppose that there are attitude-independent facts that make the belief or presentation correct. How, then, should sentimentalists understand fittingness? My own hypothesis, which I can only sketch here, is that evaluative attitudes have both descriptive content and normative content suitably related to the descriptive content. The descriptive content presents things as being in a certain non-normative way, and the normative content refers to the related desires of a subject who is authoritative in one way or another. For example, the content of admiration is something along the lines that the target has done something challenging that is of great worth. It is an ordinary empirical question whether the agent has done something challenging for her, but whether it is of great worth is a different matter. My suggestion is that here we need to turn to the desires of, say, an aesthetically or morally authoritative subject and ask, roughly, whether such a subject would desire that the target make the challenging effort and desire that others emulate the target. So whether it is morally fitting to admire Mahatma Gandhi (or more specifically his non-violent campaign for independence) depends both on whether what he did was difficult and whether any morally authoritative subject would want him to have done so and want others to do likewise (mutatis mutandis, of course). On this picture, whether the attitude is fitting is jointly determined by non-normative facts and the relevant reactions of one or another kind of authoritative subject. In virtue of the latter feature, evaluative or normative properties are ontologically subjective or attitude-dependent: attitudes come first in the order of explanation.

The strategy of approaching normative issues in terms of the reactions of an idealized subject, or of our own responses when we're at our relevant best, was characteristic of traditional sentimentalism of Hume and Smith. Such approaches have not been popular recently. In particular, views that specify the characteristics of an ideal subject in naturalistic terms face many serious objections. Even if we leave aside general objections to naturalism in metaethics, as I will do here, there are specific challenges that Rawls (1971), for example, nicely pointed out. His objection to impartial spectator accounts can be formulated as a kind of dilemma: Either the impartial spectator is underspecified, so that no normative conclusions follow from the metaethical account, or the account conflates impartiality with impersonality.

Here it is crucial that there are many alternative and competing ways of specifying a morally authoritative subject. What Rawls had in mind was a specification of the impartial spectator that I'll call the Utility Hare.[2] The Utility Hare takes on the preferences of everyone as his own and desires the action or adoption of the rule that maximizes his expected utility. On such views, famously, the distinction between persons disappears, as it is just the satisfaction of preferences that matters, regardless of who gets the benefit and who pays the cost.

One might reject such an account on the basis of its normative consequences, as Rawls does. But I think the Utility Hare is independently implausible as a specification of a morally authoritative advisor. The point of idealizing, as classical sentimentalists saw it, is to guide our non-ideal sentimental responses so that we can robustly get along without continual strife, on terms that everyone can live with (see Kauppinen 2014b). For such guidance, we need to look to or become someone who lacks the features that predictably cause the relevant problems for human beings and has features that predictably help them avoid them. The fact that we actually defer to or aspire to become certain kinds of agents when making moral judgments reveals that we regard certain perspectives as authoritative. On this view, then, the idealizations involved in an authoritative moral perspective are importantly continuous with our practice. The problem with the Utility Hare is that it is not a solution to any problem of ours – treating people as distinct individuals whose boundaries matter is not what gets us into trouble, and aspiring or deferring to a humanly unattainable perspective won't get us out of it. Consequently, it is hard to make the case that we somehow tacitly refer to the Hare's responses when we issue moral verdicts, or that we should accord authority to them while moralizing.

What should we expect a morally authoritative subject to look like, then? Here is what I think is a pretty good model, an impartial spectator I'll call the Nagelian Imp. The Nagelian Imp is an average ordinary everyday self-respecting rational Joe (or Jenny) with some special abilities.[3] He is capable of occupying the perspectives of each involved in an action and its salient

---

[2] In tribute to R.M. Hare, who laid out this kind of approach very clearly (Hare 1981).
[3] The notion of self-respect I am using here is not meant to be theoretically loaded – just the ordinary sort of opposite of self-abasement.

alternatives, and keeping track of the responses he would have in each position. Those responses depend on two kinds of desire. As a rational and self-respecting agent, the Imp has the kind of basic desires we all do as such. He wants to be able to make up his own mind, and to ensure that, he wants there to be checks and balances against others bypassing or manipulating or incapacitating his decision-making. In short, he cares about his *status* or standing relative to others, as humans generally do. Otherwise, the Imp is chameleon-like, and to some extent takes on the contingent desires of the people whose position he occupies, but they take a backseat to his own desires.

As impartial, the Imp does not give any more or less weight to responses from any position but does not aggregate the positive and negative responses into a big bundle. Rather, he prefers the action (or attitude) that is least unacceptable to the person for whom it is most unacceptable, to use Nagel's (1979) famous phrase. That is, if there are possible actions, $x$ and $y$, that bear on what the Imp wants in the shoes of A, B, and C, he'll compare the strength of the strongest preference against $x$ to the strength of the strongest preference against $y$. If, say, he disprefers $x$ in A's position more than $y$ in either B or C's position, he'll prefer $y$ to $x$. Consequently, if the Imp would not want you to do something, it will be something you would not want done to yourself in somebody else's position, insofar as you are a rational and self-respecting agent with the desires that come with those features. If you did it, someone else would be worse off than you will be if you do not do it. So the Imp's responses will be authoritative at least to those who care about living with others on terms that can be expected to have sway with them without external sanctions, as long as they, too, are willing to moderate their demands.

I have argued elsewhere (Kauppinen 2014b) that the Imp's responses and fittingness of attitudes are connected as follows: an attitude is morally fitting if and only if any morally authoritative subject would endorse it. By endorsing an attitude I mean roughly wanting the subject to manifest it. The underlying assumption is that part of what makes an attitude what it is can be found in what it motivates or disposes us to do or feel – for example, fear essentially motivates us to flee, admiration to emulate, and intention to act. So, for example, admiration is morally fitting in part if and only if and because the Imp would endorse emulating the target.

## 2    Blameworthiness and Reactive Attitudes

The reason why being right or wrong is a hard case for a sentimentalist is that such deontic properties are not obviously related to our sentiments, and it is particularly tempting to think they are independent of our attitudes altogether. It makes more sense to think we'll never realize that something is wrong than to think we'll never realize something is disgusting, even if we're acquainted with it. But sentimentalists have attempted to make the connection. For example, Allan Gibbard argues that wrongness can be understood in terms of blameworthiness, and other properties in terms of wrongness. Here is how he links blame, blameworthiness, and wrongness:

> A person is *to blame* for an act if it makes sense for others to be angry at him – from a standpoint of full, impartial engagement [...] – and if it makes sense for the person himself to feel guilt for what he has done. Morally wrong act are not always acts a person is to blame for; there are excuses. [...] *Wrong acts*, roughly, are acts a person would be to blame for if he chose them in a normal state of mind. (1990: 223)

There are two steps here: first blameworthiness is determined by fittingness of blame, and then wrongness in terms of possibly counterfactual blameworthiness. The second step is what I've called the Blame-Wrongness Link. I'll get to challenges to it in the next section, but first, let us focus on fitting blame.

Let us assume that at least the relevant kind of blame consists of reactive attitudes, most centrally guilt and the form of anger that we call resentment.[4] On the neo-sentimentalist picture I sketched, the fittingness of these sentiments depends on their descriptive content and the related desires of suitable subjects. So let us start with descriptive content. First, I want to reject what seems to me to be a deeply problematic orthodoxy, represented by Jay Wallace's influential account. He maintains that "To be in a state of reactive emotion, one must believe that a person has violated some expectation that one holds the person to" (1996: 19). At the same time, he says that "To hold someone to an expectation, I maintain, is to be susceptible to the reactive attitudes in one's relations with the person" (1996: 18). So reactive attitudes are defined in terms of beliefs about normative expectations, and normative expectations in terms of dispositions to reactive attitudes. This "mutual dependence" of attitudes and expectations may not be strictly circular, but it is at least uninformative and confusing. I believe the way out of this problem is to reject the first claim and hold on to the plausible thesis that to have a normative expectation of someone is to be disposed to negative reactive attitudes when they fail to perform as desired. Thus, the test for whether I normatively expect you to open the

---

[4] This view of blame is defended, among others, by Strawson (1962) and Wallace (1996). It is challenged by Scanlon (2008). I have argued that there is good reason to think that blame comes in both varieties, since forgiveness does too (Kauppinen 2016).

door for me when my hands are full of heavy stuff is whether I am disposed to blame you if you do not open it.

What, then, is the distinctive descriptive content of reactive attitudes? Strawson (1962) was no doubt right in saying that they are responses to the "quality of the will" of their target. My claim is that they present their target as having either a *desirable* or *undesirable* quality of the will. I am using the term "will" fairly broadly, to cover both the thought process that led the target to their plans or intentions, and the plans and intentions themselves. Two agents who take the same means to the same end (and thus have the same maxim in the Kantian sense) may display a different quality of the will, if they have arrived at the intention by way of different practical reasoning. Your *reactive* attitudes toward me target the way in which my reasoning and plans take your *own* will into account. In that sense, they are essentially intersubjective and will not be fitting toward beings who lack a capacity to take another's will into account in their planning. Consider resentment. Let me borrow D'Arms and Jacobson's (this volume) method and try to interpret resentment in terms of its typical elicitors, motivational tendencies, and attenuators. Among other things, we resent being betrayed or misled, being taken advantage of, and failures to reciprocate. Such actions motivate us to take steps that force the target to acknowledge that we matter more than their behavior suggests. As Adam Smith says,

> The object . . . which resentment is chiefly intent upon, is not so much to make our enemy feel pain in his turn, as to make him conscious that he feels it upon account of his past conduct, to make him repent of that conduct, and to make him sensible, that the person whom he injured did not deserve to be treated in that manner. (Smith 1759/1982, II.iii.1.5)

I think that the best take on this phenomenon is that resentment presents its target A as having failed to appropriately constrain her planning by the subject B's will – that it does not count for the target as it should. It is fitting if this is indeed the case. Here the strictly descriptive content is that A's planning is not constrained or shaped by B's will in way *w*. The response-dependent normative content is that it is morally desirable that A's planning is constrained or shaped in way *w*, and also that it is morally desirable to impose costs on A to ensure that it is (since resentment manifests itself in behavior that imposes some cost on its target to get her to take the subject's will into account). The old-fashioned sentimentalist way of cashing this out is to say that any suitable impartial spectator would want, indeed insist, A to constrain or shape her planning in way *w*. Since I have briefly argued that the relevant kind of impartial spectator is a Nagelian Imp, my proposal is that blame is fitting if and only if and because the agent fails to constrain or shape her planning and intentions as a well-informed Nagelian Imp would want her to do, so that any such spectator would endorse resentment and guilt on the part of the agent.

What I have said above is formal and normatively neutral in the sense that it involves taking no stand on what particular things merit blame. Two people who accept the analysis could still disagree about when blame is fitting – indeed, on the kind of neo-sentimentalist account I have sketched, this kind of moral disagreement comes to disagreeing about how a Nagelian Imp would react. But as it turns out, accepting a characterization of a morally authoritative subject does have normative consequences, so that the scope for reasonable and informed disagreement is at least reduced. (This is where the metaphysical sentimentalist move from the "is" of a certain kind of subject's reactions to the "ought" of fittingness happens.) For given the concerns and capacities of the Nagelian Imp, it is not an open question how he would want people to constrain and shape their other-involving plans.

The Imp, recall, is concerned first of all with his standing relative to others. So he wants people to rule out certain options with regard to him. Since he wants to make up his own mind, he wants others not to bypass his capacity to make choices, or manipulate it to someone else's advantage, or to disable it by depriving him of basic necessities. When his plans rely on others doing their part, he wants those others to at least make an effort, or they will turn out to have acted in such a way that they might as well have manipulated him into doing his part. For brevity, let me adopt the popular, though potentially misleading phrase, and say that he wants others to rule out using him as mere means for their ends, and to make promoting his capacity to pursue form and pursue his ends as one of their own ends.[5] As Adam Smith puts it,

What chiefly enrages us against the man who injures or insults us, is the little account which he seems to make of us, the unreasonable preference which he gives to himself above us, and that absurd self-love, by which he seems to imagine, that other people may be sacrificed at any time, to his conveniency or his humour. (Ibid.)

What's more, the Imp wants others not to be in a position to use him for their ends, which is to say he wants there to be costs for others if they fail to rule out using him. Since the Imp occupies everyone's position serially and keeps track of the responses, adopting the strongest preference as his desire, he will be against anyone using another for her ends, and for protecting everyone from being used or neglected. By the standard proposed here, then, blame will be fitting response to anyone acting on a maxim of treating another as a mere means, or failing to treat them as ends. However, the Imp will not mind if an action benefits one person more than another,

[5] The echoes of Kant's Formula of Humanity are obviously not a coincidence.

as long as this doesn't affect people's relative standing in this fundamental respect. Thus, if someone adopts a plan that aims exclusively at her own benefit or at the benefit of someone she cares about, the Imp does not necessarily desire that she change her plan even if she could do something else that would maximize benefit, considered impersonally. For the Imp is an *impartial*, not an *impersonal* spectator. And impartiality doesn't mean wanting the best outcome, but giving equal weight to everyone's grounds for resentment and other blaming attitudes. As Smith's formulation hints, not every preference given to oneself (or someone else) is "unreasonable," of the sort that would manifest a blameworthy quality of will. I'll return below to what these facts about the Imp's reactions means for the permissibility and impermissibility of actions.

## 3     Why the Blame-Wrongness Link Doesn't Hold

We now have a sketch of when negative reactive attitudes are fitting on neosentimentalist grounds. If it is indeed the case that an act is wrong if and only if it is fitting to blame the agent, in the absence of an excusing condition, it seems that we have the analysis that sentimentalists need to connect deontic properties with our attitudes. While wrongdoing doesn't entail blameworthiness because of the possibility of excuses and exemptions, blameworthiness does entail wrongdoing, if the Blame-Wrongness link holds. This link is thus crucial to the Gibbardian strategy of moving from fitting attitudes toward agents to the moral status of actions.

Alas, in recent years even nonconsequentialist ethicists have presented powerful arguments against the Blame-Wrongness Link, which consequentialists have always found problematic. Perhaps most notably, Thomas Scanlon (2008) argues that there is a fundamental difference between the two moral dimensions of *permissibility* and *meaning* of an action. On his view, blame and blameworthiness have to do with the meaning of an action, or what it says about a person's relations to others:

[T]o claim that a person is blameworthy for an action is to claim that the action shows something about the agent's attitudes toward others that impairs the relations that others can have with him or her. (Scanlon 2008: 6)

This is compatible with what I said above about blameworthiness. However, Scanlon goes on to argue that questions of permissibility are strictly distinct from questions of blame, since they concern actions themselves and not the process whereby the agent arrived at the action. Not only is it possible to perform impermissible actions without blame, but it is also possible to be blameworthy for performing permissible actions. For a simple example, consider one of Frances Kamm's variants of the standard trolley case, in which it is possible to divert a trolley threatening to kill five people to a side track on which it will kill one person:

> Suppose that it is a bad person who sees the trolley headed toward the five. He has no interest in saving the five per se, but he knows that it is his enemy who will be the one person killed if he redirects the trolley. He does not want to be accused of acting impermissibly, however, and so while he redirects the trolley in order to kill the one, he does so only because he believes that (i.e., on condition that) a greater good will balance out the death. Hence, he would not turn the trolley unless he expected the five to be saved (Bad Man Case). His redirecting the trolley is still permissible, I believe, though he does it in order to kill his enemy. (2007: 132)

Here Bad Man is surely blameworthy, but his action is morally permissible (assuming it is such in the original trolley case). Surely one can do the right thing for the wrong reasons, and so merit blame. (For reasons of space, I'll leave aside here other kinds of purported counterexamples to the Blame-Wrongness Link, such as so-called suberogatory actions and doing the right thing accidentally or in the mistaken belief that it is wrong.[6])

Beyond intuitions about cases, critics of the Blame-Wrongness Link and mental state accounts of permissibility in general appeal to a difference between different contexts in which we can ask questions about the moral status of an action (Thomson 1999, Scanlon 2008). One context is criticizing others, in which case the agent's mental states such as intentions matter. But another is *deliberation and advice*. When deliberating, we ask whether an option is permissible or not. Here our own mental states do not seem to matter. In the context of deliberation, we are trying to decide what to do – intentions are the output of such deliberation, not inputs to it. So when we are deliberating, we need criteria for permissibility that do not depend on which intention we end up with afterward. The same goes for advice to others – it is no use to say that something is permissible if you do it with one intention and impermissible if you do it with another intention. So it seems that permissibility of an action cannot depend on intentions, or more broadly on the quality of will of the agent.

Here, in brief, is the challenge these considerations pose for sentimentalism:

1. Reactive attitudes are fitting on the basis of the agent's quality of will.
2. For sentimentalists, facts about moral permissibility and impermissibility are grounded in fitting reactive attitudes.
3. If facts about moral permissibility and impermissibility are grounded in fitting reactive attitudes, they are determined by the quality of the will with which the agent acts.

---

[6] For discussion of such cases, see Capes (2012).

4. Facts about moral permissibility and impermissibility are independent of the quality of the will with which the agent acts.
5. So, facts about moral permissibility and impermissibility are not grounded in fitting reactive attitudes.
6. So, sentimentalists cannot account for moral permissibility and impermissibility of actions.

There are several ways that a sentimentalist might try to avoid the conclusion. The first premise is unassailable and accepted on all sides, and the third seems to follow from the first two. So the first salient possibility is rejecting the second premise. After all, sentimentalists do not think that all normative or evaluative facts are grounded in reactive attitudes in particular. Perhaps that is one way to understand what Hume is up to in his discussion of artificial virtues in *Treatise* 3.2 (Hume 1739–1740/2009), when he switches focus from motives to consequences of rules for the general good. On this type of view, facts about permissibility are determined by rules that would be impersonally desirable for people to live by or internalize. Blame might then be fitting derivatively when one culpably violates such a rule.

However, it would be surprising and radically revisionary if the correctness of reactive attitudes depended on such impersonal quality of the will as following a useful rule. If you frivolously break a promise you have made to me, you have (pro tanto) wronged *me*. My response to you is not some sort of general disapproval because you have violated a socially desirable rule, but resentment for what *you* did to *me*. What it is fitting for *other* people to feel is different. Were my resentment fitting because of your attitude toward beneficial rules and not because of your attitude toward me in particular, there would be no reason for any asymmetry between my attitudes and those of third parties. My resentment is a *second-personal* response, in Stephan Darwall's (2006a) language. Indeed, reactive attitudes are arguably *essentially* second-personal, since they make no sense from the perspective of a detached observer who stands over and above human affairs. Rather, they are potentially fitting in the context of an interpersonal relationship, in which we make demands of each other and expect a response. This seems to rule out the alternative of the fittingness of blame depending on something other than the quality of the will the agent displays toward another person.[7]

---

[7] As Remy Debes pointed out, sometimes following rules itself displays my attitudes toward other people. However, insofar as the rules in question are impersonally desirable ones, it is possible that there is a divergence between the attitudes the agent manifests toward people in general and the second-personal attitudes they manifest toward the person they're interacting with. The point I am making is that it is the latter that makes *reactive* attitudes fitting.

To be sure, someone rejecting the second premise might argue that this is just more evidence that blame and permissibility must be judged by different criteria. Perhaps what I've said above about fitting blame is right, but has nothing to do with right and wrong. But this, too, amounts to biting a bullet, since it means that the blameworthiness of someone who does something wrong and the wrongness of her action have nothing to do with each other. To borrow a point Paul Hurley (2006) has made in a slightly different context, morality is supposed to make *demands* of us, not just provide standards for our actions. If what we are to blame for and what it is wrong for us to do match only *accidentally*, it is unclear in what sense morality demands us to avoid wrongdoing. Hurley puts the point in terms of our having *reason* to do the right thing, but on my view, this comes down to our being accountable for giving sufficient weight to doing the right thing in our practical thinking – in short, blameworthiness is conceptually prior to having reasons (see Kauppinen 2015). So other things being equal, I think it is better to pursue a different approach that does not leave it to chance that we are blameworthy for bad actions and praiseworthy for good actions.

So instead of denying the second premise, sentimentalists might join those who have resisted separating impermissibility and the agent's mental state, thus rejecting the fourth premise. To be sure, the case is far from closed, but I believe that the kind of considerations Scanlon, Thomson, and others have put forward mean that defenders of mental state accounts of permissibility are on the back foot. I will therefore assume in the following that the fourth premise holds.

What is there left for a sentimentalist to do? I believe the best strategy is to reject the third premise. It does not, after all, strictly follow from the first two. This is because although reactive attitudes are fitting on the basis of the agent's quality of will, rightness and wrongness might be *indirectly* rather than directly grounded in them. That is, a sentimentalist need not appeal to a blameless quality of will in explaining the permissibility of an action. Instead, permissibility might be a matter of whether it is possible to perform the act in the circumstances without manifesting a blameworthy quality of the will. In such circumstances, even if one is to blame for one's actual quality of the will, one could have performed the same act without meriting blame, so that blame is not *externally supported*, as I will put it in the next section. It is the external support for blame, or its absence, that will be crucial for explaining impermissibility and permissibility.

---

A sincere Stalinist who ruthlessly sacrifices a comrade in the name of progress, out of love for humanity, still does something the comrade may rightly resent.

## 4    External Support for Blame

How could blame be somehow supported regardless of the agent's actual state of mind? My proposal is simple: sometimes we find ourselves in circumstances in which it is *not possible* to achieve a certain end by certain means without meriting blame, assuming that we are competent, informed, and lack any other kind of excuse. (I will give concrete examples soon.) If that is the case, taking the means is morally impermissible. There is external support for blame for A-ing in C, if it is not possible to A in C without being to blame while fulfilling the conditions for accountability. At other times, we find ourselves in circumstances in which it is *possible* for us to achieve a certain end by certain means without meriting blame, even if we are competent, informed, and lack any other kind of excuse. If that is the case, taking the means is morally permissible.[8] There is no external support for blame for A-ing in C, if it is possible to A in C without being to blame, even if one fulfills the conditions of accountability. The key to the solution is that in the latter kind of scenario, even if we do in fact merit blame in virtue of our actual quality of the will, we *could have* performed the act we did blamelessly, without needing an excuse. Since external support is missing, the action is permissible, although the agent is blameworthy. Yet the permissibility or impermissibility of the action is still a function of fitness of being held accountable, albeit indirectly. What I call the Indirect Blame-Wrongness Link still holds.[9]

This brief sketch raises various questions. Above all, what is it that determines whether it is possible (or not) to take some means to some end without meriting blame? Clearly, the answer to whether there is external support for blame must depend on what means to what ends are available in the agent's circumstances. To put it in more objective terms, the question is what kind of causal chains the agent can initiate and how desirable the outcomes of these causal chains are. So, whether there is external support hangs on the causal-evaluative structure of the agent's options, or what Frances Kamm, whose work I will draw on in what follows, calls the "objective correlative" of possible plans (Kamm 2007, 136).

Probably the best way to put flesh on these bones is to look at concrete cases, laying out their causal-evaluative structure and examining how it relates to potential blameworthiness. I am going to focus on the two most basic trolley cases, Switch and Footbridge, which throw into sharp relief some morally relevant features of real-life actions, in spite of their artificial quality. Here is the first one, Switch:

---

[8] This principle is directly inspired by Frances Kamm's (2007, chap. 5) non-state-of-mind theory of deontological constraints.

[9] For a similar move with reference to Kant, see Nyholm (2012).

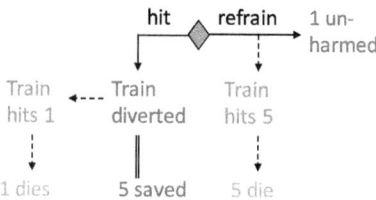

In Switch, a bystander has the choice of either hitting a switch to turn a runaway train to a side track or refraining from action. If the bystander refrains, the train will hit and kill five people, while one person on the side track will be unharmed. (Note that harmful events, or events that involve someone in non-consensual harm, are marked with dotted lines, and good consequences are marked with solid lines.) If the bystander hits the switch, the train is diverted to the sidetrack, which amounts to saving the five. Unfortunately, the train then hits the one person, who will die. Note here that it is the greater good (saving the five) that causes the lesser evil (the harm to and death of the one). In analyzing the case in terms of its causal-evaluative structure, Kamm maintains that what explains the permissibility of hitting the switch in this case is the fact that the harm is causally down-stream from the benefit (Kamm 2007: 138ff). (I will return below to why and how this matters to permissibility.) She offers many other variants to illustrate the same idea. For example, it is permissible to save five people from being killed by the trolley, even if the result is that they tumble down a cliff and their combined weight kills one person.

Here is the causal-evaluative structure of the Footbridge case:

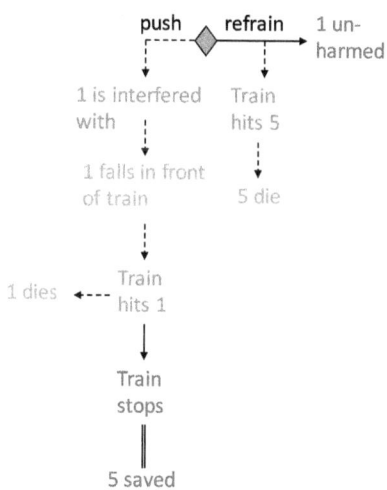

In the Footbridge case, too, the agent faces the choice between letting five die or killing one. But here the causal structure is different. While refraining from action has the same consequences, the only alternative is pushing a heavy person off a footbridge to stop the train before it hits the five, thus killing the one person. Here the event that involves the one in harm, which I will call the lesser evil, is causally necessary to bring about the good event, stopping the train, which in this context amounts to saving the five. Here doing bad things to one causes good things to others. Kamm maintains that this is what explains why pushing the heavy person is impermissible. Again, Kamm presents an impressive list of variants, such as Quinn's (1989) case of driving over an innocent person in an ambulance to save the lives of five patients (which involves harm as a side effect rather than means in mental state terms).

It is an obvious question at this point just *why* causal structure should have such moral significance. Again, Kamm does provide a persuasive deeper rationale appealing to the relative status of the people who are involved in the causal relationships. What happens in the Switch case, for example, the One person is *substituted* for the Five others as a victim when the bystander hits the switch. When harm to someone is causally downstream from the good to others, involving the person in harm does not serve the interests of the others. The good thing for the Five has already happened when the trolley is turned, and before it hits the One. In this important respect, the One and the Five are in the same position vis-à-vis each other. By contrast, in Footbridge, if the One is pushed down, she is made to serve the others in an important sense. As Kamm puts it, one person is *subordinated* to another, when specifying her causal role in a scenario "makes essential reference to his usefulness to achieving a good for that other person" (Kamm 2007: 165). So causal structure matters morally, because subordination matters morally.

But why does subordination matter morally? Why should it matter what kind of causal role one plays in producing an outcome? Is it just a brute normative fact? Kamm and other pure externalists about permissibility are plagued by such questions. Alastair Norcross, for example, is puzzled by Kamm's non-mental-state account:

If the notions of respect or inviolability . . . really just amount to constraints on the permitted causal routes to and between harms and benefits, it is hard to see them as anything other than fetishizing certain causal processes. . . . How could this be relevant to justified moral concern for others? (Norcross 2008: 16)

This is where sentimentalism promises a further explanation in terms of accountability. When the only causal chain available to bring about an end involves subordinating one person to another, there is no way to pursue the end without gaining the blame of an impartial spectator of the Nagelian Imp type (unless, perhaps, the stakes are high enough). This isn't to say that a morally authoritative subject's reactions are *normatively* fundamental. To that extent, I agree with Kamm's claim that the "objective correlative" of plans (in other words, what I have called the causal-evaluative structure of the possible act) is primary. But the sentimentalist claim is that the fact that initiating certain causal chains is impermissible is *metaphysically* grounded in subjective evaluative reactions. It is no fetishism to care about whether possible actions involve people in ways that any impartial spectator would object to (or that you would yourself object to in the victim's shoes).

Consider the causal-evaluative structure of the trolley cases from this perspective. In Section 3, I quoted Kamm's Bad Man case as a counterexample to the Blame-Wrongness Link. The Bad Man, recall, is in the Switch situation but turns the train only in order to kill the One on the side track. Since we are assuming she is innocent, future life is good for her, and she has not consented, Bad Man is surely blameworthy because of his plan. But it would have been *possible* for someone in the Bad Man's place to act with the intention of saving the Five, and without wishing anything ill for the One or using the One as a means to save the Five.[10] In other words, it would have been possible to perform the action without protest from the Nagelian Imp.

In Footbridge, in contrast, it is *not possible* for the agent to involve the One in harm in a way that does not merit blame. More precisely, it is not possible for the agent to do so, insofar as she is rational, knows the relevant facts, and meets the general conditions of responsibility. No doubt she will be more blameworthy if her end is to kill the One, and saving the Five is just a side effect. But even with the best of intentions, she will have to intend to make the One her instrument, insofar as she's rational. She'll have to act with a quality of will that the Nagelian Imp would want her not to have. To use Kamm's (2007) terms, I think it is a credible conjecture that, other things being equal, if A-ing necessarily involves nonconsensual harm that is not downstream(ish) from a comparable good to more people, any plan involving A-ing, even with the best of intentions, requires making a person serve the good of others regardless of their will. Taking into account what I've said about the likely reactions of the Nagelian Imp, it seems that he would endorse blaming the agent for any such plan. Thus, it is very plausible that subordination (among other things), defined solely in terms of the causal structure involving harms and benefits to people, externally supports blame.

---

[10] I am here assuming that Thomson's (2008) change of heart about the Switch case is a mistake, as FitzPatrick (2009) convincingly argues.

To sum up, I think these cases illustrate two related general theses that we can formulate as follows:

*External Support for Blame*
Blame for A-ing in circumstances C is externally supported if adopting any plan involving A-ing in C would make blame fitting, assuming the agent is rational, informed, and meets the general conditions of accountability.

*Indirect Blame-Wrongness Link*
A-ing in C is morally impermissible if and only if and because blame for A-ing in C is externally supported.

In the interest of keeping the things simple, I will not discuss other cases put forward as a challenge to the Blame-Wrongness link here. But what about the more principled objection that we should firmly distinguish between contexts of critical assessment of the agent, on the one hand, and advice and deliberation, on the other? A proponent of the Indirect Blame-Wrongness Link agrees that we need a notion of permissibility that is distinct from blameworthiness, and that when we deliberate or give advice, we do not consider what quality of the will we would be acting with. Rather, in deliberation and advice we consider the features that would or would not lend external support for blame, for example, whether taking certain means to our end would involve subordinating the good of some to the good of others. To take a standard case, if an air force commander asks the Prime Minister whether he should bomb a munitions factory to speed up the end of a just war, when the consequences include killing children in a nearby kindergarten, there is no suggestion that she should reply "it depends on whether killing the children is part of your plan for killing the war or whether it is just a regrettable side effect," although his blameworthiness does depend on his plans (cf. Thomson 1999). Instead, what is pertinent to moral advice and deliberation is whether the bombing is likely to achieve the goal of shortening the end of the war by way of killing the children (and the grief it causes) or by way of reducing available ammunition, and whether the alternative is that even more innocents die if the war is prolonged. So what the Prime Minister should say is that the air force may bomb only if doing so is necessary to avoid sufficiently awful consequences *and* destroying the factory is sufficient to promote this aim without involving innocents in harm (even if they will be harmed in actual fact). She might also say, less informatively but truthfully, that the air force may bomb only if it is possible to arrive at the decision by reasoning that doesn't make a morally authoritative subject resent them. Thus, with the Indirect Blame-Wrongness Link, the crucial distinction between contexts of deliberation and assessment is preserved, even though ultimately the criteria of permissibility derive from fitting reactive attitudes.

## 5          Conclusion: From Metaethics to Normative Ethics?

In this paper, I've been exploring the possibility of ambitious neo-sentimentalism, a form of sentimentalism that proposes to ground not only evaluative properties like being funny or being shameful but also deontic properties like being right and being wrong in fitting sentimental responses. My sketch is obviously not intended to be the final word on the matter. For one thing, I have focused only on the sentimentalist analysis of permissibility and impermissibility, and have said nothing about how such fundamental notions as rights or reasons might be grounded in fitting attitudes (for the latter, see Kauppinen 2015). But even so, what I have said may seem overambitious to some eyes. I have, after all, breached one of the red lines of contemporary metaethics: I have argued that although we can defend a particular characterization of a morally authoritative subject in non-moral terms, a sentimentalist fitting attitudes analysis has substantive normative implications. This is to move from a metaethical "is" to a normative ethical "ought."[11]

To be sure, there is precedent for such a move. I quoted earlier Hume's summary of his version of sentimentalist metaethics. This is how the passage continues:

We then proceed to examine a plain matter of fact, to wit, what actions have this influence [of giving rise to approbation in a suitable spectator]: We consider all the circumstances, in which these actions agree: And thence endeavour to extract some general observations with regard to these sentiments. (Hume 1751/1998, Appendix 1.10; SBN 289)

The "general observations" are the normative claims that Hume makes, such the claim that character traits that are beneficial or immediately pleasing either to the agent herself or others are virtues. This methodological comment fits with Hume's actual practice: he frequently makes observations about the "plain matter of fact" concerning people's reactions in suitable circumstances and draws conclusions about what is actually right or wrong. The benefit of proceeding in this fashion in doing normative ethics is that there is no appeal to controversial moral intuitions but only to what follows from the putatively neutral foundational facts about morality. In

---

[11] I have set aside expressivist sentimentalism. However, it is worth mentioning that for a hybrid expressivist like Michael Ridge (2006), the question of who is a morally authoritative subject (an ideal advisor) is already a first-order question – if we disagree morally while agreeing on non-moral facts, our disagreement consists in the fact that we regard different kinds of subject as authoritative. Thus, what my variant of ambitious neo-sentimentalism treats as a metaethical question is already a normative question for Ridge, and the debate about the best specification of the ideal advisor is fought at least partially on normative grounds.

this move, Hume is not alone: on a plausible reading, Kant and modern-day Kantians do just the same, only with a rationalist conception of metaethical foundations.

Although the view I have defended is not rationalist, there is a discernible Kantian flavor to the normative conclusions I claim will follow from the best kind of sentimentalist framework. That is no accident, since both my variety of the impartial spectator view and Kantianism focus on the possible quality of the agent's will, specifically the way in which the agent's reasoning and plans take the will of others into account. The key difference is that a sentimentalist is skeptical of deriving the requirement to never treat others as mere means, for example, from the very nature of practical rationality. Instead, it is founded on our contingent (though deeply rooted) tendency to resent those who treat us as having lesser worth, suitably idealized to serve a practical function for social animals like us.

There is a somewhat more modest conclusion to draw here, however. Instead of saying that the best form of neo-sentimentalism supports non-consequentialist moral theory, we might say that for neo-sentimentalists, the metaethical and normative inquiries must proceed hand in hand. In this framework, someone whose first-order intuitions are consequentialist must dispute the characterization of the morally authoritative subject whose reactions ground moral properties, or argue that it is something like an impartial spectator's preferred rules rather than reactive attitudes that determine what is and isn't permissible. Although I've given some reasons here to go one way rather than another, I cannot pretend that those considerations are in any way decisive. In any case, this kind of dispute is not just a matter of headbutting first-order intuitions or finding the best way to systematize them. It requires making the case that the Utility Hare, for example, is after all a more suitable model of a morally authoritative subject than the Nagelian Imp, and doing so requires reflection on such issues as human nature and the function of morality. I believe that shifting focus to such matters – pursuing a sentimentalist metaethics along with normative ethics – may offer a fruitful new approach to old debates concerning first-order questions about right and wrong.

# 8    Reactive Attitudes and Second-Personal Address

*Michelle Mason*

## 1    Introduction

Resenting a colleague's unfair treatment of you, feeling hurt by a lover's oversight or guilty about shirking an obligation, experiencing indignation at an official's abuse of office, contempt for another's egregious cruelty, or shame at one's own – these attitudes respond to the wrong and the bad in human action and character. They are joined by a more attractive group of sentiments attentive to the right and the good: pride in a sacrifice one makes for another, gratitude for a favor granted, and certain forms of love.[1] Arguably, all of these sentiments belong to the class that P. F. Strawson famously dubbed the "reactive attitudes": attitudes that register "...how much we actually mind, how much it matters to us, whether the actions of other people – and particularly some other people – reflect attitudes towards us of good will, affection, or esteem on the one hand or contempt, indifference, or malevolence on the other."[2]

Subsequent philosophers have found it notoriously difficult to offer a plausible account of the reactive attitudes as a unified class, and despite Strawson's suggestion that the term moral sentiments "would be quite a good name" for the attitudes that concerned him, even his most prominent admirers reject an account that would include them all as *genuinely* moral

---

[1] In what follows, I speak interchangeably of sentiments and (reactive) attitudes. For reasons to prefer the latter term, see my 2003: 239. I read Strawson as himself taking the reactive attitudes to be a subclass of sentiments, a subclass whose significance he defended in part as a corrective to a state of affairs where, he lamented, "talk of the moral sentiments [had] fallen out of favor" (Strawson 1962: 79).

[2] Strawson (1962: 63). I say that "arguably" all of these sentiments belong to the class as Strawson understands it to mark the fact that Strawson includes all of the preceding *except* for contempt and pride in his lists of reactive attitudes. For reasons I discuss below, I believe a strong case can be made for including among them a form of pride as a self-reactive attitude and of contempt as a reactive attitude toward others. Other attitudes Strawson cites as reactive attitudes include forgiveness (ibid.: 62), a "sense of compunction" and remorse (ibid.: 72).

sentiments.[3] R. Jay Wallace, for example, explicitly rejects what he calls an "inclusive interpretation of the reactive attitudes" that would embrace the full range of attitudes I cite as moral attitudes.[4] He does so on the grounds that the inclusive interpretation precludes an informative account of the reactive attitudes as a unified class of responsibility-constituting attitudes. *Bona fide* reactive attitudes, on Wallace's view, are inextricably tied to a stance from which we hold each other responsible to normative expectations and demands. Embracing resentment, indignation, and guilt as paradigmatic reactive attitudes, Wallace proceeds to develop an account of distinctively moral resentment, indignation, and guilt according to which the particular normative expectation to which they hold people responsible is that of compliance with their *moral obligations*.[5]

More recently, Stephen Darwall has argued that the reactive attitudes of blame, reproach, resentment, and indignation are distinctively moral attitudes in virtue of holding their targets accountable to "[obligations] those to whom we are morally responsible have the authority to demand that we do." For Darwall, these obligations "just are the standards to which we can warrantly hold each other as members of the moral community."[6] The way in which the distinctively moral reactive attitudes hold their targets accountable, on Darwall's view, is by addressing (perhaps only implicitly) demands for compliance with moral obligations to those targets.[7]

Given that Strawson includes among reactive attitudes not only resentment, indignation, feeling bound or obliged, feeling guilty or remorseful, but also gratitude, forgiveness, love, hurt feelings, feeling compunction, and "the more complicated phenomenon of shame," the moral reactive attitudes are for Wallace and Darwall a proper subset of Strawson's original class.[8] It is, moreover, a subclass that modern moral philosophers purportedly have reason to privilege because of their role in constituting deontic

---

[3] Strawson (1962: 79). Strawson himself offered a failed attempt to distinguish a distinctively moral subclass of reactive attitudes in his original article, an attempt he later rejected in Strawson (1980). The difficulties in understanding the reactive attitudes as a unified class were earlier noted in Bennett (1980).

[4] Wallace (1996: 11).

[5] Wallace (1996: 36). Not only are not all reactive attitudes moral reactive attitudes on Wallace's view, neither are all moral sentiments moral reactive attitudes, since there are on Wallace's view nonreactive moral sentiments. Among the latter Wallace includes shame and contempt, which on his view need have no connection with the kind of requirements and prohibitions associated with moral obligations (see, e.g., Wallace 1996: 38).

[6] Darwall (2006a: 14, 17). More precisely, blame, reproach, resentment are for Darwall distinctively *modern* moral attitudes. This reflects Darwall's view that modern moral philosophy is distinguished by an interest in morality in the admittedly "narrow" sense that interprets it in terms of moral requirements and obligations. I treat this qualification as understood in what follows.

[7] The relevant notion of address traces its origins to Nagel (1972); see, too, Watson (1994).

[8] Strawson (1962: 72).

relations between persons as such, holding them mutually accountable to what is morally required, prohibited, or permitted.[9] The negative moral reactive sentiments on such accounts are responses to wrongs understood as violations of moral requirements or performances of the morally prohibited. Positive moral reactive sentiments, to the extent they are discussed at all, presumably will include a form of respect.[10] Call this the *deontic, imperative* view of the reactive moral sentiments. In calling the view *deontic*, I mean to mark the *modality* of the normative expectations whose flouting, compliance, or exceeding the relevant attitudes register: these prescriptions are of standing moral *necessities or requirements* that entail *conclusive* reasons for action.[11] These expectations concern what the target, as member of the moral community, *owes, is prohibited from doing*, or *is permitted to do* to another qua member of the moral community. In calling the view *imperative*, I mean to mark the *mood* of the expectations whose flouting, compliance, or exceeding the relevant attitudes register: these expectations are *addressed as commands to* or *demands of* their targets.

I find much to admire in both Wallace's and Darwall's work on the reactive attitudes, I appreciate the precedents for conceptualizing the domain of modern moral philosophy as the narrowly deontic domain, and I do not wish to deny that reactive attitudes such as resentment, guilt, and indignation have a significant role to play in a compelling meta-ethics of moral obligation. However, I aim here to recover for the Strawsonian reactive attitudes a unifying thread that risks being lost in the shadow cast by the deontic, imperative view of the reactive moral sentiments. Heeding Strawson's claim that "there is a whole continuum of reactive attitude and feeling stretching on both sides of [resentment and gratitude] and – the most comfortable area – between them,"[12] I argue that although the reactive attitudes are properly conceptualized as forms of address, their modality is not invariably deontic nor their mood invariably imperative. For reasons that will emerge, I dub the latter reactive attitudes *aretaic, appellative* sentiments. In calling the sentiments *aretaic*, I mean to mark the *modality* of the

---

[9] Deontic relations obtain between persons as such or, as Darwall puts it, between "members of the moral community."

[10] What *are* the positive correlates of guilt and resentment? One anticipates a richer vocabulary here, to supplement – if not supplant – the focus on generic moral praise. On my view, forms of reactive love and pride are subordinate instances of the superordinate moral praise, just as resentment, guilt, and indignation are subordinate instances of the superordinate moral blame.

[11] Understanding here by "standing" moral necessities those moral obligations, if any, that are in force for each and every member of the moral community, simply as generic persons. The intended contrast is not just with special obligations but with the kind of non-deontic normative expectation I discuss further below.

[12] Strawson (1962: 64).

normative expectations whose flouting or compliance the relevant attitudes register: these prescriptions are of *non-jural* ideals of conduct or character. In calling the sentiments *appellative*, I mean to mark the *mood* of the expectations which the relevant attitudes manifest: these expectations are offered as *appeals* to comport oneself in the manner befitting the ideals at issue.[13]

The resulting, inclusive conception of the reactive attitudes accommodates Strawson's original cast of reactive attitudes and others, among them reactive forms of contempt and pride. It is not so expansive, however, to fall victim to the charge of failing to distinguish reactive sentiments from "disengaged aesthetic reactions" to the beautiful and ugly in human action and character.[14]

After investigating how best to understand the affective element central to the reactive attitudes' status as sentiments, I consider a challenge to distinguishing reactive moral sentiments from nonreactive aesthetic sentiments. I then take up Darwall's influential claim that the reactive attitudes presuppose what he dubs a "second-person standpoint" from which they address demands to others and ourselves.[15] On Darwall's account, reactive attitudes such as resentment, guilt, and indignation relate persons as *claimants* or *obligees* issuing imperatives to persons as *obligors*, thus constituting deontic accountability relations between persons.

On the inclusive conception of the reactive attitudes that I proceed to defend, members of the class do not in every instance implicate persons as claimants or obligors addressing imperatives to obligees in deontic accountability relations. Instead, the reactive attitudes as a generic class comprise a continuum of sentiments whose unifying thread is this: a reactive attitude, as such, relates persons in reciprocal prescription and recognition of legitimate expectations of conduct or character regulation, accordance with which is necessary for aspiring to relationships of value to beings like us.[16] It is, as a whole, a class of sentiments that values and disvalues persons by regarding them as answerable for their suitability (or not) to commune with us in not only the generic relationship of person to person

---

[13] Both Colleen Macnamara and Adrienne Martin have likewise challenged the view that the reactive attitudes are best conceptualized as addressing deontic demands. Macnamara (2013b), for example, questions both the purportedly demand-like and deontic character of the reactive attitudes as philosophers such as Darwall and Wallace understand them. Martin (2014) defends an account of normative hope that underwrites an understanding of forms of gratitude and disappointment as reactive attitudes. Indeed, in a pair of forthcoming articles, Darwall has begun to carve out conceptual space for a set of second-personal non-deontic attitudes, among which he includes forms of trust and love. It remains to be seen just how Darwall will eventually place these attitudes with respect to the deontic moral attitudes on which he had previously focused.

[14] The objection is one that, e.g., Darwall raises against Hume in Darwall (2013).

[15] Darwall (2006a).    [16] Cf. Mason (2003: 244).

but the more specific relationships of sibling, lover, spouse, tinker, tailor, soldier, spy. This, I conclude, might suffice to earn them the title of moral reactive sentiments.[17]

## 2          The Reactive Attitudes as a Class of Sentiments

I take as common ground that sentiments are, whatever else they are, affective phenomena.[18] We *feel* gratitude, resentment, hurt feelings, indignation, guilt, remorse, contempt, shame, pride, and love. If it is appropriate to speak of the reactive attitudes as sentiments, however, they are at most a proper subset of sentiments. I follow Strawson in understanding them to be that proper subset of sentiments whose necessary conditions of warrant include their target's manifestation of certain attitudes toward us or those of concern to us: namely goodwill, affection, or esteem (on the one hand) or contempt, indifference, and malevolence (on the other).[19]

The reactive attitudes are also a proper subset of attitudes.[20] Consider, for example, another subset of attitudes: the propositional attitudes. One respect in which the reactive attitudes resemble propositional attitudes is that both take intentional objects. According to a standard view, propositional attitudes (such as, beliefs and desires) are object-directed states that

---

[17] Unless, as previously noted, we stipulate from the start that morality, as we propose to treat it, concerns only the domain of obligations owed by one to another, where both are understood as generic persons or members of the moral community. It is one thing to stipulate as much in order to limit one's theoretical ambitions and another to suggest that morality, properly understood, concerns only this much. The latter substantive claim demands defense.

[18] In so saying, I mean to leave open the possibility that sentiments have cognitive content and are amenable to modification in response to rational control. Ruled out, however, are views according to which sentiments or emotions *just are* cognitive judgments, a view suggested in, e.g. Solomon (1980) and Nussbaum (2001). For a recent argument that normative judgments are neither part of the content of, nor implied by, the reactive attitudes, see Deigh (2012). For an argument that the cognitive-noncognitive distinction is itself confused in much of the relevant debate, see Debes (2009). For an account of the fraught history of the terms in play here, see Dixon (2012).

[19] Strawson (1962: 63). Hume, in contrast, takes what we might call the standing normative expectations presupposed by the warrant of a moral sentiment to concern whether the conduct or character is useful or agreeable to ourselves or others, as assessed from his common point of view. (Hume 1978, Book III, Part iii, Section 3). Darwall takes the reciprocal recognition of the authority to make demands as central on his account of the reactive attitudes' conditions of warrant (Darwall 2006a: 58, 60).

[20] Understanding by "attitude" here, as Darwall suggests, "any [mental state] that can be regulated by a norm" (Darwall 2006a: 157). "Attitudes are states of subjects that subjects can have for reasons, that is, where not only is there some non-rationalizing, say causal, explanation (explaining reason) of their having the attitude, but there is also something that is *the subject's reason* for having it, namely, some consideration or considerations the subject herself takes as a normative reason or reason and acts on" (Ibid. 157–158).

relate those persons in the relevant states to propositions.[21] Reactive attitudes, in contrast, place persons in relation not to propositions but to persons as their intentional objects, or targets.[22] The relation thus established between the subject and intentional object of the reactive attitudes necessarily is inter*personal* (or, in the case of the self-regarding reactive attitudes, *intra*personal). This is not so in the case of propositional attitudes such as belief and desire.

Second, when one resents a colleague's unfair treatment of oneself, feels hurt by a lover's oversight or guilty about shirking an obligation, experiences indignation at an official's abuse of office, contempt for another's egregious cruelty, or shame at one's own, one thereby experiences an attitude toward a person that cannot be reductively identified with affectless propositional attitudes, such as beliefs, desires, or their conjunction. Of course, it might be that a specific set of beliefs about oneself or another reliably causes a person to experience a particular reactive attitude insofar as the person is typical or rational. It might be that, for example, the belief that you've wronged me reliably causes resentment in me. Alternatively, it might be that such a belief when conjoined with a desire that you recognize the moral reasons against doing so reliably causes resentment insofar as a person is typical or rational.[23] Even allowing that such causal antecedents can give rise to resentment, resentment is a distinct, negative-affect laden attitude. Although I cannot undertake the task here, one could likewise show for each candidate reactive attitude that it resists reductive identification with propositional attitudes such as belief or desire (or conjunctions thereof), however plausible the view that such propositional attitudes are among their causal antecedents.[24] The class of reactive attitudes thus is a set of attitudes distinct from that of the propositional attitudes.

---

[21] Or to the constituents of propositions. On the latter view, individuals may be among the constituents of propositions (for example, in the case of my belief that John went to the store for cigarettes).

[22] I now believe I was not sufficiently clear on this point in Mason (2003). Writing there about resentment, e.g., I suggested that it was not person-focused in the way that contempt can be. I am now of the view that resentment can be no less person-focused but that the grounds for resentment and reactive contempt diverge – with the grounds for the former typically referring to a state of affairs picked out by the that-clause in reports such as "I resent that _____." For an argument that love is not a propositional attitude, see Velleman (1999). As will become apparent, the reactive attitudes do not, on my view, relate persons merely as such – that is, we should not understand the reactive attitudes to relate persons qua persons as opposed to persons qua friends, lovers, countrymen, or parties to any of a variety of interpersonal relationships.

[23] For a defense of a belief-desire theory of blame, see Sher (2006).

[24] That beliefs, as such, can be affectless I take here as common ground. As for desires: Even understood as motivational (or conative) states, desires do not necessarily share the affective quality I here regard as a necessary constituent of the reactive attitudes. For an argument against the reductive identification of emotional attitudes with beliefs and desires, see Goldie (2000).

Finally, I follow those theorists of emotion who take emotions to appraise their target's significance for the subject, in light of the subject's concerns. On my view, the reactive attitudes are emotions that appraise the significance of *persons' conduct and character* for the subject's concern with the quality of regard that the others manifest toward her or those of concern to her. Just as fear, for example, appraises its target as a threat, resentment appraises its target as having violated a particular standard of conduct or character.[25] In virtue of this person-appraising feature of the reactive attitudes, I call them *person-focused*.[26] This feature suggests a schema that the reactive attitudes, as such, share:

x [a subject] bears reactive attitude R toward y [R's intentional object, or target] in response to – and only insofar as – y's conduct or character manifests goodwill, affection, or esteem (on the one hand) or ill will, indifference, and malevolence (on the other) [R's possible formal objects] toward x or those of concern to x

According to this schema, resentment and gratitude are no less person-focused than are reactive forms of contempt and love.[27]

Thus far, the reactive attitudes are sentimental attitudes that take persons as their intentional objects and are warranted responses to those persons only if – and to the extent that – they have manifest, in their conduct or character, goodwill, affection, or esteem (on the one hand) or ill will, indifference, and malevolence (on the other) toward us or those of concern to us.

Are these conditions sufficient, however, to carve out a class of moral sentiments? Do they distinguish, for example, disengaged distaste at another's conduct from reactive resentment for the same?

## 3    Nonreactive Moral Sentiments and "Third-Personal Sentimentalism"

To appreciate the worry, consider Darwall's criticism of what he calls Hume's "third-personal sentimentalism" about moral evaluation. Subsequently, we can ask whether Hume's third-personal sentimentalism and Darwall's "second-personal" alternative exhaust the possibilities for carving out a class of moral sentiments in a compelling way.

---

[25] For candidate appraisal theories, see, e.g., Scherer (2005) and Roseman (2013).

[26] Mason (2003).

[27] Again, I was insufficiently clear on this point in Mason (2003). One way of glossing this feature concerning the intentional objects of contempt, shame, pride, and love – a feature I previously referred to as their person-focus – is by way of contrast with the arguably act-focus of resentment, guilt, and indignation, that is, the latter's feature of taking as intentional objects discrete actions. I've come to think that this gloss on the intentional objects of contempt, shame, pride, and love as opposed to so-called act-focused reactive attitudes engenders confusion. It is worth noting here that Strawson, albeit indirectly, eventually endorsed Bennett's view that "reactive attitudes are directed towards people viewed as 'morally expressive' and thus taken as wholes." See Bennett (1980: 33).

What Darwall dubs the second-person standpoint is "the perspective you and I take up when we make and acknowledge claims on each others' conduct and will."[28] Darwall contrasts this with a third-person standpoint from which I view another, not in their relation to myself, but only as how they are "objectively."[29] We should resist the inclination to assimilate Darwall's contrast to the linguistic distinction between the grammatical first ("I"), second ("you"), and third person ("he/she/it"). Suppose a (grammatical) third person observes conduct between an agent and patient and experiences a reactive attitude toward the agent in virtue of that conduct (as, for example, when Alice experiences indignation at Ben's wronging Caroline); in doing so, the third person occupies the second-person standpoint toward the agent (in this case, as Alice does toward Ben) because Alice thereby presumes an authority to demand Ben's compliance with his moral obligations concerning his treatment of Caroline.

Occupying the third-person standpoint does not, then, correspond to the grammatical third person; it instead corresponds to viewing the agent "objectively." One might suppose that this occurs when person A presupposes no authority to demand of person B that B recognize an expectation to comply with a moral obligation. For example, such is my situation with respect to my neighbor's boyfriend and the expectation that he bathe regularly. Suppose I react with disgust to my neighbor's boyfriend for his failure to bathe regularly. In doing so, I presume no authority to demand of her boyfriend that he bathe – whether for my sake or my neighbor's. Now, disgust is the kind of attitude that Darwall has in mind as a third-personal sentiment. However, by speaking of the third-person standpoint as one from which I view another objectively, he draws attention to a different feature of such a case: namely the failure of my disgust (like other nonreactive, third-personal sentiments) "to presuppose any capacities in [its object] to relate back in some way that might reciprocate the response."[30] Darwall refers to such a capacity as second-personal competence. Now, as I imagine the case, my neighbor's boyfriend in fact possesses such a capacity but Darwall's point is that the conditions on my disgust's intelligibility and warrant do not require that he do so. In this respect, my disgust for him is akin to my disgust for the maggot-ridden garbage at the bottom of the trash bin. Conversely, my awe of his brute physical beauty (underneath all that grime!) no more presupposes his capacity to reciprocate my response than does my awe of a particular Rothko painting.

---

[28] Darwall (2006a: 3). Compare here Strawson on the "participant" stance (Strawson 1962: 67).
[29] Darwall (2013: 11), quoting Strawson.    [30] Darwall (2013: 10).

Hume's understanding of the moral sentiments, as Darwall interprets it, is distinctively third personal in the sense just canvassed: the sentiment one experiences when considering whether the mental qualities or traits of another are useful or agreeable – a form of esteem or love – presupposes for its warrant neither any authority on my part to demand you express those qualities or traits in certain ways rather than others nor any capacity that you be able to reciprocate my love by complying in recognition of my authority. On Darwall's reading, Hume thus lacks the resources to distinguish reactive moral sentiments from nonreactive aesthetic responses.

Having identified the worry, we can take a closer look now at how the deontic imperative view of the moral sentiments purports to avoid it.

## 4 The Deontic Imperative Conception of the Reactive Moral Sentiments

On the deontic imperative conception, moral reactive attitudes relate persons not simply in virtue of being *responses* to a person's quality of will but, moreover, in *addressing* their targets.[31] That which is addressed is a conclusive-reason-entailing *imperative* or *demand* that any generic person, as member of the moral community, has authority to make of any other person who has second-personal competence. This is the nature of the I-thou relationship that we occupy when we regard each other from the second-person standpoint.

It is only from this second-personal standpoint that the reactive attitudes come into play, on Darwall's view, because it is only from this standpoint that reasons of the right kind to warrant the reactive attitudes issue. How so? Appealing to a point Strawson raises against utilitarian justifications of blame, Darwall argues that the desirability of an outcome (such as the desirability of getting lazy Tommy to do his homework, say) is a reason of the wrong kind to warrant reactive attitudes (in this case, it is a reason of the wrong kind to warrant blaming Tommy).[32] It is the wrong kind of reason to warrant a particular reactive attitude because to be a reason of the right kind, on Darwall's view,

a consideration must justify the relevant attitude in its own terms. It must be a fact about or feature of some object, appropriate consideration of which could provide someone's reason for a warranted attitude of that kind toward it.[33]

Recall the preceding schema for the reactive attitudes. According to that schema, a reactive attitude targets a person (its intentional object) in virtue

---

[31] Darwall (2006a: 20–22).    [32] Darwall (2006a: 15).    [33] Darwall (2006a: 16).

of the fact that the person's conduct or character manifests goodwill, affection, or esteem (on the one hand) or ill will, indifference, and malevolence (on the other). Darwall's view of the conditions of warrant of a particular reactive attitude requires that its object's conduct or character is such that appropriate consideration of *it* – not of the desirability of the subject's taking up the attitude itself – provides the subject's reason for the attitude.

Consider Strawson's hand-treading example: When I occupy the second-person standpoint toward you, the consideration that you have manifest ill will in violating a demand that I have authority to press simply in virtue of being a member of the moral community (that is, a moral obligation) – which demand entails the existence of a conclusive reason (which you have the competence to recognize) for you not to tread on my hand – provides me a reason of the right kind for resenting you.[34] Moreover, my warranted resentment does not merely represent you as a wrongdoer, as might a belief that you have violated a right I have authority to press. My resentment has, according to Darwall, something akin to an Austinian illocutionary force: namely, the imperative force of (perhaps only implicitly) *addressing a demand* to you and thereby calling on you to recognize a (second-personal) reason to not tread on my hand.[35]

Assuming the illocutionary force of reactive attitudes as (quasi) speech acts, Darwall suggests, metaphorically, that they come with "an implicit RSVP."[36] The demands addressed by the reactive attitudes thus call for a response from their target. In the case of my resenting your treading on my hand, the reciprocating response is that you refrain from treading on my hand *and* do so for the reason that you are obligated to me

---

[34] The "felicity conditions" on reactive attitudes as forms of address require the presuppositions of second-personal authority and competence if they are to succeed in providing the addressee with a reason for complying with the demand as opposed to, for example, arationally goading or coercing her. See, e.g., Darwall (2006a: 75).

[35] Coleen Macnamara takes issue with Darwall's (admittedly orthodox) view that what are addressed by the reactive attitudes as such are demands and, in the process, distinguishes three uses of "demand" in the relevant literature: one that understands them as "models or metaphors" of the standing requirements of morality; a second that understands them as speech acts; and a third figurative use that marks the fact that negative reactive attitudes seek a response. (See Macnamara 2013b). I agree that not only are these uses present in the literature, they are often present in the case of a single author, as in the case of Darwall. Here my emphasis is on the nature of the interpersonal relationship secured by the emphasis on understanding the reactive attitudes as (quasi) speech acts. Macnamara pursues the speech act analogy elsewhere, arguing that the expressed reactive attitudes have *recognitive* illocutionary force, i.e., they recognize their target as having done something wrong or bad. See Macnamara (2013a).

[36] Darwall (2006a: 145; see also 40, 42, and 256).

to do so. This second-personal reason is importantly different from other reasons you might have to not tread on my hand. For example, Darwall contrasts a case where I appeal to your sympathy in order to give you a reason to stop causing me pain. In appealing to your sympathy, I might succeed in getting you to want to stop causing my pain; here, your desire would represent this cessation as a good state of affairs. You would thereby accept (or not) a state-of-the-world-regarding, agent-neutral reason to ameliorate my pain – as opposed to an agent-relative reason that you not cause me pain.[37] The reason at issue when I regard you with a warranted reactive attitude, in contrast, is the agent-relative one. The reciprocating response that my resentment seeks thus requires second-personal competence in the target in the form of a capacity to recognize that my authority provides sufficient reason to comply with my demand. In contrast, I do not manifest my second-personal competence when I recognize the all-things-considered undesirability of your being in pain nor when my (third-personal) recognition of the badness of your pain motivates me to remove my foot from your hand out of sympathy.

These features of the deontic imperative view of the moral reactive attitudes – i.e., that they address accountability-seeking demands to their target, which address is warranted by the target's violation of a moral obligation that the subject has authority to press as a representative person – ensure that they constitute paradigmatically deontic relations between persons related as *claimants* or *obligees* to persons as *obligors*. In this way, the view equips its proponents to avoid the objection Darwall levels against Hume's third-personal moral sentimentalism: that it is unable to sustain a contrast between reactive moral sentiments and nonreactive aesthetic reactions.

Hume's view is not the only option available to a sentimentalist, however. More to the point, the objection does not extend to Strawson's own conception of the reactive attitudes. Accepting the deontic, imperative interpretation of the reactive attitudes comes at the cost of obscuring a more unified account of them as a class, an account that does not sustain privileging the generic relationship of claimant/obligee to obligor. Moreover, it is a cost one need not bear in order to defend an account of the reactive attitudes that distinguishes them from disengaged aesthetic reactions. I propose, then, to offer an interpretation of the reactive attitudes that heeds Strawson's advice to consider the variety of particular relationships that provide contexts for their warrant. Considering those contexts will show

[37] Darwall (2006a: 5–6).

that the conditions for second-personal address sufficient to distinguish reactive from nonreactive attitudes does not require that what is addressed implicate the parties in deontic relations that each enjoys simply as one stranger among others.

## 5     Toward a More Inclusive View of the Reactive Attitudes

Suppose we accept that it is correct to conceptualize reactive attitudes so that, like literal forms of address, their felicity conditions include a possibility of uptake and answer. Just as one does not issue written invitations among the illiterate, one does not sustain reactive attitudes toward the second-personally incompetent. So far, so good. The aretaic, appellative conception of the reactive attitudes likewise accepts these as felicity conditions on the reactive attitudes. I have doubts, however, about the requirements the deontic imperative view imposes on how and what the moral reactive attitudes thereby address their targets.

Darwall's appeal to the metaphor of the address coming with an RSVP is telling here. First, an RSVP – "Répondez, s'il vous plaît" or "Please reply" – in fact addresses a polite request or appeal to its addressee. It is in the appellative, not the imperative, mood. Indeed, this form of address would completely misfire were it to be made in the form of an imperative demand. Second, if the addressee cares about etiquette and about you, she will regard you as providing her an agent-relative reason to respond politely. However, this differs from how the deontic imperative view understands what moral reactive attitudes address: namely, conclusive agent-relative reasons. Even granting a conception of reactive attitudes as (quasi) speech acts that come "with an implicit RSVP," then, does not force one to grant that they must have imperative, as opposed to appellative, illocutionary force (or mood) and deontic content.

In spelling out a conception of the appellative mood, one does well to proceed by recalling the direct interpersonal relationships that serve as Strawson's prime contexts in introducing what he called the non-detached reactive attitudes (among them gratitude, resentment, forgiveness, love, and hurt feelings). Strawson includes among the relevant relationships those of sharers of a common interest, members of the same family, colleagues, friends, lovers, as well as "chance parties to an enormous range of transactions and encounters."[38] In order to appreciate both the variety and the unity in the phenomena of concern, consider each of the direct interpersonal relationships Strawson cites in turn.

---

[38] Strawson (1962: 63).

Consider, first, the relationship of sharers of a common interest and reactive attitudes of resentment, hurt feelings, and gratitude. Imagine you and I each enjoy gardening. Meeting at a community garden, we fall into cultivating a common plot. If we are to bring our fruits and vegetables to harvest, we will prepare our soil by a certain date, plant and fertilize our seeds or seedlings, and regularly water and weed. If, each day as I arrive at the field, I find that you have under- or overwatered, or carelessly allowed the weeds to overtake the seedlings – all while I am doing my share – it is quite reasonable for me to judge that you have fallen short of the standards of good gardening that should inform the pursuit of our common endeavor. Moreover, barring excuses, it is reasonable to take that failure to manifest toward me an attitude of indifference or disregard. This is true, moreover, despite the fact that you never promised your help. Indeed, to attempt to excuse yourself by insisting that you never made any promises would only reveal you to be more indifferent or disregarding of me. If the relationship is one I value, I'm warranted in responding with resentment or hurt feelings. If it is one you value, you will respond. An unexpected cold front has set in and I arrive at the field one morning anticipating that our seedlings will have been desiccated by the frost. Unbeknownst to me, you received word of the impending cold snap and arrived sometime in the night to cover the garden. As I peek at our seedlings thriving under your blankets, I am overcome with gratitude for your stewardship.

Familial relationships are also a misfit for understanding in terms of deontic relations of obligation and right. Consider, for example, how siblings can foment resentment and hurt feelings or earn gratitude. It is my birthday and, as usual, you have failed to acknowledge it with a card or phone call. A common theme in our relationship, I'm able to predict as much. Still, I'm always ready with flowers for your birthday and you are, after all, my only sister; even our otherwise absent-minded brother can be counted on for a card. To you, I respond with resentment or hurt feelings; to him, I respond with gratitude.

Colleen Macnamara offers a compelling example of the operation of resentment in the relationship of friends. She describes a friend who refuses to release you from a promise. You are to meet for dinner but unexpectedly someone you've been anxious to date has asked you out on the same night. You ask your friend to release you from your promise but, for no good reason, she refuses to release you from the obligation. You respond with resentment. If such resentment strikes you as warranted, as it does me, then we have another case where warranted resentment does not require of its subject authority as individual or representative person to demand another's compliance as a matter of right, in this case that your friend release you from your promise. We can find further support considering the colleague who betrays a lack of solidarity in your common cause,[39] or the associate who refuses, for no good reason, to perform a simple favor, or the close friend whom you resent for failing to do something that is morally supererogatory.[40]

Finally, in the relationship of lovers, Strawson suggests we can find a reactive form of love. Perhaps you once had a homely admirer. You met him or her at a friend's party or a book club or a bar and were, at first meeting, decidedly unimpressed. Events conspire, however, to send him or her into your path again. And again. And again. Over time, he reveals to you his wicked wit, a gentle manner with shelter dogs and young children, intellectual curiosity, and inability to tell a lie. He reveals to you, in short, that he is a great person. Before long a transformation is in progress. Eventually you find yourselves basking in a warm glow and planning a life together. Your esteem has reciprocated his and you are, alas, in love.

In each of the vignettes introduced here, we have more or less determinate normative expectations of manifest goodwill, regard, or esteem in play.[41] These normative expectations derive from an ideal of the special relationship; hence just which normative expectations are operative depends on the relationship in question. The relationship likewise determines what counts as goodwill, affection, or esteem (on the one hand) or ill will, indifference, or malevolence (on the other) in the context. Our proneness to responding to these manifestations of good- or ill-will partly constitutes our valuing the other as an accountable party to the relationship, a partner who in reciprocally valuing us both recognizes the normative expectations constitutive of the specific relationship and a more general ideal of mutual answerability for succeeding or failing to comply with legitimate normative expectations.

Note, however, that in none of these vignettes is the relevant normative expectation plausibly regarded as a *demand* as understood on the deontic imperative view of the reactive attitudes. To be sure, the expectations in question prescribe (rather than predict) manifestations of goodwill, regard or esteem and, thus, appear to underwrite a corresponding claim (on my

---

[39] I thank Peter Railton and Simon Blackburn for the example

[40] I thank Remy Debes for discussion of the relevance of the supererogatory in this context.

[41] R. Jay Wallace (1996) writes of "holding a person to an expectation (or demand)," apparently not intending to mark a distinction between normative expectations and demands (and taking both to concern standing moral requirements). Coleen Macnamara introduces a use of "normative expectation" according to which it refers to "the stance that leaves us susceptible to the reactive attitudes" (Macnamara 2013b: 149 n. 11). On my proposed use, a normative expectation is, pace Wallace, contrasted with a demand. Non-deontic normative expectation is a stance that leaves us susceptible to certain reactive attitudes that respond to failures to conform to legitimately imposed interpersonal ideals.

part) and obligation (on yours).[42] These are not, however, the kinds of claims or obligations that characterize deontic relations. The demands of concern on the deontic, imperative view, recall, entail conclusive reasons for compliance and presume an authority that any generic person, simply as member of the moral community, has authority to exercise over any generic second-personally competent target. These are not at issue in the vignettes, however. What does emerge from the vignettes is a conception of reactive attitudes that address accountability-seeking appeals to their target, which address is warranted by the target's violation of an ideal that the subject has authority to press as a party to some special relationship.

Admittedly, Strawson himself speaks variously of the reactive attitudes resting on or reflecting a demand, involving or expressing a demand, and as correlating with a demand.[43] However, all that is required to maintain the prediction-prescription distinction is that a normative expectation of goodwill, affection, or esteem and absence of ill will or indifference be operative. One need not appeal, that is, to the particular normative expectation that one comply with moral obligations. A reactive attitude thus can be an intelligible and, indeed, warranted, response to conduct or character that recognizes, flouts, or exceeds a legitimate normative expectation without a demand for compliance with a moral obligation being at issue.

If we nonetheless insist on calling what the attitudes cited in my vignettes address "demands," then, we must at the same time caution that these are demands only in an attenuated (as opposed to robust) sense. This is because the demands common to the reactive attitudes as such need impose no deontic burdens on their targets.[44] They at most call on another to comply with whichever first-order normative expectations constitute the normative ideal of the relationship in which you stand to her, that is, the relationship toward whose ideal the relevant parties aspire. This attenuates the demand-like feature common to all reactive attitudes by making whatever force the demand might have derivative of the first-order prescriptions that constitute the normative ideal of the relevant relationships: first-order prescriptions that need not themselves be deontic.[45]

---

[42] The expectation does not describe an anticipated course of action (in that sense of expectation, one's expectation may well be that another, given their past conduct, will <u>not</u> manifest goodwill toward you).

[43] Strawson (1962: 71, 72, and 77).

[44] For further discussion of the more robust understanding of demands prevalent in the literature, including that according to which they *do* impose deontic burdens, see Macnamara (2013b: 144).

[45] In Mason (2003), for example, I argue that the conditions of warrant for reactive contempt included the legitimacy of one's expectation that another live up to a legitimately imposed ideal of character.

To return to the previous examples, insofar as we value our common horticultural interest, we will have certain normative expectations regarding how we should tend our garden. Moreover, in valuing each other as participants in this relationship, we'll be susceptible to resentment and hurt feelings should we find one another flouting those expectations. The warrant for these attitudes requires no presumption that you or I have a generic authority, as representative person, to address a demand (in any robust sense) that the other tend to the garden as one believes it should be tended and neither of us violates an obligation simply for failing to do so. My resentment or hurt feelings presuppose only our valuing each other as persons responsive to – and appropriately held responsible to – the standards of conduct and character necessary for maintaining our shared interest as a common pursuit. The reactive attitudes here address not demands that entail agent-relative conclusive reasons but appeals that entail agent-relative pro-tanto reasons to comport oneself as befits a companion in gardening.

Neither does it seem plausible to construe the consideration one sibling pays another in remembering her birthday as an obligation, far less as something that is owed a sibling as her right. And, however beautiful a soul my homely beloved possesses, even *reactive* love is not a response to how he fares with respect to what I in any case have authority to demand of him as a person.[46]

In short, once we recognize that conceptualizing the reactive attitudes so that they are distinct from third-personal sentiments does not require that we understand them in exclusively deontic imperative terms, we can appreciate that the continuum of reactive attitudes is continuous *not* in virtue of its every element implicating persons as claimants or obligors addressing imperatives to obligees in deontic accountability relations. Instead, the reactive attitudes as a unified class comprise a continuum of sentiments whose every element relates persons in reciprocal prescription and recognition of legitimate expectations of conduct or character, regulation in accordance with which is necessary for aspiring to community in a wide range of relationships of value to beings like us.

## 6     Conclusion

I want to close with a few words concerning how what I have presented as a reclamation of sorts of Strawson's conception of the reactive attitudes is nonetheless likely to prove revisionary. Among those attitudes that emerge on the aretaic appellative view as candidates for bona fide reactive attitudes

---

[46] For an insightful treatment of reactive love, see Abramson and Leite (2011).

are Strawson's own candidates of shame and love. But so, too, in my view, do what I take to be their correlates: reactive contempt and pride.

Reactive shame is self-reactive. On the appellative aretaic interpretation, it involves a person reflecting on his own conduct and character, and self-addressing an appeal to recognize the reasons one has for aspiring to a better self, holds oneself accountable to that better self. A correlate attitude to reactive shame, reactive contempt, responds to the conduct and character of another, and addressing an appeal to recognize that one gives the other reason to aspire to a better self, holds the other accountable to oneself for realizing their better self. Reactive love, like gratitude, is a form of esteem. Whereas gratitude responds to manifestations of goodwill that go above and beyond that which one can legitimately demand of another as a matter of obligation or right, however, reactive love responds to another as, among other things, manifesting a self one takes to be above and beyond that which anyone can reasonably demand. Reactive pride, finally, just is self-reactive love.

A full account of the quartet of reactive shame, contempt, love, and pride – a topic for another day – will acknowledge they are forms of disesteem and esteem for persons. If esteem were an "essentially third-personal observer's response," as Darwall interprets Hume's conception, then this quartet would correctly be denied the status of reactive attitudes. They would be so on the grounds that they do not presuppose the capacity for uptake or reciprocal recognition characteristic of the reactive attitudes as such. If my sketch of an appellative aretaic conception of reactive attitudes is on the right track, however, it opens the door to allowing such esteem to manifest itself in forms of second-personal address. Once that door is open, on what grounds would the moral philosopher presume to continue to privilege resentment, guilt, and indignation as moral sentiments? Why continue to accept a conception of the moral domain according to which it is simply the domain of deontic relations and imperative prescriptions? Does a focus on what each of us, simply as a person, *owes to*, *is prohibited from doing to*, or *is permitted to do to* others home in on our most significant responsibilities or most egregious faults? It is one thing to stipulate such a focus in order to limit one's theoretical ambitions and another to suggest that morality, properly understood, concerns only this much.

Those skeptical of the latter suggestion should, with Strawson, remain suspicious of "claiming as essential features of the concept of morality in general, forms of these attitudes which may have a local and temporary prominence."[47] In so doing, we may find our way toward defending

---

[47] Strawson (1962: 80).

a conception of all reactive attitudes as moral sentiments, sentiments that address us not only as conscripts in the army of duty but as sharers of a common interest, family members, colleagues, lovers, and friends called on, and presumed capable of, fashioning better selves in response to legitimate expectations of as much.

The Authority of Empathy (Or, How to
Ground Sentimentalism)

*Remy Debes*

When observing or considering the emotions of other people, real or imagined, we sometimes come to feel the same emotions. Or if not exactly the
same, close enough to satisfy us that our two emotions – theirs and ours –
are "in accord." Call this the fact of empathy.

There has been considerable debate over how to explain this fact. But
the growing consensus seems to be that more than one explanation is possible. Humans enjoy multiple pathways to empathy. Correspondingly, insofar as any real dispute remains about what empathy is, it is a dispute about
whether or to what extent differences in these pathways make for genuinely different forms of empathy, and, in turn, what the ramifications of
these divergences might be. For example, some researchers worry about
cross-species comparisons of empathic ability; others worry about justifying claims to knowledge of other minds. However, this paper is not about
the nature of empathy – not in and of itself anyway. Instead, I examine how
the fact of empathy bears on a related fact of ethical discourse, what I will
call "empathic judgment."

I take my lead from Adam Smith. At the outset of *The Theory of Moral
Sentiments* (1759/1982), Smith observed that we routinely make judgments
about the propriety of emotions on the basis of empathy, though he and his
contemporaries called it "sympathy."[1] Smith focused on cases of empathy
resulting from imaginative simulation, by which I mean, cases in which we
imagine being in the situation of another person – cases where we imagine the "object" or conglomerate of objects, both social and environmental, to which the person's emotion is a response. If by dint of such reflection we come to feel as the other does, then, Smith argued, the consequent
empathic accord prompts us to approve her emotion. And if our feelings

---

[1] The term "empathy" was not in use until 1909, when the American psychologist Edward
Titchener coined it to translate the German concept of *Einfühlung* (feeling into). See Debes
(2015: 286–322).

diverge, or to the extent that they do, this lack of empathic accord prompts us to disapprove her emotion.[2] Smith writes,

> The man whose sympathy keeps time to my grief, cannot but admit the reasonableness of my sorrow . . . He who laughs at the same joke, and laughs along with me, cannot well deny the propriety of my laughter. On the contrary, the person who, upon these different occasions, either feels no such emotion as that which I feel, or feels none that bears any proportion to mine, cannot avoid disapproving my sentiments on account of their dissonance with his own. (1759/1982, I.i.3.1)

In this paper, I take for granted that we do sometimes judge emotions on the basis of empathy, as Smith suggested. My question is, are these judgments legitimate? That is, do we understand what we mean when we make them? And can we justify them?

I stake out answers to both questions as follows. (1) In the first section, I clarify what empathic judgments are, descriptively. In particular, I clarify the sense of "approval" in question. I argue that empathic judgments involve a distinctly "gray" shade of approbation, in the sense of lying in the normative space between proscription and prohibition, or what I will sometimes call *the space of permission*. Moreover, this permission is distinctly weak, in the sense of being easily defeasible in the face of other normative standards for emotion, like prudence or fittingness.[3] Admittedly, one might wonder whether such a weak normative standard has much significance for ethical theory. The second part of my argument, however, should mitigate this worry.

(2) Although the content of empathic judgments turns out to be very weak, Section 2 argues that the *form* of this judgment reveals itself to be grounded on the fundamental status or "dignity" we ascribe to ourselves as moral agents – albeit, not in the usual sense of agency. Empathic judgment isn't premised on the dignity we assume for ourselves as rational agents – our "autonomy" – but the dignity we assume for ourselves as *affective* agents. It is thus not rational dignity that grounds empathic judgments, but affective dignity. Defending this claim, and thereby delivering the normative grounds for (at least some) sentimentalist judgments, is the ultimate goal of this paper.

---

[2] For the purposes of this paper I make no distinctions between emotions, feelings, sentiments, etc. Those distinctions can be important, but not, I think, for the argument I build here.

[3] "Fittingness" refers to the claim that a given emotion F is fitting just in case its object is really F-able, e.g., my fear is fitting when its object is really fearful or dangerous. The terminology of fittingness has been popularized principally by the work of Daniel Jacobson and Justin D'Arms; see, e.g., D'Arms and Jacobsen (2000a).

# 1        The Description

Empathy research is flourishing in every corner of the arts and sciences. The downside is, the meaning of "empathy" has become so eclectic that no perfectly general definition now seems possible. My opening definition would certainly be too narrow. Restated more technically, I defined empathy as any non-accidental process leading to affective accord between persons. But "empathy" is sometimes used to connote a similar process in non-human animals, or just the end state of such a process in humans or animals, i.e. the resulting affective accord between sentient creatures. Others argue empathy can be "cold": we can come to know what others feel, without actually feeling their emotions ourselves.[4] Or again, "empathy" has been used to indicate a correspondence of thought rather than emotion. The term has even been used to denote a distinct emotion rather than a process or capacity to feel emotions.[5] I have no objections to these various uses so long as there is no objection to mine. And if any problematic vagueness remains in mine, hopefully the following will clear the way.

## 1.1      This Empathy, that Empathy

To preserve the starting intuition that empathy underwrites a species of approval for emotion, I will constrain my discussion to cases of empathy involving some consciously accessible, intermediate reflection on the situated object of the other person's emotion. Some theorists of mind call this, "high-level" simulation.[6]

Obviously, this is a rough definition. But we should resist the urge to refine it now. "Simulation" has become a complicated subject in its own right, and those complexities are not relevant to my argument if it will be granted, what is surely true, that (1) *sometimes* we consciously consider or imagine the situations of others; and (2) based on this reflection, *sometimes* we come to feel an emotion. This narrow sense of "simulative empathy" is all I need. In exchange, I'm happy to make two concessions.

First, I grant there are other processes that satisfy my opening definition of empathy – in particular, contagion and so-called mirroring – which do

---

[4] See n. 9 and n. 25.

[5] See, e.g., Gallagher (2012). Note also that the foregoing is not intended to be exhaustive. For a fuller rendering of alternatives, see Stueber (2014) and Sherman (1998). Sherman critiques the Smithian view I springboard from, for being *overly* focused on empathy that leads to actual emotion correspondence (91). Still, Sherman seems to concede the basic Smithean intuition, namely, that actual emotion correspondence can be the basis of a normative judgment.

[6] The most prominent contemporary precedent for this distinction comes from Goldman (2006).

*not* require an intermediate reflection on the relevant situation, and thus do not fit my constrained definition.[7] Obviously I must exclude these forms of empathy. Merely seeing my smile as I walk into a room is apt to communicate something of my joy to you. But this contagion can in no way license you to make a normative judgment about the propriety of my joy: as yet, you have no idea why I am smiling. So I am not interested in these kinds of empathy.

Second, I am happy to grant that the boundaries between all these processes (mirroring, contagion, and simulative empathy) are not perfectly firm. Moreover, these processes surely sometimes co-occur. Correspondingly, I grant that there will be in-practice confusions that complicate empathic judgment, but of course these confusions are in-principle irrelevant to my argument.

### 1.2    The Narrative Paradigm

Empathic judgment is best situated in the context of the familiar, narrative style of explanation we routinely use for our emotions.[8] If I tell you how my day went, or describe some personal misfortune, or lament the passing of my childhood best friend – these are all candidate cases of narrative. What makes them genuine narratives, however, turns on whether they play a particular explanatory role. A narrative – one properly so-named anyway – aims at more than merely conveying facts or chronicling events. It aims at conveying understanding.[9] For example, if all I wanted was for you to *know* that I'm grieved over the death of my childhood friend, then I don't tell you how as boys we shared every secret, nor do I recount the many clubs we invented to share and safeguard those secrets. I don't tell you the details of our adventures, or that most of those adventures were only imaginary, ranging no further than the backyard. And I don't tell you that when, on September 11, 2001, he suddenly left this world forever, so did a part of me. This extra detail has a manifest further purpose, namely, to recount

---

[7] Mirroring refers to the 1996 discovery of single-cell "mirror neurons" in macaque monkeys and the ensuing swell of research on neural networks or pathways in the human brain, which pathways are stimulated similarly under "action" conditions *and* "observation" conditions – that is, simultaneously.

[8] Many philosophers have noted the close connection between emotion and narrative. See, e.g., Martha Nussbaum (1988), Ronald de Sousa (1987), and Peter Goldie (2003). Goldie takes several of the same preliminary steps I do, but he stops short of explaining narrative as a paradigm for the normative assessment of emotion.

[9] I'm here borrowing from an observation David Velleman develops at length in Velleman (2003), see esp. p. 1–4. Velleman in turn partly credits his account to Peter Brooks (see Velleman's n. 1).

my friend's passing in a way that renders my particular grief, in some sense, *understandable* to you.

So, what kind of understanding distinguishes a successful narrative? The diversity of theory about both "narrative" and "understanding" makes any perfectly general answer to this question suspect. However, in the delimited context of narratives purporting to explain emotions, I think the answer is clear enough. We aim at empathic understanding.[10]

Consider: Whatever else understanding is, it is never atomic. As the twentieth-century British philosopher Neil Cooper (1994) put the point, "It is a commonplace that understanding involves connecting and unifying. Knowledge may be bitty, but understanding never is." Now, in the case of emotions, our explanatory stories are also plainly aiming at "connecting and unifying." Indeed, the success of our stories lies in presenting a *sufficiently* unified account of the various events, background setting, persons, and actions that we take ourselves to be responding to, where the operative "sufficiency" is settled by the earned empathy of our audience. Correspondingly, to empathize with the narrative just is to understand *both* the story and the subject emotion.[11]

But this is not all. I'm also claiming that in the narrative paradigm, empathy purports to be normative. To recall Smith's insight, if I tell you an autobiographical story that successfully earns your empathy, you must, in some sense, approve of how I feel. For, you don't just know that I feel some way or other. It must make sense to you that I feel as I do. How could it not? You feel the same way. Perhaps you would not commend my feeling in the sense of recommending or prescribing it. After all, just because it makes sense to you that I feel as I do does not require you to think that everyone similarly situated ought to feel this way. No such categorical requirement is entailed. But neither can you categorically *condemn* my feeling. Not without some explanation anyway. For, to reiterate, in virtue of empathizing you constitutively concede some normative space for my explanation of how I feel. Let me recast this critical point.

Empathy with narrative involves more than a simple accounting of a person's reasons to feel as they do. That is, it is not simply a way to identify the "why" of the emotion. It is not even simply an acknowledgment that

---

[10] By contrast, David Velleman argues that the distinguishing explanatory characteristic of narrative is the production of an "emotional resolution." However, Velleman is working with a much broader conception of narrative than I am. I think narratives can be limited to stories meant to explain emotion *per se*. Construed this way, I don't think Velleman and I are in serious disagreement.

[11] To be sure, building empathy is not always an explicit aim of such narratives. Sometimes we try to explain how we are feeling without explicitly identifying any emotions (ours or anyone else's).

the "why" is intelligible. Empathizing as the result of narrative is instead a particular *way* of acknowledging the intelligibility of the "why," namely, it is to *accept* the emotion *in light of* the "why" – in light of the reasons offered in a narrative.[12] And it is to accept that emotion on the basis of those reasons precisely because one feels the same way as the narrator. In other words, empathy draws us across the line from *admission* to *acceptance*. If we empathize on account of a narrative explanation, we do not imply that we simply admit the intelligibility of the narrator's reasons-to-feel. Instead, we imply that we accept her reasons in the stronger sense of making those reasons in some sense, "our own." Why? *Because we feel the very same emotion on the very same grounds* – that is, for the very same reasons. Correspondingly, we canot condemn the emotion, no matter how much we might hesitate to prescribe it – not, at least, if such condemnation entails total rejection of the relevant reasons.

To be clear, the sense in which we make the relevant reasons "our own" through empathy is quite weak. More exactly, the acceptance that empathy purports to commit us to is easily swamped by competing considerations, namely, from other normative standards for emotion. I will say more of this as we go along. For now, simply note that if someone still wanted to resist my basic descriptive premise – that empathy has normative purport – she could not do so by merely positing some case or other where she thinks she could empathize but still not approve. For, I've just conceded this very possibility, albeit by suggesting that all such cases could be explained away as cases of "swamping."

I also take this point about swamping to mitigate the worry that my account will end up licensing certain kinds of "nasty" emotions, for example, the envy, resentment, or hatred characteristic of racist prejudice. Thus one might object that once we understand the typical situation of people who harbor such feelings – unemployment, poor education, social oppression, etc. – it is not particularly difficult to empathize, to some degree, with their feelings; and yet, surely these feelings are always loathsome. But again, plausibly our categorical blame for such emotions is explained by the fact that other normative standards are swamping our judgment. For example, racist hatred is usually based on such grossly false beliefs or such obviously entrenched social conditioning that we never lose sight of how *unfitting* it is. Moreover, for many of us, racist hatred is plainly *immoral*, reflective of the most undesirable social vices. In short, most nasty emotions are so wildly normatively imbalanced, it is not surprising that a very weak sense of

---

[12] Typically, the narrative purports to represent the narrator's reasons. Of course, a narrator might dissemble or be confused about his own reasons. I must pass over this wrinkle.

approval, like what I am attributing to empathy, could be hard to detect in our thinking, normatively or psychologically.

## 1.3    The Space of Permission

All my talk of "approval," which I took over from Smith, risks mucking up the intuitive space I am grabbing at. So hereon let's call the weak species of normative judgment, which empathy implies, *sanction*, in full appreciation of the fence-riding connotation of this word. To sanction an emotion is to accept it into the normative space between categorical rejection and recommendation – and perhaps, to barely accept it. Let me elaborate.

"I see how you could feel that way." "Oh, how miserable! No wonder you're a wreck." "He said what?! I'd be mad too!" "Honestly, I don't know if you should be worried. Personally, I don't fret about such things." These are familiar bits of our daily discourse, and they smack of empathic judgment (both for and against feeling a certain way). Assuming, then, that empathic judgment purports to convey *something* normative, is the content of that normative purport best captured as a kind of sanction?

I acknowledge there are other options. In particular, one might think that empathy's normative purport is better disambiguated as fittingness. On this line of thought, empathic accord is a way of discovering or verifying that another person's emotion *fits* the object. Indeed, Smith's own view is open to this interpretation.[13] Thus, Smith writes, "In the suitableness or unsuitableness, in the proportion or disproportion, which the affection seems to bear to the cause or object which excites it, consists the propriety of impropriety, the decency or ungracefulness of the consequent action" (1759/1982, 1.1.3.6).[14] This challenge requires a reply. But to make that reply, I first need to finish fleshing out the positive proposal for sanction. To this end, then, consider a further distinction in how we use the concepts of "intelligible" or "understandable," but now in the case of action.

For example, suppose it's the end of the baseball season and you decide to catch one more game. It's a blustery day, so you decide to drive. As you get close to the ballpark, you start anticipating the extra pinch on your purse for parking, when, amazingly, you spot a car pulling out of a free spot on the street. You let the car ease out and pull forward to parallel park. Just as you shift into reverse, a small, nimble sports car slips into the spot from behind. "What the hell!" you blurt out, and pull back to address

---

[13] See also Antti Kauppinen's contribution to this volume.

[14] Smith famously argued in this same stretch of text that the overall "virtue" of an emotion can be considered "under two different aspects": its propriety (discussed above) or its merit (the beneficial or hurtful nature of its intended effects). I must gloss over the second aspect.

the driver. "Hey buddy," you call out your window to the man already starting to walk away, "I was waiting on that spot." "Tough luck, sucker!" the stranger retorts, as he turns to wave his own tickets in your face. "Oh really, well, the same to you!" you say, as you knock his tickets into a big gust of wind, before pulling away.

Now, it seems we might call your action "intelligible" or "understandable" in two different ways. We might mean there is a plausible causal or psychological explanation for why you slapped the tickets away. By contrast, we might mean there is a plausible normative explanation for what you did (if only in the offing). In particular, I suggest that in cases like this, where we dub some action or other "understandable," we sometimes mean to signal that we don't think what you did was *totally* wrong. Certainly, when we call actions "understandable" we typically mean not to recommend the action – that is, as what anyone similarly situated ought to do, morally speaking. When we want to recommend actions, we use different expressions. We call actions "right," or say that it is what one "should" have done. By contrast, in calling an action "understandable," we seem to want to signal that an action is "right" in a peculiar, narrow sense of its being "alright" – that is, "not wrong." That is, by calling what someone did "understandable," we seem to want to convey something much weaker than recommendation – something more like "toleration," or, as I deemed it, "sanction."

Or consider the same point from a slightly different direction: In judgments of "intelligibility," both causal-psychological-leaning ones and normative-leaning ones, we think something explains the action. But in causal-leaning cases, the given or assumed explanation is *merely* explanatory – your action is *merely* intelligible. In normative-leaning cases, however, we treat the given or assumed explanation as excusing you, at least from categorical blame. Moreover, the explanation seems to excuse you in a distinct sense. That is, your explanation does not simply acquit you. That would be closer to suspending judgment and a mere-intelligibility explanation can already do that. Instead, when we call actions intelligible or understandable in a normative sense, we treat the explanation as excusing the person from blame by *vindicating* the action – though once again, not by crossing over into the stronger normative space of recommendation. I think the sanction that empathic approval conveys is like this. Empathic sanction excuses an emotion from blame, but in a way that goes beyond mere acquittal (albeit not much beyond).[15]

---

[15] This loose analogy might help: In a legal insanity defense a bona fide causal-psychological account of what drove the accused to act a certain way might convince us he should not be punished for that action. He's "off the hook" we might say, as we acquit him. But notice

Admittedly, all this could use further refinement. But then again, there currently aren't any established conventions for describing the normative space I'm gesturing at. Ethicists haven't spent much time working on what lies between rejection and recommendation, which is unfortunate. In a pluralist liberal society, everyday morality might well benefit if we thought more about gray normative space, and less about distinguishing "right" from "wrong." In any event, my rough description of empathic sanction should suffice for the next stages of my inquiry.

### 1.4    Two Objections

I have argued that empathic sanction hangs on a listener coming to feel the narrator's emotion in virtue of the narrator's description of her reasons-to-feel, where what counts as a reason-to-feel are whatever features of the situation the narrator takes to explain her emotion. However, it could be objected that an actual emotion sensation is an unnecessary feature of the way we make empathic judgments, for two reasons. (1) Sometimes when we claim to empathize, we don't *actually* feel an emotion. Even construing "sensation" broadly (so as not to limit it to bodily sensations), if an actual emotion sensation is necessary, how do I explain counterfactual judgments where we mean that we *would* feel as another although we are not *now* feeling this way? (2) If empathic understanding depends on the reasons given in narrative, why think listeners must *feel* the emotion in order to judge it understandable? Can't we, for example, understand the reasons for somebody feeling jealous or betrayed simply because she tells us her partner is having an affair, without feeling jealousy or betrayal?

Reply to (1): I grant that when we say, "I empathize," we sometimes intend a counterfactual claim. But such judgments typically imply a general rule. And these rules either fold into my argument or can be explained away. Thus, on the one hand, the rule might derive from our past experiences of actually simulating narratives about emotions, and, in turn, of actually feeling something as a result of that simulation. It takes only a few poignant reactions to stories of unrequited love to form a belief about how we tend to react (empathically) to stories of heartbreak. It takes only a few poignant reactions to stories of tragic loss to know how we tend to react (empathically) to stories of grief. And so on. Obviously, the modality in this kind of counterfactual is consistent with the principle of my argument.

that even if we are convinced by a causal-psychological account against blaming him, we might still consistently disapprove of his action. "We understand he couldn't help himself," we might say, "but it was a terrible way to act." This implies that the explanation in question does not yet legitimate his action. He is excused, but not vindicated. So too for emotions, I am suggesting.

On the other hand, the general rule might stem from our first-personal emotional experiences. If, for example, I am always elated when my articles are accepted into journals, I might tell my jubilant graduate student with her first big acceptance, "I empathize," even though I'm quite placid at the moment. However, in cases like this, the meaning of empathy has simply changed. Recall, in the paradigm case, the purported normativity of empathy stems from the way the reasons-to-feel, which a narrative expresses, are "taken up" by the listener through her simulated feeling. But there is no such uptake here. Instead, there is an application of something like a personal theory of fittingness. I'm applying a theory about the "proper" object of professional elation, which theory I've developed, if only tacitly, from my own first-order reactions to professional success. And I express the application of this theory by saying, "I empathize." But this judgment makes no essential reference to literal empathic accord (not even derivatively, as in the first kind of counterfactual). So, if we want to, we can call this second kind of counterfactual judgment "empathic," but it does not bear on the principle of my argument.

Reply to (2): Can a narrator's reasons-to-feel by themselves suffice to judge that an emotion is "understandable?" Yes and no. One *could* judge an emotion this way. But then, as with the second kind of counterfactual just considered, this is no longer a sanctioning empathic judgment. It is a fittingness judgment. The sanctioning judgment comes only from accepting reasons-to-feel in the light of a narrative and in virtue of feeling as the narrator feels.

However, there is a more challenging way to interpret objection (2). Thus, one might wonder whether literal empathic accord produced by simulation can itself be construed as something like a "direct" fittingness judgment? That is, given that simulation gives the listener a virtual "direct look" at the object of the narrator's emotion, isn't any resulting empathic accord just another way for a listener to verify that the narrator's emotion "fits" the object? For example, when I experience literal empathic accord with your grief over the death of a friend, the grief I feel might be said to be proof positive that I (personally) take your grief to *fit* the facts – that your friend's passing is really grieve-*able*. In short, can't the sanctioning judgment of empathy be reduced to a fittingness judgment?

I stipulate that simulative empathy could be used to make a fittingness judgment. Correspondingly, I concede that sanctioning judgments sometimes get tangled up with fittingness assessments in practice. Nevertheless, the reductionist would have to say much more than this to show that the *concept* of sanction, as I have defined it, and which I've independently shown empathy can support, collapses into fittingness. Indeed, I defined "sanction" partly by contradistinction from fittingness; in particular, I defined it in terms of its weak normative connotation relative to fittingness. It thus makes more sense to conclude that empathy can play more than one role. Empathic accord *always* commits us to sanctioning the given emotion. But empathic accord sometimes *also* serves as evidence that the emotion is fitting.

Further to this point, there are familiar cases where fittingness and empathic sanction pull apart – cases where we all tend to feel unfitting emotions, even when we have the evidence that renders them unfitting. For example: When we make a decision under uncertainty and things go badly, we have tendency to kick ourselves even if we could not have foreseen the way in which they went sour. This seems like unfitting regret. And yet, it is a completely understandable feeling, precisely in the sense that we can empathize with such regret. Indeed, it seems we can empathize with it while still thinking it unfitting. Or again, think about a case where we get angry with a whining toddler, or with the cat that claws our new couch, or even with the corner of a cabinet that we smash our head on. These seem like cases of unfitting anger insofar as toddlers, cats, and cabinets have diminished or nonexistent agency. On the other hand, such anger seems totally understandable in the sense of being a feeling we easily empathize with. Granted, we would be quick to condemn any consequent violent action on the basis of that anger, that is, against the child, cat, or cabinet. But that's a separate issue. The point at hand is about the emotions themselves, the anger or the regret. In this respect, if empathic sanction reduces to fittingness, we'd be forced to say that there is *no* normative space for such instances of regret or anger: they are *altogether* wrong. And I suspect most of us will find this patently unintuitive. So let's avoid this result by admitting sanction does not reduce to fittingness.[16]

## 2    The Grounding

It might be worried that the argument so far raises to the level of normative any emotion for which one can find another empathizer, no matter how crazy or contemptible the emotion might seem. This could be as trivial as when a shoe fetishist finds another shoe fetishist, but could be as horrifying as when millions of Nazis found in one another someone who shared their hatred of Jews, or, as is still true today, millions of white Americans find in one another someone who shares their contempt of black Americans. Is this a legitimate worry?

---

[16] I am grateful to Justin D'Arms for discussion of this specific point, especially the regret example.

In one sense, empathic sanction for crazy or contemptible emotions is grist for my mill. After all, shoe fetishists, Nazis, and many white Americans do seem to approve of each other's feelings in precisely the way my theory predicts, namely with a kind of sanctioning attitude engendered by the smoothness with which they imaginatively identify or simulate each other's perspectives.[17] On the other hand, if I set aside descriptive accuracy in order to think about the normative viability of my theory, then I concede there is a legitimate challenge here – indeed, there are two. The first could be put like this: Can empathic judgments transcend the subjective perspective of particular judges? Can emotions be *objectively* empathically justified? After all, regardless of the descriptive accuracy of my theory, we surely do want to say that sexualized adoration of shoes is crazy in both fetishists, despite their mutual empathy. Likewise, we want to say that hating Jewish or Black people simply because they are Jewish or Black is not "alright" – not sanctioned – no matter how many people feel such vehemence.

The second challenge can be put this way: Suppose we grant that there is a correct way to make empathic judgments – perhaps some objective perspective from which we ought to make these judgments. And thus suppose you make your judgment of my emotion in this way or from this perspective, and find me wanting. My emotion is objectively empathically *un*intelligible and so not sanctionable. And suppose you tell me just this. So what? What rationally requires me to take your judgment "into account" – by which I mean, what requires me to count or even consider your judgment as a reason to do or think something? What requires me to treat your judgment as a reason to apologize for what I feel, take measures to stop feeling it, feel guilty about feeling it, and so on? In short, can we vindicate the normativity of empathic judgment?

In attempting to answer this second challenge, it is important not to confuse the *kind* of normativity empathic judgment involves, with the *authority* of that normativity. The first part of the paper has already addressed the first point: Empathic judgments involve a sanctioning kind of normativity. Now we are asking about authority. Correspondingly, nothing that follows will involve arguing that the judgment somehow transforms into a new, stronger kind of approval. It will remain a kind of sanction. Instead, my strategy will be to show, first, that the *form* of empathic judgments commits those who make them to a distinctive moral acknowledgement of those to whom they are made, namely, of the latter's agential *status*. And, second, I will show that this acknowledgment of status goes hand in hand with conceding to this other person the authority to make empathic judgments "in

---

[17] Of course, some go further, normatively speaking, by believing their emotions to be fitting.

return." That is, we constitutively concede to whomever we judge empathically the normative authority to be our judge in turn.

## 2.1    The First Challenge: Objectivity

Thus far it has been an open question whether the empathic perspective any given person has on anyone else is sufficient for making empathic assessments that are themselves genuinely justified. In this section I will try to close this question.

So consider again: When we ask how we can know if any given emotion is objectively empathically intelligible, what are we asking? It seems we're asking for some kind of normative epistemology. We want some independent principle that dictates the way in which an empathic judgment must be made in order for us to know that the judgment is itself justified. In the context of empathy, then, what kind of principle might satisfy this demand? Is there some ideal perspective from which, were we to empathize with an emotion, we could conclusively decide on the intelligibility of that emotion? A ready candidate suggests itself: an impartial perspective. The empathic stance uninfluenced by personal bias or the psychological peculiarities and foibles of a particular judge. The stance not of you or me, the fetishist or the bigot, but of "anyone."[18] In other words, what plausibly determines whether a given emotion is objectively sanctionable is its being found intelligible by impartial empathy.

This kind of move to impartiality has an obvious payoff, given that emotions like erotic adoration of shoes and racist hatred will now be struck down. Those emotions aren't objectively sanctionable because only those who share some peculiar psychological or axiological starting point can share in those feelings. However, this kind of move to impartiality is also banal in normative ethics and that banality conceals a series of complications. First, what "impartiality" itself amounts to is not obvious. Second, ideals like "impartiality" and "neutrality" have been long-time targets of criticism, especially within feminist theory and certain strands of critical theory. So we cannot simply assume them as ideals. Worse, "impartiality" might not seem in the spirit of my own argument anyway. Simulative empathy involves imaginatively casting oneself into a narrator's situation. And although bracketing one's personal axiological biases and psychological foibles plausibly would facilitate such imaginative simulation, why think we are any good at detecting our biases and foibles? Moreover, won't such bracketing be helpful only because it will help us take on the narrator's reasons? But aren't the narrator's reasons also likely to be based on biases and

---

[18] This formulation is due to Stephen Darwall (2002).

foibles? And so, won't that cut against an ideal of impartiality? After all, the narrator might be the racist.

The last worry is the most serious. But answering it requires replying to the preceding points first. To begin, then, the general question of what foibles or biases we *can* detect (in ourselves) is irrelevant. If empathic sanction is a philosophically defensible standard for emotion, then it suffices to say we *ought* to bracket such foibles and biases – as best we can anyway. Assuming it is not totally impracticable, our weakness to live up to the standard is not a mark against the theory – it is a mark against us. Moreover, empathic sanction needn't be thought of as an all-or-nothing kind of judgment in the first place. If the combination of your biases and foibles with my biases and foibles is such that we cannot reach perfect empathic accord, this still does not entail total rejection. Unlike deontic judgments, judgments of permission can be graded. As long as we don't end up in a type-mismatch (e.g., you laugh about what makes me angry), then imperfect empathic accord will result in a mixed judgment focused on the *intensity* of feeling. I feel *like* you do, only not as strongly, or not as weakly. In these cases empathy lends itself to mixed judgments, expressed by familiar judgments such as, "I think you are overreacting." We tend to hear such judgments for their negative implication, but they also imply a positive judgment as well, namely, that what we are feeling is in the ballpark – which is to say, it is not altogether wrong.

What, then, of the meaning of impartiality itself? By speaking of the stance of "anyone," I don't mean an a-perspectival stance. I don't mean a situation-less perspective. It is not the stance from "nowhere." On the contrary, as I've construed it, empathy is all about getting into the situation of the narrator. "Impartiality" thus denotes a constraint on *how* we get into that situation. The listener attempts to get into the narrator's situation as if she were "anyone." Less metaphorically, my appeal to impartiality doesn't rule out an end-point that would be isomorphic with the peculiar perspective of a narrator. It rules out getting to that point by relying on one's own existing biases or foibles, or by adopting in brute fashion the biases or foibles of the narrator. The white racist cannot describe blacks as "contemptible," full stop, and win "impartial" empathy. Just as empathy with anger is not won by simply describing the object as "maddening." Such brute description works only when a listener is already primed to find the object-in-question in the situation-in-question "contemptible" or "maddening," in which case we should suspect either partial empathy or a counter-factual empathic judgment. Instead, then, narrators must describe what it is about the object that *makes* it maddening or contemptible to them. They must give details of their personal history with such objects, or circumstantial detail about the situation that might explain why, in this particular instance, they feel angry or hateful. Only this sort of approach can win the empathy of a listener who is actively trying, best she can, to bracket her biases and foibles.

This brings us back to the final, serious worry. For, is it not possible that the awesome powers of poetry, prose, or cinema might weave such a poignant and delicate narrative, even of the most atrocious subject like racial hatred, such that, by story's end, the narrative could win a glimmer of impartial empathy and in turn claim objective sanction? Perhaps just the right story of some particular Nazi soldier, which skillfully detailed the gradual process and peculiar events by which this solider came to feel anti-Semitic hatred, could raise in others an imaginative hatred for Jews – even from an impartial perspective? This is an uncomfortable prospect. The question is, what can be said in reply that amounts to more than an *ad populum* appeal about the limitations of such a narrative?

My reply to this final bit of the first challenge about objectivity requires developing my answer to the second challenge about normative authority. This in turn requires a conceptual segue.

## 2.2    *A Segue: Emotional Agency*

Grant for a moment that appealing to impartial empathy answers the challenge about objectivity. Still, what entitles us to appeal to impartial empathy in the first place? Is there anything internal to my argument that motivates such a move? Yes. But the explanation may at first seem oblique.

All persons, I submit, are entitled to demand of one another respect for what I shall call their *emotional agency*. To say persons are emotional agents is to say that a fundamental aspect of how we conceptualize ourselves as agents requires reference to our essentially emotional point of view on the world, or what I call, our *affective perspective*. Let me elaborate.

We are rational agents, to be sure. And in virtue of our rational agency, or our autonomy, we are entitled to demand what is often called "recognition-respect" from others.[19] This is largely both an uncontroversial claim about personhood and an uncontroversial value claim. And in principle I endorse both claims: (i) Our rational autonomy underwrites a certain moral status, which we often speak of under the rubric of "dignity" or sometimes "humanity"; and (ii) we can demand recognition from one another precisely because we are creatures with dignity. However, my present point is that this rationalist conception of agency and its attendant notion of dignity don't go far enough. They are both conceptually impoverished because we are *also* emotional agents.

[19] See Darwall (1977).

By this I don't mean to signal only that agents *have* emotions. That would be banal. I'm arguing that affectivity – being emotional – is itself a fundamental aspect of what it is to be a human agent. More exactly, part of what it means to be a human agent is to have an essentially emotion-laden perspective. Moreover, I assume this perspective is peculiar. That is, individuals have unique affective perspectives. Reformulated, then, the claim is as follows: In order to recognize you fully for the individual agent you are requires recognizing your particular point of view, which point of view is in principle always partly emotional. To say otherwise is intuitively to miss something crucial about what it means to be *you*.

It follows that as persons we have both rational dignity *and* affective dignity. For, of course, if conceiving ourselves as emotional agents is fundamental to personhood, then we can add a value claim to the notion of emotional agency that parallels the one connected to rational agency. All persons, we can say, are (also) fundamentally valuable in virtue of their status as emotional agents. But to say this is essentially to say persons have "dignity" in virtue of their emotional agency, and, in turn, that all persons are entitled to some recognition-respect for this status?

Now, whatever else such respect requires, it would seem to require that we do not ignore the affective perspectives of other persons wholesale. In virtue of being creatures with affective dignity, persons can demand to be taken account of *as* emotional agents, which, in the light of the foregoing speculations, seems to mean that all persons can justifiably demand to have their affective perspectives taken account of by other persons. Taken all together, your being a person gives others a moral reason not simply to pay attention to your emotions but also to pay attention to your emotions from *your* point of view.

Here, then, is the crucial last move: to satisfy this particular kind of recognition respect just is to empathize with particular emotions – or at least, to try to empathize with those emotions. Consider: What else could it mean to genuinely take account of the emotions of others, and to take account of them from *their* point of view, but to try and simulate the situation they are in and as they understand that situation? But, of course, this is how I defined empathy in the paradigm narrative case. Thus, if what's at issue when it comes to respecting persons as emotional agents is taking account of their affective perspectives, then anything less than simulative empathy will make a claim to respect ring hollow.[20]

---

[20] At a minimum, given that empathy obviously has the capacity to satisfy a demand for individual, affective recognition, the burden of proof lies on anyone who would suggest an alternative means for such recognition.

So now consider what the hypothesis of affective dignity (speculative as it may be) yields for the discussion of impartiality. Given the assumption that our status as affective agents entails a special kind of status or dignity, and given an attending right to demand respect for this status, and given our own psychological capacity to empathize – given all this, we can now derive an *implicit* commitment to impartial empathy. For, how else could we possibly expect to meet, reliably, a general demand to respect the affective dignity of others unless we were willing to bracket our own biases and peculiarities and attempt to empathize as "anyone?" I can think of no way. And this works in both directions, that is, regardless of whether I'm assessing the emotions of another person or I'm the person being assessed. In order to reliably take up the affective perspectives of other people, we must, each of us, accept a constraint of impartiality.

## 2.4    *The Second Challenge: The Authority of Empathy*

What compels us, normatively, to take account of the empathic judgments that others make of us? It is the status they have as agents with affective dignity. Because empathic judgments originate from within an affective perspective, and because all persons have a legitimate demand to have that perspective recognized (for that is simply what affective dignity entails), then their empathic judgments inherit a demand to be taken account of – that is, by us, in our practical deliberation. Correspondingly, if we simply ignore this demand, we disrespect the affective dignity of our judges and in turn open ourselves to justified blame. This, in short, is the sense in which the affective dignity of persons "grounds" their empathic judgments, and, in turn, the sense in which those judgments can be said to carry "authority." Let me unpack this argument a bit.

First and foremost, the claim isn't that we are committed to endorsing every empathic judgment others make of us. Again, affective dignity grounds a demand for recognition-respect, namely, for a person's affective perspective. So, to satisfy this demand is to "take account," in our practical deliberation, other people's perspectives and the judgments they make from that perspective. Affective dignity thus demands that we *consider* the perspectives of others, and, in turn, their empathic judgments. It does not entail that those judgments are themselves moral, or correct, or conclusive, etc. This can be made clearer with a distinction between "unavoidability" and "trumpability." Many believe that morality (if it exists), issues reasons that *trump* other kinds of reasons, in the strong sense that they override those other reasons. But we don't need anything this strong to explain the authority of empathic judgment. Instead, we need something like, "unavoidablity." Consider: Whatever else dignity is, we think it is the sort of value that makes negligence of its presence distinctly blamable. So let us say that a judgment grounded on dignity is "authoritative" in the sense that it should not be *ignored* within practical deliberation. Thus, in the case of affective dignity, to say that affective perspective has authority is to say that it may not be ignored, even if it may be trumped (e.g., if particular judgments issuing from it can be trumped). Correspondingly, we can say that one makes a distinctive kind of moral mistake if she deliberatively ignores the affective dignity of others or the empathic judgments they make. So, although empathic judgments constitute only weak kind of reason-to-feel, they are grounded in an awesome authority. They may not be ignored, even if they are ultimately overridden.

I grant that the hypothesis of affective dignity raises new questions – more than I can address here. But two questions deserve quick mention before we turn back to the puzzle that put all this in motion, namely, empathy with nasty emotions.

First, what is the relation between the dignity we enjoy in virtue of our rationality (viz. a more classic Kantian conception of dignity) and that which we enjoy in virtue of our affective agency? Second, what is the scope of protection offered by affective dignity? In particular, do non-human animals have affective dignity? Non-human animals (or some of them anyway) undeniably feel emotions, even if those emotions differ in various ways from how humans experience them. Does this suffice to establish that such animals have affective perspectives and thus a kind of dignity?

Regarding the first question, I grant that there may be subtleties worth drawing out about the connection between rational and affective dignity. But for my purposes it is enough to note that there is no obvious tension. Just as affective dignity grounds the authority of claims to a distinctive kind of recognition, rational dignity is often taken to ground the authority of its own distinctive claim for recognition, namely, for a person's recognition as a rational agent. So the two standards look complementary. They fit together to give us a better, more complete understanding of what respect for persons involves.

Regarding the second question, I take it to be a feature rather than a bug that affective dignity plausibly includes non-human animals, and for that matter children and the mentally impaired. One long-standing worry about rationalist theories of dignity is that they draw prima facie lines around adult humans. Proponents of these theories have a variety of stock moves they can make to redraw these lines, but it is an advantage of my theory that it requires no contortion to get children and mentally impaired humans into the scope of dignity. True, for the same reason it invites in non-human animals. But then again, I share the pre-philosophical intuition that non-human animals do have dignity. Of course, this invites a question about how non-human claims to dignity are balanced against human ones. But in this regard, facts about the relative complexity, depth, and qualitative richness of human affectivity could quickly be appealed to. Moreover, humans can make a further appeal to rational dignity, which may not be open to non-human animals – though I hasten to add, this does not erase the import of acknowledging that humans aren't the only creatures with affective dignity. Perhaps non-human animals neither actually *judge* us nor actually *make* claims of us, but their affective dignity still requires that we not ignore their perspectives. Like us, their perspectives are unavoidable.

## 2.5    *Puzzles Solved*

Suppose you try to empathize with me but ultimately cannot. The emotion you feel after simulation does not match mine, even approximately. According to my argument, your emotion forms the basis of your (disapproving) judgment for how I feel. But now suppose that your emotion required as part of its cognitive structure a *denial* of my affective dignity. That is, suppose that part of the constitutive attitudes or beliefs that made it possible for you to feel as you do, involve either contempt for or outright rejection of *my* status as a being with affective perspective. In this case, your judgment loses its authority. Here is why:

The basis of authority for your judgment is your status as a being with affective agency: this is what normatively grounds a requirement that I heed your judgment. Or, what amounts to the same thing, your status as an affective agent is what grounds a requirement that I take into account your perspective, which perspective was the source of your emotion, which emotion in turn is the basis of your normative judgment. But this is just to say that in judging me empathically, you already *assume* the existence of something like affective dignity for yourself. That is, you assume *you* have a status that provides *me* with a sufficient reason to take into account *your* empathic judgments of *my* emotion. But if all this is correct, then you must in a sense contradict yourself if your emotion – which is the basis of your judgment – requires for its existence denying affective dignity to me. For, of course, the principle of affective dignity is perfectly general across persons with affective perspectives. Certainly, it can't be denied arbitrarily. You also cannot pretend that I do not have an affective perspective that is at least prima facie *like* yours. Otherwise, it would be nonsensical to address me with any empathic judgment in the first place. If you really *address* an empathic judgment to me, you assume that I have the requisite capacities to understand that judgment, namely, that I have an affective perspective and a capacity to empathize. And these capacities are precisely what qualify one as having affective dignity. The upshot is, I'm free to disregard your (contradictory) judgment of my emotion. Indeed, I have grounds for criticizing you.

We now have the means to give a definitive reason why, even if we could bring ourselves to empathize with something like a particular and vivid account of a Nazi's hatred of Jews, the normative import of our empathy is precluded. The Nazi's hatred is a paradigmatic candidate of an emotion that depends for its very existence on a denial of affective dignity to others (at least implicitly, though probably often explicitly). It is simply hard to imagine how else hatred for a race of people, to the point where one could indiscriminately torture and kill those people, could subsist without some kind of blanket assumption that those people are less than persons.[21] In particular, it seems the Nazi must assume that Jews needn't have their fears, sorrows, and sufferings taken account of. Consequently, we have grounds to judge the hatred the Nazi feels is *altogether* impermissible – truly outside the space of sanction. In virtue of its constitutive denial of affective dignity to others, that hatred loses its right to be recognized in the first place, regardless of what we might be brought to feel by some exquisite rhetorical manipulation.

But there is also this. I have leaned on intuition when it comes to the idea of affective dignity. However, the foregoing final argument for how a certain kind of contradiction might arise between the empathic judgments one makes and what one must take as a principle of authority for those very judgments, namely, the existence of one's own affective dignity, suggests something far-reaching: *any* empathic judgment assumes the principle of affective dignity. The implication is thus a constructivist argument for affective dignity itself. To address an empathic critique to another person is to implicitly commit oneself to a generalized *right* of recognition-respect for affective dignity. This final claim, though in need of further defense, suggests an internal self-sufficiency to the overarching thesis of this paper. At least, it suggests such self-sufficiency for us – we humans already caught

---

[21] Perhaps such driving hatred could be built on the premise that a particular race is one's mortal enemy, without any belief that these people are less than human or lacking affective dignity. However, in this case it is not clear the hatred is still morally problematic. Hating a person or group of persons because they are bent on one's destruction or the destruction of one's kin, culture, or nation seems a perfectly intelligible emotion. Of course, were such "enemy-hatred" true of any Nazis, the hatred would still be wrong because the beliefs underlying that hatred should or could be known to be false. That is, the hatred would be a case of "mistaken" emotion because the Jews were not *in fact* the Nazi's mortal enemy.

in a web of empathic judgment with one another. For us, empathy carries its authority with it.[22]

[22] I am grateful to the authors of this volume for their feedback during the manuscript work-shop at Holy Cross in 2014 and to Karsten R. Stueber for his comments on the penulti-mate draft. I am indebted to Stephan Blatti for invaluable comments on a very early draft of this essay, and to Stephen Darwall and David Velleman who helped me work out some of my foundational ideas about empathy, justification, and dignity many years ago. I'm also deeply grateful to the John Templeton Foundation, which provided me with research support.

# 10 Smithian Constructivism: Elucidating the Reality of the Normative Domain

*Karsten R. Stueber*

## 1 Introduction

The contemporary metaethical debate and the more general debate about normativity and normative reasons are certainly not for the philosophically faint-hearted. One can be easily overwhelmed by a plethora of finely tuned and meticulously articulated positions that are often distinguished in regard to only minute technical details. Within this context, constructivism has in the last few years gathered quite a bit of attention. It promises to transcend the established metaethical oppositions and to set us onto the right path of doing metaethics.[1] Yet many philosophers have been puzzled by these claims as they have a hard time discerning how exactly constructivism differs from more established realist or expressivist/antirealist positions. They have even raised doubts about whether constructivism is a genuine metaethical position rather than a first-order normative one.[2]

This essay will argue that there is something fundamentally right about conceiving of the metaethical project in a constructivist manner, particularly as articulated by Christine Korsgaard. I view constructivism as a position that attempts to account for the whole domain of normative discourse, rather than as a position that is more restricted and limited to issues of justice or morality like Rawls (1980) or Scanlon (1998). Nevertheless, it seems to be a constraint on such a general account of normativity that it also allows for the possibility of a normative perspective that issues categorical demands irrespective of the particular group one belongs to.

At the heart of the constructivist perspective lies the conviction that to make sense of the objectivity of normative discourse we have to grasp how such discourse can provide us with reasons for deliberation about how to act, reasons in light of which our action and deliberation can also be

---

[1] See Korsgaard, "Realism and Constructivism," in her 2008, particularly 324/5; especially the infamous ftnte 49.

[2] In this respect, see particularly Darwall, Gibbard, and Railton (1992: 137–144), Hussain and Shah (2006) and (2013). For a more sympathetic presentation of constructivism and its relation to expressivism consult especially Wallace (2012). See also Street (2010) for articulating the advantages of constructivism over expressivism and quasi-realism.

appropriately and objectively judged to be right or wrong, good or bad, rational or irrational. According to this view, to call stealing and killing wrong is not a judgment that addresses the other person merely from an external perspective by expressing a subjective disapproval of an action and by exerting pressure to make somebody conform to the behavior of the group. Rather it should be understood as expressing a judgment from a perspective that belongs intrinsically to the person to whom the judgment is addressed.[3] Constructivists generally tend to "solve" the philosophical task of accounting for such judgments by suggesting that it is best to conceive of the nature and objectivity of normative discourse as being in some sense dependent on what Street (2010) calls a "practical point of view," its underlying principles and logical structure. They differ, however, in how they understand these principles and structure.[4]

Pace Korsgaard, I will argue that Kant does not provide us with the best orientation for developing a plausible constructivist position. As I will show in the next section, Korsgaard's constructivism is from the very start undermined by a too narrow and too individualist conception of an agent's deliberative perspective. But rather than turning to Hume, as is common, I will suggest that constructivist aspirations are easier to fulfill if we take our lead from Adam Smith and his *Theory of Moral Sentiments.* As a moral sentimentalist, Smith provides us with an analysis of the practical domain of agents' deliberation that is psychologically and empirically plausible. Smith's starting point is indeed a contingent one. Yet, as we will see, Smith's manner of conceiving of the practical domain has not only the advantage of being plausible from the third-person scientific perspective. It also resonates with the first-person deliberative perspective to which normative propositions are addressed, since he links our ability of making normative judgments to our empathic capacity of imaginatively reenacting another person's perspective, his or her thoughts, emotions and feelings. Most importantly, we should follow Smith and conceive of the impartial spectator perspective and the principle of impartiality as quasi-a-priori commitments of our folk psychological practice of making sense of each other's actions through empathic perspective taking. It is in terms of

---

[3] See in this respect also Darwall (2006a). A discussion of Darwall's second-person perspective has to wait for another occasion. Ultimately, however, I am not fully sure how Darwall meets, what I will call, the naturalism constraint.

[4] For a good discussion of the various manners of formulating the constructivist position, see Ridge (2012) and particularly Street (2008, 2010, 2012). Constructivism about reasons in its Kantian form is generally understood as asserting that the reality of normative reasons is a constructed one, they are seen as the "outcome of a suitable procedure" of deliberation, decision making, agreement reaching, and so on, a procedure with the help of which we solve normative problems. For an overview of the broad range of contemporary constructivism see also the anthologies by Bagnoli (2013), and Lenman and Shemmer (2012).

such commitments that we can also explicate the intersubjective validity and objectivity of normative reasons, especially of moral ones.[5]

## 2     Evaluating the Promise of Korsgaardian Constructivism

Let me start my brief exploration of Korsgaard by focusing on her conception of the constraints that any plausible account of normativity has to satisfy, a conception that I largely share. In the *Sources of Normativity*, she argues that normative questions arise essentially within the first-person deliberative perspective. Similar to Frankfurt, for Korsgaard agency involves the ability to distance oneself from the situation one faces – including one's own psychological drives and states – and ask how one should best respond to it. In this manner one is no longer merely driven by one's desires but rather chooses to act on some of them because one reflectively approves of them. Acting for a reason, as Korsgaard explains most fully in her later work (Korsgaard 2008 and 2009), is always an activity that is an act of self-constitution in that it purports to unify an agent within a certain normative outlook toward the world. Accordingly, normative concepts or normative facts can be understood only as answers to our normative problems that arise within our first-person deliberative perspective. Only in this manner can we also account for the objectivity of our normative discourse in a "normatively adequate" manner.

Yet a plausible account of normativity has also to be "explanatorily adequate" from the third person scientific perspective (Korsgaard 1996a: 13), that is, it has to be judged to be compatible with the philosophical framework of naturalism.[6] From within that perspective, the reality of the normative and moral domain is however anything but assured, since from the perspective of the explanatory sciences one could argue that the world does not contain any normative reasons that have the authority to demand something from me. Correspondingly, accepting naturalism as a constraint for any account of normativity seems to provide positions of radical moral

---

[5] This is also the reason why I turn to Smith rather than Hume. Moral sentimentalists, who are inspired by Hume such as Slote or Prinz, have to conceive of the normative force of moral claims in analogy to peer pressure. See Stueber (2015) in this regard. Sharon Street develops a Humean version of constructivism, according to which the truth of a normative claim is grounded "within the practical point of view, where the practical point of view is given a formal characterization" (2010). In contrast to sentimentalists who emphasize emotions and empathy, Street takes the attitudes of valuing or subjective normative judgments as her starting point. Here is not the place to engage in an extensive discussion of Street's view. In the end I fail to see how Street can explicate the intersubjective normative nature of our normative and moral judgments. In this respect, I agree with Ridge (2012) that Street's view is a "sophisticated version of subjectivism."

[6] For the purpose of this essay, I assume without much argument that a reductive and naturalistic account of normativity and morality is implausible. For various ways of thinking about the framework of naturalism, see particularly De Caro and Macarthur (2010).

and normative skepticism as espoused by Mandeville or Nietzsche with a credible argumentative basis. Korsgaard attempts to circumvent this problem and satisfy the normativity and the naturalism constraints by providing a psychology of moral agency that is compatible with what the sciences tell us but that resonates also with the first-person deliberative perspective. In this manner, Korsgaard hopes to establish the normative authority of reasons even against the doubts of the normative skeptic by forcing him or her to acquiesce to their demands. As it is well known, Korsgaard opts for a Kantian framework because she regards his "ethics of autonomy" as the "only one consistent with the metaphysics of the modern world" (Korsgaard 1996a: 5).[7] Kant allows us to see that reason in its practical form is structured in a manner so that the normative authority and thus the reality of normative reasons can be grasped in light of procedures and principles to which practical reason or agents acting for reasons are constitutively committed. As Korsgaard argues, showing that a principle is constitutive "for an inescapable activity" is showing it to be "unconditionally binding" for the agent (2009: 32).

I have great sympathies for Korsgaard's constructivist project. At the same time, I am, like many others, doubtful that one can account for the authority of normative reasons in a Kantian manner relying mainly on formal principles of practical reasoning. In Korsgaard's rendering, Kant's categorical imperative is grounded in the conceptual truth that acting for a reason commits agents to think that they also have a reason to act in that manner in other circumstances that are sufficiently similar. Hence particularistic willing, as Korsgaard calls it (Korsgaard 2009: 75/76), is not a conceptual option for a rational agent. Yet the prohibition against particularistic willing could hardly explicate the normative authority of more substantial moral reasons, since it is perfectly compatible with the egoistic principle that one always should act in order to satisfy one's strongest felt desire. Korsgaard is quite aware of this line of reasoning and appeals to practical but contingent identities of individual agents as parents, citizens, lovers, friends, and so on in order to further restrict the range of maxims to be universalized. Most importantly, for Korsgaard, in acting for a reason and being committed to a contingent practical identity, we are also implicitly committed to valuing our humanity as the ultimate and inescapable identity that in some sense "stands behind our more particular identities" (Korsgaard 1996a: 121). The intersubjective authority of substantive normative reasons is hence to be explicated in light of the principle of

---

[7] Whether or not Kant himself does address the moral skeptic in the manner proposed by Korsgaard is however a topic of contention (see Stern 2013). As has become much clearer in Korsgaard's recent work (2009), her use of Kant intended to satisfy the above constraints also mirrors a much more ancient source, that is, it mirrors the philosophical and dialogical procedure as it is exemplified in Platonic dialogues, particularly the *Republic.*

generalization and our inevitable and undeniable commitment to our identity as a human being, or so Korsgaard would like us to believe.

Korsgaard's argumentative strategy has been extensively discussed in the literature. I share many of the reservations expressed in this context (see among others Cohen 1996; Enoch 2006; Hussain and Shah 2006 and 2013; and Ferrero 2009, Darwall 2006b, Street 2012). It is, for instance, questionable whether pointing to the inevitability of our identity as human beings reveals humanity as a value to which we are *normatively* committed, unless one is willing to leave the framework of metaethical constructivism and conceives of such a value in a realistic manner. For my purposes more important, however, is another related question. So far the acknowledgment of our humanity has proceeded squarely from within the deliberative first-person perspective. Moreover, acknowledging our humanity only means to acknowledge ourselves as human agents acting for reasons (see also Street 2012). I regard it as rather questionable that one can ground the objectivity and intersubjectivity of our normative discourse on such a thin basis in a manner that also explains the existence of moral obligations expressing categorical demands on me and other persons. More specifically, it needs to be explained why acknowledging my own humanity from the first-person perspective implies anything for how I have to treat other agents. Even if I were to disavow solipsism and agree that other rational agents acting for reasons exist, the argument so far has not shown, for example, that I am forbidden to treat them merely as means for the satisfaction of my needs.

To her credit, Korsgaard is quite aware of the limited nature of her argumentative strategy so far. Her ultimate pitch for her constructivist position consists in her argument for what she calls the "publicity of reason," an argument that attempts to show that in acknowledging myself as an agent acting for a reason

I must treat your reasons... as *reasons*, that is, considerations that have normative force for *me* as well as you, and therefore as public reasons. And to the extent that I must do that, I must also treat you as what Kant called an end in itself – as a source of reasons, as someone whose will is legislative for me. (Korsgaard 2009: 192)

In the *Sources of Normativity*, Korsgaard relies in her argument for the publicity of reason heavily on Wittgensteinian considerations about the impossibility of a private language (cf. also Gert 2002).[8] Yet, one has to be rather careful in distinguishing between the epistemic and normative

---

[8] See Korsgaard (1996a: 136ff). While it is true that Korsgaard does not explicitly refer to Wittgenstein's private language argument in her later work, she also does not seem to fully abandon it. She rather claims her earlier use of Wittgenstein has been misunderstood. See Korsgaard (2009: 196, ftnte 12). For my take on Wittgenstein's private language argument, see Stueber (1994).

aspects of the publicity of reasons. Wittgensteinian considerations at most allow us to say that the reasons for which agents act have to be somehow epistemically accessible to other persons. These considerations do not automatically imply that I have to recognize them as reasons, which put a normative demand on me. In order to argue that the epistemic notion of the publicity of reasons essentially includes a normative aspect, Korsgaard analyzes the conversation between a student and a professor trying to find a suitable meeting time. At the time that her professor originally suggests, however, the student has another class. In this case, Korsgaard rightly suggests that the student's subjective reason for not meeting also provides the professor with a reason for meeting at another time. Nevertheless, it is not clear that we can draw any general conclusions from this case. Assume, for instance, that the professor does not think very highly of his or her colleague, with whom the student takes the class. Indeed he or she thinks that it would be more beneficial for the student to skip the class and meet with him or her. In that case the student's reasons for not meeting would not automatically be reasons for the professor. The student's subjective reasons are normatively compelling for the professor only if the student and professor interact in a realm of shared norms of behavior. Regardless of what one thinks of one's colleagues, we all agree that students should not meet with another professor during class times. The fact that a student's reasons normatively oblige me can be understood only in light of the fact that other reasons and norms are already public and make demands on me. The example thus presupposes what it intends to prove, namely, the publicity of reason. Even if one would grant Korsgaard that she has shown that our identity as a human person and as an agent acting for a reason is in some sense inescapable, she is still unable to account for the objectivity and intersubjective authority of normative reasons on this basis. It is exactly in this respect that turning to Adam Smith will be particularly helpful, even if Smith did not approach the problem of normativity within the conceptual framework of contemporary metaethics.[9]

---

[9] In turning to Smith, I also disagree with Scanlon, who argues for a realist conception of reasons and claims that the normative authority of reasons cannot be explicated. For Scanlon, the reality of reasons and the fact that we are "in their grip" have to be accepted as unanalyzable features of the intersubjectively valid domain of the discourse of reason within which rational agency happens to take place (Scanlon 2014: 98). Yet Scanlon acknowledges that the notion of an objective normative reason has its home primarily within the first person deliberative perspective where one asks oneself "What reasons do I have?" (14). But if this is so, Scanlon fails to explain how it is that reason talk from the first person perspective has any intersubjective validity for other rational agents. Why is what I regard as a reason is also a reason that another person owns? Like Korsgaard, Scanlon fails to account for the publicity of reason. He seems to suggest that he can avoid addressing this question by maintaining the existence of rational agency as a perfectly natural phenomenon (22, 54–60). Without further explicating the structure of rational agency and without further situating such agency within the natural world, Scanlon is however begging an important question.

### 3     Smith's Mental Geography of Reasons: Empathy and the Impartial Spectator

Smith accounts for the normative realm by squarely situating it within the domain of social interaction, which is constituted by the human longing for mutual recognition, understanding, and approval of each other based on our ability of imaginative perspective taking.[10] Accordingly, I take Smith to suggest anchoring the normative realm in the explanatorily autonomous domain of folk psychology within which we make sense of other people in terms of their mental states and considerations that speak for their action. It is a practice that I understand, like Smith, to depend centrally on our ability to simulate and recreate another person's state of mind. In this manner I also intend to satisfy the naturalism constraint of the metaethical project as conceived of in this article. That folk psychology constitutes an explanatory autonomous domain, within which empathic perspective taking (what Smith refers to as sympathy) is indeed epistemically central, is a claim for which I have argued more extensively elsewhere (see especially Stueber 2006, 2008, and 2013). In this essay, I take it for granted.

More important for our purposes, we have to understand why Smith thinks – or better how we should think with Smith – that our ability of empathic perspective taking, grounds the normative domain. For Smith, empathy is not only a means of knowing other minds (see Stueber 2006) but it is also the primary psychological mechanism enabling us to judge the normative quality of another person's action according to what he calls its propriety and merit. In judging an action to be proper we judge it according to the "suitableness or unsuitableness" which the inner sentiment that moved the agent "seems to bear to the cause or object which excites it." In judging an action to have merit, however, we judge it according to its "beneficial and hurtful nature," that is, its consequences judged in terms of whether or not the feeling of gratitude or resentment by an affected person toward the agent is appropriate and proper (Smith 1759/1982 I.i.3.7 and II.i–iii). Significantly, empathy as imaginative perspective taking is not solely oriented toward the inner mental realm of the other person or his bodily expression of this inner mental realm, rather it is oriented toward his situation. In

---

[10] Here I am not concerned with defending the textual and historical adequacy of my take on Smith, even though I think of it as providing a coherent interpretation of the *Theory of Moral Sentiments*. Rather I am primarily interested in articulating a specific Smithian perspective that speaks to the contemporary constellation of philosophical problems. Within this context, my understanding of Smith's moral philosophy has profited first and foremost from Griswold (1998). In addition, besides Fleischacker (1999), it has benefitted from Debes (2012a), Forman-Barzilai (2001) and (2010), Griswold (2001), Harman (2000), and Sayre-McCord (2010) and (2013). For an excellent and historically astute survey of the sentimentalist tradition in moral and political theory, consult also Frazer (2010).

empathizing with another person, we try to reenact his sentiments in light of the relevant aspects of the situation that the agent faces. In general, Smith suggests that we approve of the sentiments, thoughts, and actions of other agents in terms of propriety and merit if empathy/sympathy (conceived of as imaginative perspective taking) allows us to bring the agent's sentiments and thoughts *home to ourselves*.

Smith puts a particular sentimentalist spin on this insight in regard to judgments of the propriety of another person's actions and sentiments. Not only do we have to be "affected in the same manner as he is" but "we must [also] perceive this harmony and correspondence of sentiments between him and ourselves" (Ibid. II.i5.11). In addition, the perception of such harmony is supposedly tied to an "agreeable and delightful emotion" and it is this emotion "in which the sentiment of approbation properly consists" (Ibid. I.iii.1.9n). Unfortunately, not only is such an emotional conception of approbation psychologically implausible, it also does not allow us to account for the intersubjective validity of any of our normative judgments, particularly the categorical nature of our moral verdicts. First of all, as already questioned by Hume, it does not seem to be the case that in noticing agreement between our sentiments when taking the perspective of another person, we always take pleasure in such correspondence. Think about the other person as somebody whom we utterly dislike (or think about a rather distasteful joke told by another that we somehow find funny in our imagination). More importantly, any approval understood as the expression of such subjective enjoyment carries no normative force, that is, it cannot be viewed as the expression of a normative obligation that the other person has to take seriously. We all probably like to be liked (most of all by our friends), but that does not seem to be the foundation of a normative perspective from which we also make categorical moral commands leaving behind the framework of personal relations where we distinguish between friend and foe.[11]

More significant for our purposes, Smith does not tie the judgment of merit directly to an enjoyable emotion caused by the observation of a congruence of sentiments. Judging the merit of an action is a more complex process. It requires us to take the perspective of the agent in order to grasp his or her intentions for acting. It also involves putting ourselves in the shoes of the affected subject in order to determine whether we would feel any gratitude or resentment toward that agent in light of our empathic

---

[11] Notice also that Smith does not escape the diagnosed conundrum merely by pointing to the perspective and reactions of the impartial spectator. It still would need to be explained why anybody should be normatively obliged even by that person's enjoyment in observing a congruence of sentiments.

appreciation of his or her intentions (Ibid. II.i.5.1). We can, however, judge an action to be meritorious regardless of whether the affected subject himself feels any gratitude since we might differ in our empathic evaluation of the intentions of the agent. This could occur, for example, if we think of the agent as altruistically motivated while the affected subject regards him as a selfish jerk. For that reason, Smith explicitly says that for the judgment of merit "no actual correspondence of sentiments, therefore, is here required." (Ibid. II.i.5.11).

In light of those passages, Smith's account of the psychological mechanisms underlying our judgment of merit is best understood as describing the manner in which we grasp the intentions of the agent as considerations that speak for feeling gratitude from the perspective of the affected subject. It allows us to grasp his or her subjective reasons for gratitude. Indeed, regardless of whether it corresponds neatly to everything that Smith says, I would suggest that in order to develop a position of Smithian constructivism it is best to consider empathy as being primarily concerned with a form of imaginative perspective taking that allows us to grasp aspects of another person's situation as his subjective reasons for acting. Such empathy constitutes what I have referred to as reenactive empathy in my earlier work (Stueber 2006). Even in judging the propriety of an action or a sentiment, we approve of an action not because we enjoy the observation of correspondence between sentiments. Rather in reenacting his thoughts and sentiments the other person's actions become intelligible to me since his thoughts are grasped in this manner as his reasons for acting, as reasons for which I also might have acted in his situation. Accordingly, understanding the Smithian contribution to the metaethical project means grasping the normative relevance of our ability to pick up on an agent's subjective reasons through our ability of reenactive empathy. Most significantly, since Smith analyzes the normative relevance in this way, it implies understanding how a practice of reenactment also commits us to an impartial spectator perspective.

For that purpose, we should remind ourselves of the Smithian starting point for the philosophical explication of normativity. Smith implicitly acknowledges a widely shared conception of rational and self-reflective agency according to which agents are persons who are able to say something in favor of their actions and who can situate their actions vis-à-vis their environment in light of considerations that from their perspective speak for them. As a sentimentalist, Smith is however not interested in making any claims regarding the constitutive features or constitutive aims of agency as is common among authors influenced by a more Kantian perspective (see also Velleman 2009). Instead, for him it is sufficient to take certain features of human agency to be empirically contingent but standard features of human nature. Sentimentalists in general do not see the need for a transcendental argument establishing that those features of our agency are inescapable and therefore somehow normatively obligatory.[12] Even if we think of the moral skeptic as one of the main interlocutors for the metaethical project, it is a mistake to conceive of such a skeptic as a psychopath rather than as somebody who shares the standard human abilities to relate to other people. There is no transcendental cure for psychopathy.

Because of his empirical orientation, Smith also conceives of agency and the intelligibility of agency from the very start as a social phenomenon. Like Hume, he recognizes that "the minds of men are mirrors to one another" (Hume 1739–1740/2000: 2.2.5.21; SBN 365) in that we are able to resonate on different levels of cognitive complexity with the sentiment of others. Yet we also serve as mirrors through our emotional reactions toward others and thereby provide them with some orientation regarding the social appropriateness of their actions and sentiments; a fact that contemporary research on social referencing has amply demonstrated. Already infants make sense of their surroundings and their place within it in light of the emotional reaction of others, particularly their caretakers. Lack of any emotional reaction on part of their caretaker seems to increase anxiety on part of the infant, indicating a loss of a source of orientation (see Thompson 2006: 33ff.).It is thus in a social context that we humans experience each other as being like-minded in resonating with each other's happiness and sorrow. We also pick up on social expectations and norms in light of other people's reactions toward our actions and mature as rational and reflective agents who make sense of our own and other's agency in terms of reasons for acting.

---

[12] In this manner, one also avoids the agency/shmagency debate that has recently plagued the discussion of constructivism. See Enoch (2006, 2010), and Velleman (2009: 136–144). My account developed here has very much benefitted from reading Velleman's work. Yet in his "Kinda Kantian strategy" (2009: 149), Velleman also conceives of practical reasoning in too individualistic a manner and regards a common social form as developing merely because of the rational "pressure towards generality" (151). Moreover, he seems to align himself with a theory–theory conception of folk psychology according to which "I don't share your egocentric perspective" but only "a third-personal perspective from which you are a creature … to be understood in folk-psychological terms" (2009: 60). In his 2013, however, Velleman focuses more on the "drive towards sociality" (58) that he sees grounded in human nature. Unfortunately, Velleman still overlooks the important role that empathy plays in constituting the social realm. More significantly, he does not sufficiently take into account that interpretation and empathic reenactment is possible (even if difficult) across the boundaries of different communities. It is exactly in this context that I suggest we locate the possibility and ideal of a moral and impartial stance that is not bound by the particularities of a community, rather than in our very limited propensity for love and friendship (2013: 71ff).

Philosophers influenced by the sentimentalist tradition have therefore appropriately emphasized the importance of reactive attitudes in the moral context. But Smith is absolutely right to think that empathy has to be seen as the central psychological mechanism in the social context. Empathy in its basic form allows us to notice the emotions expressed by others and it enables us in its cognitively more advanced form to understand and reenact the reasons for which another person acted or for which he felt a certain way.[13] Moreover, in experiencing others in that manner we experience them as being like-minded, as creatures that have similar sentiments and that act on the basis of those sentiments as reasons for acting. A fortiori, within a social context we view ourselves and our reasons for acting as something that another like-minded person could potentially reenact and could, at least in his or her imagination, regard as reasons for acting. In that sense the intelligibility of our actions (which is central for our self-conceptions as agents) is not merely a subjective or solipsistic notion. It is an intersubjective one since the very intelligibility of our actions can be mirrored in other minds. Those expectations about the intersubjective and mutual accessibility of our considerations for actions are confirmed when we are able to recognize the other as acting for reasons that we would have acted on. They are disappointed when mutual understanding breaks down.

Accordingly, an interpreter's puzzlement due to the inability to reenact another person's sentiments and reasons that might be expressed in the form "I just don't get you. Why did you do it?" potentially challenges the intelligibility of that person by suggesting that there is no reason for him (even from his subjective point of view) to take ownership of his actions. This challenge is particularly severe in everyday situations – situations that do not require particular theoretical or technical sophistication – where we normally experience the other person as like-minded. Particularly in those ordinary situations, such judgments challenge the foundation of a person's agency in that they seem to deny the fundamental fact of like-mindedness that has been the basis of my social interaction and experience so far. Accordingly, it seems that they constitute what I would call a very low-grade normative judgment, a judgment that I have reasons to care about because if such judgments would proliferate throughout a society they would constitute an effective expulsion from the domain where my agency can thrive.

But it is not only the judged subject that has an interest in addressing the inability of the interpreter to reenact him or her. From the

---

[13] For an elaboration of the distinction between basic and reenactive empathy, see Stueber (2006, chap. 5) and (2012). Smith himself does not distinguish between both forms of empathy.

interpreter's perspective, the inability to reenact another person's reasons constitutes an explanatory problem that he or she would like to address. Notice however, in order for such explanatory problems to occur we presuppose that the interpreter has also experienced the subject as being otherwise in some sense like-minded and has also succeeded in interpreting him to some extent.[14] In these situations, very often the explanation of why an interpreter fails to reenact the other person's considerations as that person's reasons has to do with the fact that the interpreter was subjectively biased in that he projected all of his beliefs, desires, and values onto the other person. He was engaged in what psychologists refer to as "self-oriented perspective taking," and imagined only how he would feel in the other person's position. Quite often then an interpreter will be able to reenact another person's considerations for acting and understand them as his reasons by taking into account the relevant differences between him and the other person, and engage in what psychologists refer to as "other-oriented perspective taking." Here I do not want to dwell on the difficulties involved in this project particularly in cases of great cultural differences (see Stueber 2006, chap. 6 and 2011). For my purposes it is sufficient to note that I will be able to reenact your reasons successfully if I am able to locate the differences in our psychological attitudes, imaginatively take up the attitudes that I do not share with you, and quarantine the attitudes that you do not share with me while simulating your thoughts and deliberating about the situation that you encounter from your perspective.

When Smith talks about perspective taking in his *Theory of Moral Sentiment*, he tends to obscure the difference between self-oriented and other-oriented perspective taking. Yet he does so with a purpose. In emphasizing the affirmative and evaluative character of empathy/sympathy, Smith underscores the fact that we have to bring the other person's case home to ourselves. On the other hand he also wants to allow for individual or cultural differences and does not want to conceive of moral evaluation as an expression of self-love.[15] Yet other-oriented perspective taking does not bring another person's sentiments sufficiently home to ourselves so that we could wholeheartedly agree with another person's reasons for acting. I have only taken up the other person's perspective in the imagination. From

---

[14] In this respect I tend to agree with Davidson that concrete disagreement presupposes some areas of agreement. See also Stueber (2006, chap.2). Equally important, as I have argued elsewhere, making sense of each other in terms of reasons for acting and with the help of our folk psychological repertoire presupposes that we experience each other as having the capacity for skillful goal-directed bodily movement and as expressing emotions. I view this ability as a developmentally early capacity that I refer to as basic empathy. See Stueber (2013).

[15] See particularly Smith (1759/1982: VII.iii.1.4).

within that imaginative stance I understand why the other person would approve of his actions, but not necessarily why I should also approve of it from the perspective that I actually occupy. In this manner, Smith has at most accounted for what one might call the epistemic publicity of subjective reasons for acting. He has however not shown how such reasons can be understood as reasons that have any normative authority over me. Moreover, it would still need to be explained why approving of another person's actions from my own subjective perspective has anything to do with a moral approval that expresses a normative and categorical demand for the other agent. So far then Smith's account seem to face the same problem as Korsgaard's more Kantian-oriented constructivist position.

Smith attempts to "solve" this conundrum by appealing to the perspective of the impartial spectator. Moral judgments for him are judgments constituted by the ability of the impartial spectator to reenact another person's sentiments and reasons for acting. The most immediate question in this context, however, is not how exactly Smith describes the impartial perspective. The more urgent question has to be why he thinks that an approval from such a third perspective (not mine or yours) possesses any normative force, that is, why empathizing from the impartial perspective should provide us with normative reasons for the evaluation of our actions. Smith's distinction between a desire for praise and a desire for praiseworthiness, the latter being supposedly satisfied by approval from the impartial spectator perspective, is rather unhelpful in this context (Smith 1759/1982: III.2.1). Pointing to different desires does not address the question of why we ought to satisfy one rather than the other desire.

In understanding the normative relevance of the impartial spectator perspective it is better to follow Smith's suggestion of thinking about the impartial spectator perspective as the "highest tribunal of appeal."[16] In reenacting another person's subjective reasons for acting through other-oriented perspective taking, I do not necessarily recognize his reasons as reasons that I would have in his situation. Nevertheless, I recognize them as reasons that I could have were I to adopt all of his background beliefs, values, and commitments that are different from mine. As a result, his reenacted thoughts have a status similar to my considerations when I hypothetically reflect on various courses of actions. I might, for example, consider what would be the best car to buy based on various principles and past experiences in light of which I entertain considerations that speak for one

---

[16] While the exact term does not appear in Smith, it corresponds to one strand of his thinking about the impartial spectator perspective in the context of which he does speak of appeals and tribunals. See particularly Smith (1759/1982), draft variants included by the editors in III.2, p. 128.

car rather than another. Based on past driving experiences I might choose car x, considerations about fuel efficiency might favor car y, while attention to reliability might speak for buying car z. Ultimately, I have to settle on one option in coming to an all things considered judgment by "weighing" these various considerations against each other. Another person's reasons, which I grasp in a reenactive mode, are in principle reasons or considerations that can engage me in the same manner as a critical reasoner. Such reenactment potentially raises the question of whether the attitudes that I quarantined in the reenactment (a quarantine that allowed me to grasp the other person's thoughts as reasons) need to be reconsidered and should be given up, a question that requires a rational response. Insofar as I am in this case negotiating among considerations of at least two different persons, the perspective within which those reasons (mine and the other person's) are evaluated against each other has to be regarded as more than my own or the other person's subjective perspective (Smith 1759/1982: III.3.3). It has to be regarded as a perspective that is impartial in this respect, since it is a perspective within which both of us struggle to get our reasons for acting corroborated as being intersubjectively valid for both of us. In "surviving" such evaluations, subjective considerations are revealed also as objectively valid reasons for acting.

Smith tends to be rather sparse in his analysis of the characteristics of an impartial spectator. He certainly emphasizes that the impartial spectator perspective is a perspective that looks at agency from a distance and corrects for the merely momentary and overly selfish concerns of agents involved in the "heat of the action." As has also been noted by Smith's interpreters, the impartial spectator perspective is not a perspective in which we are omniscient about all of the consequences of an action or in which we are stripped of our normal emotional attunement toward the world and are without the human capacity for love, friendship, and so on. Even for an impartial spectator it is only in light of such emotional attunement to the world and each other that certain considerations speak for our actions.

In addition, Smith is aware of the fact that it is rather difficult for human beings to adopt an impartial perspective and that it is undermined by a variety of corrupting factors. The question of whether impartiality has been realized in a particular judgment can always be challenged in light of the presence of morally irrelevant factors that have been shown to have a corrupting influence on our judgment. In order to adopt an impartial perspective, human beings with fallible and limited cognitive capacities have to become aware of such corrupting influences. Reflection on the nature of the impartial perspective and how various factors influence or corrupt our moral sentiments has to be seen as being an integral part of the impartial spectator perspective itself. And it is exactly in this respect that research from empirical psychology might be helpful. It is particularly important in allowing us to become aware of our biases and natural "laziness" in utilizing our empathic reenactive capacities, most prominently among them the so-called here and now biases according to which we empathize with others more easily if we perceive them to be similar or near to us in a variety of dimensions. Such insights might allow us, to give a contemporary example, to evaluate more appropriately the merit or demerit of a police officer's actions and his defense that shooting another person was a justified course of action.

If my reconstruction of our commitment to the impartial spectator perspective is plausible, that perspective has to be seen as the dimension within which attention is paid to a potentially infinite number of agents from a vast array of cultural backgrounds who like me act for reasons and whose reasons for acting I attempt to reenact in order to find their behavior intelligible. In that sense, Smithian impartiality is, as Amartya Sen calls it, an open form of impartiality that does not limit itself to members of a particular group (Sen 2002). The commitment to impartiality is characterized by the recognition "that we are but one of the multitude, in no respect better than any other in it" (Smith 1759/1982: III.3.4), since in reenacting other persons' sentiments I recognize them as persons like myself attuned to the world and others and who in light of their attunement have reasons for acting. In reenacting their reasons, I thus speak on their behalf and attend to them as persons whose reasons have to be given attention by the impartial spectator in the same manner that my own reasons and considerations have to be given attention. Being impartial then first and foremost requires me to make sure that I have indeed been sufficiently open and attentive to another person's perspective and have taken sufficient care in my attempt to reenact it.

In some sense however the debate in the contemporary Smith literature about how concretely we should conceive of the impartial spectator perspective and whether or not it is possible to ever fully adopt such a perspective is one-sided (see Forman-Barzilai 2001 and Griswold 2001). It assumes that the impartial spectator perspective constitutes only the stance that we need to adopt so that our judgments of propriety and merit have proper normative and moral force. Smith himself (and the manner in which contemporary sentimentalists generally think about the moral appropriateness or fittingness of our reactive attitudes) has certainly encouraged this debate. One however should distinguish between the question of whether or not we are able to fully adopt the perspective of an impartial spectator and the question of why we are committed to the standard of impartiality in the first place.[17] Within the context of agents who act for reasons and who grasp and negotiate each other's reasons through reenactive empathy impartiality is indeed a quasi-a-priori commitment. If that is so, then impartiality has also to be conceived of as the fundamental standard to which we can directly appeal in arguing for the validity of certain normative expectations.[18] Yet this later point has in my opinion not garnered sufficient consideration in the Smith literature (see, however, Sayre-McCord 2010, Debes 2012a, and this volume). Paying more attention to it opens up paths of thinking about the moral domain that have been less traveled within the context of sentimentalism. It allows us also to distinguish between two ways of justifying normative claims. On the one hand, we can justify them by pointing to the reactions of a supposedly impartial spectator. So far this manner of justification has been regarded to be the only one within the context of moral sentimentalism. Yet I would suggest that normative claims and standards can similarly be justified because the idea of impartiality as the dimension within which different subjective points of views are negotiated commits us also to certain kinds of behavior. It commits us to norms of behavior acknowledging that we are but one among a multitude of "like-minded" agents acting for reasons. Accordingly, the norm against killing is justified because killing is a denial of my access to the very dimension in which my reasons for acting can get their proper (even if not necessarily affirmative) hearing. More concretely, the civil rights and women rights movements are best understood as reactions to a perceived inconsistency between our ordinary practices of interacting with each other and our implicit commitment to the norm of impartiality.[19] Both movements have argued for a recognition of the status of women and

[17] Utilitarianists also claim to be committed to impartiality. Yet within the consequentialist literature it is not always clear why we should be committed to such a standard. It speaks for Smith that he has an answer to such foundational question.

[18] This is not to deny that even within the Kantian framework, philosophers have started to pay more attention to the role of emotions as constitutive aspects of moral agency. In her interesting "Emotions and the Categorical Authority of Moral Reason" (in Bagnoli 2011), Bagnoli emphasizes the role of respect. Prima facie, however, it is difficult to see how one can meet the naturalism constraint in this manner. Respect presupposes the objective validity of norms and values and is thus a normatively soaked feeling in contrast to our natural capacity for empathy.

[19] Compare also Robert Kane (2010), who conceives of moral norms as the framework that allows us to discuss the question of a good life with a sufficiently open mind appropriate for the conditions of modernity. Kane, however, conceives of the decision to engage in such discussion about the good life as a personal choice, while I view it as emerging from within our empathic engagement with each other that forms the basis of human sociality among agents acting for reasons. Moreover, I do not see such engagement as limited to a discussion about the good life. My Smithian constructivism echoes also themes in Habermas's discourse ethics. An exploration of this echo will have to await another publication.

African-Americans that fully acknowledges their existence as agents acting for reasons whose reasoning we are more than willing to reenact in our everyday encounter. All of this does certainly not deny that killing and so on is also behavior that is emotionally horrifying from the impartial spectator perspective and that such emotional reaction strengthens the case for the norm against killing. Yet the important point to make here is that sentimentalism has also the resources to think of the justification of certain norms by addressing the question of how our behavior in general respects the standard of impartiality we are committed to in our intersubjective practice of empathic reenactment.[20]

Let me conclude the paper with a metaphysical note on the underlying ontology of normativity associated with the view I'm proposing, a view that I refer to as Smithian constructivism. It would be a mistake to characterize my constructivism as claiming that normative and moral reasons are in some sense constructed facts as Korsgaard has claimed. As others have pointed out (see particularly Enoch 2009), if we understand reasons to possess a "constructed reality" (Korsgaard 2008: 324), we undermine rather than explicate their normative authority. From the first-person perspective, it is hard to reconcile the claim that I have an objective reason for doing x with the admission that it is only a reflection of the structure of my subjectivity, even if that structure is inescapable. Instead, I refer to my position as a position of Smithian constructivism because it allows us to address the metaethical project as originally conceived of by Korsgaard. It provides us with an account of the normative domain that meets both the normativity and naturalism constraint without having to postulate irreducible normative facts in addition to ordinary scientific facts. To use a "theological" device common in the philosophy of mind and analytic metaphysics, after creating all the facts (to be studied by the physical sciences and so on) and creating among those facts human beings who engage with each other in the empathic and reenactive manner described above, God did not need to sprinkle the world with additional normative or moral facts as robust

---

[20] The above example illustrates another difference between my Smithian and Korsgaard's Kantian constructivism. Behaving immorally, for Korsgaard, violates constitutive principles of rational agency. Immoral agency for Korsgaard is thus agency "falling apart" or agents "losing their identity" (Korsgaard 2009: 180 and 1996a: 102). From my perspective immoral agents do not live up to the commitment of impartiality implicit in our explanatory folk psychological practice. As I see it, the question of whether or not we should adopt that explanatory stance is primarily not a moral but an epistemic one. It concerns the question of whether that stance provides us with an explanatorily rich account of human agency. I see that stance as one that we tend to adopt naturally and as one to which we do not possess a plausible alternative to account for individual agency.

normative realists seem to suggest.[21] In my view, normative facts are nothing but plain facts that can be grasped from the impartial spectator perspective as considerations that speak for an action or adoption of certain attitudes toward the world. In that sense the existence of normativity is indeed intrinsically tied to a "practical point of view." Being an intrinsic feature of our practical point of view does however not mean that the domain of normativity is less real. It means only that it is as real and natural as the practical point of view from which it emerges. But the stance that agents (as natural organism with a certain organization of their brain) take toward each other in order to make sense of their behavior as intelligible agents is not something that can be explained away or that we are free to negotiate about. The stance is part of the natural world, even if it is a stance that does not have its equivalent in the natural sciences. It speaks for the position of Smithian constructivism developed here that it allows us to appreciate the normative splendor of the world without any philosophical and ontological regrets and resentments, as any impartial spectator is prone to agree.[22]

---

[21] Interestingly, in defending a position of robust realism (in contrast to the more attenuated internal realism of Scanlon), David Enoch (2011, chap. 3) appeals to the "intrinsic and instrumental indispensability" of deliberation. Notice, however, that in conceiving of deliberation mainly as a first-person phenomenon he fails to validate the intersubjective validity of such reasons.

[22] The paper has benefitted from its discussion at the Moral Sentimentalism conference at the College of the Holy Cross in November 2014. More significantly, I would like to express my gratitude to Andrea Borghini, my co-editor Remy Debes, Larry Cahoone, Michael Frazer, Robert Kane, and Brit Smith for their astute and helpful comments on drafts of this essay.

# 11     A Modest Feminist Sentimentalism: Empathy and Moral Understanding Across Social Difference[1]

*Diana Tietjens Meyers*

Sentimentalism has held a central place in feminist ethics from the beginning of the mid-twentieth century philosophical movement. This philosophical project gained considerable momentum in response to Carol Gilligan's studies of the contrast between moral deliberation guided by the Justice Perspective and moral deliberation guided by the Care Perspective. Although some feminist philosophers evinced skepticism about grounding ethics in care, others were inspired by Gilligan's discovery that some women construe moral problems in terms of constellations of relationships and regard maintaining relationships as a key value. Proponents of care ethics, including Annette Baier (1995), Eva Kittay (1999), and Virginia Held (2006), embraced this approach in part because it is anchored in and valorizes the roles women are expected to assume, as well as the kinds of experience typically regarded as feminine.

However, care is not the sole sentimentalist theme in contemporary feminist ethics. The topics of anger and trust are also salient. Elizabeth Spelman (1988), Naomi Scheman (1993), and Alison Jaggar (1989) point out that warranted anger is gender-coded masculine and that women's anger is dismissed as arbitrary and pathological. Rejecting this baseless and inequitable view of women's negative affect, all three maintain that women must claim their anger as a signifier of injustice and a signpost for feminist political action. In contrast, Karen Jones (1996) explicates trust as an affective attitude, and Annette Baier (1986) argues that trust, not contract, is the foundation of social relations. Without the prior establishment of social relations of mutual trust, no one could count on others to adhere to the agreed-to provisions of the social contract. Jones's and Baier's accounts of trust differ, for Jones's is more emphatically sentimentalist. Nevertheless, nothing in Jones's account prevents trust from serving as the

[1] I am grateful to Remy Debes and Karsten R. Stueber for their very helpful comments on earlier drafts of this chapter. I am also grateful to Lori Gruen for countless conversations about empathy, its relevance to ethics, and the nuances of our points of agreement and disagreement. As well, I thank audiences at many conferences and colloquia over the years for input that helped me refine my views.

fundamental social glue that is a precondition for voluntaristic social arrangements. Thus feminists invoke sentimentalist themes not only to ground feminist social critique but also to correct for shortcomings in familiar moral and political theories.

My goal in this chapter, however, is to evaluate the potential of sentimentalism for addressing a challenge internal to contemporary feminism. Shifting away from the use of anger to critique patriarchal institutions and practices and the role of trust in securing social cooperation, I take up what feminists and critical race theorists call "the problem of difference." The problem of difference arises as a result of the vast experiential chasms separating women in societies that differentially position persons according to race, class, sexuality, nationality, and other markers of privilege and subordination. Insofar as differential positioning shapes the needs and priorities of different groups of women, their political agendas conflict. Audre Lorde (1984), for one, vividly articulates the corrosive syndrome of anger and mistrust among diverse women that these differences can generate and ardently defends African American women's anger and mistrust toward white middle-class feminists. I'll return to Lorde's argument later. The immediate point is that the resulting factionalism divides women and imperils the cause of gender justice. Once feminist philosophers came to grips with the political implications of women's diversity, the need to theorize how to promote respect, understanding, and solidarity across social divisions among women became pressing. To meet this demand, feminists offered a variety of proposals for bridging the rifts that prevent women from making common cause, yet these proposals fall short in various ways (Section 1). Hence my positive project here. Taking into account the weaknesses in these existing proposals, I'll argue that empathy is a condition for the possibility of solidarity among diverse women.

Still, there is ample reason to be wary of my proposal. For one thing, students of empathy note that the philosophical and social scientific literatures are awash in variant definitions of empathy.[2] Since there is no consensus about what empathy is, it is not clear what is meant by the suggestion that empathy can shrink the distances separating women who occupy different social locations.

The German term we translate as empathy originated in aesthetics. Robert Vischer invented it to characterize the experience of art works as a process of "feeling into."[3] Soon thereafter the idea gained currency in philosophy of mind and moral philosophy. Since each of these fields poses

---

[2] See Nussbaum (2001: 301–302, 331), Gruen (2009: 26), Stueber (2006: 27), Coplan and Goldie (2011, esp. "Introduction"), Aaltolta (2014: 76–77), Debes (2015).
[3] See Debes (2015: 296).

a different set of questions, it is unsurprising that conceptions of empathy answering to those disparate questions proliferated. In philosophy of mind, empathy is a candidate answer to various questions raised by the problem of other minds – such as (1) how do we know that other minds exist? and (2) how do we know what anyone else is thinking and feeling? In ethics, empathy is a candidate answer to such questions as the grounds for the distinction between right and wrong and the source of moral motivation. Spanning these two philosophical fields are questions about social cohesion and coordination, and here too empathy is a candidate answer.

Philosophers of mind, Karsten R. Stueber (2006: 21, 147) and Alvin Goldman (2011: 36–38), offer bi-level accounts of empathy. Lower level empathy exploits neuro-muscular mirroring processes that enable you to rapidly grasp that someone is experiencing this or that emotion or that someone intends to accomplish such-and-such a goal. Higher level empathy exploits your imaginative powers to construct a representation in your own mind of what someone else is thinking or feeling. Both are forms of simulating others' subjectivities, and proponents of the major alternative to simulationist views – so-called theory-theory – do not invoke empathy to account for our knowledge of other minds.

Whether empathy has any role in ethics and how empathy should be conceptualized for ethical purposes are also disputed. Some moral philosophers foreground affect as the core component of empathy and treat emotional contagion as a rudimentary, automatic form of empathy.[4] The concept of emotional contagion relies on the metaphor of pre-consciously catching an emotion that someone else is experiencing without sharing the other's reasons for feeling the emotion. For example, you might begin to feel sad at a funeral despite not feeling any grief over the loss of the deceased or on behalf of her family and friends. Another form of empathy is purposeful and effortful. When seeking to empathize with someone in this conscious and deliberate way, you try to imagine how that person feels and perhaps what she is thinking from her perspective. No one excludes imagining other people's emotional states from this type of empathizing, but Jesse Prinz (2011a: 215) and Martin Hoffman (2011: 233) seem to bar imagining other aspects of people's subjectivity from it. Those who favor a more expansive view of this type of empathy include Stephen Darwall (1998: 266, 2011: 13), Peter Goldie (2000: 198; 2011: 302), and Martha Nussbaum (2001: 327). Unlike Prinz and Goldie, however, Hoffman, Darwall, and Nussbaum find a place for empathy in moral relations.

In light of this welter of conceptualization, my suggestion that empathy might pave the way to solidarity among diverse women and help resolve

---

[4] See Slote (2007: 13), Prinz (2011b: 212), Darwall (2011: 8–9).

the problem of difference might seem baffling. Moreover, that the circumstances shaping women's lives vary enormously on both qualitative and quantitative measures and give rise to intense hostility and fear that condition relations among different groups of women compounds this definitional quandary, for empathy seems to work best when the empathizer and the person she is empathizing with are similar. Of concern as well, vocal critics of empathy Jesse Prinz and Peter Goldie hammer away at the value of empathy as a moral tool (Section 2). Although I agree with Prinz that empathy is not the foundation of morality, and I agree with Goldie that empathy is not a necessary condition for each and every moral act, I undertake a defense of empathy as a conduit to solidarity among women.

To understand a contribution of empathy to moral sentimentalism and to clarify a contribution of sentimentalism to feminist ethics, I develop an account of visceral imagination and explain how intellect constrains empathetic engagement anchored in visceral imagination. In my view, empathy is best understood as an embodied, affectively valenced, proto-moral grasp of the values in play in a given situation. Because empathy is crucial to apprehending what is at stake in situations that involve individuals from disparate backgrounds as well as individuals from similar backgrounds, empathy is indispensable to a feminist account of moral relations. Although students of empathy explicate this concept in widely varying ways, I argue that the account I offer is consonant with paradigmatic ascriptions of empathy in everyday interactions and that empathy with different others makes important contributions to moral epistemology. Conceived as I propose, empathy prompts moral questioning and reconsideration. Moreover, it is vital to addressing the problem of difference, for it enables women from different social groups to recognize and make sense of seemingly counter-intuitive political objectives and priorities (Section 3). Finally, I take up the charge that empathy is detrimental to moral insight and action because empathizers are biased in favor of people like themselves. Against this view, I argue that feminists facing the problem of difference and conscientious agents generally are cognitively equipped and highly motivated to resist this bias (Section 4). If so, feminists and moral sentimentalists who take seriously the moral quandaries that bedevil our culturally pluralist, inegalitarian world ought to embrace empathy.

## 1    The Problem of Difference

At the height of second wave feminism during the 1960s and 1970s, activists and theorists who were by and large white, middle class, and heterosexual presumed a universal sisterhood based on membership in the category "woman" and generalized freely about the needs of women based on their ostensibly common interests. Of course, this heedlessness did not go unnoticed among women who did not share this relatively privileged background. Alienated from the women's movement, women of color, poor women, and lesbians soon challenged the legitimacy of the theories and goals that animated it. In so doing, they articulated the problem of difference and raised doubts about the feasibility of solidarity among diverse women. This is not the place to recount in detail the emergence and evolution of this line of criticism. However, I need to sketch its principal points before I can consider how empathy might bear on overcoming the divides separating women of different races, classes, and sexualities.

In the late 1970s and early 1980s, Audre Lorde (1984) penned a series of essays and talks that captures the disconnect between prominent feminist intellectuals and women of color. In "An Open Letter to Mary Daly," Lorde calls out Daly's book *Gyn/Ecology* for its selective appropriation of Black women's experience and writing:

Then I came to the first three chapters of your Second Passage, and it was obvious that you were dealing with noneuropean women, but only as victims and preyers-upon each other. (67)

Then, to realize that the only quotations from Black women's words were the ones you used to introduce your chapter on African genital mutilation made me question why you needed to use them at all. For my part, I felt you had misused my words, utilizing them only to testify against myself as a woman of Color. (68)

In "The Master's Tools," she exposes the hyperbolic and deceptive rhetoric commonly found in then-contemporary feminist theory and accuses that theory of racism:

Poor women and women of Color know there is a difference between marital slavery and prostitution because it is our daughters who line $42^{nd}$ Street. If white american feminist theory need not deal with the differences between us, and the resulting difference in our oppressions, then how do you deal with the fact that the women who clean your houses and tend your children while you attend conferences on feminist theory are, for the most part, poor women and women of Color? What is the theory behind racist feminism? (112)

Nor are the erasures of poor women and women of color merely theoretical. "The Uses of Anger: Women Responding to Racism," Lorde's keynote address to the National Women's Studies Association, charges the organization with hypocrisy as well as exclusion:

Yet the National Women's Studies Association here in 1981 holds a conference in which it commits itself to responding to racism, yet refuses to waive the registration fee for poor women and women of Color who wished to present and conduct workshops. (126)

Affirming her profound anger at the forces of racism and heterosexism, Lorde endorses strategic separatism (78). Nevertheless, she does not eschew dialogue with women who have theorized and acted in such purblind and reprehensible ways (130–133). She seeks solidarity with white, middle-class, heterosexual feminists but not at the price of suppressing the rage she rightly feels or losing the insight into power relations her rage discloses.

It is easy to call for mutually respectful, mutually enriching dialogue, but extremely hard to achieve it in a context of multiple, reinforcing types of social stratification and the divergent, sometimes opposed interests they foster.[5] However, María Lugones and Elizabeth Spelman offer suggestions about how to overcome this communication logjam. In a co-authored article in which Lugones speaks as a Latina feminist and Spelman as a white/Anglo feminist, they maintain that feminist theory should be developed jointly across difference (1983: 580). They go on to analyze the interpersonal conditions under which this endeavor could succeed, and they urge that because of existing power hierarchies white/Anglo women must assume the onus of adjusting their mindset and behavior:

[Y]ou will need to learn to become unintrusive, unimportant, and patient to the point of tears, while at the same time open to learning any possible lessons. You will also have to come to terms with the sense of alienation, of not belonging, of having your world thoroughly disrupted, having it criticized and scrutinized from the point of view of those who have been harmed by it, having important concepts central to it dismissed, being viewed with mistrust, being seen as of no consequence except as an object of mistrust. (Ibid.)

Raising the bar even higher, they add that white/Anglo women must accede to this unsettling regimen out of friendship, not out of self-interest or a sense of obligation (581). In later work, Lugones reframes these ideas in her influential account of "world-travelling" in a spirit of "loving playfulness" (1987: 15–17), and Spelman proposes correcting for power imbalances among women by modeling relations between privileged women and women of color and poor women on an apprenticeship of the former group to the latter two (1988: 178 and 181).

To redress inequalities that pit groups of women against one another, Lugones and Spelman prescribe attitudes and motives that they think conduce to communication across difference and coalition building. But even supposing that these attitudes and motives are appropriate, something is

---

[5] For discussion of the ways in which remedial initiatives that work well for white, middle-class women fail to meet the needs of women of color, see Crenshaw (1991). For discussion of ways in which the interests of lesbians are at variance with those of heterosexual women, see Calhoun (1994). The difficulties are magnified when we take up issues of transnational feminism, global justice, and human rights. However, I do not have space to go into these matters here.

amiss, for it is unclear how the requisite spirit of (one-sided) friendship and stance of epistemic humility are to develop. If they were already in place, there presumably would not be so much mistrust and anger separating relatively privileged women from those disadvantaged by race, class, or sexuality. According to Sandra Bartky, what is missing is an account of "a knowing that transforms the self who knows, a knowing that brings into being new sympathies, new affects as well as new cognitions and new forms of intersubjectivity" (1997: 179). There is no single practice that can guarantee such personal transformation. But Bartky urges that Scheler's theory of Sympathie (fellow-feeling) provides a platform for explicating politically constructive interaction between differently situated women.

Sally Scholz is skeptical of both of these positions. In her view, solidarity is an egalitarian relationship among individuals committed to a political goal, and solidarity often precedes empathetic engagement (2010: 25–26). For Scholz, empathy is neither necessary nor sufficient for political solidarity across difference (23). Still, Scholz grants that epistemic empathy – "negotiat[ing] the importance of claims in a loving way that affirms the relevance of any given perspective toward a cause" – conduces to identifying the best ways to advance a movement's cause (26). In Section 3, I defend a conception of empathy that I believe improves on Bartky's and Scholz's views by showing how empathy brings unfamiliar values and disvalues to the attention of the empathizer and that clarifies empathy's contribution to moral epistemology. But before I take up that task, I need to consider arguments against assigning empathy a central role in ethics.

## 2      Two Critiques of Empathy

Empathy skeptics Jesse Prinz and Peter Goldie mount sustained attacks on empathy from different angles. As a moral sentimentalist, Prinz asks whether empathy is necessary for moral competence. Concerned principally with issues in the philosophy of mind, Goldie asks whether empathy is a good way to grasp what others are thinking and feeling.

Prinz characterizes empathy as "a kind of vicarious emotion" – "feeling what one takes another person to be feeling" (2011b: 212). Although his antagonism toward empathy is unequivocal in some respects, it is interestingly ambivalent in others. He definitely holds that empathy is not a causal, developmental, motivational, epistemic, or normative precondition for moral judgment and action.[6] I will not rehearse his arguments regarding these claims, for they are not germane to the question of empathy's possible role in overcoming the problem of difference. But Prinz also catalogs

---

[6] See Prinz (2011a) and (2011b).

various hazards of empathetic thinking: It can be manipulated easily; it is subject to similarity, proximity, and other biases; it encourages unequal treatment; and so on (2011a: 225–226; 2011b: 227–228). Although he acknowledges that no moral emotion is perfectly reliable, he insists that unlike other moral emotions empathy is "intrinsically biased," and he speculates that empathy may lead other moral emotions astray (2011a: 229; 2011b: 227). These are objections that my account of empathy will need to circumvent.

This barrage of criticism notwithstanding, Prinz makes an important concession to empathy:

> It is undeniable that empathy sometimes leads us to see good and bad actions whose status we might have otherwise missed. This is especially clear when we move beyond paradigm moral categories, such as murder and charity, and consider isolated cases whose worth depends on emotional impact. (2011a: 223)

Elsewhere Prinz maintains that moral approval and disapproval attach to action-types (See 2011a: 214; 2011b: 220). But in this passage, he hints that empathy may catalyze moral awareness, say, by exposing unjust practices that had heretofore been deemed acceptable. Likewise, empathy may have something to offer where moral perplexity has taken hold. Perhaps when you doubt that the standard way of classifying a particular type of behavior is justifiable, when you are not sure of the scope of a moral category, when you suspect that a new moral category may be needed, when you are torn between outrage and open-mindedness, empathy is needed to help you sort things out. Coupling this point with Prinz's observation that empathy may enrich empathizers' lives and strengthen their interpersonal relationships, it seems that he might grant that empathy should play a part in solving the problem of difference (2011b: 229).

Although Goldie seems to be a harsher critic of empathy than Prinz, Goldie's antipathy stems largely from the extremely exigent conception of empathy he posits to flesh out the simulationist view of mentalizing. With the aim of debunking simulationist accounts of understanding other minds, Goldie distinguishes in-her-shoes imagining from empathy (2000: 195–203; 2007: 79; 2011: 302–303).[7] Both are forms of central imagining or perspective-shifting – you imagine a scenario from the standpoint of one of the protagonists. But they should not be confused. When you engage in in-her-shoes imagining, you centrally imagine how you would feel if you were in the other's situation. You cast yourself in someone else's role in a scenario, and you imagine what you would think and what you would do from the inside. For example, you might pretend that you (I am assuming

---

[7] Here and elsewhere I have altered Goldie's terminology for the sake of gender parity.

that you are not Nepali) were visiting Kathmandu when the 2015 earth-quake started and imagine how you would feel and what you would do given your own configuration of beliefs and desires. In in-her-shoes imag-ining, you shift your circumstances but keep your identity. In contrast, when you empathize, you centrally imagine being another person in a situation different from your own. You take on someone else's personality, and you imagine thinking what she would think and doing what she would do from the inside. For example, you might imagine the feelings and actions of a res-ident of Kathmandu whose beliefs and desires have been shaped by Nepali culture as if you were that person during the 2015 earthquake. In empathiz-ing, then, you shift both your circumstances and your identity. Although in-her-shoes imagining allows you to access another's subjectivity when the other's relevant traits match your own and the other's situation and options are clear-cut, it is unreliable when the other's psychological profile differs from yours and the other's situation and options are complex. In the lat-ter types of cases, a different imaginative project is called for. And if that imaginative project must be a project of central imagination, it will have to be empathetic imagination.

But, Goldie argues, empathizing so understood is impossible. To empathize, you must have a "substantial characterization" of the other – a subtle, detailed portrait of the other's desires, values, abilities, affective dispositions, and so forth – and you must imagine the other as if those attributes were your very own (2000: 195; 2011: 308). In other words, the characterization must remain in the background and must function "holis-tically" as it does when you're centrally imagining yourself as the protag-onist (2000: 198–199; 2011: 308–309). Moreover, if empathy is to succeed in anticipating how someone will feel and act, it must take into account non-rational influences on her decisions, such as moods and temptations (2000: 206; 2011: 311–313). Initially, Goldie held that empathy is contin-gently impossible because managing these bourgeoning demands exceeds our imaginative powers (2000: 205). However, he ultimately concluded that empathy is conceptually impossible because an empathizer cannot "oper-ate with the appropriately *full-blooded notion of first-person agency* that is involved in deliberation" (2011: 303). Only the agent can take this stance toward her subjective states and values, for she alone is authorized to inter-pret or prioritize them (313–316). So empathy is necessarily impossible.

In view of this unconditional repudiation of empathy, it is clear that empathy can have no place in Goldie's moral philosophy,[8] and at this point

---

[8] So his remarks in earlier work to the effect that empathy may deepen and strengthen sym-pathy must be set aside. See Goldie (2000: 180 and 214).

Goldie's and Prinz's views converge. Although Goldie adopts the vocabulary of sympathy and Prinz adopts the vocabulary of concern, both hold that caring about someone's plight, as opposed to sharing her suffering, is ethically crucial, for it motivates ameliorative action (Goldie 2000: 213–215; Prinz 2011a: 230). In addition to sympathy, Goldie recommends taking what he calls the external perspective on others (2007: 70–72). In order to treat someone well, what you need to do is to assiduously think about her while attending to how her needs, beliefs, and feelings and her perspective on the world differ from yours (2000: 181; 2007: 70, 82, 83; 2011: 302).[9] You need to sympathetically dwell *on* the other's state of mind and circumstances in life, not empathetically *in* them. For Goldie, this discipline is an antidote for mistaking the other's feelings and troubles for ones you've experienced as well as for agentic paralysis due to submersion in the others' feelings and troubles (2007: 72, 81, 83). He notes that thinking about others from the external perspective does not suppress emotion or imagination (77). Indeed, he has no objection to acentrally imagining-how-it-is for someone else (2011: 305–306). For example, you might imagine what a Nepali resident of Kathmandu felt and did during the 2015 earthquake from the standpoint of your safe place elsewhere and with your own beliefs and desires intact. In acentrally imagining-how-it-is for someone else, you imagine someone else's subjectivity without imaginatively changing your own identity or situation.

Because Goldie's discussions of thinking about someone from the external perspective repeatedly accent how different that person may be from you and how morally necessary it is to apprehend these differences, his views hold promise for addressing the problem of difference. Capitalizing on this potential, Catriona Mackenzie joins Goldie in rejecting empathetic imagination as a pathway to understanding across difference (2006: 307). Like Goldie, she endorses sympathetic imagining from the external point of view (322–323). To make my case for empathy, then, I'll need to argue that sympathetic imagining from the external point of view poses problems that Goldie and Mackenzie overlook and that empathetic imagining augments moral insight in ways they ignore.

Now, it's important to note that Prinz (2011a: 231) and Goldie (2007: 70–71; 2011: 303–305) do not deny that there are tenable conceptions of empathy other than the ones they criticize. If the project is only to devise

---

[9] Goldie's position on thinking about others from the external perspective resembles Iris Young's account of asymmetrical reciprocity, wonder, and enlarged thought in several respects. Among other things, both invoke the trope of gift giving to develop their views, and each affirms that it is logically impossible for one person to assume another's identity in some way that empathy requires. See Young (1997: 38–59).

an account of empathy that satisfies the theoretical objectives of simulation theory, Goldie's extremely exacting conception of empathy may fit the bill, and his bleak assessment of empathy may be justified. However, moral philosophers have an assortment of projects and, Prinz notwithstanding, might be able to demonstrate the value of empathy without contending that empathy is the foundation of morality. Indeed, my comparatively modest aim is to theorize how it is possible to fathom someone else's subjectivity and life circumstances well enough to appreciate the values that are at stake for her and to envisage the sort of response those values call for.

## 3    A Feminist Conception of Empathy

In setting out my view of empathy, I advert to insights from the western philosophical tradition, contemporary accounts of empathy, and current US colloquial usage. My aim is to provide an account of empathy that benefits from these sources and that also recommends itself in virtue of its potential to address the problem of difference and its fruitfulness for moral philosophy more generally.

Perhaps because of empathy's role in simulationist theories of mind-reading, many philosophers hold that empathy is morally neutral in the sense that it can serve moral or immoral purposes.[10] In my view, however, there is no reason to suppose that ethics must inherit whatever conception of empathy makes sense in philosophy of mind. On the contrary, considering that the conceptions of empathy in simulationist philosophies of mind are artifacts of a controversial research program, but the vernacular conception is embedded in ordinary moral discourse and moral relations, there is reason to think that the vernacular conception should take precedence in ethics.

The claim that empathy is morally neutral flies in the face of colloquial usage, which differentiates empathy from sizing people up based on their respective motivations. People size each other up for relatively benign as well as nefarious reasons. A shrewd real estate agent tries to figure out how high a price a prospective buyer would be willing to pay. An astute torturer tries to divine a prisoner's vulnerable points. In pursuit of their ends, both might "channel" – that is, centrally imagine – their targets. But in ordinary speech it would be exceedingly odd to call what they're doing "empathy" because attributing empathy to someone normally implies a measure of moral approval. In many career niches, sharp sizing-up skills are prized, but for tactical rather than moral reasons. In contrast, practitioners of the helping professions rely on empathy to do their ameliorative work. That

---

[10]  See Goldie (2000: 215), Darwall (1998: 261), Nussbaum (2001: 331).

we ascribe empathy to good nurses and social workers but not to successful real estate agents and torturers, at least not in their professional capacities, argues for building a presupposition of concern for the other into the concept of empathy. Unlike sizing others up, empathizing presupposes sufficient concern for the other to rule out an unabashedly instrumental attitude toward her.

I follow philosophical precedent, though, and assign pro-social motivation to sympathy but not to empathy. If an altruistic motivation were incorporated into empathy, the problem of difference would seem more tractable than it actually is. In other words, to equate empathetic concern with sympathetic concern would be to underestimate the magnitude of the rifts among differently positioned women and the intensity of the anger and mistrust that fuel the problem of difference. Accordingly, I propose that empathetic concern is something like taking a humane interest in another individual with a distinctive point of view, an interest that stops short of entailing a desire to help but that does not reduce to bare non-maleficence.[11] Whereas empathetic concern for a person jumpstarts and frames the task of imagining her experience from her point of view, sympathetic concern for a person prompts you to respond to her perceived needs by providing assistance. If so, empathy is not what moves members of helping professions to provide benefits to their clientele, nor is it what moves women with clashing interests to compromise and forge alliances. Instead, duty, sympathy, or solidarity must motivate the provision of aid and the construction of feminist coalitions.

It stands to reason that empathy cannot solve the problem of difference in one fell swoop because empathy is first and foremost a form of "experiential understanding." Motivated by proto-moral concern, empathy seeks to understand another person "from the inside" by imaginatively replicating the other's subjective experience, including its cognitive, affective, corporeal, and desiderative dimensions. As Amy Coplan urges, you understand someone else by having an imaginative experience of what it is like to be her, as opposed to analyzing the causes of her experience (2011: 17). Still, it remains to ask what epistemic pay-offs empathy furnishes that acentrally

---

[11] In two recent papers, Pierre Jacob and co-authors Frédérique de Vignemont and Pierre Jacob argue that a caring condition is necessary for empathy. On the surface, their view seems similar to mine, but I am not sure how far the similarity goes. Jacob maintains that the caring condition rules out the possibility that empathy is the default response to noticing another person's affective state (2011: 523–524). De Vignemont and Jacob argue that the caring condition ensures that empathy is other-directed – that is, not egoistic (de Vignemont and Jacob 2012: 307). However, my reading of this work suggests that they are not using the terms "care" and "other-directed" in a moral or even a proto-moral sense. They seem to be saying that in order to empathize you must take an interest in the other, not that you must take a humane interest in the other.

imagining-how-it-is for someone and thinking about her from the external point of view do not.

Scholz maintains that epistemic empathy enables individuals with a shared commitment to a cause to resolve their differences in a spirit of mutual caring (2010: 26). However, she does not say what enables participants in these discussions to surpass mere civility and mutual respect and to sustain their solidarity despite serious disagreements. Bartky's reading of Scheler provides a possible explanation: "there is a difference between a mere knowing-that (even a knowing that can list concretely and in detail the circumstances of the case) and a 'vicarious visualization' that causes these circumstances to come alive in the theater of my mind" (1997: 192). Nussbaum adds that by empathizing with someone you recognize "another world of experience," the "reality and humanity" of the other (2001: 333). But it seems that done well, acentral imagining brings the other vividly to life and shows respect for the other's unique subjectivity. What more may be gained through empathy?

In my view, empathetic imagination is special because it opens a window on the values and disvalues that are being experienced or can be experienced by someone whose situation is profoundly different from your own. Empathetic encounters with values and disvalues are not to be confused with in-her-shoes imaginings that reproduce your value system as you project yourself into an alternative set of circumstances. Nor are they to be confused with grasping inventories or theoretical distillations of alternative value systems, for in empathizing you are viscerally apprehending what the values and disvalues mean concretely in the life of another human being. Consider an individual who feels humiliated because she has been disrespected, an individual who despairs because her job applications never get uptake, or an individual who is enraged by police violence against members of her social group. In empathizing with these individuals, the empathizer viscerally apprehends the experiential meanings of the disvalues of disrespect, discrimination, and oppression for those who suffer their psychocorporeal corollaries – such as, humiliation, despair, and rage. If so, empathy imparts something more than third-person imaginative representations that you take in intellectually or respond to emotionally, and empathetic imagining yields a kind of understanding that exceeds that of acentrally imagining the same person. What is missing from the latter is the *poignancy* of the other's interiority. This poignancy may be what Nussbaum is getting at when she says that by empathizing with someone who is suffering you get a "sense of what it means for her to suffer that way" (2001: 331) and what Darwall is getting at when he says that empathizing with someone accesses what she is "going through" (2011: 13).

The poignancy of the other's interiority that is captured by empathetic imagining makes it a potent impetus for moral questioning and reconsideration, which in turn can lead to discerning heretofore-unnoticed wrongs. Not only is readiness to confront moral uncertainty and alertness to the possibility of overlooked wrongs of paramount importance to leading a moral life, but also both are clearly vital to addressing the problem of difference. Here I wish to reiterate that Prinz allows that empathy may be helpful in these very respects.[12] It seems, then, that we might agree that moral philosophers should regard explicating empathy's role in prompting moral perplexity as a core philosophical project.

Still, my suggestion about the distinctive sort of knowledge that empathy yields may strike some readers as implausible. If so, I would venture that one reason is that Goldie and Mackenzie would have us believe that the line between acentrally imagining someone and centrally imagining her is sharper than it is. Suppose you are imagining your friend receiving news of her promotion to a coveted new position. You certainly can acentrally imagine her behavior – her ear-to-ear grin, her characteristic exclamations, and so forth – and you can think that she's feeling gleeful. But to imagine *her* glee, you must centrally imagine her subjectivity – that is, you must empathize. What, after all, would it be like to acentrally imagine someone else's feelings of glee? Of course you could imagine feeling gleeful yourself, and you could infuse your picture of her happy visage and joyous utterances with that feeling. However, her feeling gleeful is not an affective tint coloring her behaviors. It is a gleeful feeling. Whereas your infusion strategy misses her subjectivity, empathetically imagining her glee attends to her subjectivity as such. Consequently, your third-person perspective on your friend is likely to segue into her first-person perspective as you attempt to grasp her experience. That is, imagining-how-it-is for her is likely to segueway into empathetically imagining her, and much is lost by limiting yourself to imagining-how-it-is for her.

Still, Goldie maintains that empathy is impossible when it is not trivial. In requiring that your substantial characterization of the other stay in the background and function holistically as you centrally imagine her, Goldie turns empathizing into something like a waking dream in which you are possessed by someone else's identity and a story unfolds from that point of view, but somehow you know that it's just a dream and retain

---

[12] I would add that Prinz (2011a: 223) is mistaken if he thinks that such moral uncertainty and the need for moral reflection arise only in isolated, unusual cases. Only recently, after all, have the rights of gays and lesbians gained a purchase in most Americans' moral imaginations, and discriminatory, often violent treatment of gays and lesbians remains an all but ubiquitous problem worldwide.

your awareness of your independent identity. I welcome Goldie's insistence that empathizing is a demanding imaginative endeavor. But I do not see the advantage of treating the process of developing a characterization of another person as a precondition for, but not a constituent of empathy.

Whereas an actor playing a role must, so to speak, shed her identity and become her character for the duration of the performance, you do not fail to empathize by making use of the hermeneutic process of rallying various faculties and feeling your way along. Given that people are not transparent to one another, accurate empathy requires gradually building up propositional and intuitive knowledge of the other that is then fed into an imagined situation, which may in turn be corrected and reimagined after further observation and thought, and so on. In other words, alternating between the first-person perspective of the individual you are empathizing with and your own third-person perspective on her is part and parcel of empathy.[13] Presumably, psychotherapists work back and forth between the third-person and the first-person perspectives – characterizing and reasoning about their clients, on the one hand, and imaginatively entering into their emotional lives and patterns of thought, on the other. According to clinical theory, what they are doing is empathizing. In a more casual way, friends constantly accumulate propositional knowledge about one another and become attuned to one another's shifting states of mind. As a result, they can empathize with one another with relative ease. Thus, empathy always requires empathizers to obtain considerable background knowledge concerning the other, but empathizing may be more or less difficult depending on the nature of the relationship between the empathizer and the other.

If we agree that empathy need not be a pure feat of central imagining, we can also agree that empathy is often difficult yet possible. It seems to me that this is the right conclusion for moral philosophy to reach because in everyday parlance empathy is something that people actually do. Although it is important (1) to bear in mind that it is impossible to completely imagine another individual's life from the inside and (2) to stand ready to modify your empathetic imaginings if disconfirming information turns up, it is clear that empathetically imagining a person can afford you a substantial acquaintance with the subjectivity of another distinctive individual and that this acquaintance may spark questions about the propriety of your moral beliefs and conduct.

---

[13] Here I agree with Amy Coplan, who characterizes empathy as a "complex imaginative process" that mobilizes cognitive as well as affective capacities (2011: 5).

## 4      Difference, Empathy, and the Problem of Bias

I now turn to Prinz's empirically-based charge that empathy is intrinsically biased – that it is intrinsically partial in a number of ways and therefore morally misleading. In light of the anger and mistrust that perpetu-
ate social divisions among women and interfere with a cohesive feminist
politics, Prinz's objections to empathy are all too pertinent. Moreover, if
his objections hold up, it follows that the arguments I have made so far on
behalf of my account of empathy come to naught. Sobering as this prospect
is, I shall attempt to vindicate the value of empathy by addressing the biases
that Prinz enumerates.

In the context of the problem of difference, Prinz's claim that you can
empathize only with someone different from you by foregrounding her similarity to you may be his most worrisome charge (2011a: 228). However,
I'm not sure what to make of it. Since he states it without citing empirical evidence or offering an argument, I shall focus on the biases that he
substantiates:

1. cuteness effects (2011b: 226)
2. high selectivity (2011b: 226)
3. similarity biases (2011a: 227; 2011b: 226)
4. salience effects (2011b: 227)
5. proximity effects (2011b: 226–227)

Some of these biases pose greater difficulties for my view of empathy than
others.

Cuteness effects and salience effects are less likely to bewitch women
who are committed to gender justice. Cuteness effects – the tendency to
empathize more with more attractive people – are unlikely to interfere with
empathy among women who are schooled in the harms of objectifying
women and valuing them mainly for their looks. Likewise, salience effects –
the tendency to empathize with people affected by events that are getting
a lot of media attention – are unlikely to interfere with empathy among
women whose feminist orientation sensitizes them to the many ways in
which women's voices are routinely silenced and women's issues are routinely sidelined. It seems to me that cuteness effects and salience effects
would be disruptive only if you assume, as Prinz and the studies he cites
often seem to, that empathy is something that just happens or does not, not
something difficult that you strive to achieve. But since my account puts
empathy solidly on the purposeful and effortful side of this dichotomy, I
discount the invidiousness of cuteness and salience effects.

Still, high selectivity, similarity bias, and proximity effects present serious challenges to my account. High selectivity allows your own interests

to interfere with empathizing – for example, you may downplay and fail to empathize with an opponent's feelings and concerns. On the one hand, I have urged that empathy is motivated by a form of concern that I characterized as taking a humane interest in the other. Endowed with a disposition to take a humane interest in others, empathetic individuals wouldn't be so disposed to overlook the feelings and concerns of others when they conflict with their own. But on the other hand, empathetic individuals might find it all but impossible to take a humane interest in people who are angry and distrustful of them. While acknowledging this impediment, I believe that my replies to the charges of similarity bias and proximity effects will go some distance toward moving beyond anger and mistrust and achieving empathetic concern.

Similarity bias disposes you to empathize with people who are like you but to withhold empathy from people who are not like you. Since difference is the mainspring blocking empathy among women in socially stratified societies, this bias is particularly troubling. However, I think that in conjunction with my conception of empathy, the logic of moral relations undercuts the claim that the similarity bias prevents empathy across difference.

No one can deny that some sort of imagination across difference is possible unless she is prepared to aver that belonging to different social groups precludes moral relations. I think it is safe to say, though, that moral relations between members of different social groups are common (though by no means common and intimate enough) in contemporary western societies. Neither Goldie nor Prinz says otherwise. But both reject empathy and advocate sympathy or concern as responses to the wrongs suffered by others. Yet, sympathy and concern – feeling for someone's suffering – presuppose that you know she has been wronged. Being present at a transgression and witnessing a morally unacceptable type of action as it is taking place can arouse sympathy or concern for the victim. So can being told about a transgression and imagining-how-it-is-for the victim arouse sympathy or concern for her. Absent immediate experience of wrong-doing, it is by imagining a scenario and attaching a name to the offending action in the scenario that sympathy and concern are aroused. So it seems that proponents of sympathy must allow at least for acentrally imagining-how-it-is for someone, for otherwise it would be unclear how you could come to sympathize with or feel concern for a different, possibly distant other, which Prinz plainly thinks you can do (2011a: 230).[14]

---

[14] Prinz cannot respond that acentrally imagining-how-it-is for someone is no more probable across difference than empathy, for that would leave him with a single unpalatable alternative. He would need to claim that imagining-how-it-is-for anyone to be subjected to

Assuming, then, that the ability to imagine-how-it-is for someone is a component of moral competence, I now explore the implications of this type of imagination with regard to the feasibility of empathy across difference. Recall that far from magically transporting one person into another's consciousness, empathy requires navigating between imagining the other's first-person perspective and gathering relevant information about her from your own third-person perspective – that is, communicating with a different other or otherwise educating yourself about what it is like to be her, gradually expanding your understanding, and hence refining your imaginative representation of her point of view. The aim of shifting back and forth between third-person inquiry and central imagining is to sort out how you differ from the other and to learn what she experiences that you do not in order to avoid imaginatively misrepresenting her.

Granted that imagining-how-it-is for a person from a different social group is possible despite the similarity bias, it follows that empathy with this person is possible too. If you can sufficiently suppress irrelevant features of your identity while sufficiently mobilizing relevant ones to succeed in acentrally imagining someone different from you, you can also sufficiently suppress irrelevant features of your identity while sufficiently mobilizing relevant ones to centrally imagine the other's experience from her own point of view. In other words, you can empathize with a person from a different walk of life. Adopting a realistic conception of empathy implies that significantly different backgrounds and attributes are no more formidable a barrier to empathy than they are to acentral imagining. In light of empathy's contribution to revealing wrongs you had not previously been aware of, it is necessary to espouse a conception of empathy, such as the one I propose, that counteracts the similarity bias and allows for empathy with different others.

Proximity effects discriminate in favor of people who are culturally or geographically nearby and against those who are culturally or geographically distant, and empathy is subject to proximity effects. In an era of global media, however, the geographical distances between people are shrinking. Moreover, as educators offer curricula designed to teach multicultural literacy, understanding of and respect for diverse cultures is on the rise. As a start, then, institutional changes can help to mitigate proximity effects. Increased social and economic diversity in schools and workplaces coupled with extensive media coverage of events and trends beyond the bounds of

---

an immoral action-type suffices to feel concern. But this generalized imaginative exercise would hold up only in cut-and-dry situations. In many situations, however, whether a particular immoral action-type is applicable depends on who the parties are and what they are like as individuals.

the target western, middle-class audience can reduce proximity effects on empathy.

Storytelling is a particularly effective vehicle for overcoming proximity effects, similarity biases, and high selectivity. Although Iris Young is no friend of empathy, her discussion of personal storytelling across difference helps to explain why narrative conduces to empathy.[15] According to Young, narrative:

1. discloses the particularity of the storyteller's experience,
2. explains what experiences and values mean to the storyteller, and
3. depicts what listeners' values and conduct mean to the storyteller. (1997: 72–73)

Summing up, she affirms that "narrative provides an important way to demonstrate need or entitlement" (71).[16] If we supplement this point with her comment that rhetorical devices "pull on thought through desire," it becomes evident that a well-told personal story can overcome the obstacles to taking a humane interest in the other as well as diminishing the impact of the similarity bias and proximity effects (Ibid.). If so, Prinz overplays his case in declaring: "We can no more overcome [empathy's] limits than we can ride a bicycle across the ocean" (2011a: 229). Moreover, to the extent that a well-told personal story suppresses these biases, a story can kindle moral transformation in auditors (or readers). In precipitating empathy with the experience of a different other and the meanings attaching to that experience for her, a personal story gives audience members reasons to consider modifying their moral convictions and practices.[17] But there is more. By deploying familiar mediating concepts, such as human rights, to interpret your empathetic imaginings, you can readily extend the scope of your moral reflection to whole groups of people. If you empathize with the story of one woman trafficked into prostitution – viscerally imagining how

---

[15] I note, though, that Young objects to a conception of empathy that is more like Goldie's than mine. For related discussion of the problem of imaginative resistance in relation to personal story-telling, see Meyers (2016, chap. 3, Section 4). There I consider the accounts of imaginative resistance advanced by Tamar Gendler (2006), Julia Driver (2008), and Karsten R. Stueber (2011) and show how a former child soldier's recounting of his participation in a morally heinous incident overcomes readers' imaginative resistance.

[16] I defend a similar claim in Meyers (2009).

[17] Remy Debes develops a line of thought that reinforces the point I'm making here. He maintains that empathizing "with a narrative meant to explain emotion . . . is just what it means to understand both the story *and* the subject emotion." Moreover, experiencing this sort of empathy entails that you "condone" my emotion inasmuch as it *makes sense* to you that I feel as I do," for you are feeling the same way (2010: 223). If Debes is right, empathizing with a personal story of humanly inflicted, humanly remediable woe obliges you to give credence to the complaint implicitly being lodged and to adjust your moral thinking to accommodate it.

threats against family members, social isolation, and sexual violence instill fear and secure compliance – and if you link your empathetic understanding to moral concepts such as slavery and exploitation, you have reason to become an opponent of the sex trafficking industry and an ally of the countless women worldwide who are vulnerable to its predatory machinations. Thus, empathy can eventuate in reconfigured judgments about what justice to diverse social groups requires. If so, Prinz's assertion that empathy's "focus on affected individuals distracts us from systemic problems" also overstates his case (2011a: 228). Far from "push[ing] partiality into prejudice," personal storytelling links empathy to solidarity across difference (229).

As Audre Lorde makes clear, feminists are not complacent about the problem of difference. They want to give voice to their concerns, and they want to be heard across difference. Thus the emotional climate surrounding the problem of difference is an admixture – anger and mistrust, to be sure, but also longing for connection and solidarity. For this reason and also because of the doubts I have raised about the power of the various biases Prinz tars empathy with, I do not think it is out of the question to expect feminists who come from different backgrounds and whose priorities differ to take a humane interest in and to empathize with one another. If I am right that empathy paves the way to moral perplexity and conscientious reflection, empathy is an indispensable tool in the search for feminist alliance.

# 12     Moral Sentimentalism in Early Confucian Thought

*David B. Wong*

This essay is an exploration of what Mencius (fourth century BCE) and
Xunzi (fourth and third centuries BCE) in the classical Confucian tradition have to say about cultivating goodness in persons.[1] One of the benefits
of such an exploration is that it can help us go outside well-worn Humean
and Kantian grooves of thinking about the relationship between reason on
the one hand and desire and emotion on the other hand. Mencius tries to
change how kings feel and what they desire, by getting them to engage in
reflection about what they feel. These feelings stem from innate affective,
perceptual, and reflective dispositions. Mencius metaphorically describes
these dispositions as "sprouts" and holds that they can be "grown" into
fuller forms of goodness. I shall suggest that central to this conception of
growing one's sprouts is a kind of reflection that is itself a feeling. Mencius
holds that affect-laden reflection has the power to shape us. His view is a
corrective to two opposing one-sided tendencies in Western thinking about
reflection and emotion: either to hold that emotion is irrelevant or distract-
ing from proper rational motivation to be moral or to hold that reflection
is purely instrumental to goals established by emotion. Xunzi also relies
on a kind of "felt" reflection to induce internal change in moral motivation, albeit within a broader set of practices involving observance of rituals
and music that involves the mind's taking charge of and shaping its psychic economy, and this is done in great part through shaping one's cultural
environment.

Let me first clarify and set in context the question about the relation
between reflection and feeling. I use the word "reflection" rather than "reasoning" to cover a wider array of thinking that involves identifying reasons
for doing something or living in a certain way that do not necessarily involve
following rules. Sentimentalism in the West, with its roots in the Scottish
enlightenment thinkers, addresses two distinct questions in ethical theory:
first, there is the question of how is moral judgment made, where it comes

---

[1] Many thanks to Remy Debes and Karsten R. Stueber for many comments and suggestions
on the earlier draft of this essay.

from; second, there is the question of what roles reflection and feeling play in the motivation to act on moral judgment. Though the two questions are distinguished in the sentimentalist tradition, they often receive parallel answers. Hume provides a good example: the sentiments, rather than reason, are the source of moral distinctions and judgments; and the sentiments are necessary for motivating action on moral judgment rather than reason, which is motivationally inert on its own.

Mencius and Xunzi express views that can be understood as answers to the question about the source of moral judgment.[2] Mencius, as shall be discussed below, is less systematic, and the relevant passages do not determine a definitive interpretation of his views on this matter. Xunzi systematically defends a view of the source of moral judgment that involves both the cognitive and affective. For him, the intellect takes charge of redesigning a person's psychic economy, but that psychic economy is not completely plastic and puts constraints on what could be the best redesign.

Both Mencius and Xunzi have much to say about the second question of moral motivation and how to become good. Mencius' and Xunzi's concerns were overridingly practical in a way that is unusual in the Western tradition. They addressed the troubling situation in China in which the centralized authority of the Zhou Dynasty kings had steadily eroded and in which the various Chinese states increasingly acted on their own, the larger powerful ones swallowing up or least dominating the smaller ones. Those who held power in these states often acted in purely self-interested ways and exploited their subjects rather than caring for their welfare. Mencius and Xunzi sought to understand how this situation could be remedied, and they held in common the belief that leadership needed to undergo a moral transformation, one in which their policies, and their hearts and minds, would be guided by moral values.

The Western tradition, especially in its modern form, has been more focused in a purely theoretical way on the question about the source of moral judgment. It has developed an arsenal of distinctions and frameworks that allows a sophisticated discussion of the alternative answers to be given. Western moral psychology, on the other hand, is comparatively thinner on a conception of how people become good. Mencius' and Xunzi's moral psychologies are full of rich insights about the way that

---

[2] In articulating views from the eponymous texts as the views of the persons Mencius and Xunzi, I am following a convention of the scholarship, but it should be noted that it cannot be taken for granted that the texts were respectively single-authored by these persons. It is quite possible that they come to us as collectively authored texts by many persons working within a school of thought focused on the teachings of Mencius and Xunzi. My interpretation of the views mentioned here is based on my judgment of what makes the best total sense of each text taken as a whole.

feeling and reflection can interweave and mutually influence one another in the course of one's moral development. Their insights can present alternatives to well-worn grooves of thinking in the Western tradition about the relation between reflection and feeling in moral development of character. In what follows, I shall lead with a discussion of what Mencius and Xunzi said about the practical question of how to become good, because that is truer to their primary focus. I close the discussion of each thinker by addressing his view about the source of moral judgment.

## 1     Mencius: Feeling Reflection

With Mencius, we immediately start slipping outside well-worn grooves in thinking about the relation between reflection and feeling when we recognize that there is no good equivalent to "reason" as a faculty distinct from feeling and desiring. He does distinguish between great and small parts of one's body (6A14). If one nurtures the small parts, such as the ones disposed to eating and drinking, one becomes a small person. If one nurtures the great parts, by which Mencius means the feelings and intuitions that constitute the basis for developing ethical excellence, one becomes a great person. Feelings and intuitions come from *xin* 心, the word which literally means "heart," but which came to stand for the seat of both thinking and feeling, the mind. Not only are thinking and feeling construed as coming from a single source, but that source, the mind, is not conceived dualistically as separate from the body but rather is *of* the body as it is composed of the psycho-physical energy stuff called *qi* 氣. Human *qi* on Mencius' view has inborn cognitive and affective tendencies to move in certain directions. He calls these tendencies the four *xin* 心 (hearts or feelings) that can develop into ethical virtues.

The first heart, *ceyin zhi xin* 惻隱 之 心 (compassion), can develop into *ren* 仁 (human-heartedness or the virtue of loving or caring for others). The second, *xiuwu* 羞惡 (shame and dislike), can develop into *yi* 義. *Yi* has two meanings. It can be a property of actions. It is often translated into English as "rightness," but it more specifically is a kind of appropriateness or fittingness to the circumstances in which the action is performed. *Yi* can also be a virtue of persons. It is often translated into English as "righteousness" but should be glossed as "a firm and constant dedication to doing what is right." Shame and dislike are negative affective reactions to actions perceived as shameful or inappropriate, and can grow into the virtue of righteousness. The third heart, *ciran* 辭讓 (deference and yielding), can develop into *li* 禮 (observing ritual propriety, or observing customary practices that signify respect for others through expressing the attitudes of deference and yielding to them). The fourth, *shifei* 是非 (the disposition to make distinctions between "this" and "not this"), can develop into *zhì* 智 or wisdom (making accurate distinctions between things, categorizing them appropriately, including actions as appropriate or inappropriate, and making good judgments that allow a person to live an ethically excellent life). Thus wisdom seems to the virtue required to complete the other three virtues.

The first three hearts are clearly affective, but Mencius talks about them in ways that do not rule out cognitive components in these feelings. To respond to someone's suffering is to perceive him or her as suffering. Furthermore, Mencius in 1A7 and 3A5 links the feeling of compassion with perceiving the one who is suffering as innocent, or as undeserving of the suffering. King Xuan in 1A7 is led to spare an ox being led to ritual slaughter because its terror reminds him of an innocent man being led to execution. In 3A5, Mencius links the compassion we feel for a child about to fall into a well with her not having done anything to deserve such a fate. The feelings of shame and dislike also include thoughts that it would be shameful to perform a certain action. 6A10 provides an example of this feeling in the beggar who rejects food offered with abuse on the grounds that it would be shameful to accept the food. Deference and yielding are affective attitudes one adopts toward one's parents or elders, for example, and involve thoughts of what is proper and respectful. The fourth heart might be conceived as purely cognitive, but "*shi/fei*" can have the connotation of accepting or rejecting, which is why they are sometimes translated as "approval/disapproval." So it is not definitive but plausible to interpret Mencius as conceiving all four of the hearts as simultaneously cognitive and affective. They can be conceived as affective reactions that are infused with thought and meaning-conferring perception.

In what way are these hearts the basis for becoming good? The way Mencius addresses this question is not without ambiguity, but his most plausible metaphor for them is that of sprouts or seedlings.[3] They have an inborn direction of growth (a barley sprout cannot grow into a wheat plant), but by themselves they do not constitute fully-grown or mature goodness. Take the heart of compassion. People spontaneously feel compassion for a small child about to fall into a well (2A6), but a king, despite having the heart of

---

[3] In *Mencius* 6A2, he compares the tendencies in human nature toward the ethical with the tendency of water to flow downward unless it is dammed up or struck with one's hand. The implication of this water metaphor is that people will become good unless there is interference. The sprout metaphor, on the other hand, implies that the ethical tendencies need positive nurturance such as a secure livelihood, ethical education, and the personal effort to reflect on one's sprouts. I have argued that in fact these two metaphors imply significantly different views about the character of the four hearts that raises important issues about what it is for something to be innate. See Wong (2015).

compassion, readily drafts his people into wars of territorial expansion and throws their lives into chaos; people have an inborn sense that it would be shameful to accept food offered in an abusive way, but despite having the heart of shame and dislike they can accept a morally compromising job for the sake of a big salary (6A10). The occasions when people react as they should are indications of the inborn tendencies of the sprouts or of their proper growth; the occasions when they fail to react as they should are indications of unrealized growth or even worse, the withering of the sprouts.

In 6A7, Mencius compares the inborn hearts or feelings to barley seeds planted into the earth. Differences in the yield are not due to the seeds but rather to differences in "the fertility of the soil, the nourishment of the rain and the dew, and the human effort invested" (translation by Bloom 2009: 125). Moral growth depends on having the right developmental conditions. In 1A7, he stresses that for people to have "constant minds" (minds reliably set on becoming good) they must have constant livelihoods. When poverty and inconstant livelihood prevail, such that people must be preoccupied with mere survival, crime burgeons, and the king who lets such conditions prevail and then punishes his people for their crimes is laying a trap for them (1A7).

The environment is crucial to a person's moral growth, but so is the person's effort invested into growing the sprouts. This effort begins with *si* 思 (6A14–15), often translated as "thinking" but having more specific meanings of "pondering," "considering," and "reflecting." In his conversations with kings of Chinese states, Mencius urges them to reflect. He is trying to get them to re-evaluate their priorities, which typically are focused on consolidating and extending the power of their states and securing their status as rulers. They are understandably preoccupied with holding onto power in the aptly named "Warring States" period. But Mencius is trying to get them to question their assumptions about the basis of power and in particular about the basis of the loyalty, or lack of it, that their people have toward them.

In 1A1, King Hui asks Mencius for advice on how he could profit his state. Mencius warns that by modeling for his people an overriding concern for profit, the king encourages them to focus on what is of profit *for themselves* and in doing so endangers the state. Mencius suggests that if the king were to attend only to *ren* 仁 (human-heartedness), and *yi* 義 (rightness), his state will be in far better health and his subjects would be wholeheartedly loyal to him. Thus Mencius deflects the king's focus on profit by presenting the way to strengthen his people's allegiance. Ultimately, however, ethical excellence requires wholehearted devotion to *ren* and *yi* for their own sakes and not just as means. In his subsequent conversations with the kings,

Mencius appeals to the hearts he believes they possess as human beings, such as compassion and shame and dislike. He believes kings can be moved by their people's suffering to care for them properly (and thus to achieve *ren*). It is also right for kings to promote their people's welfare, and Mencius believes he can appeal to their sense of how shameful it would be to fail in this duty (and thus help them to achieve *yi*).

In 1A7, King Xuan asks whether someone like him could protect the people, as Mencius has been urging. In response, Mencius asks about the occasion on which the king spared an ox being led to ritual slaughter for consecration of a bell. The king recalls that he spared the ox because he could not bear its trembling, like an innocent person being led to the execution ground. The king also decided that the ritual consecration must go on and ordered that a sheep take the ox's place. The king heard that the people understood his act to be motivated by cheapness: substituting the less expensive sheep for the ox. Mencius assures the king that it was his compassion that motivated him, because he witnessed the ox's suffering. An exemplary person must respond to an innocent's suffering once he sees it, which is why he chooses to stay out of the kitchen. He goes onto suggest that surely the king could extend the compassion he felt toward the ox to his people. In fact, he goes on to imply that it would be shameful for the king to spare the ox but not to spare his own people. To say that he could spare the ox from compassion but not spare his people, says Mencius, is like saying he can see the tip of an autumn hair but not a cartload of firewood.

Sometimes we do not understand why we do things. The story of 1A7 has enough psychological complexity so that it is quite understandable why the king is not so clear on why he spared the ox. Mencius is trying to get him to *si* on his motivations in trying to persuade him that he has the motivational wherewithal to be a true king. This part of the 1A7 passage contains a characteristic form of Mencian reasoning: reflecting takes the form of turning over in one's mind certain elements of one's past and present experience so that certain patterns or analogical associations emerge. In this case, it is the association between the innocent man and the ox, and then the ox and the king's suffering people.

It is not just the reflection on relevant similarities that Mencius urges upon the king. It is *feeling* from relevant similarities. When we recall an emotionally significant event, we typically re-feel it to some degree. Some of the same neural circuitry re-activates. Indirect evidence for this claim is provided by observations of the psychologists Clore and Ortony to the effect that an object can acquire emotional meaning through "reinstatement," which is frequently non-conscious and based on resemblance between features of the past situation that provoked the emotion and those of the present situation.[4] Reinstated emotion can unconsciously result from *irrelevant* similarities between the past and present situation. The fact that one's work colleague looks very much like the classmate bully in one's child-hood is not a good reason for being irritated at him. However, reacting to the present on the basis of resemblance to a past situation can be warranted and/or a conscious matter. In getting the king to recall what he felt about the ox and reminding him of his people's suffering, Mencius is trying to get the king to reinstate his compassion in a way that warrants the reoccur-rence, and where the warrant is the fact of his people's suffering.

But the king substituted a sheep for the ox so that the ritual could go on. Does this mean he was mistaken to have spared the ox?[5] Was his emotional reaction to the terrified ox based on its resemblance to the innocent man mistaken in the way that irritable reactions to one's colleague are mistaken? King Xuan showed some uncertainty about his own motivation for sparing the ox. Mencius explains his motivation in a way that is plausible, as well as flattering, to the king: that ultimately it was more important for the rit-ual to be performed than for an animal to be spared, but once having seen the ox, the king was right to give expression to his compassion for the ox. Mencius says it is the working of human-heartedness in the exemplary per-son (the most prominent Confucian character ideal) that if he sees animals alive, he cannot bear to see them die. So he stays out of the kitchen. Though we may rightly be disturbed at the thought that the exemplary person will have someone else who is lower in the social hierarchy do his killing for him, *a different part* of Mencius' justification is plausible: compassion as respon-siveness to the suffering of another must be nurtured through expressing it, and trying to regulate its expression too tightly, turning it off in the face of suffering, even suffering one rightly inflicts, might result in dulling one's responsiveness.

## 2     Pleasure in Acting on the Sprouts

The point of getting King Xuan to remember his sparing of the ox may have been not only to remind him that he is capable of feeling

---

[4] Clore and Ortony go on to characterize these processes in ways I do not necessarily think are the most useful. They hold that direct computation of emotional meaning is "theory-based," i.e., rule-based computation of emotional meaning based on "underlying" aspects of the situation rather than "surface" features that are perceptually accessible. Reinstatement is "prototype"-based processing that goes on the similarity of perceptually accessible features (2000: 37) possessed by a present situation to that of a past situation that has triggered an emotion, resulting in reinstatement of that emotion in the present. This categorization neglects the possibility that the similarity between situations that can reinstate an emotion need not be based on surface similarity. This possibility will be explored shortly.
[5] Emily McRae (2011) argues that the king was mistaken, but I hold this is true only if he had not seen the ox. Mencius clearly justifies what the king did after having seen the ox.

compassion. It reminds him of how satisfying it felt to act on his compassion. The remembered pleasure of acting on a moral sprout can spur one to act on it again when the opportunity arises, or it can help one overcome reluctance to act when it has a cost to the self. The role of analogical reflection is well known in Mencius, but what is not so well recognized is that according to Mencius desires can grow along analogical lines, often guided by thinking that is also feeling at the same time. Mencius is trying to get the king to recognize *and* re-live that he experienced pleasure upon sparing another being from suffering. The king can then realize in affectively moving fashion that he can experience such pleasure again if he spares his people.

Realization of the potential to grow one's compassion, then, is reinforced by what we might call today a feedback loop mechanism based on the pleasure of acting compassionately, a feedback loop that can be guided by analogical reflection on what has given one pleasure in the past. The self-feeding feature of the mechanism is why Mencius said that knowing how to fill out the moral beginnings is like a fire starting up or a spring breaking through (2A6). Once the process of growth gets going, it can accelerate.

This does not mean that Mencius has a hedonistic picture of human motivation. To derive pleasure from sparing another from suffering or rejecting the shameful is not equivalent to doing it for the sake of pleasure. But neither is pleasure the mere by-product of dispositions to do these things. It is also a signal from the body that one has done something that is good for it, something that sustains and expands its powers. On a dualistic view of the person, of course, pleasure may be associated with the body and not the mind, and on such a view, the pleasures of the body may not be a reliable signal of what expands the powers of the mind. But on a Mencian view of mind as an especially important *part* of the body, the pleasures of acting on compassion and doing what is right have credibility as signals for what is good for the whole person. Of course, one might ask how Mencius knows that the pleasures of compassion and rightness are to be given priority over the pleasures of the "small part" of the self such as the pleasures of eating and drinking.

## 3    Coming to Know Moral Priorities Through Reflection

Sometimes it looks as if Mencius simply asserts that it is part of our inborn moral knowledge to know priorities such as doing what is right over continuing to live in case one must choose between them. In 6A10, he says that all human beings, and not just exemplary persons, have the mind that desires some things more than life and detests some things more than death. At other times, he provides a reflective path to realizing the satisfactions of acting in accord with such priorities. It is fairly easy for him to slide between these different ways of talking about human knowledge of moral priorities given his conception of the innate beginnings of morality as incomplete dispositions that need further development. Thus we may have some intuitive notions of the priority of rightness over life, but not in all cases where this priority holds true. In 6A10, Mencius says that a beggar will reject food that is offered with abuse even if he is in danger of starving to death. But he also observes that plenty of people will accept a large salary without regard for propriety or rightness. That is why development of the four hearts or feelings of goodness is necessary, and reflection plays a crucial role in such development.

Here is one reflective path that is charted by Mencius. Tranquility in the face of tumultuous circumstance is highly valued in early Chinese philosophy.[6] In 2A2, Mencius is asked, if he were appointed a high minister of Qi (King Xuan's state), and if the king were to become a hegemon or even king of the entire country, would his heart remain unperturbed (more literally, would his heart remain "unmoved")? Mencius replies that his heart has been unperturbed since he was forty. Perturbation here is best interpreted as disturbance or anxiety. Success, as well as failure, can cause such perturbation. The higher one climbs, the farther one can fall. In explaining how one achieves tranquility, Mencius says that he heard a saying of Confucius: "If, on looking inward, I find that I am not upright, I must be in fear of even a poor fellow in coarse clothing. If, on looking inward, I find that I am upright, I may proceed against thousands and tens of thousands" (2A2, Bloom 2009: 29). Mencius is suggesting that identifying with rightness allows one to forget the anxieties one has about oneself: concern about getting social honors and rank, for example (6A16), which one is bound to lose in the end, along with one's life.

Consider a conception of agency that in one important respect is close to the Mengzian view of human beings: Harry Frankfurt's view (1971) that our actions are only fully our own when we are able to endorse the desires we act on, i.e., when we have second-order desires to act from our first-order desires. On Frankfurt's view, such reflective endorsement is appropriate for the kind of creatures we are. Reflective endorsement is what Mengzi has in mind, and when he spells out what happiness must be for such reflective creatures, he says, in effect, that it cannot be separated from our attempts to find meaning in what we do for the short time we are here. As in the case of Mencius getting the king to remember what it felt like to spare the ox

---

[6] Consider *Analects* 4.2, where the Master said, "Those persons who are not human-hearted (*rén* 仁) are neither able to endure hardship for long, nor to enjoy happy circumstances for any period of time. The human-hearted are content in being human-hearted; the wise (*zhì* 知) flourish in it" (translation adapted and modified from Ames and Rosemont, 1998, Kindle location 1729–1731).

while reminding him of his duties to his people, *detached* reflection will not achieve the desired psychological change. To appreciate the appeal of identifying with something larger than the self, one must have at least some of the relevant kinds of experience, both of anxiety for the successes and failures of the self *and* of liberating forgetfulness of the self. It is felt reflection that has the power to change.

Affect-laden reflection has the power to shape us. Mencius' conception of how emotion can be transformed and extended through affect-laden reflection is a corrective to two opposing one-sided tendencies in Western thinking about the relation between reflection and emotion. One tendency, represented by Kant, is to think of emotion as a threatening distraction from the kind of dispassionate and objective thinking that ideally guides human conduct. The other tendency, represented by Hume, is to think of emotion as the dominant force in human life, dictating our ultimate aims and assigning to reason, if it is up to it (and on some interpretations of Hume, it is not up to even that), the task of figuring out how best to realize those aims. This dichotomization of reflection and emotion leaves out the ways that the two can interact and interweave: through its marriage with feeling, reflection becomes motivationally effective, and through being guided by moral reflection, the feeling becomes intelligent.

## 4          What did Mencius think about the Source of Moral Judgment?

As indicated earlier, at least three of the four hearts that Mencius believes to be the bases of becoming good are clearly affective with cognitive components. The prominence of the affective in his theory might prompt some to liken him to Western moral sentimentalists, as holding a kind of moral sense theory. However, the cognitive components of the Mencian affective attitudes complicate the picture. If the feelings of shame/dislike, for example, can involve the thought that something would be shame*ful*, perhaps the hearts involve certain intuitive judgments that in principle are separable from the affective components. Along the same lines, the thought that something is shameful could be plausibly taken to imply that it would be seriously wrong. This interpretation of Mencius would not justify saying that he identifies the source of moral judgment as feeling *rather than* a cognitive apprehension of moral properties such as rightness. Rather, what is apprehended is simultaneously cognized as well as felt.

There is a way of expanding on this idea of the felt intuition or felt reflection that may explain why they are found together. This way involves the further idea that apprehensions or judgments reflect what the agent cares about. We do not come by knowledge by being detached, neutral observers of the world. We notice and inquire into matters we care about. And what we care about is bound up with our feelings. On Mencius' view of human nature, we have it in us to care about the suffering of others, about doing right by others or by ourselves, and to behave properly and with respect toward others and oneself. The fact that we care about these things helps to explain why our duties to do something about them become salient to the intellect and why we have the motivation to act on them. One need not reduce moral judgment to an expression of sentiment in order to see why judgment and sentiment typically accompany one another.

This interpretation is compatible with Mencius' belief that the inborn hearts are implanted in human nature by *tian* 天 (2A7, 7A1), which literally refers to the sky, and is usually translated as Heaven. *Tian* in Mencius has the status of an ordering force in the world, and it is sometimes characterized as having a plan for human beings to fulfill. Mencius regards the way for human beings to live, *rendao* 人道, as a proper part of *tiandao* 天道 or Heaven's Way. In order that human beings may come to know the way they are meant to live, Heaven implanted in them thinking and feeling dispositions that enable them both to know and to live according to the human way.

Thus on one plausible interpretation of Mencius, Heaven endows human beings with the dispositions to make correct intuitive judgments, e.g., that someone is suffering and in need of help, or that accepting food offered with abuse or in an insulting way would be a shameful thing to do. Such judgments are made spontaneously and without deliberation or calculation, and are rooted in the inborn dispositions that form the beginnings of morality. These intuitive or what one might call "baseline" judgments do not provide the answers for all occasions on which one asks what is the right thing to do or how to go about living an ethically excellent life. However, they form a kind of basis for deriving the answers through analogical reasoning. When we are wondering what to do, we try to find the closest analogy between the present situation and a past situation in which we have made a baseline judgment. We then identify a response to the present situation that most resembles the response embodied in the baseline judgment. For example, a baseline judgment that has to do with compassion is that it is right or appropriate to try to prevent a child from falling into a well (*Mencius* 2A6). A feature of that situation that Mencius holds is relevant to its rightness is the child's innocence (3A5). Reflecting on whether one should help another person, therefore, involves reflecting on cases such as the child and the well, and then determining whether the person in question is suffering and innocent.[7] If Mencius does have a theory that human

---

[7] I expand on the 2002 work in an essay, Wong, "Feeling, Reflection, and Reasoning in the *Mencius*" forthcoming by Springer in the *Dao Companion to Mencius*, edited by Xiao Yang.

beings arrive at moral judgments through intuition and analogical reasoning, and if this theory is metaphysically realist (if moral properties exist independently of how human beings respond to them), we have a theory that recognizes the relevant cognitions to be also affective, to come embedded in feelings, and to form the basis for a realistic and insightful moral psychology of how people can become good.

## 5    Xunzi: The Power of the Mind to Tame and Reshape the Self

About half a generation later Xunzi arises as Mencius' rival for the mantle of defender of Confucius' teachings. In the chapter entitled 性惡 xing e ([Human] Nature is Bad), Xunzi asserts that human nature contains a love of profit, envy, and hatred, and desires of the eyes and ears that lead to violence and anarchy. To avoid these consequences, it takes wei 偽 (conscious activity, deliberate effort), models and teaching, guidance through observing ritual propriety and yi 義 or appropriateness (Knoblock translation 1988–1994, hereafter abbreviated 'K' with chapter and section, volume and page following, K23.1b, v. 3, 151). "Xing" names the raw psychological material that human beings have to work on, and hence it is part of what is unlearned and unacquired. However, both the Mencius' and the Xunzi's references to the xing of human beings should be translated as "human nature" only with significant qualification. It should not be taken to imply any essentialism about what it is to be human, as Roger Ames (1991, 2002) points out. It also obscures the fact that Xunzi attributes unlearned capabilities to human beings that he does not subsume under their xing. Among these is the capability of the heart and mind (xin 心) to approve or disapprove of the desires and emotions arising from xing. It is this capability that enables us to recognize that xing urgently needs transformation.

In arguing for the need of transformation, Xunzi says, "If one acts with only profit in mind, loss is certain" (K19.1d, v. 3, 56). In more contemporary terms, his point is that one must be genuinely willing to forgo advantage for oneself in order to be a trustworthy partner in cooperation and therefore in order to benefit from cooperation. Xunzi's point is not far from identifying the solution to "the problem of emotional commitment," as characterized by the economist Robert Frank (2001). Frank has noted that forms of mutually beneficial cooperation are hindered or made impossible by the inability to trust one's potential partners. One needs assurance that others will not take advantage of one's cooperation and "bail out" of the agreement when it comes time for them to do their part. Frank proposes that evolution's answer to this fundamental problem for human cooperation is the capacity to make verifiable emotional commitments to others even if those commitments foreclose ways of acting that are beneficial for the self.

Showing sympathy with others makes one more trustworthy because it provides them with some assurance that one will live up to one's agreements even if one can gain an advantage by breaking them.

Xunzi is in fact proposing such a solution: to become a trustworthy partner in cooperation, one must show emotional commitments to others that go beyond ones that are motivated by calculating self-interest. This commitment cannot be generated merely from the intellectual recognition that one's long-term self-interest requires it, because long-term self-interest is still calculating self-interest. There must be other-concerned motivations that are already within human nature. In fact, there are places in the text where he says exactly that. In the chapter on ritual, Xunzi asserts that all creatures of blood and *qi* 氣 love members of their own kind, and of these, human beings do so the most because they have awareness (K 19.9b, v. 3, 69). Such natural desires and feelings have the potential for supporting the kind of trust in others that is necessary for cooperation.

That Xunzi had this more complex view of human nature is not so apparent in the *xing e* chapter, where he is concerned to express disagreement with Mencius' emphasis on human *xing* as good or at least congenial to the development of goodness. Perhaps partly to distinguish his position from that of Mencius, and perhaps because he thinks that Mencius is dangerously optimistic, Xunzi highlights what is *e* in our *xing*. But in chapters where he is not criticizing Mencius and more concerned with explaining *how* moral development can actually happen, he acknowledges that human beings have unlearned motivations that are congenial to goodness.

Ultimately, then, Xunzi must envision moral cultivation as a complex process in which one must not only restrain the pursuit of self-interest for the sake of self-interest but also deliberately strengthen and cultivate natural concern for others. This is a plausible view of the complexity and diversity of motivations that come with our biology. We have unlearned motivations that both resist and depart from goodness and unlearned motivations that could be nurtured toward goodness – not necessarily because they are already good, but because their direction of growth is congenial and susceptible to being channeled and shaped toward goodness.

In sum, although Xunzi does seem to believe we have the right emotional stuff for trustworthiness, he is careful to stress that this stuff does not make us automatically so. Instead, the emotions that go into trustworthiness need to be strengthened *in relation to* the desires for gain and profit and related emotions such as envy. In this respect, Xunzi's understanding of how the emotional commitment problem is to be solved is *superior* to Frank's. Frank sometimes writes as if the biologically given capacities were all that are needed, revealing excessive confidence that biological evolution provides all of the solution. What Xunzi understood is that however these emotional capacities got there, they need to be cultivated and refined through culture to do the sort of job that both he and Frank think they do.

At the end of the *xing e* chapter, Xunzi says, "If you do not know your son, look at his friends; if you do not know your lord look to his attendants. It is the environment that is critical! It is the environment that is critical!" (K 23.8, v. 3, 162). An especially important part of the environment is culture, and for Xunzi an especially critical cultural tool is ritual. Rituals include ceremonies that mark major passages of life such as birth, coming of age, marriage, and death, but also ceremonies and customs woven into the fabric of everyday life, such as the drinking ceremony that begins a banquet in a village, or ways to respectfully greet another or to give and receive gifts. To perform such rituals correctly is most of all to focus on expressing the respect and care that others deserve. Observing such rituals helps to correct the undue concern for the self that is a large part of our natural inheritance. One feature of ritual that might have appealed to Xunzi is its pervasiveness in human life and recurrent performance. It is embedded into the fabric of life because it marks the major passages and because it constitutes the protocol of various types of social interaction. The pervasive and repetitive training effect makes ritual most suitable for the task of taming the powerful and troublesome part of human nature.

That task is the reason why Xunzi chooses not the metaphor of growing sprouts but a craft metaphor such as a potter molding a dish from clay (K 23.4a v. 3, p. 157) to convey that human beings must work with their own nature to transform it from something that is initially bad into something good. But to fully explain how rituals can have a powerfully transformative effect, Xunzi must acknowledge that the function of rituals is not simply to constrain the troublesome emotions and desires, it turns out, but also to strengthen and give expression to the morally constructive emotions. Consider Xunzi's argument that the mourning period for parents must extend into the third year because of the natural emotions involved (K 19.9c, v. 3, 70). Xunzi says the length was established to be equal to the emotions involved: "The greater the wound, the longer it remains; the more pain it gives, the more slowly it heals" (K 19.9a, v. 3, 69). Though Xunzi is not persuasive when he insists that natural emotion dictates a precise mourning period for parents, the underlying idea is plausible.

Emotions and desires cannot simply be repressed or their expression in action simply held in check by the mind's capacity for approval and disapproval. Rather, they must be given, under the direction of the mind, an appropriate measure of satisfaction and expressed in socially beneficial ways. Rituals that "fit" the love one feels for parents and the intensity and duration of one's grief upon losing them give expression to and strengthen the dispositions to have these emotions more consistently. Another ritual that performs both the restraining and expressive functions is the protocol of the village drinking ceremony, in which all villagers drink from a single cup in order of the seniority. In drinking according to seniority, the young learn to restrain their impulses and defer to the older, but in all drinking from the same cup, the common bond is affirmed. So understood, Xunzi is not, in the end, categorically opposed to Mencius' position, especially if Mencius acknowledges that desires and emotions, when given undue priority, could grow to be weeds, choking the growth of the moral sprouts. Still, Xunzi can object, and I think rightly so, that the troublesome part of human nature is far more powerful than Mencius thinks it was.

Xunzi's metaphor of the craftsman is appropriate given the emphasis he places on the role of the mind to construct and order the human psyche. Its tools are rituals that must have the right form do the job: mourning rituals that have the right length to give expression to grief; rituals such as the drinking ceremony to restrain the tendency to give undue emphasis to the self and to express and strengthen feelings of unity with others. The moral craftsman must shape and select the tools he uses to fit the material he works on. To bring home this point, let me extend the craft analogy. Raw material has a structure that must be respected by the craftsman because it, together with the function the artifact is meant to fulfill, constrains the nature and shape of the final product. Analogously, to produce beings capable of sustained self-restraint with respect to desires for material goods and sensual gratification, the artisan heart-mind needs to identify structural properties of the human psychic economy that make self-restraint not only bearable but also necessary for a far greater and more deeply satisfying good.

We have already identified love of one's kind as one of the most important features of the material that the moral craftsmen must work with. But how must the craftsman deal with the potentially troublesome features, the desires for gain and sensual satisfaction? Xunzi acknowledges that the craftsman mind cannot merely strive to eliminate or repress desires such as those for material goods and sensual satisfaction. In seeking to remove the causes of conflict between people, one must assure some measure of satisfaction of these desires. Human beings are born with desires, he says, which if not satisfied cannot but lead them to seek to satisfy them (K 19.1a-b, v. 3, 55). To avert the conflict that would ensue, claims Xunzi, the sages *sheng* 生 ("generated," "produced") ritual and moral principles so as to regulate the human pursuit of the goods for satisfying desires and at the same time to assure that these goods would not be exhausted (K23.1c, v. 3, 152). The meaning of ritual, concludes Xunzi, is to nurture (K 19.1b, v. 3, 55).

Is it sufficient, then, to simply allot some goods for a measure of satisfaction and for the heart-mind simply to judge that such measure is enough?

Xunzi's position is much more insightful than that. For him, there is no absolute amount that constitutes sufficient material gain and sensual satisfaction. The intensity of a desire interacts with other desires within a person's psychic economy. The *Xunzi* says that a serene and happy heart-mind will be satisfied with colors less than ordinary, with sounds less than average, and a diet of vegetables and a broth of greens that nurture the mouth (K 22.6e, v. 3, 13). On the other hand, if that security and peace is missing, no amount of material goods will be experienced as enough (K 22.6d, v. 3, 137–138).

That serenity and happiness is based in natural emotions and desires that could be deeply satisfying and sustaining of social cooperation when channeled in the right directions. When love of one's own kind and gratitude to them for one's nurturance are fostered and strengthened through ritual activity, they provide a context within which self-restraint eventually is no longer felt as a burden but rather enabling of a greater contentment than could ever have been possible otherwise.

Happiness achieved through the cultivation of love and gratitude by the right forms of ritual places the satisfaction of troublesome motivations in a new psychic context, where they become much less urgent and less demanding of our attention and personal resources. And going in the other direction, we can see how moderating the desires for material gain and sensual gratification might make it possible for us to dedicate more of our attention and personal resources to the cultivation of love and gratitude. Restraint of the troublesome motivations is not sufficient by itself, but it can provide some psychic space within which we can begin to experience some of deep satisfactions of relationship. And such experience can help motivate further restraint, which in turn can make possible taking deeper satisfaction in relationship.

Thus Xunzi conceives of an expansive role for the mind's reflections on how to change the self. But he, like Mencius, acknowledges the importance of feeling reflection. For the Confucians, one of the aims of dedicated practice at the performance of ritual is that one need not think about the basic mechanics of knowing how to do it so that one may reflect on and feel the meaning it is supposed to express. As Fingarette (1972: 9) remarked about one of our contemporary rituals of greeting, one who knows how to shake hands does not have to self-consciously direct the motions of her hand, but rather spontaneously coordinates with the other. The point is not to be *mindless* during this dance of hands, but to liberate oneself from having to think about how to do it so that one can be *mindful* of the moral and emotional significance of what one is doing. As Raposa (2004: 115) observes, ritual activity "organizes and directs the attention of its participants, supplying a distinctive frame for human experience." Xunzi's description in the chapter on ritual of the proper form of rites of mourning illustrates this idea of disciplining and focusing attention. Preparation of the body, he says, should prevent its being "hideous" so that the mourner can keep in mind duties of grief and respect for the person who has been lost. Over the course of mourning, the body is progressively moved farther away so that one's attention gradually returns to the ordinary course of life whereby one cares for the needs of the living. (K19.5a, v. 3, pp. 64–65). The ritual helps one focus properly on the dead and to meditate on their importance while helping one in the transition to caring once again for the needs of the living.

The emphasis on ritual as a crucial tool in crafting the self raises the question of whether we have available to us anything like its equivalent in our cultures. Most of us are academics who live much of our lives in institutions that are structured and perhaps sustained by many rituals, and if this is generally true, or more true than we at first thought, our next step is to become much more self-conscious of how we are deliberately, or more likely inadvertently, shaping ourselves to be. There is a natural worry about how ritual activity could be used as a tool of self-cultivation in a big, culturally pluralistic society. While there are some common rituals such as the pledge of allegiance in schools or the playing of the national anthem at sporting events with the audience taking the customary stance of hand over the heart and facing the flag, one might think these common rituals are too few and do not sufficiently pervade the fabric of everyday life in the way Xunzi had in mind. But here I think Confucians such as Xunzi overemphasized the importance of homogeneity in rituals. Culturally pluralistic societies can be harmonious in their diversity. In the United States, many of us have become accustomed to the fact that different communities have different ritual forms for expressing respect and concern, and it is possible to appreciate that this diversity adds to the richness of our societies. Though I do not know how to shake hands in the way that some younger people do, I can recognize and delight in at least roughly the moral and emotional meanings that their rituals convey.

It is clear that for Xunzi, the mind, in its capacity of judging whether it would be a good thing to pursue the satisfaction of a desire, is no Humean slave to the passions. Xunzi envisions the mind to take charge of its feelings and desires and embark on a program of training and reshaping the psychic economy. On the other hand, this is no Kantian program. The mind is not judging what is right or rational independently of its feelings and desires. It is judging which of these motivational items need to be tamped down and restrained, even if satisfied in due measure, and which of its feelings and desires, many of which may only be latent or suppressed in a situation of conflict with others, should be fostered and strengthened in the appropriate environment.

## 6    What did Xunzi Think about the Source of Moral Judgment?

Xunzi presents a startlingly different alternative theory to Mencius'. Rather than *tian*'s implanting baseline moral intuitions or judgments in human nature, Heaven (or "Nature" as some translators such as Knoblock think is a more accurate translation of Xunzi's idea of *tian*) produces creatures whose nature is troublesome, even destructive to others and to themselves. Instead of Mencian contentful inborn intuitions about what is right, *tian* provides human beings with the intelligence to identify the problem of conflict created by powerful forms of narrow self-concern and the ingenuity to generate rituals to reshape the psychic economy. Human intelligence also devises standards of rightness to structure the benefits and responsibilities of social cooperation so that our self-regarding desires and feelings receive a proper measure of satisfaction but within a larger social and psychological context in which the desires and feelings of others also receive a proper measure of satisfaction.

In light of such claims about the origin of rituals and standards of rightness, it is tempting to call Xunzi a kind of moral constructivist: morality consists of the norms that would be invented and adopted so as to most optimally address the end of preventing destructive human conflict, or more positively, to reshape human psychology so as to prevent the depletion of natural resources to satisfy human desire and to provide for the widespread satisfaction of such desire. Insofar as the existence of moral rules depends on human adoption of the purpose of preventing destructive conflict and promoting widespread satisfaction of human desire, the theory is not realist but nevertheless purports to provide an objective basis for moral norms. These norms are justified insofar as they accomplish the purpose of morality.

On the other hand, Xunzi might seem to have the view that there is a "best" shape for human psychology to take, or at least that there are shapes it could take that are bad for human beings. The bad shapes are ones in which the desire for sensual satisfaction and material goods are pursued without restraint. Greater satisfaction is obtained when this desire gets tamped down and the social desires are fostered and strengthened through ritual. In this regard, one might be tempted to call Xunzi a moral realist, about human well-being and about the best way (or at the very least about the better and worse ways) to foster that well-being in society.

As indicated at the end of the last section, it is apparent that Xunzi envisions a great deal of sophisticated reflection and reasoning to go into the design of ritual and correct moral principles. On the other hand, the type of reflection and reasoning that is relevant is firmly anchored in the structure of the human psychic economy. Even if the project of becoming good involves significant transformation of our given natures, it is constrained by certain aspects of the structure of our natures. We cannot simply disregard our desires for material goods, for example, but see to it that these desires receive a measure of satisfaction in a way that is compatible with satisfaction of our social desires and for the measure of meaning that rituals confer on life. Xunzi cannot be called a rationalist if being one involves bypassing these aspects of our affective nature. It is in this sense that reflection and feeling must both play necessary roles in arriving at moral judgment.

## 7    How to Place Mencius and Xunzi in the Context of Western Ethical Theory

It is best to use extreme caution in applying a categorical metaethical label (such as "moral sentimentalist," "constructivist," or "realist") derived from the Western tradition to either Mencius or Xunzi. They did not explicitly pose the same set of questions that Western metaethicists posed to themselves. Those textual remarks that can be interpreted as supporting one or another metaethical position appear in the course of laying out and defending conceptions of how human beings can become good, which was their overriding theoretical concern. To the extent that we can identify metaethical views about the source of moral judgment in the texts, they can hold a great deal of interest, especially Xunzi's, who seems at times to have great affinities with contemporary naturalistic approaches to ethical theory. It should expand our sense of philosophical possibility to see how these two philosophers, who both take the role of feeling in morality very seriously, depart from the sort of metaethical theory that Western sentimentalists have provided.

It should also expand our sense of philosophical possibility to see what kinds of philosophical discourse emerge from a tradition that pays a great deal of attention to *how* one realizes its moral ideals. Mencius' and Xunzi's theories are informed by a concrete sense of specific practices that could and were used. These practices involve complex interweavings of reflection, feeling, and desire that resists reduction to the dominance of reason over emotion and desire or to its submission as an instrument for the fulfillment of emotion and desire. The Western sentimentalists did appreciate the need to educate sentiments so that they could become truly moral, but often they are handicapped by an overly simplified conception of the relation between feeling and reflection, so there is not nearly as much informative explanation of how sentiments actually do become educated. In charting the future of moral sentimentalism, we would do well to look at resources the Confucians have provided.

# 13 Whither Sentimentalism? On Fear, the Fearsome, and the Dangerous

*Justin D'Arms and Daniel Jacobson*

The task of writing an essay titled "Whither Sentimentalism?" is daunting in several respects, not least because of the diversity of important projects focused on the role of emotions in evaluative thought. We welcome this development and think it salutary for moral philosophy. Nevertheless, our approach in this chapter is to seek a common thesis definitive of sentimentalism that unifies a research program, without impugning those projects that deviate from this paradigm. We think a common thesis can be identified that captures much of the historical tradition as well as many modern approaches to sentimentalism; and we have a view, no doubt controversial, about the direction this program should take, and the outstanding questions it must answer.

We propose to understand *sentimentalism* as the thesis that values depend essentially upon emotional response.[1] Thus a sentimentalist theory of humor identifies the funny with what causes or, more plausibly, what merits amusement. Sentimentalists differ over which values they aim to explicate and how they understand the relevant dependence, as well as in their account of the emotions on which values depend. But they are united in this response-dependency thesis; they agree that the relevant values cannot adequately be explained without appeal to the emotions. Since sentimentalism is committed specifically to the emotion-dependency of the values it explicates, this is what we will mean by response-dependency, not any of the broader notions of that thesis sometimes advanced.[2]

Much of the philosophical literature on sentimentalism advances it either as a generic theory of value or specifically about morality: good and bad, vice and virtue, right and wrong. We would not try to defend such an inclusive sentimentalist theory of value, and we will here treat the adequacy of a sentimentalist theory of morality as an open question, for reasons to

---

[1] Let this be a stipulation for purposes of this paper. Other authors in this volume may understand sentimentalism differently, but we will not attempt here to defend our terminological preference.

[2] Cf. Pettit (1991) who offers perhaps the broadest conception of response dependence.

be explained. In our view, the most promising candidates for a sentimentalist treatment are those values most closely tied to the emotions, which we call the *sentimental values*: the shameful, the fearsome, the funny, and so forth.[3] These values are widely underrated in importance by philosophers and therefore under-theorized. The sentimental value concepts wear their affiliation with specific sentiments on their sleeves. These are evaluative concepts, because thinking that something is funny or shameful is thinking it is good or bad (respectively) in some way, and they are sentimental at least inasmuch as they refer to specific emotions. They will be our focus here. Hence our first answer to the "Whither Sentimentalism?" question is: toward a focus on the sentimental values.

Sentimental values are a promising focus for sentimentalism because the sentiments with which they are associated are plausibly *natural emotions*: psychological kinds that (we claim) are prior to the values they help to explain, and that belong to a common human nature.[4] As we will illustrate in §3, the priority of natural emotions to values enables sentimentalism to meet a familiar challenge from the predominant cognitivist theory of the emotions – which holds that emotions are at least partly constituted by evaluative thoughts – concerning the order of explanation between sentiment and value. And the focus on pan-cultural emotions ensures that the sentimental values have a claim to be human values, not just the values of a specific time or place. This means that all human beings have a stake in them, and that disagreements between cultures over what is shameful or disgusting have a common subject matter: they are about the fittingness of emotions all parties share. Just how many natural emotions there are, and thus how many sentimental values there might be, are questions left for another day.

The pride of place we give to the sentimental values invites the question of how they fit into a volume called *Ethical Sentimentalism*. It is now common for philosophers to draw a distinction between ethics and a narrower notion of morality.[5] Ethics takes as its subject matter all answers to the broadest questions of how to live, if not all of practical reason. The narrow notion focuses much more specifically on obligation and questions of right

[3] We will use such expressions as *the* disgusting and *being* disgusting interchangeably with *disgustingness*, and likewise for analogous expressions about other sentimental values. Each is a way of referring to the generic feature that disgusting things (e.g.) have in common.
[4] About the natural emotions, we reject the idea that there is no priority between property and response, as mooted by Wiggins (1987) and McDowell (1998), though this may be true about other states called emotions. We cannot here defend the claim that a class of emotions are pan-cultural psychological kinds, but it is crucial to note that this is not at all to say that these or any emotions have the same eliciting conditions across times and cultures, which is clearly false.
[5] See Williams (1985: 6).

and wrong, which it often takes as giving overriding or even silencing reasons – perhaps not just to humans but all rational agents. Such sentimental values as the shameful and prideworthy are obviously central to ethics, but so too is the disgusting, which is associated with norms concerning purity.[6] Even the funny plays a subtle but important role in the mores that structure much of social life.

Nevertheless, modern moral philosophy tends to concentrate on the narrow notion, which raises more complex issues. It proves to be a partly empirical question whether wrongness or blameworthiness can be understood in terms of guilt and anger, as seems necessary in order for these concepts to count as sentimental values.[7] Even if the central moral concepts are not sentimental values, however, we contend that sentimentalism has important implications for narrowly construed morality, by constraining the demands of morality so as to cohere with the ineradicable sources of motivation provided by guilt and anger. Although there is much more that needs to be said about these issues, we cannot do more than raise them here.

According to the view we call *neo-sentimentalism*, which is a version of fitting attitude theory, sentimental value judgments invoke a distinctive kind of standard for emotional responses. To think something φ (shameful, funny, etc.), in one important and familiar sense, is to think it *fitting* to feel F (shame, amusement, and so forth) toward it. Equivalently, this is to think the object *merits* response F. To think an emotion fitting is to endorse it specifically as correct. This contrasts with some other considerations about whether to have an emotion. It might be better for an actor not to be frightened of an upcoming performance attended by some influential critic, if fear will inhibit her performance, but that fact does not speak against the fittingness of her fear. The consideration that she is better off not being afraid is irrelevant to whether the performance merits fear: that is, to its fearsomeness. It is a good reason not to be afraid, if she can help it, but it is a reason of the wrong kind.[8]

Several disparate factors suggest the same direction for sentimentalist research. Neo-sentimentalism needs a way of distinguishing considerations of fittingness from wrong kinds of reason. In our view, this requires piecemeal investigations of the natural emotions, interpreting their characteristic appraisals so as to understand which considerations speak to their distinct concerns. The focus on the sentimental values that we advocate

---

[6] See Haidt (2001).

[7] See Mill (1963) and Gibbard (1990) but cf. D'Arms and Jacobson (1994).

[8] See D'Arms and Jacobson (2000b) and (2014a), Rabinowicz and Ronnow-Rasmussen (2004).

requires an argument both for the existence of natural emotions and for their priority to the values that sentimentalism would use them to explain. The plausibility of a sentimentalist theory of morality hangs on whether guilt and anger, or perhaps some other natural emotion, can capture the central (narrowly) moral concepts. In short, we suggest that the overarching answer to the question "Whither Sentimentalism?" is: toward a more profound engagement with the philosophy of emotion. Moreover, such engagement will provide the resources needed to address a trenchant challenge that threatens all forms of sentimentalism, even about those values most amenable to the theory. In what follows, we develop this challenge and answer it on behalf of sentimentalism.

## 1    Sentimentalism and Shadow Skepticism

This paper addresses a skeptical challenge that applies to all sentimentalist views. We call the challenge *shadow skepticism*, because it suggests that the values essentially tied to the emotions are mere shadows of more important, emotion-independent values. Shadow skepticism about the disgusting, for example, typically claims that the evaluatively significant property in that vicinity is contamination. Either the disgusting just is the contaminated – which in this view can be understood without reference to disgust – or else it is not an important value. If so then that would show sentimentalism about the disgusting to be either false or (relatively) insignificant.[9] One reason shadow skepticism presents a fundamental challenge to sentimentalism is that it offers an alternative account of the connection between emotions and values. Although the sentimental values seem most congenial to sentimentalism, in virtue of their obvious affiliation with specific emotions, it does not follow that sentimentalism is true even for these values.

Some philosophers claim that the tie between amusement and the funny, for instance, is merely epistemic rather than constitutive. It is not that the funny just is whatever causes amusement or even what merits

---

[9] The skeptic might grant that a dispositional account of the disgusting (better termed the disgust-causing) identifies a category of psychological or anthropological interest. But he will claim that being such as to cause disgust is not the important bad-making feature of disgusting things; the normatively significant property in the neighborhood is contamination. This argument is analogous to the argument we will soon consider at length about fear and the dangerous. In both cases, the emotion might be claimed to have an adaptive function best specified in terms of a response-independent property such as danger or contamination. Our contention is that insofar as these properties are response-independent, they are inadequate to what matters in the vicinity of disgust and fear. See Kelly (2011) who gives a plausible account of the function of disgust, without making the shadow skeptical move of equating the disgusting with the contaminated. See also D'Arms and Jacobson (2014b) for argument that the importance of the disgusting in moral psychology outstrips contamination.

it; rather, amusement is our (human) way of perceiving something that can be understood without reference to the emotions. According to the incongruity theory of humor, one of the most philosophically influential accounts, the funny is simply the incongruous – where incongruity is construed as a response-independent property: the sort of thing that a pattern-detecting alien without a sense of humor could identify. But the theory either founders on counterexamples or abandons any response-independent notion of incongruity. As Roger Scruton (1987: 162) puts it, "To know what is meant by 'incongruous' you would have to consult, not some independent conception, but the range of objects at which we laugh." We agree. Indeed, since we endorse a sentimentalist theory of the funny, we are committed to denying that any such response-independent account can be adequate.

We have been couching our dispute with the skeptic in terms of the response-dependency of *values*, but this requires some clarification. In the first place, our claim is about the response-dependency of the sentimental value concepts: we offer an account of them that appeals to (fitting) emotions, and we contend that what it is to think something shameful or funny cannot be adequately explained without appeal to the relevant emotional response (inter alia). Sometimes shadow skeptics express their claims in the language of properties, however, by claiming that the property to which a given emotion is sensitive is response independent. Although we dispute the substance of these claims, we prefer to remain neutral on some issues about the metaphysics of properties. This allows us to accept that there is a sense in which the sentimental value properties can be said to be response independent, while denying that this sense supports shadow skepticism.

We take the sentimental values to be analogous to colors in this respect. It is plausible that the concept of redness is response dependent, in that it invokes an object's disposition to produce certain visual experiences. Still, it might be possible to construct a disjunctive spectral-reflectance property that is identical to redness. But this property will not have a wide cosmological role: it will not figure in explanations of anything but human color vision and the like, though it is very useful for those anthropocentric purposes.[10] Similarly, it might be possible in principle to construct a disjunctive response-independent property that realizes funniness. Even so, we claim that any interesting explanatory and normative roles this property might play will run through its connection to amusement. That is the point that matters to us, not whether a jury-rigged physicalist description of the same property as red or funny can be given.[11] If we are correct, then it

[10] Cf. Wright (1992).
[11] We are indebted to Matt Bedke for helpful discussion of these issues.

gets things backward to suggest that what merits amusement is a shadow of some response-independent property; rather, the contours of the putatively response-independent property are determined by what merits amusement. Whereas if a robust, response-independent rationale unites the things that merit some emotion, then the shadow skeptic would be right about that sentimental value, and we would be wrong.[12]

Shadow skepticism challenges sentimentalism quite generally, because it contradicts the response-dependency thesis that is its central commitment, but our response will utilize some claims that are specific to neo-sentimentalism. Although we are defending the response-dependency thesis common to all forms of sentimentalism, our argument thus offers an important consideration in favor of neo-sentimentalism in particular. Our response to the skeptic will focus on the case of fear and danger, an example that seems especially amenable to shadow skepticism and has been used to mount this challenge in influential recent work. Since this is the skeptic's best case, and the structure of our response can be deployed elsewhere, a convincing response should diminish the appeal of shadow skepticism across the board. In order to generalize this argument, the sentimentalist needs an account of how best to interpret each natural emotion, which requires the deeper engagement with the philosophy of emotion we have previously advocated.

The case of fear is particularly conducive to the shadow skeptical challenge because danger appears to be a response-independent concept. And if the fearsome is anything other than the dangerous, then it seems less important. Hence the response-independent value trumps the response-dependent one in the same vicinity, just as the shadow skeptical challenge claims. There are two other related reasons why fear and danger seem so conducive to this challenge. One motivation for shadow skepticism about the sentimental values in particular is that natural emotions are arguably adaptive syndromes, which exist to respond to emotion-independent features of the environment that pose special problems or opportunities for survival and reproduction. Nowhere is this more plausible than with fear. Surely fear is an adaptation. The human fear syndrome is homologous with syndromes in other animals, and it exists and many of its features

---

[12] A response-independent rationale need not be characterized in causal or naturalistic terms. If what merits pride and shame could be identified with what is virtuous and vicious, for instance, and a compelling response-independent account of virtue and vice can be found, then shadow skeptics would be right about the shameful and the prideworthy – even if that theory of virtue and vice turns out to be a normative one, and the associated properties are not natural properties. But the prideworthy and the shameful cannot be identified with the virtuous and the vicious. We simply assert that for now, to indicate another example of what is at stake in our dispute with the shadow skeptic. A few relevant considerations will emerge in our later discussion of pride.

exist because of the role they played in helping our ancestors, including non-human ancestors, survive various threats (LeDoux 1996). Hence it is plausible to suppose that fear is a fast and frugal heuristic that alerts us to danger, however imperfectly, and motivates us to avoid it.

Furthermore, it just seems obvious that fear is *about* danger: that it presents its object as dangerous, and thus that it is fitting just in case the object really is dangerous. This suggests that the fearsome (what merits fear) just is the dangerous (understood as what threatens harm). Indeed, Jesse Prinz takes this claim to be supported by the idea that fear is an adaptation. Prinz holds a teleosemantic account of the representational content of emotions, according to which an emotion represents whatever it is "set up to be set off by" (2004: 54). Since fear is set up to be set off by danger, he contends, that is what it is about. One need not embrace Prinz's teleosemantics to reach the same conclusion. Every account we've seen of what fear is about – whether put in terms of its generic appraisal, core relational theme, paradigm scenarios, or constitutive thought – inevitably points to danger or some near synonym, such as the threat of harm.

Although these thoughts are conducive to shadow skepticism, they do not entail it. Fear could be an adaptation, the function of which is to respond to dangers by motivating avoidance behavior, and best understood as being about danger – and yet *danger* could still be a response-dependent value that cannot be understood except by appeal to fear. This is in fact our view. Nevertheless, philosophers who treat fear as being about danger typically assume it to be response-independent. Prinz is explicit about this commitment, claiming: "Fear represents the property of being dangerous . . . [it] does not represent a response-dependent property" (2004: 64). Prinz does not argue for the response independence of the dangerous, he simply asserts that if fear is about danger then it is about something response independent. We will argue in what follows that this assumption is false, but it is worth noting why the assumption appears so plausible. In the first place, the adaptive syndrome picture can seem to support response independence even though it does not entail it. Second, the cognitivist tradition in the philosophy of emotion, which holds (roughly) that a necessary condition of being afraid is that one believes oneself in danger, makes the same assumption. Since Prinz is one of the leading non-cognitivists about the emotions, and the cognitivist tradition in the philosophy of emotion is committed to response-independence as well (for reasons to be discussed in §3), this consensus makes shadow skepticism about fear and danger hard to resist.

The shadow skeptic argues that the important values to which emotions are sensitive, however imperfectly, are response independent. But he need not deny the existence of emotion-dependent concepts or properties. He can say that what it is to be "scary" is to be disposed to make people afraid

(Prinz 2004: 60–61). And he can grant that there is some point to thinking about the scary, for instance when picking a Halloween costume. He will rightly claim that the scary is distinct from the dangerous, and that it pales in importance by comparison.[13] Indeed, the shadow skeptic can even grant us the coherence of sentimental value concepts such as the fearsome, explicated in terms of what merits fear. But he must hold that these concepts are either epistemic devices for thinking about a property with a response-independent rationale (such as danger), or else they are about something comparatively unimportant (like the scary).

Francois Schroeter presses just this line. He argues that sentimentalism is suited only to make sense of various relatively trivial questions, such as what is fearsome or guilt-worthy. But these response-dependent values are insignificant in comparison with the response-independent ones in their vicinity: danger and wrongness. As Schroeter puts the point: "Even if fear is one of our most important emotions, we don't care that much about when it is appropriate: once we know whether a situation is dangerous, we typically have little interest in finding out whether it warrants fear" (2006: 346). Thus shadow skepticism poses a dilemma concerning the sentimental values: they are either response independent or relatively insignificant. In particular, if the fearsome is stipulated to be what merits fear, then either it should be identified with the dangerous or else it does not matter much in comparison. And the same goes for the other values that sentimentalism proposes to explicate.

## 2     Fear and the Dangerous

What is at issue between the sentimentalist and the shadow skeptic is whether there is a value that is *independent* of any associated emotion (as danger seems to be independent of fear), yet to which the emotion seems *sensitive* (as fear seems sensitive to danger, however imperfectly). Shadow skepticism must offer a value that meets both criteria in order to pose its distinctive challenge. Without independence, the theory is sentimentalist. Without sensitivity, it is a different and more radical skeptical claim, akin to the claims of the Stoics who proposed that one should ignore emotional concerns – such as with danger, contamination, slights, and so forth – because these are all matters of indifference. In this view, one should not care about the sentimental values at all. Rather than take up this radical

---

[13] Indeed, the contours of the scary can be explained by fear's function of responding to danger, even when the scary and dangerous diverge. Probably the scariness of roller coasters and fierce masks is explained by the danger of precipices and aggressive animals.

suggestion, we propose to address a form of skepticism that grants the significance of the things with which emotions are concerned, while aiming to understand those properties and their significance in response-independent terms.

We contend that it is more difficult to give a response-independent account of the dangerous than it appears, and that attempts to do so fall prey to the same problems besetting incongruity and contamination as accounts of the funny and disgusting. Schroeter's attempt to explicate dangerousness is illustrative of the general problem. He writes:

> [S]omething is dangerous just in case it is *liable to cause harm*. The crucial question one needs to answer when it comes to evaluations of danger is whether an object or situation poses a threat, especially to the relevant subject's bodily integrity. (Schroeter 2006: 343; emphasis added)

This exemplifies the shadow skeptic's commitment to finding some empirical or thinly evaluative (and hence response-independent) property to which an emotion characteristically responds, and then argue that this is what matters in the vicinity. But though it seems plausible to claim that something is dangerous just in case it is liable to cause harm, what exactly does that mean? There are two issues here, concerning the concepts of harm and liability, which we will treat sequentially.

Consider what Schroeter identifies as the crucial question: does something pose a threat to the subject's bodily integrity? Since the goal is to locate a (perhaps complex) property to which fear is sensitive, such a narrow focus on the subject and her bodily integrity will not suffice. Threats to other things than the subject's bodily integrity have to count as dangers, Schroeter ultimately concedes, though he seems to consider this a minor difficulty that can be solved by extending the notion of harm to include "damage to the subject's mental well-functioning and even to conditions which might incapacitate subjects in fulfilling important functions in their lives – as, for instance, loss of economic independence or social status" (2006: 344). But even this expansion is inadequate. We have been supposing that harm is an empirical notion, connected in the first place to something like bodily injury and now widened to include psychological damage and even vague malfunction, but this progression in what must be allowed to count as harm demonstrates the difficulty facing the shadow skeptic.[14] Minor threats to bodily integrity, such as trivial pain or hair loss, pale in comparison to serious threats to other things people care about. A broken

---

[14] All these terms (danger, threat, harm) have wobble. One might expand the notion of harm instead. But we will give "harm" to the shadow skeptic, understood as something like bodily integrity plus psychological functioning and incapacitation. But danger must then include other threats than harm.

nail is nothing as compared to a broken heart. Various misfortunes merit fear even if they do not threaten one's mental functioning or other basic capacities.

The crucial point here is that if harm really is so circumscribed, and if danger just is liability to such harm, then the dangerous no longer seems more important than the fearsome. Grave threats to your well-being, such as the collapse of a marriage or financial disaster, matter more than many harms. Moreover, the suggestion that danger must threaten harm to the subject himself is surely wrong; it can also threaten other people and things he cares about deeply. Hence the range of what can be threatened must be expanded considerably, moving away from any empirical notion of harm toward some broader category of bad outcomes for you and the things you most care about, which better captures what merits fear.[15] Still, shadow skepticism is not committed to identifying the sentimental values with empirical properties – such as contamination, incongruity, and harm – but with emotion-independent properties. So for the sake of argument, let us grant the shadow skeptic a notion of self-interest that might take the place of harm without trading illicitly on fear.[16] He can then say that something is dangerous just in case it threatens a significant setback to one's interests.

Even if the shadow skeptic is willing to abandon the restriction to harms in favor of a broader notion like interests, we doubt that he can give a plausible response-independent account of danger, because the notion of liability proves as problematic as harm. The claim we're now considering is that for something to be dangerous is for it to be *liable* to set back your interests. But there is no ordinary sense of "liable" on which that is plausible. If liable means possible, then the claim is false; plenty of things that could just possibly damage one's interests are not dangerous. If liable means likely, that too is false; some things that probably will not harm you, like a game of Russian roulette, are nevertheless dangerous. But if liability is neither of these things, then it is not at all clear what it is, and the attempt to specify a response-independent notion of danger is in jeopardy.

We see two possible responses for the shadow skeptic. First, he can insist that anything that can possibly damage your interests is indeed dangerous, while noting that some things are much less dangerous than others.

---

[15] In ordinary language, it may be more common to speak of physical harms than other threats as dangers. We think it perspicuous to let the class of dangers include the many important risks that are not bodily harms, and this is how we shall speak in what follows. But we could instead restrict the dangerous to physical harms without concession to shadow skepticism. This would simply make the dangerous a less important category than it seemed, and less important than the fearsome in particular – which is just what we conclude about harm.

[16] This notion of self-interest might even be response dependent in a more capacious sense, for instance by appealing to the satisfaction of informed desires.

This response is not intuitively plausible, since unlikely prospects of minor inconveniences are not ordinarily regarded as dangers. More important, to treat them as such seems to undermine the central role of the concept of danger, which is to pick out certain importantly bad prospects for special attention. (This was precisely what Schroeter attempted to do with threats to bodily integrity and mental functioning.) If the shadow skeptic's best proposal for a response-independent explication of danger is in terms of possible setbacks to one's interests, then he would not have located the most important value in the neighborhood of fear.[17]

A second option seems more promising. The skeptic can instead reply that danger is a function of two interacting, response-independent factors: how likely a prospect is and how bad it is. Dangers are prospects that reach some threshold of *expected* badness. People routinely face miniscule risks of death fearlessly. Yet they are often afraid when a less serious prospect, such as social humiliation, looks more probable – in anticipation of a public performance, for instance. Indeed, they typically endorse such fear as fitting. This proposal seems to ensure that dangers will be important – because they rise above the relevant threshold – while satisfying the sensitivity constraint by conforming to familiar patterns in what elicits fear.[18]

Although this proposal is on the right track, we think it ultimately runs afoul of the independence constraint, because there is no good response-independent rationale for setting danger thresholds. The question is: what justifies setting the threshold that determines whether something is dangerous in one place rather than another? *That is the problem to which fear can be seen as the solution.* What is dangerous is whatever counts as sufficiently likely and sufficiently bad that it merits one's immediate and complete attention on avoiding the threat. Nico Frijda (1986) calls this phenomenon, which characterizes emotional motivation, *control precedence*. A bout of fear focuses attention (almost) exclusively on some threat, prioritizes its avoidance, and prepares the body for action. Thus the point of the threshold notion invoked by the concept of danger can be found in contingent but deeply seated aspects of moral psychology. The focused attention and goal prioritization that are central to fear are costly, and they do not scale downward incrementally in ways that could match degrees of

---

[17] This suggestion fails to capture the sensitivity constraint, because fear is not concerned with merely possible setbacks. The two most commonplace criticisms of unfitting fear are that the feared prospect is either insufficiently bad (as with fear of spiders) or insufficiently likely (fear of flying). The shadow skeptic needs to provide an account of danger that makes sense of these commonplace criticisms.

[18] This is not to suggest that an account of danger must track actual dispositions to fear perfectly. Any plausible account should allow that fear is sometimes unfitting, and there are some familiar human tendencies to irrationality, such as loss aversion, that produce predictable but unfitting fear.

expected badness. Hence one cannot help but set thresholds in thinking about what things merit fear: a prospect must reach some level of expected badness before it makes sense to prioritize it in attention and motivation. This, of course, is a response-dependent account of the danger threshold. Yet without this appeal to fear, it would be mysterious what makes a prospect count as likely and bad enough to be dangerous.[19]

We are not providing a standard that dictates just how likely and bad something has to be in order to be dangerous. In the first place, the threshold is vague, and where it gets set in any given circumstance is surely context-sensitive in various ways.[20] Even more important, people often disagree about whether certain prospects are dangerous (though they agree about easy cases). And these disputes can persist even when both sides agree on the facts. An account of the concept of danger need not settle such substantive disputes; it should explain what is at issue. Neo-sentimentalism identifies the subject matter as disagreement over whether or not a given prospect merits fear.

From the response-independent ("objective") point of view, however, there seems to be no rationale for distinguishing, among the many negative changes in one's prospects, which to count as dangers. Any particular specification of likelihood or severity would be arbitrary, and it would create unmotivated distinctions between admitted dangers that just barely rise above the threshold and putative non-dangers that fall just short. We are not unreasonably insisting that the shadow skeptic owes us an account of danger with no vagueness at its boundaries. The point is rather that, however vague the threshold may be, the skeptic must explain what is at stake in placing something on one side of it rather than the other. Our sentimentalist proposal claims that there *is* an important question at stake in such disputes: whether this amount of expected disvalue merits fear.[21] Hence the appeal to thresholds too is ultimately response-dependent, and it does not help the shadow skeptic meet the independence constraint.

Indeed, we think the problem cuts even more deeply against the shadow skeptic. From the objective perspective, the very project of identifying a

---

[19] Of course we are not denying that some activities, such as walking through a lion's den, are dangerous for a perfectly obvious reason that can be understood without recourse to fear: it is likely to kill you.

[20] Neo-sentimentalism can accommodate this context sensitivity by holding that what merits fear depends upon the baseline, such that something dangerous in suburbia is not so in a war zone.

[21] Note that our claim is about the concept of danger, not about what passes through one's conscious mind when thinking about particular dangers. In wondering whether a dog is dangerous, one does not think about fear but about the dog's size, its demeanor, and how secure the fence is.

class of dangers seems misguided. According to rational choice theory, a decision-maker should govern his actions on the basis of expected utility, not danger, taking account of both positive and negative expectations only in proportion to their contribution to the overall calculation. This makes fear's concern with thresholds seem gratuitous: a kind of predictable irrationality. None of this implies that humans would be better off fearless, however, and that conclusion seems highly unlikely to us. Insofar as humans are also subject to other forms of predictable irrationality, such as being overly tempted by salient goods in our immediate vicinity, a form of systematic negative bias such as fear might be salutary. Even if this advantage depends on other deeply seated human characteristics that look like flaws from the perspective of pure practical rationality, nevertheless we are stuck being human. The ideal decision-maker of rational choice theory, who is unencumbered by fear and other emotions, may not be a model that humans would generally be well advised to emulate. We grant that the sentimental values are anthropocentric, of no inherent interest to rational but dispassionate aliens: they are human values.

Hence we conclude that in order for danger to matter as the shadow skeptic intends – for it to be "what ultimately interests us in our most important evaluative judgments" (Schroeter 2006: 346) about the objects of fear – it must be covertly response dependent. The human concern for threats and the dangerous leads inevitably to a response-dependent account. By contrast, a thoroughly objective point of view would treat all prospects equivalently, without giving any gratuitous privilege to threats. It thus requires a far more radical revision than the shadow skeptic can accommodate: one that gives up on danger as an important evaluative concept altogether. Although this radical suggestion eventually requires a response from the sentimentalist, for now we take ourselves to have shown that the dangerous is best understood as a response-dependent property. If so then the shadow skeptic is mistaken even about his most promising case. To be dangerous just is to be fearsome: that is, to merit fear.

## 3     The Direction Forward

Since the previous argument refutes shadow skepticism about danger by relying on details specific to neo-sentimentalism, as we anticipated, it is not available to every form of sentimentalism. A simple dispositional sentimentalism cannot answer the challenge, because it is not plausible that the scary – that is, what people are disposed to be afraid of – is the significant value in the vicinity of fear. The scary is much less important than the dangerous. It is only by appealing to what merits fear, not what causes it, that neo-sentimentalism can capture what is at stake in questions and disputes about what is dangerous. And, although we cannot argue this in detail here, the same holds for the other sentimental values.

This result raises both a general question and a more pointed problem. The question is how to understand and justify assessments of emotions as fitting. Recall that to judge an emotion fitting is to endorse it specifically as being correct, which requires neo-sentimentalists to provide some account of how to assess emotions for correctness. The problem is that the most straightforward and familiar answer to this question comes from an account of the emotions that conflicts with sentimentalism: the cognitive theory of emotion. All of the various forms of this theory hold that emotions are (at least partly) constituted by certain evaluative thoughts, which serve to differentiate and type-identify them.[22] If the emotion of guilt is even partly constituted by the belief that you have done wrong, for example, then it seems to follow that your guilt is fitting just in case that belief is true. Indeed, it is commonly held to be a virtue of cognitivism that it can explain and justify such assessments. But this simple explanation of fittingness turns out to be unavailable to sentimentalists, because they must reject the cognitive theory, for reasons to be explained. We will contend that cognitivism's apparent advantage in accounting for emotional fittingness is specious, however, and that sentimentalism can generate the resources for a better account only by conducting the substantive engagement with the emotions that we have counseled.

Although cognitivist theories differ in detail, they all identify some evaluative thought that is claimed to be a necessary condition for having a given emotional state. Philippa Foot states this commitment of cognitivism especially clearly, with respect to pride, when she writes: "I do not mean, of course, that one would be illogical in feeling pride towards something one did not believe to be in some way splendid and in some way one's own, but that the concept of pride does not allow us to talk like that" (1978: 76). Foot is similarly explicit about another point that is implicit in cognitivism but not always overtly stated, by insisting that the belief necessary for pride is comprised of concepts (*splendid* and *mine*) that are not themselves emotion-dependent.[23] Moreover, Foot uses this suggestion to ground

---

[22] For instance, Martha Nussbaum writes: "It seems necessary to put the thought into the definition of the emotion itself. Otherwise, we seem to have no good way of making the requisite discriminations among emotion types" (2001: 30).

[23] We need not dispute "cognitivist" theories that do not have this commitment, and we certainly grant that emotions involve various cognitive processes. But we think it clear that all the influential cognitivist theories presuppose response independence. If the thoughts Nussbaum claims necessary to put into the definition of emotions (see fn. 23) were themselves response dependent, they would not serve to discriminate emotion types as she and other cognitivists intend.

a rejection of Humean sentimentalism. Contrary to Hume, "the explanation of the thought comes into the description the feeling, not the other way round" (Foot 1978: 76). Foot aspires not only to identify a belief or thought that constitutes a necessary condition for having an emotion, but also to specify it in emotion-independent terms. This is the basis of her objection to Hume.

Although this conflict between sentimentalism and cognitivism is fundamental, it is somewhat oblique. Sentimentalism is a theory of value, in the first place, but it requires a compatible theory of the emotions. If the prideworthy is to be explicated by way of fitting pride, as rational sentimentalism has it, then pride had better not be even partly constituted by the response-independent belief that something is splendid and one's own, as Foot claims. In that case the prideworthy (for me) would be a mere shadow of what is splendid and mine, a response-independent value by hypothesis.[24] Cognitivism is a theory of the emotions, in the first place, but it has implications for the sentimental values due to its claim that the content of the emotions can be given by way of emotion-independent constitutive thoughts. If so then an emotion would be fitting, and the sentimental value instantiated, just in case this thought is true. Although their primary subject matter differs, sentimentalism and cognitivism are incompatible, and this incompatibility is directly related to our debate with the shadow skeptic. Indeed, the argument against shadow skepticism can be turned against the cognitivist theory of emotion.

Our argument about fear and danger purported to show that the most significant value in this neighborhood is emotion-dependent: the dangerous just is the fearsome, which is to say, whatever merits fear. But cognitivist accounts of fear invariably analyze it as involving the thought that something is dangerous (or in terms of some synonym such as threat or harm). Moreover, they at least tacitly assume that *dangerous* is a response-independent concept. Hence our argument shows that the sentimentalist order of explanation is correct, at least for this case, contrary to Foot's challenge to Hume.

We think the same argument applies, mutatis mutandis, to the other natural emotions and sentimental value concepts. We cannot here develop this argument adequately for every case, however, and we merely asserted it for the funny and the disgusting (with respect to amusement and disgust). Yet it will be helpful to illustrate the central dispute over response dependence from the emotion side, in addition to the evaluative side, by considering Foot's account of pride. We thereby aim to illustrate what we take to be

---

[24] Foot gives her account in terms of what is "one's own," but we will move freely between that formulation and other possessive notions (such as mine or yours).

a general phenomenon. In order to avoid rampant counterexamples, cognitivist accounts of the constitutive thoughts of emotions must become covertly response-dependent. Which is to say, they inevitably belie cognitivism. If this argument proves convincing then, although sentimentalism must shoulder the burden of finding a compatible theory of emotion, there is reason to think that cognitivism takes the wrong side of the order of explanation issue that puts it at odds with sentimentalism.

Yet we have noted that cognitivist theories seem to offer a straightforward and compelling account of emotional fittingness, namely as the truth of an emotion's constitutive thought. If in order to be proud of something, you have to think it in some way *splendid and yours*, then something merits your pride just in case it is indeed both splendid and yours. This seems like a simple conjunction of a response-independent evaluative claim (it is splendid) and a matter of fact (it is yours). The cognitivist theory of pride thus motivates shadow skepticism about the prideworthy: it would merely be a shadow of the response-independent property of being splendid and mine. But this suggestion proves untenable.

Consider your winning lottery ticket in this regard. It is splendid, to be sure: worth a fortune! And it is certainly yours: you bought it, you own it, and it is in your possession. But is it prideworthy? Clearly not, we contend.[25] It was blind luck that you won the lottery. Perhaps your athletic talent, beauty, and native intelligence are also lucky, in that you are not responsible for possessing them, but they still reflect something about you, in virtue of being traits of yours. By contrast, there is nothing about you that caused you to win the lottery – at least if it is granted that luckiness is not a trait. Though the ticket is splendid and yours, its splendor does not connect to you in the right way: the pride-y way. So Foot's proposal about pride does not capture the important value with which pride is concerned – a kind of splendor that must redound to the credit of its owner, so to speak, in order for pride to be fitting.

Note that precisely what a cognitivist account of pride cannot do is to covertly rely on an idea like "splendid and mine *in the pride-y way*." That would be to embrace the response dependence of the content of pride and the prideworthy. Since the real significance of Foot's conceptual claim, by her lights as well as our own, is that it purports to contradict sentimentalism, her larger argument cannot allow the thought putatively constitutive of pride to be pride-dependent. Yet that is exactly our conclusion – not only

---

[25] This normative judgment seems obvious, and we expect most readers to agree, but it is not indisputable. Yet it must be granted that someone can think the lottery ticket splendid and his without deeming it prideworthy, which suffices to show that *splendid and mine* does not fully capture what pride is about.

for pride but for all cognitivist attempts to capture the generic emotional appraisal of natural emotions. Our central argument about fear and danger can be seen as another example, developed at greater length.

We offer the lottery ticket example not *exactly* as a counterexample to Foot's account of pride. She claims that the belief that something is splendid and yours is a necessary condition on being proud of it, not a sufficient condition.[26] So Foot could perhaps grant that the lottery ticket is splendid and yours but not prideworthy, by allowing that a full specification of pride's defining thought would add more cognitive content.[27] There is no indication that Foot thinks that her gloss needs any such supplement, though, and other cognitivists have not offered any better specification. While there are several alternative cognitivist accounts of pride, they are competitors to Foot's gloss rather than supplements, and we think they all fail for the same reason. None succeeds in offering an adequate response-independent account of the evaluative content of pride, and the cognitivist's promise of explaining emotional fittingness goes unfulfilled.

While this brief discussion cannot exhaust the options available to the cognitivist, we believe that it illustrates something crucial and insufficiently appreciated: that the evaluative content of natural emotions is distinctive and cannot be captured in response-independent terms. If that is true, it motivates a sentimentalist approach that treats natural emotions as distinctive species of evaluative concern and seeks to explain sophisticated human thinking about what is shameful, dangerous, and so forth as arising out of our common human emotional repertoire. These suggestions leave sentimentalism with two large tasks. It owes an account of the natural emotions, and an account of how they can be assessed for fittingness if not by appeal to some constituent evaluative judgments.

In our view, the best account of the natural emotions is a motivational theory, which understands them as distinctive kinds of motivational state. Emotional motivation is characteristically irruptive, engages specific action tendencies, and exhibits control precedence: the suite of tendencies mentioned earlier, including goal prioritization and directed attention.[28] These features explain the susceptibility of natural emotions to recalcitrance – arising in conflict with evaluative judgment – and their tendency to

[26] Although she only claims it to be a necessary condition, Foot is attempting to gloss the content of pride in emotion-independent terms. So the question is whether *splendid and mine* suffices to capture pride's evaluative content and thus determine what is prideworthy.

[27] It is also open to Foot to hold that no belief alone is sufficient for pride – perhaps a certain feeling or behavior is also required – which might explain why she claims that the belief is just a necessary condition. But although adding non-cognitive conditions improves the account, it does not change the standard of what merits pride, for the cognitivist, so this does not matter for the issue at hand.

[28] See e.g. Frijda (1986), Scarantino (2014).

produce various kinds of irrational but intentional action.[29] We recruited a motivational account of fear already, in defense of the suggestion that fear explains the role of thresholds that are central to the concept of danger.

If a motivational theory is correct, then the question becomes how these motivational syndromes can be assessed as fitting. This is a difficult challenge. Our preferred approach is to try to understand emotions as involving appraisals, as distinct from evaluative judgments. We look to the motivational role of the emotion, to its paradigmatic elicitors, and to its characteristic phenomenology in order to justify *interpretive* claims about how someone in the grip of one of these natural emotions is best understood to be appraising the situation. Then we can say that considerations of fittingness are those that speak to whether or not the object is as one appraises it to be, in the throes of the emotion. For instance, the kinds of thing people fear, the characteristic action tendencies of fear (such as flight and other forms of threat avoidance), and the directed feelings of dread that are typical of it support an interpretation of fear as an appraisal of danger.

Although fear was the most difficult case for us in one respect, because it is so natural to think of danger as response independent, this discussion reveals another respect in which it is a relatively easy case. Characterizing fear's appraisal seems easy: it is uncontroversial that fear is about danger. But other natural emotions are more difficult to interpret in natural language in ways that are at once adequate to their evaluative content and somewhat informative. It is not easy to say how pride appraises its object, for instance, and we have already shown that Foot's suggestion is inadequate.

It can be disputed just what articulation of a generic emotional appraisal makes best sense of the data. But in our view such disputes must be grounded in the nature of the emotions themselves, not in substantive convictions about what is prideworthy (or enviable, shameful, etc.). Thus, sentimentalism will distinguish considerations that bear on fittingness from other kinds of reasons for and against evaluative responses in part through empirical investigations of the emotions at issue. Settling on an interpretation of these appraisals will not settle contested evaluative questions about what merits pride or shame, but it will circumscribe what kinds of considerations bear on disputes about such questions, and thus help to constrain the evaluative debates that sentimentalism aims to explicate.[30]

---

[29] See D'Arms and Jacobson (2003) and Jacobson (2013).

[30] We would like to thank the editors of this volume for their support and patience, as well as good advice. Thanks are also due to David Shoemaker and readers of the PEA Soup Blog for their helpful comments on a central argument, and to audiences at Holy Cross and Washington University in St. Louis.

# References

Aaltolta, E. 2014. "Affective Empathy as Core Moral Agency: Psychopathy, Autism, and Reason Revisited," *Philosophical Explorations* 17: 76–92.

Abramson, K. and Leite, A. 2011. "Love as a Reactive Emotion," *Philosophical Quarterly* 61: 673–699.

Adler, H. E., Menze, A., and Palma, M. (tr. and eds.). 1997. *Herder on World History: An Anthology*. Armonk, NY: M. E. Sharpe.

Alicke, M. D. 2000. "Culpable Control and the Psychology of Blame," *Psychological Bulletin* 126: 556–574.

Ames, R. T. 1991. "The Mencian Conception of Ren Xing: Does It Mean Human Nature?," in Henry Rosemont Jr. (ed.), *Chinese Texts and Philosophical Contexts: Essays Dedicated to Angus C. Graham*. La Salle, IL: Open Court, 143–175.

Ames, R. T. 2002. "Mencius and a Process Notion of Human Nature," in Alan Kam-leung Chan (ed.), *Mencius: Contexts and Interpretations*. Honolulu: University of Hawai'i Press, 72–90.

Appiah, K. A. 2008. *Experiments in Ethics*. Cambridge, MA: Harvard University Press.

Audi, R. 2013. *Moral Perception*. Princeton, NJ: Princeton University Press.

Ayer, A. 1936. *Language, Truth, and Logic*. London: Penguin.

Bagnoli, C. (ed.). 2011. *Morality and the Emotions*. New York: Oxford University Press.

Bagnoli, C. (ed.). 2013. *Constructivism in Ethics*. New York: Cambridge University Press.

Baier, A. C. 1980. "Hume on Resentment," *Hume Studies* 6.2: 133–149.

Baier, A. C. 1986. "Trust and Anti-Trust," *Ethics* 96: 231–260.

Baier, A. C. 1991. *Progress of Sentiments: Reflections on Hume's Treatise*. Cambridge, MA: Harvard University Press.

Baier, A. C. 1995. *Moral Prejudices*. Cambridge, MA: Harvard University Press.

Bartky, S. L. 1997. "Sympathy and Solidarity: On a Tightrope with Scheler," in D. T Meyers (ed.), *Feminists Rethink the Self*. Boulder, CO: Westview, 177–196.

Bedke, M. 2009. "Intuitive Non-Naturalism Meets Cosmic Coincidence," *Pacific Philosophical Quarterly* 90: 188–209.

Behrens, T. E. J., Hunt, L. T., and Rushworth, M. F. S. 2009. "The Computation of Social Behavior," *Science* 324: 1160–1164.

Behrens, T. E. J., Hunt, L. T., Woolrich, M. W., and Rushworth, M. F. S. 2008. "Associative Learning of Social Value," *Nature* 456: 245–250.

Beierholm, U. R., Quartz, S. R., and Shams, L. 2009. "Bayesian Priors are Encoded Independently from Likelihoods in Human Multisensory Perception," *The Journal of Vision* 9 (5), 23: 1–9.

Beiser, F. 1992. "Kant's Intellectual Development: 1746–1781," in P. Guyer (ed.), *The Cambridge Companion to Kant*. New York: Cambridge University Press, 26–61.

Bennett, J. 1980. "Accountability," in Z. Van Straaten (ed.), *Philosophical Subjects: Essays Presented to P. F. Strawson*. New York: Oxford University Press, 14–47.

Berker, S. 2014. "Does Evolutionary Psychology Show that Normativity is Mind-Dependent?," in J. D'Arms and D. Jacobson (eds.), *Moral Psychology and Human Agency: Philosophical Essays on the Science of Ethics*. New York: Oxford University Press, 215–252.

Bernecker, S. 2011. "Keeping Track of the Gettier Problem," *Pacific Philosophical Quarterly* 92 (2): 127–152.

Blackburn, S. 1988. "How to Be an Ethical Antirealist." in S. Blackburn (ed.), 1993. *Essays in Quasi-Realism*. New York: Oxford University Press, 166–181.

Blackburn, S. 1998. *Ruling Passions: A Theory of Practical Reason*. New York: Oxford University Press.

Blair, R. J. R. 1995. "A Cognitive Developmental Approach to Morality: Investigating the Psychopath," *Cognition* 57: 1–29.

Bloom, I. (tr.). 2009. *Mencius*. Edited by P. J. Ivanhoe. New York: Columbia University Press.

Butler, J. 1983. *Five Sermons Preached at the Rolls Chapel and a Dissertation Upon the Nature of Virtue*. Edited by S. L. Darwall. Indianapolis, IN: Hackett Publishing Company.

Calhoun, C. 1994. "Separating Lesbian Theory from Feminist Theory," *Ethics* 104: 558–571.

Capes, J. 2012. "Blameworthiness Without Wrongdoing," *Pacific Philosophical Quarterly* 93 (3): 417–437.

Cartwright, D. E. 1987. "Kant's View of the Moral Significance of Kindhearted Emotions and the Moral Insignificance of Kant's View," *The Journal of Value Inquiry* 21: 291–304.

Churchill, T. (tr.). 1966. Herder's *Outlines of a Philosophy of the History of Man* (originally published 1800). New York: Bergman Publishers.

Clarke, S. 1964. "Discourse upon Natural Religion," in L. A. Selby-Bigge (ed.), *British Moralists*, vol. 2. Indianapolis and New York: Bobbs-Merrill Company, 3–56.

Clarke-Doane, J. 2012. "Morality and Mathematics: The Evolutionary Challenge," *Ethics* 122 (2): 313–340.

Clore, G. L. and Ortony, A. 2000. "Cognition in Emotion: Always, Sometimes, or Never?," in R. E. Lane and L. Nadel (eds.), *Cognitive Neuroscience of Emotion*. New York: Oxford University Press, 24–61.

Cohen, G. A. 1996. "Reason, Humanity, and the Moral Law," in Korsgaard (ed.), *The Sources of Normativity*. New York: Oxford Univeristy Press, 166–188.

Collingwood, R. G. 1946/1994. *The Idea of History* (revised edition). New York: Oxford University Press.

Confucius, 1998, *The Analects of Confucius: A Philosophical Translation*. Translated and edited by Roger T. Ames and Henry Rosemont, Jr. New York: Random House Publishing.

Cooper, J. M. 1999. *Reason and Emotion: Essays on Ancient Moral Psychology and Ethical Theory*. Princeton, NJ: Princeton University Press.

Cooper, N. 1994. "The Inaugural Address: Understanding," *Proceedings of the Aristotelian Society, Supplementary Volumes* 68: 1–26.

Coplan, A. 2011. "Understanding Empathy: Its Features and Effects," in Coplan and Goldie (eds.), *Empathy: Philosophical and Psychological Perspectives*. New York: Oxford University Press, 3–18.

Coplan, A. and Goldie, P. (eds.). 2011. *Empathy: Philosophical and Psychological Perspectives*. New York: Oxford University Press.

Courville, A. C., Daw, N. D., and Touretzky, D. S. 2008. "Bayesian Theories of Conditioning in a Changing World, " *Trends in Cognitive Sciences* 10: 294–300.

Craig, E. 1990. *Knowledge and the State of Nature*. New York: Oxford University Press.

Crenshaw, K. 1991. "Mapping the Margins: Intersectionality, Identity Politics, and Violence against Women of Color," *Stanford Law Review* 43: 1241–1299.

Crowe, M. J., ed. 2008. *The Extraterrestrial Life Debate, Antiquity to 1915: A Source Book*. South Bend, IN: University of Notre Dame Press.

Cuneo, T. 2003. "Reidian Moral Perception," *Canadian Journal of Philosophy* 33: 229–258.

Cuneo, T. 2007. "Recent Faces of Moral Nonnaturalism," *Philosophy Compass* 2 (6): 850–879.

D'Arms, J. and Jacobson, D. 1994. "Expressivism, Morality, and the Emotions," *Ethics* 104: 739–763.

D'Arms, J. and Jacobson, D. 2000a. "Sentiment and Value," *Ethics* 110: 722–748.

D'Arms, J. and Jacobson, D. 2000b. "The Moralistic Fallacy," *Philosophy and Phenomenological Research* 61: 65–90.

D'Arms, J. and Jacobson, D. 2003. "The Significance of Recalcitrant Emotions (or, Anti-Quasijudgmentalism)," *Philosophy*, Supp. 52: 127–145.

D'Arms, J. and Jacobson, D. 2006. "Sensibility Theory and Projectivism," in D. Copp (ed.), *Oxford Handbook of Ethical Theory*. New York: Oxford University Press, 186–218.

D'Arms, J. and Jacobson, D. 2014a. "Wrong Kinds of Reason and the Opacity of Normative Force," in R. Shafer-Landau (ed.), *Oxford Studies in Metaethics*, vol. 9. New York: Oxford University Press, 215–244.

D'Arms, J. and Jacobson, D. 2014b. "Sentimentalism and Scientism," in J. D'Arms and D. Jacobson (eds.), *Moral Psychology and Human Agency: Philosophical Essays on the Science of Ethics*. New York: Oxford University Press, 253–278.

Damasio, A. 1994. *Descartes' Error*. New York, NY: Harper.

Damasio, A. and Van Hoesen, G. W. 1983. "Emotional Disturbances Associated with Focal Lesions of the Limbic Frontal Lobe," in K. M. Heilman and P. Satz (eds.), *Neuropsychology of Human Emotion*. New York, NY: Guilford Press, 85–110.

Darwall, S. 1977. "Two Kinds of Respect," *Ethics* 88: 36–49.

Darwall, S. 1983. *Impartial Reason*. Ithaca: Cornell University Press.

Darwall, S. 1997. "Reasons, Motives, and the Demands of Morality: An Introduction," in S. Darwall, A. Gibbard, and P. Railton (eds.), *Moral Discourse
and Practice: Some Philosophical Approaches*. New York: Oxford University
Press.

Darwall, S. 1998. "Empathy, Sympathy, Care," *Philosophical Studies* 89: 261–282.

Darwall, S. 2002. *Welfare and Rational Care*. Princeton, NJ: Princeton University
Press.

Darwall, S. 2006a. *The Second-Person Standpoint: Morality, Respect, and Accountability*. Cambridge, MA: Harvard University Press.

Darwall, S. 2006b. "Morality and Practical Reason: A Kantian Approach," in
D. Copp (ed.), *The Oxford Handbook of Ethical Theory*. New York: Oxford
University Press, 282–320.

Darwall, S. 2011. "Being With," *Southern Journal of Philosophy, Spindel Supplement*
49: 4–24.

Darwall, S. 2013. "Morality's Distinctiveness," in *Morality, Authority, and Law:
Essays in Second-Personal Ethics I*. New York: Oxford University Press,
3–19.

Darwall, S. 2017a. "Love's Second-Personal Character: Reciprocal Holding,
Beholding, and Upholding," in E. Kroeker and K. Schaubroeck (eds.), *Love,
Reason, and Morality*. London: Routledge, 93–109.

Darwall, S. 2017b. "Trust as a Second-Personal Attitude (of the Heart)," in
P. Faulkner and T. Simpson (eds.), *The Philosophy of Trust*. New York: Oxford
University Press, 93–109.

Darwall, S., Gibbard, A., and Railton, P. 1992. "Toward Fin de Siècle Ethics: Some
Trends," *The Philosophical Review* 101: 115–189.

Dasgupta, S. 2015. "The Possibility of Physicalism," *The Journal of Philosophy*
111 (9/10): 557–592.

Dayan, P. and Daw, N. D. 2008. "Decision-Theory, Reinforcement Learning, and
the Brain," *Cognitive, Affective, & Behavioral Neuroscience* 4: 429–453.

De Caro, M. and Macarthur, D. 2010. *Naturalism and Normativity*. New York, NY:
Columbia University Press.

de Sousa, R. 1987. *The Rationality of Emotions*. Cambridge, MA: MIT Press.

de Vignemont, F. and Jacob, P. 2012. "What is it like to feel another's pain?" *Philosophy of Science* 79 (2): 295–316.

Debes, R. 2009. "Neither Here Nor There: The Cognitive Nature of Emotion,"
*Philosophical Studies* 146 (1): 1–27.

Debes, R. 2010. "Which Empathy? Limitations in the Mirrored 'Understanding' of
Emotion," *Synthese* 175: 219–239.

Debes, R. 2012a. "Adam Smith on Dignity and Equality," *British Journal for the
History of Philosophy* 20: 109–140.

Debes, R. 2012b. "Recasting Scottish Sentimentalism: The Peculiarity of Moral
Approval," *Journal of Scottish Philosophy* 10: 91–115.

Debes, R. 2014. "Moral Rationalism and Moral Realism," in Aaron Garrett
(ed.), *The Routledge Companion to Eighteenth Century Philosophy*. New York:
Routledge, 500–534.

Debes, R. 2015. "From Einfühlung to Empathy: Sympathy in Early Phenomenology and Psychology," in E. Schliesser (ed.), *Sympathy: A History*. New York:
Oxford University Press, 286–322.

Decety, J. and Chaminade, T. 2003. "When the Self Represents the Other: A New Cognitive Neuroscience View on Psychological Identification," *Consciousness and Cognition* 12: 577–596.

Deigh, J. 2012. "Reactive Attitudes Revisited," in Bagnoli (ed.), *Morality and the Emotions*. New York: Oxford University Press, 197–216.

Dick, S. J. 1984. *The Plurality of Worlds: The Extraterrestrial Life Debate from Democritus to Kant*. New York: Cambridge University Press.

Dixon, T. 2012. "'Emotion': The History of a Keyword in Crisis," *Emotion Review* 4: 338–344.

Döring, S. 2007. "Seeing What to Do: Affective Perception and Rational Motivation," *Dialectica* 61: 363–394.

Doris, J. 2005. *Lack of Character*. New York: Cambridge University Press.

Driver, J. 2001. *Uneasy Virtue*. New York: Cambridge University Press.

Driver, J. 2008. "Imaginative Resistance and Psychological Necessity," *Social Philosophy and Policy* 25: 301–313.

Du Bos, J.-B. 1719. *Critical Reflections on Poetry, Painting, and Music*, vol. 1., T. Nugent (tr.). London: John Nourse.

Dworkin, R. 2011. *Justice for Hedgehogs*. Cambridge, MA: Harvard University Press.

Enoch, D. 2006. "Agency, Shmagency: Why Normativity Won't Come from What is Constitutive of Agency," *Philosophical Review* 115: 169–198.

Enoch, D. 2009. "Can there be a Global, Interesting, Coherent Constructivism about Practical Reason?," *Philosophical Explorations* 12: 319–339.

Enoch, D. 2010a. "Shmagency Revisited," in M. Brady, (ed.), *New Waves in Metaethics*. Basingstoke: Palgrave/Macmillan, 208–233.

Enoch, D. 2010b. "The Epistemological Challenge to Metanormative Realism: How Best to Understand It, and How to Cope with It," *Philosophical Studies* 148 (3): 413–438.

Enoch, D. 2011. *Taking Morality Seriously: A Defense of Robust Realism*. New York: Oxford University Press.

Enoch, D. and Schechter, J. 2008. "How are basic belief-forming methods justified?" *Philosophy and Phenomenological Research* 76.3: 547–579.

Eskine, J. K., Kacinik, A. N., and Prinz, J. J. 2011. "A Bad Taste in the Mouth: Gustatory Disgust Influences Moral Judgment," *Psychological Science* 22: 295–299.

Ewing, A. C. 1947. *The Definition of the Good*. New York: Macmillan.

Ferrero, L. 2009. "Constitutivism and the Inescapability of Agency," in R. Shafer-Landau (ed.), *Oxford Studies in Metaethics*, vol. 4, New York: Oxford University Press, 303–333.

Festa, L. 2006. *Sentimental Figures of Empire in Eighteenth-Century Britain and France*. Baltimore: John Hopkins Press.

Fine, K. 2002. "Varieties of Necessity," in T. Gendler & J. Hawthorne (eds.), *Conceivability and Possibility*. New York: Oxford University Press, 253–281.

Fingarette, H. 1972. *Confucius: The Secular as Sacred*. New York: Waveland Press.

FitzPatrick, W. 2009. "Thomson's Turnabout on the Trolley," *Analysis* 69.4: 636–643.

FitzPatrick, W. 2015. "Debunking Evolutionary Debunking of Ethical Realism," *Philosophical Studies* 172.4: 883–904.

Fleischacker, S. 1999. *The Third Concept of Liberty: Judgment and Freedom in Kant and Adam Smith*. Princeton, NJ: Princeton University Press.

Foot, P. 1978. *Virtues and Vices*. New York: Oxford University Press.

Forman-Barzilai, F. 2001. "Whose Context? Which Impartiality? Reflections on Griswold's Smith," *Perspectives on Political Science* 30: 146–150.

Forman-Barzilai, F. 2010. *Adam Smith and the Circles of Sympathy*. New York: Cambridge University Press.

Forster, M. N. (tr. and ed.). 2002. *Herder: Philosophical Writings*. New York: Cambridge University Press.

Frank, R. H. 2001. "Cooperation through Emotional Commitment," in R. M. Nesse (ed.), *Evolution and the Capacity for Commitment*. New York: Russell Sage, 57–76.

Frankfurt, Harry G. 1971. "Freedom of the Will and the Concept of a Person," *The Journal of Philosophy* 68.1: 5–20.

Frazer, M. 2010. *The Enlightenment of Sympathy: Justice and the Moral Sentiments in Eighteenth Century and Today*. New York: Oxford University Press.

Frijda, N. 1986. *The Emotions*. New York: Cambridge University Press.

Gaier, U. *et al.* (eds.). 1985. *Johann Gottfried Herder, Werke in Zehn Bänden*. Frankfurt am Main: Deutscher Klassiker Verlag.

Gallagher, S. 2012. "Empathy, Simulation, and Narrative," *Science in Context* 25: 355–381.

Gendler, T. S. 2006. "Imaginative Resistance Revisited," in S. Nichols (ed.), *The Architecture of the Imagination*. New York: Oxford University Press, 149–174.

Gert, J. 2002. "Korsgaard's Private-Reasons Argument," *Philosophy and Phenomenological Research* 64: 303–324.

Gibbard, A. 1990. *Wise Choices, Apt Feelings*. Cambridge, MA: Harvard University Press.

Gibbard, A. 2003. *Thinking How to Live*. Cambridge, MA: Harvard University Press.

Gill, M. B. 1996. "A Philosopher in his Closet: Reflexivity and Justification in Hume's Moral Theory," *Canadian Journal of Philosophy* 26.2: 231–256.

Gill, M. B. 2000. "Shaftesbury's Two Accounts of the Reason to be Virtuous," *Journal of the History of Philosophy* 38.4: 529–548.

Goldie, P. 2000. *The Emotions*. New York: Oxford University Press.

Goldie, P. 2003. "Narrative and Perspective; Values and Appropriate Emotions," in A. Hatzimoysis (ed.), *Philosophy and the Emotions*. New York: Cambridge University Press, 201–220.

Goldie, P. 2007. "Dramatic Irony, Narrative, and the External Perspective," in D. Hutto (ed.), *Narrative and Understanding Persons*. New York: Cambridge University Press, 69–84.

Goldie, P. 2011. "Anti-Empathy," in Coplan and Goldie (eds.), *Empathy: Philosophical and Psychological Perspectives*. New York: Oxford University Press, 302–318.

Goldman, A. 2006. *Simulating Minds*. New York: Oxford University Press.

Goldman, A. 2011. "Two Routes to Empathy: Insights from Cognitive Neuroscience," in Coplan and Goldie (eds.), *Empathy: Philosophical and Psychological Perspectives*. New York: Oxford University Press, 31–44.

Goodwin, G. P. and Darley, J. M. 2008. "The Psychology of Meta-Ethics: Exploring Objectivism," *Cognition* 106: 1339–1366.

Greene, J. and Haidt, J. 2002. "How (and Where) Does Moral Judgment Work?," *Trends in Cognitive Sciences* 6: 517–523.

Greene, J. D., Sommerville, R. B., Nystrom, L. E., Darley, J. M., and Cohen, J. D. 2001. "An fMRI Investigation of Emotional Engagement in Moral Judgment," *Science* 293: 2105–2108.

Greenspan, P. 1995. *Practical Guilt: Moral Dilemmas, Emotions, and Social Norms.* New York: Oxford University Press.

Griswold, C. 1998. *Adam Smith and the Virtues of Enlightenment.* New York: Cambridge University Press.

Griswold, C. 2001. "Reply to My Critics," *Perspectives on Political Science* 30: 163–167.

Gruen, L. 2009. "Attending to Nature: Empathetic Engagement with the More than Human World," *Ethics and the Environment* 14: 23–48.

Haidt, J. 2001. "The Emotional Dog and Its Rational Tail: A Social Intuitionist Approach to Moral Judgment," *Psychological Review* 108: 814–834.

Hamlin, J. K. and Wynn, K. 2011. "Young Infants Prefer Prosocial to Antisocial Others," *Cognitive Development* 26: 30–39.

Hare, R. M. 1981. *Moral Thinking.* Oxford: Clarendon Press.

Harman, G. 1977. *The Nature of Morality.* New York: Oxford University Press.

Harman, G. 2000. "Moral Agent and Impartial Spectator," in *Explaining Value and Other Essays in Moral Philosophy.* Oxford: Clarendon Press, 181–195.

Held, V. 2006. *The Ethics of Care: Personal, Political, Global.* New York: Oxford University Press.

Henrich, J. 2000. "Does Culture Matter in Economic Behavior? Ultimatum Game Bargaining among the Machiguenga of the Peruvian Amazon," *American Economic Review* 90: 973–979.

Henson, R. G. 1979. "What Kant Might Have Said: Moral Worth and the Overdetermination of Dutiful Action." *The Philosophical Review* 88: 39–54.

Hobbes, Th. 1994. *Leviathan.* Edited by Edwin Curley. Indianapolis: Hackett.

Hoffman, M. 2011. "Empathy, Justice, and the Law," in Coplan and Goldie (eds.), *Empathy: Philosophical and Psychological Perspectives.* New York: Oxford University Press, 230–254.

Horgan, T. 2015. "Injecting Phenomenology into the Free Will Debate," in D. Shoemaker (ed.), *Oxford Studies in Agency and Responsibility*, vol. 3, New York: Oxford University Press, 34–61.

Horgan, T. 2012. "Introspection about Phenomenal Consciousness: Running the Gamut from Infallibility to Impotence," in D. Smythies and D. Stoljar (eds.), *Introspection and Consciousness.* Oxford: Oxford University Press, 405–422.

Horgan, T. and Potrč, M. 2010. "The Epistemic Relevance of Morphological Content," *Acta Analytica* 25: 155–173.

Horgan, T. and Tienson, J. 2002. "The Intentionality of Phenomenology and the Phenomenology of Intentionality," in D. Chalmers (ed.), *Philosophy of Mind: Classical and Contemporary Readings.* New York: Oxford University Press, 520–533.

Horgan, T. and Timmons, M. 2006a. "Expressivism, Yes! Relativism, No!," in R. Shafer-Landau (ed.), *Oxford Studies in Metaethics*, vol. 1. New York: Oxford University Press, 73–98.

Horgan, T. and Timmons, M. 2006b. "Cognitivist Expressivism," in T. Horgan and M. Timmons (eds.), *Metaethics after Moore*. New York: Oxford University Press, 255–298.

Horgan, T. and Timmons, M. 2008. "What Does Moral Phenomenology Tell Us about Moral Objectivity?," *Social Philosophy & Policy* 25: 267–300.

Horgan, T. and Timmons, M. 2009. "Expressivism and Contrary-Forming Negation," *Philosophical Issues* 19: 92–112.

Horgan, T. and Timmons, M. 2011. "Introspection and the Phenomenology of Free Will," *Journal of Consciousness Studies* 18: 180–205.

Horgan, T. and Timmons, M. In Preparation. *Illuminating Reasons: An Essay on Moral Phenomenology*.

Hume, D. 1739–1740/2000. *A Treatise of Human Nature*. Edited by David Fate Norton and Mary J. Norton. New York: Oxford University Press.

Hume, D. 1740. "Abstract of a Book Lately Published." London: Borbet. Facsimile edition at www.davidhume.org/texts/abs.html.

Hume, D. 1748/1999. *An Enquiry Concerning Human Understanding*. Edited by Tom L. Beauchamp. New York: Oxford University Press.

Hume, D. 1751/1998. *An Enquiry Concerning the Principles of Morals*. Edited by Tom L. Beauchamp. New York: Oxford University Press.

Hume, D. 1975. *Enquiries Concerning Human Understanding and Concerning the Principles of Morals*, 3rd edition, L. A. Selby-Bigge (ed.) and P. H. Nidditch (rev.). Oxford: Clarendon Press.

Hume, D. 1987. "Of the Standard of Taste, " in E. F. Miller (ed.), *Essays: Moral, Political, and Literary*. Indianapolis: Liberty Fund, 226–249.

Hurley, P. 2006. "Does Consequentialism Make Too Many Demands, or None at All?" *Ethics* 116 (4): 680–706.

Hussain, N. and Shah, N. 2006. "Misunderstanding Metaethics: Korsgaard's Rejection of Realism," *Oxford Studies of Metaethics* 1: 265–294.

Hussain, N. and Shah, N. 2013. "Meta-Ethics and its Discontents: A Case Study of Korsgaard," in Bagnoli (ed.), *Constructivism in Ethics*. New York: Cambridge University Press, 82–107.

Hutcheson, F. 1728–1742/2002. *An Essay on the Nature and Conduct of the Passions and Affections, with Illustrations on the Moral Sense*. Edited with an Introduction by Aaron Garrett. Indianapolis, IN: Liberty Fund.

Hutchseon, F. 1742–1747/2007. *Philosophiae Moralis Insitutio Compenderia, with A Short Introduction to Moral Philosophy*. Edited with an Introduction by Luigi Turco. Indianapolis, IN: Liberty Fund.

Hutcheson, F. 1755/2005. *A System of Moral Philosophy*. With an Introduction by Daniel Carey. New York: Continuum.

Hutcheson, F. 2004. *An Inquiry Into the Original of Our Ideas of Beauty and Virtue*, ed. Wolfgang Leidhold. Indianapolis: Liberty Press.

Immerwahr, J. 1989. "Hume's Essays on Happiness," *Hume Studies* 15: 307–324.

Jacob, P. 2011. "The Direct-Perception Model of Empathy: A Critique," *Review of Philosophy and Psychology* 2: 519–540.

276     References

Jacobson, D. 2013. "Regret, Agency, and Error," *Oxford Studies in Agency and Responsibility* 1: 95–125.

Jaggar, A. 1989. "Love and Knowledge: Emotion in Feminist Epistemology," in A. Garry and M. Pearsal (eds.), *Women and Knowledge*. Boston: Unwin Hyman, 166–190.

Johnston, M. 2001. "The Authority of Affect," *Philosophy and Phenomenological Research* 63: 181–214.

Jones, K. 1996. "Trust as an Affective Attitude," *Ethics* 107: 4–25

Joyce, R. 2007. *The Evolution of Morality*. Cambridge, MA: MIT Press.

Kahneman, D. 2013. *Thinking Fast and Thinking Slow*. New York: Farrar, Straus, & Giroux.

Kahneman, D. and Tversky, A. (eds.). 2000. *Choices, values and frames*. New York: Cambridge University Press and Russell Sage Foundation.

Kamm, F. 2007. *Intricate Ethics*. New York: Oxford University Press.

Kane, R. 2010. *Ethics and the Quest for Wisdom*. New York: Cambridge University Press.

Kant, I. 1902–. ("KGS") *Gesammelte Schriften*. Hrsg. von der Koeniglich-Preussischen Akademie der Wissenschaften zu Berlin.

Kant, I. 1992. *Theoretical Philosophy, 1755–1770*. Translated and edited by David Walford and Ralf Meerbote. The Cambridge Edition of the Works of Immanuel Kant. New York: Cambridge University Press.

Kant, I. 1996. *Practical Philosophy*. Translated and edited by Mary J. Gregor. The Cambridge Edition of the Works of Immanuel Kant. General Introduction by Allen Wood. New York: Cambridge University Press.

Kant, I. 1997. *Lectures on Ethics* Translated by Peter Heath. Edited by Peter Heath and J. B. Schneewind. The Cambridge Edition of the Works of Immanuel Kant. New York: Cambridge University Press.

Kauppinen, A. 2014a. "Moral Sentimentalism", *The Stanford Encyclopedia of Philosophy* (Spring 2014 Edition), Edward N. Zalta (ed.), URL = http://plato.stanford.edu/archives/spr2014/entries/moral-sentimentalism/.

Kauppinen, A. 2014b. "Fittingness and Idealization," *Ethics* 124 (3), 572–588.

Kauppinen, A. 2015. "Favoring," *Philosophical Studies* 172, 1953–1971.

Kauppinen, A. 2016. "Character and Blame in Hume and Beyond," in Iskra Fileva (ed.), *Questions of Character*. Oxford University Press, 46–62.

Kelly, D. 2011. *Yuck!: The Nature and Moral Significance of Disgust*. Cambridge, MA: MIT Press.

Kelly, T. and McGrath, S. 2010. "Is Reflective Equilibrium Enough?" *Philosophical Perspectives* 24: 325–339.

Kittay, E. F. 1999. *Love's Labor: Essays on Women, Equality, and Dependency*. New York: Oxford University Press.

Knoblock, John. 1988–1994. *Xunzi: A Translation and Study of the Complete Work*, 3 vols. Stanford, CA: Stanford University Press.

Korsgaard, C. 1996a. *The Sources of Normativity*. With responses by G. A. Cohen, Raymond Geuss, Thomas Nagel and Bernard Williams. Edited by Onora O'Neill. New York: Cambridge University Press.

Korsgaard, C. 1996b. "From Duty and for the Sake of the Noble: Kant and Aristotle on Morally Good Action," in S. Engstrom and J. Whiting (eds.), *Aristotle,*

*Kant and the Stoics: Rethinking Happiness and Duty.* New York: Cambridge University Press, 203–236.

Korsgaard, C. 1997. "The Normativity of Instrumental Reason," in G. Cullity and B. Gaut (eds.), *Ethics and Practical Reason.* Oxford: Clarendon, 215–254.

Korsgaard, C. 2008. *The Constitution of Agency: Essays on Practical Reason and Moral Psychology.* New York: Oxford University Press.

Korsgaard, D. 2009. *Self-Constitution: Agency, Identity, and Integrity.* New York: Oxford University Press.

Kuehn, M. 2001. *Kant: A Biography.* New York: Cambridge University Press.

Lamm, C., Batson, C. D., and Decety, J. 2007. "The Neural Substrate of Human Empathy: Effects of Perspective-Taking and Cognitive Appraisal," *Journal of Cognitive Neuroscience* 19: 42–58.

LeDoux, J. 1996. *The Emotional Brain.* New York: Simon and Schuster.

Lenman, J. and Shemmer, Y. (eds.). 2012. *Constructivsm in Practical Philosophy.* New York: Oxford University Press.

Locke, D. 2014. "Darwinian Normative Skepticism," in M. Bergmann and P. Kain (eds.), *Challenges to Moral and Religious Belief: Disagreement and Evolution.* New York: Oxford University Press, 220–236.

Loeb, L. E. 2002. *Stability and Justification in Hume's Treatise.* New York: Oxford University Press.

Lorde, A. 1984. *Sister Outsider.* Freedom, CA: Crossing Press.

Louden, R. B. 2000. *Kant's Impure Ethics: From Rational Beings to Human Beings.* New York: Oxford University Press.

Lugones, M. C. 1987. "Playfulness, 'World'-Travelling, and Loving Perception," *Hypatia* 2: 3–19.

Lugones, M. C. and Spelman, E. V. 1983. "Have We Got a Theory for You! Feminist Theory, Cultural Imperialism, and the Demand for 'the Women's Voice,'" *Women's Studies International Forum* 6: 573–578.

Luo, S. 2007. *Classical Confucianism and Moral Sentimentalism.* Saarbrücken: VDM Verlag.

MacIntyre, A. 1966. "Hume on 'Is' and 'Ought'," in V. C. Campbell (ed.), *Modern Studies in Philosophy: Hume.* New York: Anchor Books, 240–264.

Mackenzie, C. 2006. "Imagining Other Lives," *Philosophical Papers* 35: 293–325.

Macnamara, C. 2013a. "'Screw You!' and 'Thank you!,'" *Philosophical Studies* 165: 893–914.

Macnamara, C. 2013b. "Taking Demands out of Blame," in Coates and Tognazzini (eds.), *Blame: Its Nature and Norms.* New York: Oxford University Press, 141–161.

Mandeville, B. 1988a. *The Fable of the Bees.* (2 vols.), Edited by F. B. Kaye. Indianapolis: Liberty Fund Press.

Mandeville, B. 1988b. "A Search into the Nature of Society," in Mandeville, *The Fable of the Bees* 2: 323–370.

Martin, A. 2014. *How We Hope.* Princeton, NJ: Princeton University Press.

Martin, M. A. 1994. "Hume as Classical Moralist," *International Philosophical Quarterly* 34.3: 323–334.

Mason, M. 2003. "Contempt as a Moral Attitude," *Ethics* 113: 234–272.

McBrayer, J. 2010a. "A Limited Defense of Moral Perception," *Philosophical Studies* 149: 305–320.

McBrayer, J. 2010b. "Moral Perception and the Causal Objection," *Ratio* 23: 201–307.

McDowell, J. 1998. "Values and Secondary Qualities," in *Mind, Value, and Reality*. Cambridge, MA: Harvard University Press, 131–150.

McGrath, S. 2004. "Moral Knowledge by Perception," *Philososophical Perspectives* 18: 209–229.

McGrath, S. 2014. "Relax? Don't Do It! Why Moral Realism Won't Come Cheap." *Oxford Studies in Metaethics* 9: 186–214.

McRae, E. 2011. "The Cultivation of Moral Feelings and Mengzi's Method of Extension," *Philosophy East & West* 61.4: 587–608.

Meinecke, F. 1936/1972. *Historicism: The Rise of a New Historical Outlook*. Translated by J. E. Anderson with a Foreword by Sir Isaiah Berlin. London: Routledge and Kegan Paul.

Melis, A. P., Hare, B., and Tomasello, M. 2006. "Chimpanzees Recruit the Best Collaborators," *Science* 311: 1297–1300.

Mendus, S. 1985. "The Practical and the Pathological," *The Journal of Value Inquiry* 19: 235–243.

Meyers, D. T. 2009. "Narrative Structures, Narratives of Abuse, and Human Rights," in L. Tessman (ed.), *Feminist Ethics and Social and Political Philosophy: Theorizing the Non-Ideal*. Dordrecht: Springer, 253–270.

Meyers, D. T. 2016. *Victims' Stories and the Advancement of Human Rights*. New York: Oxford University Press.

Mill, J. S. 1963. Utilitarianism, in J. M. Robson (ed.), *Collected Works of John Stuart Mill*, vol. 10. Toronto: University of Toronto Press.

Miller, D. 2013. *Justice for Earthlings: Essays in Political Philosophy*. New York: Cambridge University Press.

Moore, G. E. 1903/1993. *Principia Ethica*. Edited with an Introduction by Thomas Baldwin. New York: Cambridge University Press.

Nadler, J. and McDonnell, M. 2012. "Moral Character, Motive, and the Psychology of Blame," *Cornell Law Review* 97: 11–43.

Nagel, T. 1972. "War and Massacre," *Philosophy and Public Affairs* 1: 123–144.

Nagel, T. 1979. "Equality," in *Mortal Questions*. New York: Cambridge University Press, 106–127.

Nagel, T. 1986. *The View from Nowhere*. New York: Oxford University Press.

Nichols, S. 2004. *Sentimental Rules: On the Natural Foundations of Moral Judgment*. New York: Oxford University Press.

Nichols, S. and Folds-Bennett, T. 2003. "Are Children Moral Objectivists? Children's Judgments about Moral and Response-Dependent Properties," *Cognition* 90: B23–B32.

Norcross, A. 2008. "Off Her Trolley? Frances Kamm and the Metaphysics of Morality," *Utilitas* 20.1: 65–80.

Nunner-Winkler, G. and Sodian, B. 1988. "Children's Understanding of Moral Emotions," *Child Development* 59: 1323–1338.

Nussbaum, M. 1988. "Narrative Emotions: Beckett's Genealogy of Love," *Ethics* 98: 225–254.

Nussbaum, M. 2001. *Upheavals of Thought: The Intelligence of Emotion*. New York: Cambridge University Press.

Nyholm, S. 2012. *On the Universal Law and Humanity Formulas*. PhD Dissertation, Ann Arbor: University of Michigan.

Parfit, D. 2011. *On What Matters*. 2 vols. New York: Oxford University Press.

Pessoa, L. 2008. "On the Relationship between Emotion and Cognition," *Nature Reviews: Neuroscience* 9: 149–158.

Pettit, P. 1991. "Realism and Response-Dependence," *Mind* 100: 587–626.

Pew Research Center. 2010. "The Decline of Marriage and Rise of New Families." Retrieved October 10, 2015, from http://pewsocialtrends.org/files/2010/11/pew-social-trends-2010-families.pdf.

Pizarro, D. A. and Tannenbaum, D. 2012. "Bringing Character Back: How the Motivation to Evaluate Character Influences Judgments of Moral Blame," in M. Mikulincer and P. R. Shaver (eds.), *The Social Psychology of Morality: Exploring the Causes of Good and Evil*. Washington, D.C.: American Psychological Association, 91–108.

Potkay, A. 2000. *The Passion for Happiness: Samuel Johnson and David Hume*. Ithaca, NY: Cornell University Press.

Price, H. 2003. "Truth as Convenient Friction," *Journal of Philosophy* 100: 167–190.

Prinz, J. J. 2004. *Gut Feelings: A Perceptual Theory of Emotions*. New York: Oxford University Press.

Prinz, J. J. 2007. *The Emotional Construction of Morals*. New York: Oxford University Press.

Prinz, J. J. 2011a. "Against Empathy," *Southern Journal of Philosophy, Spindel Supplement* 49: 214–233.

Prinz, J. J. 2011b. "Is Empathy Necessary for Morality?" in Coplan and Goldie (eds.), *Empathy: Philosophical and Psychological Perspectives*. New York: Oxford University Press, 211–229.

Prinz, J. J. 2016. "Sentimentalism and the Moral Brain," in S. M. Liao (ed.), *Moral Brains: The Neuroscience of Morality*. New York: Oxford University Press.

Prinz, J. J. Forthcoming. *The Moral Self*. Oxford University Press.

Pritchard, D. 2012. "Anti-Luck Virtue Epistemology," *Journal of Philosophy* 109.3: 247–279.

Pryor, J. 2000. "The Skeptic and the Dogmatist," *Noûs* 34.4: 517–549.

Quinn, W. 1989. "Actions, Intentions, and Consequences: The Doctrine of Double Effect," *Philosophy and Public Affairs* 18.4: 334–351.

Rabinowicz, W. and Ronnow-Rasmussen, T. 2004. "The Strike of the Demon: On Fitting Pro-Attitudes and Value," *Ethics* 104: 291–423.

Railton, P. 1997. "Aesthetic Value, Moral Value, and the Ambitions of Naturalism," in J. Levinson (ed.), *Aesthetics and Ethics*. Cambridge: Cambridge University Press, 59–105.

Railton, P. 2013. "Reliance, Trust, and Belief," *Inquiry* 57: 122–150.

Railton, P. 2014. "The Affective Dog and Its Rational Tale: Intuition and Attunement," *Ethics* 124: 813–859.

Raposa, M. L. 2004. "Ritual Inquiry: The Pragmatic Logic of Religious Practice," in K. Schilbrack (ed.), *Thinking Through Rituals: Philosophical Perspectives*. New York: Routledge, 115–130.

Rawls, J. 1971. *A Theory of Justice*. Cambridge, MA: Harvard University Press.

Rawls, J. 1980. "Kantian Constructivism in Ethical Theory," *The Journal of Philosophy* 77: 515–572.

Reeder, G. B. and Brewer, M. B. 1979. "A Schematic Model of Dispositional Attribution in Interpersonal Perception," *Psychological Review* 86: 61–79.

Richerson, P. J., Boyd, R., and Henrich, J. 2003. "The Cultural Evolution of Human Cooperation," in P. Hammerstein (ed.), *The Genetic and Cultural Evolution of Cooperation*. Cambridge, MA: MIT Press, 357–388.

Ridge, M. 2006. "Ecumenical Expressivism: Finessing Frege," *Ethics* 116: 302–336.

Ridge, M. 2012. "Kantian Constructivism: Something Old, Something New," in Lenman and Shemmer (eds.), *Constructivism in Practical Philosophy*. New York: Oxford University Press, 138–158.

Roseman, I. 2013. "Appraisal in the Emotion System: Coherence in Strategies for Coping," *Emotion Review* 5: 141–149.

Rosen, G. 2010. "Metaphysical Dependence: Grounding and Reduction," in B. Hale and A. Hoffmann (eds.), *Modality: Metaphysics, Logic, and Epistemology*. New York: Oxford University Press, 109–136.

Ross, L. and Nisbett, R. E. 1991. *The Person and the Situation: Perspectives of Social Psychology*. New York, NY: McGraw-Hill.

Ross, W. D. 1930. *The Right and the Good*. New York: Oxford University Press.

Rozin, P. and Singh, L. 1999. "The Moralization of Cigarette Smoking in the United States," *Journal of Consumer Psychology* 8: 321–337.

Rozin, P., Markwith, M., and Stoess, C. 1997. "Moralization and Becoming a Vegetarian: The Transformation of Preferences into Values and the Recruitment of Disgust," *Psychological Science* 8: 67–73.

Sarkissian, H., Park, J., Tien, D., Wright, J., and Knobe, J. 2012. "Folk Moral Relativism," *Mind and Language* 26: 482–505.

Sayre-McCord, G. 2010. "Sentiments and Spectators: Adam Smith's Theory of Moral Judgment," *The Adam Smith Review* 5: 124–144.

Sayre-McCord, G. 2013. "Hume and Smith on Sympathy, Approbation, and Moral Judgment," *Social Philosophy and Policy* 30: 208–236.

Scanlon, T. M. 1998. *What We Owe to Each Other*. Cambridge, MA: Harvard University Press.

Scanlon, T. M. 2008. *Moral Dimensions: Permissibility, Meaning, and Blame*. Cambridge, MA: Harvard University Press.

Scanlon, T. M. 2014. *Being Realistic about Reasons*. New York: Oxford University Press.

Scarantino, A. 2014. "The Motivational Theory of Emotion, " in J. D'Arms and D. Jacobson (eds.), *Moral Psychology and Human Agency: Philosophical Essays on the Science of Ethics*. New York: Oxford University Press.

Schafer, K. 2010. "Evolution and Normative Scepticism," *Australasian Journal of Philosophy* 88.3: 471–488.

Schafer, K. 2013. "Quasi-Realism, Projectivism, and the Explanatory Challenge," in G. Hubbs and D. Lind (eds.), *Pragmatism, Law, and Language*. Oxford: Routledge, 136–151.

Schafer, K. 2014. "Knowledge and Two Faces of Non-Accidental Truth," *Philosophy and Phenomenological Research* 89 (2): 373–393.

Schafer, K. 2015a. "How Common is Peer Disagreement? On Self-Trust and Rational Symmetry," *Philosophy and Phenomenological Research* 91: 25–46.

Schafer, K. 2015b. "Constructivism and Realism in Kantian Metaethics (1 & 2)," *Philosophy Compass* 10 (10): 690–713.

Scheman, N. 1993. *Engenderings: Constructions of Knowledge, Authority, and Privilege*. New York: Routledge.

Scherer, K. 2005. "What are Emotions? And How Can They be Measured?," *Social Science Information* 44: 695–729.

Schilpp, P. A. 1938/1960. *Kant's Pre-Critical Ethics*. Second Edition. Evanston, IL: Northwestern University Press.

Schilpp, P. A. (ed.). 1942. *The Philosophy of G. E. Moore*. Evanston, IL: Northwestern University Press.

Schmidt, E. Z. and Bonelli, R. M. 2008. "Sexuality in Huntington's Disease," *Wiener Medizinische Wochenschrift* 158: 84–90.

Scholz, S. 2010. "Persons Transformed by Political Solidarity," *Appraisal* 8: 19–27.

Schopenhauer, A. 1840/1995. *On the Basis of Morality*. Translated by E. F. J. Payne. With an Introduction by David E. Cartwright. Providence, RI: Berghan Books.

Schroeter, F. 2006. "The Limits of Sentimentalism," *Ethics* 116: 337–361.

Schultz, W. 2002. "Getting Formal with Dopamine and Reward". *Neuron* 36: 241–263.

Schwarz, N. and Clore, G. L. 2003. "Mood as Information: 20 Years Later," *Psychological Inquiry* 14: 296–303.

Scruton, R. 1987. "Laughter," in John Morreall (ed.), *The Philosophy of Laughter and Humor*. Albany: SUNY Press, 156–171.

Seidel, A. and Prinz, J. J. 2013a. "Sound Morality: Irritating and Icky Noises Amplify Divergent Moral Domains," *Cognition* 127: 1–5.

Seidel, A. and Prinz, J. J. 2013b. "Mad and Glad: Musically Induced Emotions Have Divergent Moral Impact," *Motivation and Emotion* 37: 269–237.

Sen, A. 2002. "Open and Closed Impartiality," *The Journal of Philosophy* 99: 445–469.

Setiya, K. 2012. *Knowing Right From Wrong*. New York: Oxford University Press.

Shafer-Landau, R. 2003. *Moral Realism: A Defence*. Oxford: Oxford University Press.

Shafer-Landau, R. 2008. "Defending Ethical Intuitionism," in W. Sinnott-Armstrong (ed.), *Moral Psychology* (5 vols.), vol. 2. Cambridge, MA: MIT Press, 83–96.

Shafer-Landau, R. 2012. "Evolutionary Debunking, Moral Realism, and Moral Knowledge." *Journal of Ethics and Social Philosophy* 7.1: 1–38.

Shaftesbury, A. A. C., Third Earl of. 1711/2001. *Characteristics of Men, Manners, Opinions, Times*. Foreword by Douglas Den Uyl. Indianapolis, IN: Liberty Fund.

Shapin, S. and Schaffer, S. 1985/2011. *Leviathan and the Air Pump: Hobbes, Boyle and the Experimental Life*. Princeton, NJ: Princeton University Press.

Shell, S. M. 1996. *The Embodiment of Reason: Kant on Spirit, Generation and Community*. Chicago: The University of Chicago Press.

Sher, G. 2006. *In Praise of Blame*. New York: Oxford University Press.

Sherman, N. 1990. "The Place of Emotions in Kantian Morality," in O. Flanagan and A. Oksenberg Rorty (eds.), *Identity, Character and Morality: Essays in Moral Psychology*. Cambridge, MA: MIT Press, 149–170.

Sherman, N. 1997. *Making a Necessity of Virtue: Aristotle and Kant on Virtue*. New York: Cambridge University Press.

Sherman, N. 1998. "Empathy and Imagination," *Philosophy of Emotions, Midwest Studies in Philosophy* 22: 82–119.

Sidgwick, H. 1981. *The Methods of Ethics*. Indianapolis, IN.: Hackett Publishing.

Siegel, S. 2011. *The Contents of Perception*. New York: Oxford University Press.

Sinnott-Armstrong, W. 2008. *Moral Psychology*, 5 vols., Cambridge, MA: MIT Press.

Slote, M. 2003. *Morals from Motives*. New York: Oxford University Press.

Slote, M. 2007. *The Ethics of Care and Empathy*. London: Routledge.

Slote, M. 2010. *Moral Sentimentalism*. New York: Oxford University Press.

Smith, A. 1759/1982. *The Theory of Moral Sentiments*. Edited by D. D. Raphael and A. L. Macfie. The Glasgow Edition of the Works and Correspondence of Adam Smith. Indianapolis, IN: Liberty Fund Press.

Smith, M. 1994. *The Moral Problem*. Oxford: Blackwell.

Solomon, R. 1980. "Emotions and Choice," in A. Rorty (ed.), *Explaining Emotions*. Berkeley and Los Angeles: University of California Press, 251–281.

Soto, F. A., Gershman, S. J., and Niv, Y. 2014. "Explaining Compound Generalization in Associative and Causal Learning through Rational Principles of Dimension Generalization," *Psychological Review* 121: 526–558.

Spelman, E. V. 1988. *Inessential Woman: Problems of Exclusion in Feminist Thought*. Boston: Beacon.

Stern, R. 2013. "Moral Skepticism, Constructivism and the Value of Humanity," in Bagnoli (ed.), Cambridge University Press, 22–40.

Stevenson, C. L. 1944. *Ethics and Language*. New Haven: Yale University Press.

Stevenson, C. L. 1963. *Facts and Values: Studies in Ethical Analysis*. New Haven: Yale University Press.

Storbeck, J. and Clore, G. L. 2007. "On the Interdependence of Cognition and Emotion," *Cognition & Emotion* 21: 1212–1237.

Strawson, P. F. 1962. "Freedom and Resentment," *Proceedings of the British Academy* 48: 1–25. Reprinted in Watson (ed.). 1982. *Free Will*. Oxford University Press: 59–80. Page references are to the reprint.

Strawson, P. F. 1980. "Replies," in Z. van Straaten (ed.), *Philosophical Subjects: Essays Presented to P. F. Strawson*. New York: Oxford University Press, 260–296.

Street, S. 2006. "A Darwinian Dilemma for Realist Theories of Value," *Philosophical Studies* 127: 109–166.

Street, S. 2008. "Constructivism about Reasons," in R. Shafer-Landau (ed.), *Oxford Studies in Metaethics*, vol. 3. New York: Oxford University Press, 207–245.

Street, S. 2009. "Evolution and the Normativity of Epistemic Reasons," *Canadian Journal of Philosophy* 39, suppl. 1: 213–248.

Street, S. 2010. "What is Constructivism in Ethics and Metaethics?" *Philosophy Compass* 5: 363–384.

Street, S. 2011. "Mind-Independence Without the Mystery: Why Quasi-Realists Can't Have It Both Ways," in R. Shafer-Landau (ed.), *Oxford Studies in Metaethics*, vol. 6. Oxford: Clarendon Press, 1–32.

Street, S. 2012. "Coming to Terms with Contingency: Humean Constructivism about Practical Reason," in Lenman and Shemmer (eds.), *Constructivism in Practical Philosophy*. New York: Oxford University Press, 40–59.

Stueber, K. 1994. "Practice, Indeterminacy, and Private Language: Wittgenstein's Dissolution of Scepticism," *Philosophical Investigations* 17: 14–36.

Stueber, K. 2006. *Rediscovering Empathy: Agency, Folk Psychology, and the Human Sciences*. Cambridge, MA: MIT Press.

Stueber, K. 2008. "Reasons, Generalizations, Empathy, and Narratives: The Epistemic Structure of Action Explanation," *History and Theory* 47: 31–43.

Stueber, K. 2011. "Imagination, Empathy, and Moral Deliberation: The Case of Imaginative Resistance," *Southern Journal of Philosophy, Spindel Supplement* 49: 156–180.

Stueber, K. 2012. "Varieties of Empathy, Neuroscience and the Narrativist Challenge to the Contemporary Theory of Mind Debate," *Emotion Review* 4: 55–63.

Stueber, K. 2013. "The Causal Autonomy of Reason Explanations and How Not to Worry about Causal Deviance," *Philosophy of the Social Sciences* 43: 24–45.

Stueber, K. 2014. "Empathy," in E. N. Zalta (ed.), *The Stanford Encyclopedia of Philosophy* (Winter Edition), http://plato.stanford.edu/archives/win2014/entries/empathy/.

Stueber, K. 2015. "Naturalism and the Normative Domain: Accounting for Normativity with the Help of 18th Century Empathy-Sentimentalism," *Rivista Internazionale Di Filosofia e Psicologia* 6: 24–36.

Suphan, B. *et al.* ed. 1967–1968. *Johann Gottfried Herder Sämtliche Werke*. Originally Published 1887–1913. Reprinted Hildesheim and New York: Georg Olms Verlag.

Szendy, P. 2013. *Kant in the Land of Extraterrestrials: Cosmopolitical Philosofictions*. Translated by Will Bishop. New York: Fordham University Press.

Tannenbaum, D., Uhlmann, E. L., and Diermeier, D. 2011. "Moral Signals, Public Outrage, and Immaterial Harms," *Journal of Experimental Social Psychology* 47: 1249–1254.

Tenenbaum, J. B., Kemp, C., Griffths, T. L., and Goodman, N. D. 2011. "How to Grow a Mind: Statistics, Structure, and Abstraction," *Science* 331: 1279–1285.

Thompson, R. 2006. "The Development of the Person: Social Understanding, Relationships, Conscience, Self," in N. Eisenberg (ed.), *Handbook of Child Psychology*, 6th edition, vol. 3. Hoboken, NJ: Wiley, 24–98.

Thomson, J. 1999. "Physician-Assisted Suicide: Two Moral Arguments," *Ethics* 109.3: 497–518.

Thomson, J. 2008. "Turning the Trolley," *Philosophy and Public Affairs* 36.4: 359–374.

Tobler, P. N. *et al.* 2006. "Reward Value Coding Distinct from Risk Attitude-Related Uncertainty Coding in Human Reward Systems," *Journal of Neurophysiology* 97: 1621–1632.

Trevarthen, C. 2001. "Intrinsic Motives for Companionship in Understanding: Their Origin, Development, and Significance for Mental Health," *Infant Mental Health Journal* 22: 95–131.

Uhlmann, E. L. and Zhu, L. 2014. "Acts, Persons, and Intuitions: Person-centered Cues and Gut Reactions to Harmless Transgressions," *Social Psychological and Personality Science* 5: 279–285.

Uhlmann, E. L., Zhu, L., and Diermeier, D. 2014. "When Actions Speak Volumes: The Role of Inferences about Moral Character in Outrage over Racial Bigotry," *European Journal of Social Psychology* 44: 23–29.

Uhlmann, E. L., Zhu, L., and Tannenbaum, D. 2013. "When it Takes a Bad Person to Do the Right Thing," *Cognition* 126: 326–334.

Vaish, A., Carpenter, M., and Tomasello, M. 2011. "Young Children's Responses to Guilt Displays," *Developmental Psychology* 47: 1248–1262.

Van Straaten, Z. (ed.). 1980. *Philosophical Subjects: Essays Presented to P. F. Strawson.* Oxford: Clarendon Press.

Vauvenargues, Marquis de, Luc de Clapiers. 1857. *Introduction à la connaissance de l'esprit humain,* in D.-L. Gilbert (ed.), *Oeuvres de Vauvenargues.* Paris: Furne et Cie.

Vavova, K. 2014. "Debunking Evolutionary Debunking," in R. Shafer-Landau (ed.), *Oxford Studies in Metaethics.* vol. 9. Oxford: Oxford University Press, 76–101.

Velleman, D. 1999. "Love as a Moral Emotion," *Ethics* 109: 338–374.

Velleman, D. 2003. "Narrative Explanation," *The Philosophical Review* 112: 1–25.

Velleman, D. 2009. *How We Get Along.* New York: Cambridge University Press.

Velleman, D. 2013. *Foundations of Moral Relativism.* Cambridge: Open Book Publishers.

Wallace, R. J. 1996. *Responsibility and the Moral Sentiments.* Cambridge, MA: Harvard University Press.

Wallace, R. J. 2012. "Constructivism about Normativity: Some Pitfalls," in Lenman and Shemmer (eds.), *Constructivism in Practical Philosophy.* Oxford: Oxford University Press, 18–39.

Watson, G. (ed.). 1982. *Free Will.* New York: Oxford University Press.

Watson, G. 1994. "Responsibility and the Limits of Evil: Variations on a Strawsonian Theme," in Fischer and Ravizza (eds.), *Perspectives on Moral Responsibility.* Ithaca, NY: Cornell University Press, 119–148.

Wedgwood, R. 2007. *The Nature of Normativity.* New York: Oxford University Press.

Werner, D. 1979. "A Cross-Cultural Perspective on Theory and Research on Male Homosexuality," *Journal of Homosexuality* 4: 345–362.

White, R. 2005. "Problems for Dogmatism," *Philosophical Studies* 131: 525–557.

Wielenberg, E. 2010. "On the Evolutionary Debunking of Morality," *Ethics* 120.3: 441–464.

Wiggins, D. 1987. "A Sensible Subjectivism," in *Needs, Values, Truth: Essays in the Philosophy of Value.* Oxford: Blackwell, 185–214.

Willenken, T. 2011. "Moorean Responses to Skepticism: A Defense." *Philosophical Studies* 154: 1–25.

Williams, B. 1985. *Ethics and the Limits of Philosophy*. Cambridge, MA: Harvard University Press.

Williams, B. 1995a. "Who Needs Ethical Knowledge?," in *Making Sense of Humanity*, New York: Cambridge University Press, 203–212.

Williams, B. 1995b. "What Does Intuitionism Imply?," in *Making Sense of Humanity*, New York: Cambridge University Press, 182–191.

Winkler, K. P. 2011. "Hume and the Sensible Qualities," in L. Nolan (ed.), *Primary and Secondary Qualities: The Historical and Ongoing Debate*. New York: Oxford University Press, 239–273.

Winter, L. and Uleman, J. S. 1984. "When are Social Judgments Made? Evidence for the Spontaneousness of Trait Inferences," *Journal of Personality and Social Psychology* 47: 237–252.

Wong, D. B. 2002. "Reasons and Analogical Reasoning in Mengzi." in Xiusheng Liu and Philip J. Ivanhoe (eds.), *Essays on the Moral Philosophy of Mengzi*. Indianapolis, IN: Hackett Publishing Company, 187–220.

Wong, D. B. 2015. "Early Confucian Philosophy and the Development of Compassion," *Dao: A Journal of Comparative Philosophy* 14: 157–194.

Wood, A. 1999. *Kant's Ethical Thought*. New York: Cambridge University Press.

Wright, C. 1992. *Truth and Objectivity*. Cambridge, MA: Harvard University Press.

Wright, J. C., Grandjean, P., and McWhite, C. 2012. "The Meta-Ethical Grounding of Our Moral Beliefs: Evidence for Meta-Ethical Pluralism," *Philosophical Psychology* 26: 336–361.

Yamada, M. 2011. "Getting It Right By Accident," *Philosophy and Phenomenological Research* 83.1: 72–105.

Young, I. M. 1997. *Intersecting Voices: Dilemmas of Gender, Political Philosophy, and Policy*. Princeton, NJ: Princeton University Press.

Zammito, John H. 2002. *Kant, Herder and the Birth of Anthropology*. Chicago: The University of Chicago Press.

# Index